Going Coastal

*A geographical and historical journey
around the coastline of Britain –
by whatever road is closest to the ocean*

Late Spring 2016

Ian McBeath

Table of Contents

Introduction

Baggy Point, Croyde, North Devon

G oing Coastal is a recounting of my journey around the whole coastline of mainland Britain (and some of its islands) that I undertook in the Spring of 2016. My aim was to drive the coast by whatever road was closest to the ocean; and this is what I did, for a total of 5068 miles.

You cannot drive the coast of Britain without bumping into many interesting reminders of its history and also of the men and women who ruled and influenced the land. So, this story is not just one of the present day, but I have also sought to weave into it a history of Britain through the lives of many of the Kings and Queens of England, Scotland and Wales. The history is not written in chronological order but rather in geographical order, as I came across them on my journey.

With a Scottish father, whose mother was an Irish Kennedy and an English mother, born within the sound of Bow bells, whose father was a Welsh Morgan, I feel that I can certainly lay claim to having a very British set of genes. Though for the past seventeen years I have lived in Vancouver, Canada, ironically in Beautiful *British* Columbia, the saying "You can take the boy out of Britain, but you can't take Britain out of the boy" has become very real to me.

I was born in Cheltenham in the Cotswolds, my wife in Exeter, Devon and together we have lived mainly in either the west of England or in the Thames Valley, though with a short period of time in the north west of England. For the past eighteen years I have been happily living in Vancouver, Canada, a beautiful and spectacular place. However, for some time now, I have had an increasing feeling that I needed to reconnect with the land of my birth.

I have travelled extensively around the UK and think that I know it quite well, but the feeling of wanting to reengage with my roots was intensified when about a year ago I began to research my family history. This stimulated a desire to try and connect more deeply with the land of my birth and the home of my ancestors. The furthest ancestor I can trace on mother's side is to 1475, in Sussex and on my Father's side to 1625 in Fife, Scotland. With a name of McBeath though, I would like to feel that I belong to a particularly noble lineage in Scotland!

So it was that in 2015 I set out to plan a trip that would allow me to "capture" the whole of Britain. So much of

Britain's history is in its coastline. As an island nation Britain's heritage has been strongly influenced by the sea, including the invaders who have come from the sea. Its people are by necessity a seafaring nation and the way they have adapted and used its coastline is strongly reflected in Britain's history. Some of my earliest memories as a child are of family holidays or trips to the seaside. Rather than crisscross the country, visiting old haunts, or places that I had always wanted to see but never got there, I decided that recognising Britain is an island nation, I would travel all the way around its coastline. A coastal journey would allow me to feel that I had encircled every part of the country. It also is a route with a clear starting and finishing point. My decision to do this was further strengthened when I shared my idea with friends; they all said, "Wow, go for it. It's something I would love to do." Thus in the autumn of 2015, I began my planning and by spring 2016 I was ready to go.

I did not include Ireland on this trip. My passport states that I am a citizen of the European Union and of the "United Kingdom of Great Britain and Northern Ireland". Thus, though Northern Ireland is part of the United Kingdom, it is not part of Great Britain and my trip is a trip around Britain. That is not to deny my Grandmother's links to Ireland, but time did not permit me to make this a United Kingdom trip. However, I am determined to drive around the whole of Ireland, to seek out and feel my heritage there, at some time in the future. A lot of British history is of course interwoven with that of the island of Ireland and their peoples share a common heritage.

Britain only became Great Britain in 1707 under the Act of Union, which united Scotland and England. (The designation "Great" meaning large). Since its subjugation in

1282, Wales was considered to already be part of England and a principality, ruled by a Prince not a King, rather than a country. Although Ireland was formally included in 1801, creating the United Kingdom of Great Britain and Ireland, in 1924, with the recognition of the Republic of Ireland, the term changed to the United Kingdom of Great Britain and Northern Ireland.

In very early times what is now mainland Britain was made up of multiple kingdoms, each with its own rulers and people having strong ethnic and cultural identities, distinct within each "kingdom". Borders were very different then. For example Kings of Ireland controlled great swathes of northern England and Scotland. The Vikings similarly held sway over broad areas of what is today Britain with Ireland also being a major centre for them. The Welsh identity, developed from the Celts after the Romans left Britain. Today Wales still holds on to its ancient language, spoken by more than half the population. Gaelic also remains, spoken by some in Scotland and Ireland and there are still a few speakers of the ancient Cornish language in Cornwall. Current day England, Scotland and Wales have had not only different borders in the past but also different names. Probably, with the passage of time, they will do so again.

What follows are my observations, made as I drove around the mainland coast of the British Isles, written in the order in which I made my journey. What I recorded is what I saw and what happened to me and how I felt at any precise moment on my journey. It is a snapshot of a moment in my time. I am sure that others who know these places might have different perspectives from my attributions and observations. I only saw a particular county from its coastline and I recognise that the inland can be very different from its coast. For example, Cumbria and the Lake District are one of Britain's greatest treasures but the coast of Cumbria I found very uninteresting. Similarly I did not like the coastline of Kent, finding it bleak and depressing and overcrowded with caravan and chalet parks. However, I know that inland Kent is lovely with gems such as Canterbury Cathedral and Leeds Castle. Counties without any coastline, like my native Gloucestershire, or Berkshire where I lived for so many years, are not observed in this book. It would take a very long time to visit every county in Britain and to spend sufficient time in every place to see its diversity.

My narrative was written on the day of (or occasionally the day after) my journey. The history that is mentioned is dictated by the order of the geography of my trip and the places that I visited rather than in any chronological order of the history of Britain.

As my aim was to drive whatever road was closest to the ocean, the focus was therefore on "driving it". This intent impacted my time to visit places and it would have been more relaxing if I had taken more time. I also opted to avoid going into the center of any major town or city, choosing instead to view the harbour and beaches rather than the city center, so my observations are generally on smaller places rather than major towns or cities. My story is held together only by the cliffs, beaches and different oceans that make Britain into such an interesting, diverse and wonderful island.

I chose to undertake my journey in May and June as this is generally a good time for weather, especially so for Scotland. I must say that this proved to be a good choice as in my 34 days on the road I only had about 5 days in which it rained and then not for all of the day. The weather in Scotland, especially on the western side was spectacular. This is such a magnificent part of Britain that had it been raining and foggy I could have missed the best part.

The greater part of my journey was on roads that were no more than narrow lanes or, were just better than lanes. At one stage, in Scotland, I drove for four days on roads without any markings.

My route was planned to be continuous and following the coast. On a few occasions, if a lane was just a spur down to a solitary beach, which would mean that I would then have to return back along the same lane, I did not always drive down to the beach. However, if there was a point of particular interest such as a lighthouse or something noted on the map, I did make the drive down and back.

In some places I chose to drive around an island off the coast and miss out that part of the mainland that geographically it covered, on the basis that the outer road of the island was the one closer to the ocean. For example I took a ferry from Lymington to the Isle of Wight and drove along the southern edge of the island and then took a ferry from Ryde to Southsea, thus cutting out Southampton. Similarly I followed this logic for some of the Scottish western isles and missed off parts of the mainland that they covered. But, in the main, there is not a point on the British coastline that I did not drive along.

I also made great use of vehicle ferries, where I could, to save a long drive around an estuary. In my view the drive up and down the estuary was not really following the ocean, but had to be done if it was the only way to get to the coastline on the other side.

My plan was to leave from Exmouth in Devon on or around May 23rd 2016 and travel in an anti-clockwise direction – this meant that I would keep the ocean on my right (the driver's side of the car). I expected to arrive back in Exmouth on June 24th, so 33 days in total. My estimated mileage was 4600, and did not include ferry distances to certain islands. My total mileage ended up at 5068. The extra miles included one or two diversions such as a visit to ancestor's graves and to Loch Ness plus the inevitable back track where there was only a single road to a point, which had to be driven in reverse to get back on route.

Accommodation was generally booked no more than 24 hours ahead and in some cases only a couple of hours ahead. On one night I slept in the car! I ate mainly in pubs, but also cooked an evening meal myself on a number of occasions using a trusty butane stove. This also provided me with many a cup of tea en route! I photographed and filmed as much as possible and kept up a daily blog so that family and friends could keep up with my journey.

On three sections I was joined by good friends, which added to the pleasure of my trip. It was nice to be able to share experiences and the beauty with someone, and they proved invaluable for maintaining the accuracy of my notes.

One of my companions suggested that I should read before I set out, Paul Theroux's, "The Kingdom By The Sea – A Journey Around the Coast of Great Britain". I had to admit that I had not read this book, although at Christmas I was given Bill Bryson's "The Road to Little Dribbling", which I thoroughly enjoyed. My view and that of other reviewers of Theroux's book found him to be critical and very negative of Britain and the British. Bill Bryson's book however was a very good read. He is witty and insightful while also being endearing when he criticizes the British foibles and failings. Theroux also travelled the opposite direction to what I am doing. He went clockwise, whereas I am going anti-clockwise. He also travelled by rail and foot, whereas I am doing it all by car, with just a little bit of walking to any "interesting bits" that might be en-route. Bill Bryson on the other hand has only done Britain in chunks, not as a continuous trip. It would have been good to have had him as a companion on my trip. Perhaps I could have offered him the chance to fill in the gaps.

As far as I am aware my account will be the first that covers a complete round Britain coastal journey and one that is undertaken within a consecutive period of time. The common thing that Theroux, Bryson and myself all found was an island whose people is as varied as its scenery.

The Origins of the British People

Britain became an island nation around 8,500 years ago. This was possibly when the great ice dam, in what is now northern Canada, gave way and the sudden release of such a volume of water gave rise to flooding that cut off Britain from mainland Europe and also increased the size and height of the Mediterranean so that it flowed into and formed the Black Sea. With the development of farming around 5,000 BC, growing crops and keeping herds of animals, meant that people stopped wandering and established permanent settlements. This was the Iron Age in Britain and we now know these ancient people as the Picts. This was not a society of ignorant savages and on my visit to the Orkneys I saw remains of villages, stone henges and possibly temples that were at least as old as 4500BC. They clearly showed that these people had skills of masonry, astronomy and a hieroglyphic language. They were no doubt at least as intelligent as we think of ourselves today, though the increase and accumulation of knowledge is much faster for us thanks to a greater level of technology. The evidence for the Pictish people is strongest along the western side of Britain, particularly in Scotland.

About 2000 years ago the Celts, a people with their origins in central Europe and Gaul became dominant. However, with the arrival of the Romans in 43AD, the Celts were pushed westward, becoming restricted mainly to Ireland, western Scotland, Wales and Cornwall. Strong evidence for the Celts is also found in Brittany and in Spain.

For the next four centuries the Romans were the biggest influence on Britain, though mainly in England. Indeed at that time the Emperor Hadrian built his famous wall to keep at bay the marauding Celts from Scotland. Scotland was never tamed by Rome, though the Romans did get as far as a line roughly between present day Glasgow and Edinburgh where the less well know Antonine Wall was built. With the arrival of the Romans, Christianity took an increasing hold in Britain. However, Christianity had already reached the Celts and their influence, from Scotland and Ireland, is particularly seen today in the names of Celtic saints given to many villages and towns in Britain.

The departure of the Romans in 410AD saw the country open to invasion by Angles, Saxons and Jutes from northern Europe. It was in this time that the name Britons was given to the peoples who were concentrated in the west, especially in Wales. Britain now slipped back into a pluralistic and pagan society, though the Celtic Christians fought hard to slow this and convert people. The Christian Church in Rome was still a major force and missionaries from here came to the southeast and northeast areas of Britain. In 664 at a Synod in Whitby, the Celtic Christian movement, which generally espoused organisation of religion, but felt that unity was important, agreed to follow the doctrines of Rome.

Britain has a long religious history and multiple saints are recorded all around the land and even to this day 268 places in Britain have the title "Saint" in their place name. I have sought to include some of the stories of the saints where they are connected and relevant to the places I visited.

Writing in the 8th century, the Venerable Bede recorded that there were five languages spoken in Britain: Latin, the language of the Church; Old English, the language of the Angles and Saxons; Irish, spoken on the west coast; Brythonic, the precursor to the Welsh language; and Pictish, spoken in the north. In the ninth century, with the arrival of the Vikings, Old Norse entered the country.

From around 800AD Britain and Ireland began to be attacked by the Vikings. Many people think of the Vikings as being one race, but in reality they had three separate but simultaneous origins. The Swedish Vikings generally moved eastward, invading the Slavic nations and Russia. The Danes raided the east coast of Britain and established the Danelaw, with their headquarters based in York. Meanwhile the Norwegian Vikings became the masters of northern Scotland and around to Ireland and the western coastal regions of Britain. Their capital was Dublin, a city that they established and built around their main trade, which was slaving. The Vikings had a devastating impact upon the British Isles and came to dominate, Ireland, Scotland and the east of England. Wales, apart from its coastal areas and much of southern England remained for many years, much less impacted by their raids and subjugation.

By the eleventh century though, the Danes had gained control of most of eastern and southern England and a Danish Viking, Sweyn Forkbeard, in 1013, invaded and became King of England, ousting King Aethelred of Wessex. Sweyn though died within a year of his conquest, so Aethelred came back in 1014. However, in 1016 Sweyn's son, the famous, King Canut restored Viking rule. Indeed Canut solidified his hold on the throne by marrying Aethlered's wife, Emma.

It was clear that the Vikings were not a unified horde of invaders and they also fought for territory amongst themselves. This is evidenced by the fact that when Canut died his son Harold Harefoot, by his first wife, ruled southern England, whilst his stepmother, Emma resisted his ambitions to rule the whole of England and held-out for her and Canut's son, his half-brother, Harthacanut to return. Harthacanut was for some time having to remain in Denmark fighting against the Swedes and Norwegians who were trying to invade. After Harthacanut died, at an early age, Edward the son of Emma and her first husband, Aethelred, took the throne as Edward the Confessor and the Anglo-Saxon dynasty was restored.

On Edward's death in 1066, his brother-in-law, Harold Godwinson, whose sister was married to Edward, took the throne. However, Harold soon lost the throne, at the famous Battle of Hastings, to William of Normandy, who would become known as William the Conqueror. William was a nephew of Edward and claimed that he had earlier been named his heir during a time when Edward had fallen out with his father-in-law, Earl Godwin. Even though French, William was himself of Viking descent, being the great, great,

great grandson of a Viking warrior, Rollo. Charles King of the Francs gave Rollo an area of France in 918, as a ransom price for Rollo agreeing not to carry out any further attacks on Paris. This part of France came to be called Normandy, given its name from the "Norsemen" or men of the north. So, though Britain now became Norman, it was in effect a partial return to Viking roots.

You cannot drive anywhere in Britain without coming face to face with its history in some form or another. There are hundreds of stately homes, castles, manor houses, prehistoric settlements, stone circles, Roman remains, battlefields etc. Almost every village has a church that is likely to be at least 800 years old and a pub almost equally as old.

According to my count there are 146 castles in England, slightly more at 157 in Scotland and 41 in Wales. Every one of them has a history that is part of the rich story of Britain. Most of it is about conquest or dominance by Monarchs and invaders. It was William who introduced the stone castle to maintain his power over the land. Many castles remain only as ruins, ravaged by war or just deterioration, but many are still intact and many still lived in. Along the east coast they were built to defend from invaders from the Continent, whereas inland and on the borders of Wales and Scotland they were built to dominate and subjugate the people. Their histories are long and usually fascinating and intriguing. Whenever I passed a coastal castle I sought to find out some of its history and have included it in my narrative. Thus the recounting of my journey includes a lot of the history of Britain. It is though written in the order in which I made my journey. So it is a partial history of Britain in geographical order, rather than in any chronological order. As multiple monarchs visited castles on multiple occasions, some people will appear more than once on my trip as I come across them again in a different castle or city on my route.

The full history of Britain is much more complicated than this simple description, but hopefully it sets some of the scene for the intrigues and plots that we shall see as my journey unfolds.

The borders of England, Scotland and Wales have of course not always been as they are today. Throughout history they been broken up or combined under various regional Kings and invaders. For example, Wessex, Anglia and Northumbria had notable separate Kings. Scotland also had territory ruled by different Kings. What we know today as Strathclyde in Scotland at one time encompassed Cumbria, now in England. Similarly, Northumbria has been a separate Kingdom and at other times part of Scotland or England depending on who had the most power at any one time. A King of all of England or of all Scotland was not recognised before the late 9th century, with Alfred in England and Kenneth in Scotland and even then there were parts of Britain that they did not have full control over. Indeed a single Monarch who had control over of the whole of Britain did not occur until King James I of England and VI of Scotland in 1603.

All of these raids, invasions and power struggles have left their mark in the people who live in Britain today. The advent of genetic testing and the ability to trace the origins of our DNA has provided a unique opportunity to accurately determine who are the people of the British Isles and their origin. In 2004, a project, led by Professor Walter Bodmer at the University of Oxford, was started to try and map the genetic origins of the people of Britain. Already the early data has thrown up some startling findings. For example the DNA of the people in the Orkneys is almost completely different from anywhere else in Britain, reflecting not only the influence of the Norwegian invaders, but also that the people of these islands remained relatively static as a community over time. Similarly the people of Cornwall are distinctly different than other people in Britain and even more surprisingly are very different from the people in Devon, the next county to whom they are joined and who themselves are distinct from the majority of people elsewhere. In Wales there is a clear difference between the people of North Wales to the people living in South Wales. It is suggested that this is possibly due to language, as the people in the north traditionally have spoken Welsh rather than English and this would limit socializing and mixing.

From this work can also be seen distinctions between the catholic and protestant peoples in Northern Ireland and supports the very nature of Northern Ireland being James I's "Plantation of Ulster". In 1609 James I of England (and VI of Scotland) gave land to Protestants from Scotland as a means of negating the influence of the Irish Catholics and reducing the chances for rebellion. The DNA of many Protestants in Northern Island has matches to that of people in Scotland.

Certainly this genetic research demonstrates that the origins of the British people and indeed those that call themselves English, Scots and Welsh are not of a single source. Britain always has been and continues to be, a melting pot of ethnicities and origins. Our Kings and Queens have come not only from England, Scotland and Wales, but also from Denmark, Norway, Holland, France and Germany as well. Britain has therefore been strongly influenced and populated by peoples from right across Europe. It is ironic therefore that my journey took place at the time of "Brexit" when the people of Britain were being asked to vote on whether they should remain part of the European Union or leave and go forward outside of a unified Europe, where in fact most of their origins lie.

The island nature of Britain and its geographical location gives rise to one of the most talked about things in Britain, its weather. Weather on the east coast is influenced by Continental airflow, bringing generally warm dry air in the summer and very cold air in the winter. West coast weather is moderated by the Gulf Stream, a sixty mile wide, half a mile deep, current of warm water, that flows from the Gulf of Mexico right up to Northern Europe. This results not only in milder, more temperate weather on the west coast, but also more rainfall. The weather at both the top and bottom of the British Isles is influenced by either weather source, with the north of Scotland also impacted by air flow from the arctic at certain times of the year.

One of the wonderful things about Britain is the diversity of its Geography, packed into such a small land mass. The east coast is generally flat and is separated from Europe only by the fairly narrow English Channel, twenty miles across at its shortest point near Dover. The west coast is rugged and mountainous and apart from Ireland, about one hundred and ten miles away, there is nothing until you reach North America.

Geography and weather has greatly influenced land usage and the development and nature of communities, rooted over generations to an area, either by economic necessity for employment and income, or, through lack of travel and communication. This is reflected in the wide diversity of accents found in Britain. When people mostly lived, married, raised families and died in a small geographical area, there were few influences on the way in which they pronounced words. Many people today still live within only a few miles of where they were born; so, strong regional accents continue and indeed are thriving. An accent today is about belonging and being proud of region and home. Even the BBC, in search of inclusivity, has given up on "BBC English" and goes for diversity with all sorts of accents, sometimes the stronger the better, being heard widely.

Starting in Devon, where the accents are quite sing song, with somewhat of a raising of the voice at the end of the sentence as if asking a question, the first couple of days of my trip, along the south coast would see little change, only a flattening of the voice. When I turned the corner to travel north the differences in accents was much more noticeable, almost on a daily basis. From the cockney style accents in Essex, to the country burl of East Anglia, to the dogmatic short sentences of Yorkshire, to the very different and distinctive accent of the Geordies, eventually softening in Northumbria and becoming lilting on the Borders of Scotland and into Edinburgh. All of this adds to the glory of Britain! Direct travel from top to bottom in Britain is only about 800 miles but visit a number of places anywhere in between and you can feel that perhaps you are in a series of very different countries.

I set out to discover if the Britain I hold in my heart and in my memories still exists. My conclusion is that it does and much has remained the same and Britain continues as a wonderful and at times, magical place; this is especially so in the rural coastal areas, which form much of my journey.

Seen from its coast, Britain presents as a nation that is thriving, attractive and mostly unspoiled. Before I finished my trip though, the Brexit vote had happened with the vote being, by a very small margin, to leave Europe. Personally I found this very sad as so much of the origins of the British people are within Europe.

I hope you enjoy and are able to vicariously share in my experiences and explorations of the history and character of Britain and of its people and its islands. It offers a great place to visit and live and I am proud to say is part of my history and my heritage.

Exmouth to Ryde, Isle of Wight

185 Miles

Orcombe Point, Exmouth

Well, my coastal journey has begun. I set off this morning at 10.00am from Exmouth beach and the distinctive red sea cliffs at Orcombe Point. My destination today is Ryde on the Isle of Wight, selected, as I want to take an early morning ferry from near there across to Southsea. Orcombe Point will also be my finishing point in about 5 weeks time.

19

From a coastal seaside perspective, Exmouth is an excellent place to start a journey around Britain. It has a two-mile long beach of golden sands, with good "digging sand" ideal for sandcastles. The Esplanade runs from Orcombe Point in the east through to the harbour at the western end. It is a road of two halves. At one end, the harbour and marina is now the site of an extensive development of town homes and apartments with wonderful views over the Exe Estuary or the marina. These properties command high prices, well above those of some of the fine houses in the town. Residents are mainly out-of-towners, who don't live here full time, with apartments turned into vacation lets. Just up from the marina, facing the ocean, are lovely white Georgian houses, but, as it seems with all such properties along the coast, almost entirely turned into hotels, guesthouses or rental properties. The area behind is generally red brick, older style properties with no distinguishing architecture to make it attractive and extending into a dated 1950's style town center with little charm.

The remainder of the esplanade is generally open and very pleasant. There is a new hotel alongside a not very special restaurant and a small amusement area and bowling alley on the town side and a couple of small cafes and ice cream vendors on the seaward side, but generally the council are to be commended for not allowing any buildings that block the lovely estuary views, apart from the necessary, but magnificent, new RNLI station built right on the beach.

The River Exe at Exmouth is gradually silting up with the sandbanks moving around. In recent years it became impossible to securely launch, at all tide states, the previous Trent Class lifeboat, with its deep draft. So the station was relocated from the Marina to its new site closer to the ocean and to be outfitted with a new Shannon class lifeboat, which is a joy to see in action. It is launched and recovered by a purpose built tractor that takes it into the water. The return of the lifeboat is particularly spectacular. They just point it at the beach and run full speed, thus beaching the vessel a good way up the sand, where the tractor then collects it and returns it to the boathouse. It felt appropriate that I should be starting my journey close to a lifeboat station, having served as a volunteer with the Royal Canadian Marine Search & Rescue in Vancouver for almost 8 years.

There used to be some very large sand dunes close to where the lifeboat station is now located. These have completely disappeared over the past two or three years. Bad winter storms dispersed them, mainly across the road and the parkland opposite, or back into the ocean. In January of 2016 I drove along the Esplanade here in Exmouth and found it similar to skiing across moguls with sand inches deep covering the road.

Just past the RNLI Station I turned right and headed over the cliffs towards Littleham. The cliff road is narrow and the bank and hedgerow high so there is little sight of the sea until you reach Sandy Bay with its vast Caravan and Holiday Chalet Park called Devon Cliffs. There must be a thousand caravans and chalets here. They all appear to be good quality and I am sure meet the needs of many families looking for a seaside holiday. We found from personal experience though that you can rent a holiday home in the neighbourhood for less money than the cost of booking a caravan here for a week! For me it would be just too many people all in one place all at the same time. Unfortunately, a feature of much of today's drive has been the plethora of chalet and caravan parks right along the south coast. Though they serve a function, they are blighting Britain's lovely coastal vistas.

The next town I reached was Budleigh Salterton, surely one of the treasures of the many seaside towns of Devon. It is not much bigger than a good-sized village. It is notable in that here is the start of the World Heritage Jurassic Coast. The sandstone cliffs running eastward along the coast towards Weymouth and Bournemouth have provided some of the most exciting fossil and dinosaur remains in Britain. Budleigh has a pebble beach made up of smooth stones of the most incredible designs and colours. There is a high pebble bank running parallel to the ocean onto which the waves break. This is the remains of an ancient riverbed that thousands of years ago, apparently, was joined to Brittany in France. This high bank is an extension of the beach and stretches towards the cliffs at the northern end, but is eventually breached by the exit of the River Otter into the ocean. When the tide comes in the river cannot escape and backs up behind the shingle bank and meanders amongst channels within the mud flats. Over time this has become a haven for birds such that the "binoculared common twitcher" is seen here in droves throughout the year. The Otter Head cliffs at the mouth of the river are a famous place for photography and painting.

The River Otter was navigable for about a mile and a half up to Otterton until the 16th Century, when a huge storm drove the pebbles across the mouth of the river. Significant silting then made the river too shallow for boats. In the early nineteenth century French Napoleonic prisoners of war were used to build drainage ditches and reconstruct the land behind the pebble bank and expand the area for farming.

22

Otter Head, Budleigh Salterton, Devon

The name Salterton comes from the time, between the 12th and 15th century when the monks produced salt in the town based at Otterton Priory. They built salt pans at the mouth of the River Otter where it enters the sea. On an incoming tide seawater would enter the pans and then as the tide receded the water trapped in the pans would evaporate leaving behind a crust of salt. In the early nineteenth century, close to the river mouth a number of Lime Kilns were constructed, with coal and limestone being landed on the beach for turning into fertilizer.

Very close to Budleigh Salterton is the village of East Budleigh, which was the home and birthplace in 1552 of Sir Walter Raleigh. As a boy he would know well the beach and harbour area at Otterton and Budleigh. Indeed on the very walkable sea front, at the edge of the town, is a house, the Octagon, with a memorial to Sir John Everett Millais, who here produced his famous painting, "The Boyhood of Raleigh".

23

Sir Walter Raleigh was of course a favourite of Queen Elizabeth 1, the last Tudor monarch. The Tudors continue to have a connection with Budleigh in that it is today the home of Dame Hilary Mantel, the author of the book and television series Wolf Hall, which tells the tales of the intrigues within Henry VIIIs household. I will come across a lot more connections with the Tudors on my journey around the coast.

From Budleigh I followed the Sidmouth Road, turning off at East Budleigh and on into Otterton. Otterton today is a charming village with a mill powered by the River Otter. The mill still operates today, but now only produces small quantities of flour sufficient to be turned into bread and cakes that are sold in the café situated on the property.

It is a very pleasant two-mile walk along the River Otter from the Mill to Budleigh Salterton. It is possible to see trout glistening in the shallow water and beavers also are now making their home here. No one knows, or admits, as to how the beavers came to the river, but there are strong efforts being made to keep them secure and allow them to reestablish themselves, having been wiped out as a native species in Britain in the 16th century. This walk along the riverbank is probably one of the nicest strolls in Devon.

A tributary of the Otter runs down Otterton's small high street, but this is not so charming at times of high rainfall and on many occasions the villagers have had to use sand banks to stop the river entering their homes. Though I live in Vancouver, my first ever white Christmas was actually experienced in Otterton. In 2010, we had rented a cottage. On Christmas Eve the snow fell so quickly we could not get out of the village. But the local Pub was open and that made it all right!

Out of Otterton the road is single track. You can turn right and go down to the beach at Ladrum Bay, with, once again, a huge caravan park. Indeed it is hardly possible to use the beach here as the only parking is in the caravan and camping park. Rather than drive down and have to drive back up I continued on along the single-track road towards Sidmouth. This goes up and over the cliffs, providing spectacular views as you reach the top. The view back to Exmouth from here must be one of the loveliest in Devon. The road then drops down into a small wooded area and through the trees you get a terrific view of Sidmouth.

※

Sidmouth is another almost unspoiled little town, mainly Edwardian and a favourite of Queen Victoria; though on her first visit here as a small child, her father the Duke of York was taken ill and died. Sidmouth is also a mainly shingle and pebble beach. A lot of the pebbles were brought here in the early 1990s after storms washed away the beach and undermined the esplanade sea wall. Rock "islands" acting as groins were put in and these are now creating sandy areas as they hold back the wave action. Sidmouth is one of my favourite places in Devon with old-fashioned shops and a family department store, Fields, which prides itself on offering "service as it used to be". For the genteel folk of Sidmouth, afternoon tea at Fields is a pleasant thing to do. In the last few months though the family have sold Fields to a Chinese company, so it remains to be seen whether changes will be made. The sea cliffs here are very unstable, particularly after heavy rain and some of the footpaths and fences at the far end of the town have now fallen onto the beach, but the famous Jacob's Ladder, at the south end of the town, is still a safe and popular beach. The cliff walk from the Ladder, past the Connaught Gardens and into the town is a very pleasant thing to do. The sea front is also excellent for strolling with one or two lovely hotels where you can get a good Devon cream tea.

This is a retirement town, as are so many of the seaside towns on Britain's south coast. In 2004 the population of Sidmouth was said to be about 15,000 with 40% aged over 65. By 2011 the population had fallen to just under 13,000, but I could not find out if this was due to "natural causes" among the residents. Despite its seemingly geriatric legend, it is host to an annual Folk Festival in August, which is well attended by people from all across Britain.

If you follow the sea front to the end and then make your way through the small streets you will come to a ford, which, of course, I had to drive through at speed and make a wave! Some of the locals also gave me a wave; at least I think it was a wave, so I just waved back.

The road comes to a junction and here you turn right to Salcombe Regis where there is an observatory that still operates. Once on the main road you quickly turn off right towards Branscombe. Just past the turn off is a Donkey Sanctuary, free to enter and with 100s of donkeys living a happy retirement. Branscombe village is reached via a very narrow and steep road. You will not any find drivers from North America on this road, at least not twice! The road is not even as wide as an American parking space, yet traffic is two-way. You just have to drive cautiously and if you meet another vehicle, one driver has to use the passing places. A great way to make someone's day and receive a genuine thank you wave and a smile. About half way down is a superb National Trust tearoom, opposite the forge, offering Devon cream teas.

Probably the best pub in Devon, the Masons Arms is located in the main part of the village, but keep on going to the beach. This was the site a few years ago of a shipwreck. The MSC Napoli broke its back and was beached on a sand bank. Lots of containers were washed off and swept up onto the beach. Locals then came down to help themselves to the pickings, which even included six BMW motorbikes! Though the Police did all they could some of the loot was never recovered. Smuggling and pirating is obviously still in the Devon genes.

Just back up from the beach you follow the road to Beer. No sight of the sea as the journey is along typical sunken roads with high banks and hedges on top. Allegedly all of these roads were trodden out by cattle in times past, before tarmac was invented, hence their meandering ways. Just before you enter Beer you come across the entrance to the ancient Beer caves that go back to Roman times. These provided the white limestone blocks for many British buildings, including the Tower of London, St.Pauls Cathedral, and twenty seven other cathedrals. The hammering away at the stone was so noisy that miners would eventually go deaf giving rise to the term that someone is "stone deaf". The caves are now protected as the roost for the declining greater horseshoe bat colony. They are open to visit, for a fee.

Beer is also, almost, another one street town with the road leading to the beach. However it has great charm, made more so by the small stream that runs in a gulley alongside the pavement. On the beach are drawn up a number of fishing boats that are still very active. This is a pretty scene, made more attractive by the colourful beach huts that are lined up.

27

Beach Huts at Beer, Devon

Now the beach hut is something particularly British. Its origins are probably in the huts on wheels that were used by the Victorians to change into their swimming costumes and be hauled to the waters edge for them to swim in the ocean. Today they have no wheels, are generally brightly painted and stand side by side in long lines at the rear of the beach. They are usually owned by the local Council and can be rented for the season or longer. It is actually very difficult to find one still available to rent as families repeat book them year after year. They are basic, without electricity or water and overnight sleeping is not allowed. Hopefully, if you are lucky enough to get one, there is a toilet block an easy stroll away. Surprisingly, although it is hard to get hold of one, they never seem to be widely used. On almost any day on the beach, even the bright and sunny ones, many of the huts are locked and shuttered. If they are in use, generally their occupants are elderly and asleep by the door in a chair. You can espy a kettle and teapot inside and the ubiquitous plastic container in which sandwiches or fruitcake have been brought from home to consume. If there are younger occupants, the sandwich packages will probably be marked with the name of the local supermarket, showing that the modern generation, prefer instant food to the trouble (and pleasure) of making their own.

The footpath above the beach and onto the cliff provides wide views across to Seaton, the next town along the coast. The road to Seaton offers more coastal views, but I find Seaton a disappointing place. Though the town is tidy, its location facing directly onto the ocean, with nothing to see but sea, makes it feel bleak to me. In fact you cannot see much of the sea from the road. There is a high wall blocking any view from a parked car. You have to get out to see over it. No sitting in the car here with a cup of tea or having a doze, while the waves wash on the sand. Seaton is however saved from mediocrity by its wonderful old tramway that runs right along the Axe estuary to Colyton; absolutely worth the trip if you have the time. We have in the past had a great day out with the children on the tramway. There is also Pecorama, with its narrow track railway, which is a fun experience for children. The model railway exhibition here though has decreased in size over the years and is now slightly disappointing.

You leave Seaton crossing the mouth of the River Axe and follow up the estuary, before going down again to reach the town of Lyme Regis. Most people know Lyme as the setting for the film the French Lieutenant's Woman and the famous picture of Meryl Street standing on the end of the Cob, the Harbour Wall.

Lyme Regis and the Cob, Dorset

There is no doubt that Lyme is a very pretty place, but traffic through the town is congested and parking is awful. But a Monday in May, before the school's break up for the summer, is clearly the time to go. Previously whenever I have tried to park down by the Cob in the nearby car park it has not been possible. In the summer it must be worse and I am sure traffic jams occur as people going down the hill looking for parking, meet others coming up the hill who have given up looking. You can use the Park & Ride just outside the town for £5.

The Cob invites you to walk on it like Meryl. But be warned! It is uneven, has no fencing and slopes towards the ocean. I felt very nervous on it. The beach next to the Marina has very good sand, but I suspect that it is imported as elsewhere it is shingle. I also noticed that they had groomed it. The only other place that I have been to that does this is Miami in Florida!

To drive through the town is a challenge as there is a very narrow section, on a slope and on a bend. Rightly the town has traffic lights here to minimise collisions, but the heroes have to be the bus drivers (double deckers no less) that negotiate this hazard plus also all of the country lanes to and from the town.

On entering Lyme Regis you leave Devon behind and now are in the county of Dorset. As you take the road, which has now turned eastward, the first seaside place you come to is Charmouth, famous for the fossils that have been found here and also for Golden Cap the highest point on this coast. I well remember Charmouth as the place in which my son nearly drowned. In the hot summer of 1976 we came to Charmouth for two weeks. We were joined by some cousins for the day and being very hot, stood in the ocean to chat. I was in charge of the children. My cousin suddenly said, "Where's James?" We looked around and could not see him but his hat was floating close by. We jumped and grabbed at the hat and found that it was still on the head of a two year old that came up coughing and spluttering from beneath the water. He was too young to tell me off, but his mother certainly did!

After Charmouth the main road takes you to Bridport from where you can drop down to the ocean at the charming little place of West Bay. This served as much of the backdrop for the popular TV series, Broadchurch. The harbour here is also known as Bridport Harbour and is not a natural one so has been challenged many times over the centuries by the ravages of the sea and from silting up. The two piers, east and west, have been modernized and upgraded in recent times to provide some protection for boats from the open sea.

The coastal road is now mainly the B3157 that goes on to Abbotsbury where there are the remains of a Benedictine Abbey, originally built in the reign of King Canut in the 11th century and then later destroyed by Henry VIII in the 16th century.

The dissolution of the monasteries, by Henry VIII, beginning in 1536, was a momentous time in English history. Henry's breakaway from the Roman Catholic Church was stimulated by his anger at the Pope for refusing to give him a divorce from his first wife Catherine of Aragon. However, it was more than that. This was just the spark that lit the flame. The Pope's refusal demonstrated clearly that there was another power in the land, apparently greater than that of the King. And as well as the ability to wield power the Church owned almost half of all of the land wealth and money in Britain. The Crown, through the Barons and Earls had access only to the other half and the King was himself rationed as to how much of this he could access for his own use and the payment of wars etc. Thus in "protesting" at the Pope being Head of the Church and taking this role for himself, Henry was taking upon himself greater power. He now had the ability to write his own laws without the hindrance of Papal veto. It also gave him the ability to control the Priests, who were able to influence the thinking and loyalty of much of the population. Importantly though it also gave him access to immense wealth.

Though the protestant Church of England was now born, many of the rites and ceremonies performed by the Church continued in the old Catholic style. But this act by Henry VIII was to have significant and long-lasting repercussions, some of which are still felt today. A life order was destroyed; countless historic and architecturally important buildings were also destroyed, but more than this, thousands of people, over time, lost their lives through supporting one denomination or another. There were clearly those Roman Catholics who strongly opposed Henry's actions, but there were also those who felt that his actions did not go far enough and from this camp grew the Puritans who themselves were the stimulus for significant and bloody upheavals, with the most notable individual being Oliver Cromwell.

Abbotsbury is today famous, less for its Abbey ruins and more for its swannery. This covers a 2-acre fresh water lagoon and at times there are almost 600 swans here. It is believed that the swannery was actually started by the monks at the Abbey when swans would be provided as royal fare. As I drove by there were notices proclaiming that lots of cygnets had been born and were available for visitors to see.

After Abbotsbury the road becomes the B3159 that leads to Weymouth and Portland. The ocean frontage going all the way from Golden Cap to Portland is notable for the pebble bank formation called Chesil Beach, which is up to 15 metres high and stretches for 29 kilometers. This is a storm bank that was created by the ocean about 6000 years ago when sea levels were higher. The pebbles here are markedly different from those at Budleigh, belying their different origins. Chesil Beach is made up of very small pebbles, not much bigger than shingle.

Portland is technically an island, but is connected to the mainland by Chesil beach and a road bridge. It appears more as a peninsular of the main land. It is famous for its very tall lighthouse, known as Portland Bill at its southernmost tip. This is one of the sixty-eight lighthouses that are prominently placed around Britain's coast providing safety to mariners.

Historically Portland's two main industries have been the navy and quarrying. Portland stone is famous and has been used for many major buildings in England, including St. Paul's Cathedral, whose architect, Sir Christopher Wren, just happened to be the Member of Parliament for Weymouth and controller of the Portland quarries! The stone is almost white when quarried but fades to either a light grey or a warm yellow colour, somewhat akin to Cotswold stone.

The drive onto the island of Portland is not especially attractive as the quarries and cliffs above the town seem to overpower it. It was a sunny day and I saw at least three men walking around with no shirt on. Each of them was covered all over with heavy tattoos. Either this is the old naval tradition, or, the new fashion that seems to be afflicting so many men (and women) these days. The view from the top of Portland looking back along Chesil Beach is excellent.

Chesil Beach from Portland, Hampshire

34

Weymouth the next town on is a grand Georgian town of good size. It is in fact larger than the county town of Dorchester. It is built at the mouth of the River Wey and shops and restaurants run along this back from the sea. It has an excellent sandy beach that appears to run all the way along its seafront. Weymouth infamously, is known as the place where the Black Death was brought to Britain on board a ship that landed at Melcombe Regis, part of the town where the harbour is located.

Weymouth was the venue for the sailing competitions in the 2012 Olympics and grand plans were hatched to smarten it up in time for the Games. However, little of these materialized, due to delays and lack of finance. Some of the town was redeveloped with the addition of new bars and restaurants that have, apparently, fallen to the curse of the now common British young person's penchant for binge drinking. This is a sad situation and a blight on many towns and the undoing of many a young person. Even television in North America shows news film of young people in the UK and especially girls, spewing up or lying face down in the street after a night on the town. This is something that North America has more of a handle on with its stricter drinking laws, especially restrictions on drinking in public areas. Unfortunately it seems to be becoming a rite of passage for the British young person. In North America the bar and restaurant owners and staff, can be fined for supplying alcohol to a person beyond the level of intoxication. Certainly they can be sued if anyone is injured as a result. Such laws in the UK may be the only way to bring this to an end.

I had little time to stop in Weymouth, as I wanted to see both the great sea arch of Durdle Door and the almost circular cove at Lulworth. Unfortunately, entering yet more chalet/caravan parks and paying a fee is the only way you can experience them. At Durdle Door, it cost £4 to park so I drove in, took a photo from a distance and then drove out.

It was by this stage that I had realised that my journey planning was way too optimistic and I was averaging, with stops, only 20 miles per hour rather than the 30 I had planned for. If I hung around too much I might miss my ferry to the Isle of Wight, which had been booked and paid for. Lulworth Cove village is very small; indeed the car park seems bigger than the village, probably confirming how popular a place this is. My journey was to drive the coastal road, rather than stop and sight see at every point, so after a quick glance I carried on, but regretting that I had not stopped longer.

In my haste to get to the ferry on time, I switched on the GPS rather than use the road atlas. The GPS, despite my trying to instruct it differently took me to a main road. OK, I thought, I can make up some time. Unfortunately Dorset County Council had decided to resurface 10 miles of road by sprinkling a little bit of sticky tar and then pouring gravel over it. As this surface was then deemed to be slippy, until enough vehicles had driven on it, the Council had arranged for traffic to travel in convoy, led by a police car driving at 20mph for the whole of the ten miles. At one point, where I actually came across the workmen in the road, they had posted flag persons with stop/go boards, which meant single file traffic. The hold-ups were at least 5 miles long in each direction. My GPS gave me no alternatives so I had to stick with it.

When I eventually emerged close to the prominent ruins of Corfe Castle, I was so behind time that all I could now do was take a photo through the car window and continue on.

The castle is very much a ruin. An earlier castle stood on this spot and is noted for being the place where King Edward the Martyr was murdered, to be replaced on the throne by his half-brother Aethelred (the Unready).

Corfe was one of the first and thus one of the oldest stone castles in Britain, having been built by William the Conqueror to protect the road between Wareham and Swanage, which ran through a gap in the Purbeck Hills. Over the following years it was altered many times by numerous residents before being on the wrong side in the English Civil War and falling foul of Oliver Cromwell, who ordered its destruction.

The castle had been purchased by Sir John Bankes, who was Attorney General to King Charles I, just a few years before the Civil War started. While Sir John was absent the castle was besieged by Parliamentary troops, but with only four people to assist, his wife Lady Mary was able to resist the siege, demonstrating the power and impregnability of the castle. Eventually more supporters were smuggled in to her aid and reached as high as 80. They resisted for over three years against Parliamentary forces that numbered almost 600. Unfortunately in 1645 one of Lady Bankes' officers colluded with the Parliamentarians and on the pretext of bringing fresh reinforcements, brought in Parliamentary soldiers in disguise. The brave Lady and her guard were overpowered but she was eventually allowed to leave unharmed. However, Cromwell ordered that the castle be destroyed. When the monarchy was restored in 1660, the Bankes family was given back the castle, but it was so ruined that they instead built a large house at Kingston Lacy, near Wimborne. In 1980 the latest descendent, Ralph Bankes, bequeathed Corfe castle, the village and the manor at Kingston Lacy to the National Trust.

To get to my ferry to the IOW, I had to take another ferry from Studland and then drive through Bournemouth. The ferry from Studland to Sandbanks is a delight. The journey only lasts about 10 minutes, but you get excellent views across into Sandbanks and what are said to be the most expensive houses in Britain: £20 million, £30 million and up.

When you get off the ferry it feels like you are driving into a Mediterranean town such as Cap Ferat. The road from Sandbanks takes you into Bournemouth, which has one of the longest sandy beaches and esplanades in England. Bournemouth is mainly a Victorian town and is the largest coastal town on the south coast. Also from 2015 it can now boast that it has, for the first time in its history, a Premiership football team, known locally as the Cherries. On certain Saturdays in the year you may now find teams such as Manchester United, Liverpool, Arsenal, or Chelsea "in town".

Bournemouth can almost be described as a perfect town, with lovely houses, hotels and guest houses and despite relying heavily on tourists does not seem to have given itself over to them, keeping an "expensive" and quality residential aura. Bournemouth must be one of the youngest towns in Britain. Until 1810 the area was just open heathland. It was at this time that an army Captain in the Dorset rangers, Lewis Tregonwell, decided to build a house here. He had been given responsibility for protecting this area of coastline from Napoleonic invaders and the area was under the command of Henry Bankes of Kingston Lacey (and Corfe Castle). The town steadily grew, its expansion hastened by the building of spas and the coming of the railway. Tregonwell was much revered becoming town mayor, a magistrate and Deputy Lieutenant of Dorset, but it was only after his death in 1832 that a large secret chamber, six feet high, was discovered under the floor of the Lodge built in the grounds of his house. Such chambers were common in houses used for smuggling and it is now thought that he may well have bolstered his income by "trading" in duty free goods.

My endeavours to drive on the road closest to the ocean were somewhat thwarted by the large coach in front of me that blocked most of my view of the road signposts. Eventually I found my way and followed the ocean to Christchurch, just as pretty as Bournemouth but with a more laid back feel.

Christchurch was established back in the 7th century by missionaries sent to Wessex by St. Birinus Bishop of Dorchester (in Oxfordshire not the one in Dorset). Then it was called Twynham as it was between the two rivers of the Avon and the Stour. The castle at Christchurch was another one that suffered at the hands of Oliver Cromwell and little remains. Christchurch Harbour is very shallow having a number of salt marshes. Apparently the most lucrative trade for the town in the 1700s and 1800s was smuggling as the coastguard boats had too deep a draft to be able to follow the smugglers into the shallow harbour. Mudeford Spit protects the entrance to the harbour and has good sandy beaches with the proverbial British beach huts.

After Christchurch you continue to New Milton, which lacks the quality feel of its other two neighbours. Here again the most memorable sight was bare chested tattoo man, or at least one of his cousins. I suppose if you spend that much money on covering your body you must feel the need to uncover it and show off what you have got. However, the value of it is lost if others don't like what they see. My Father had a tattoo on his arm, in memory of his Mother. He had it done when he was in the army. Unfortunately as he grew older, so did the tattoo and it became hard to read and resembled more of a blue/black area of skin. He regretted having it done. I wonder if in a number of years young people who have tattoos today will regret them as they age and lose definition?

At Milton On Sea there was an excellent view across to my destination for tonight the Isle of Wight and the famous rock formation, the Needles, at its westerly point. But I needed to hurry to catch my ferry.

I arrived at the car park of the Wight ferry in Lymington with one minute to spare. They had me in the system and the man in the booth gave me a ticket telling me to place it on my windscreen and go into Lane 3. After all of my rushing, I sat there for 15 minutes. Then the same man from the ticket office came along and asked me for the ticket back and said I could now board the ferry! They obviously take recycling very seriously. One unusual and presumably money generating scheme used by Wight Ferries is that if you pay at the terminal rather than on line, they charge you £10 extra. However, though cheaper, if you book on line there is no refund if you have to cancel. I suppose this is the corollary of charging a "convenience fee" for the privilege of booking on line, which so many firms are now seemingly doing, which is quite outrageous in my view.

The ferry to the IOW was just 40 minutes and at £55 (or £65 if you pay at the terminal) gave excellent views of the hundreds (though probably more correct to say thousands) of pleasure boats moored in Lymington harbor and marina. Lymington was a salt producing town from the middle ages up to the nineteenth century, when its fortunes turned to shipbuilding.

I arrived at Yarmouth on the Isle of Wight and turned right out of the ferry dock to head to the Needles Park to have a closer view of these iconic structures before the light failed. Unfortunately the Park itself is a rather ghastly entertainment area. Britain seems to excel at turning wonderful geographic structures into tatty places. Rather than walk the couple of miles on the cliffs to the Needles, and be in danger of falling over in the dark, I drove into the car park, took a photo from a distance and left.

The Needles, Isle-Of-Wight

The Isle of Wight has a long and interesting history and was a favourite place of Queen Victoria who built Osborne House here for her country mansion. It also has the ancient Carrisbrooke Castle. Fortifications have been on this site from at least the time of the Romans, but the stone castle was not built until the 12th century. It has been associated with most Kings of England, but famously it was here that Charles I was kept prisoner for fourteen months prior to his execution in 1649. Ironically the castle is only a 10 minute drive from the much more recently constructed Parkhurst Prison, so the Island is still today a place where people are kept at "Her Majesty's pleasure"! The last Royal to use the castle was Princess Beatrice, daughter of Queen Victoria, whilst she acted as Governor of the Isle of Wight. It is now under the management of English Heritage.

I have fond memories of the Isle of Wight, often flying here for lunch and landing at one of its two airfields, in the days when I shared a plane based at White Waltham Aerodrome near to Maidenhead. Flying was expensive in those days, but it is even more so today. Since moving to Canada I have taken up boating instead of flying. The boat is a bit like a plane. It goes fast, has trim tabs and bounces up and down a lot. Like flying it is also an expensive hobby!

Partly because of my love of this Island, I had decided to visit here and drive around its southern end and thus omit the same geographic area that it covered on the mainland. This allowed me to feel that I really was at the furthest point of the coastline. By doing so I missed out Southampton, one of Britain's most famous maritime cities. Unfortunately, arriving late and leaving early meant that I really saw very little of this lovely island and I could have saved myself the expensive ferry fares. Indeed the Isle of Wight ferries, at £55 one way, proved to be the most expensive in Britain. If I do this coastal trip again I think I will skip the Isle of Wight altogether and drive through Southampton.

Apart from stopping at an old pub in Niton, highly touted but not overly special and with sticky, unclean tables, I arrived at my hotel, on the other side of the island, the Travel Lodge in Ryde. This had just opened and no one could direct me too it, so I rang the number listed for the hotel to find that

I was talking to a central call office at a premium rate cost for the call. They then gave me the address, but as the hotel does have its own number, why couldn't they just print that in their brochure? I expect they make a lot of money from their premium phone line, but that's certainly not the way to attract and keep customers.

The hotel when I got there was very nice, clean and comfortable with good Wi-Fi. They have no car park though, which meant that I had to park in the road; free at night but you have to move it by 8.00am in the morning. This also meant that I had to make two trips to take out all of my luggage and film equipment just to keep it safe. In the morning it would only be a short drive to the ferry across to Portsmouth.

I had the day before thought that I would use AirBnB for most of my accommodation on this trip. However, when I put in the date and my destination of Ryde, I got five pages of possible places to stay. I chose one, clicked on it and it came up as not available. This continued for two pages of selections. I then contacted AirBnB and asked why is it that they have filters for all sorts of things but not a filter to block B&Bs that are already booked on the day you want them. The young lady who replied said that if I put in the date I want to stay only those available would come up. I had put the date in, but tried it again with the same result. I emailed her again to say that this did not work, but she replied that it did, perhaps intimating that I was one of those irritating, computer illiterate idiots who can't follow instructions. Well I don't feel that I am completely computer illiterate or an idiot. I followed the instructions twice more and Air BnB, I can assure you that it did not work so don't try and tell me that it does, 'cos it doesn't. I have 33 more nights to book yet, so it does not auger well!

Isle of Wight to Hastings

Miles 185

Beachy Head, East Sussex

I had a very pleasant overnight stay in the new Travel Lodge in Ryde. I declined the hotel breakfast of a pre-packed muffin and orange juice in favour of a banana that I had brought with me and a cup of tea from the obligatory British kettle in my room.

As I was awake early I thought that I would try and catch an earlier ferry. I discovered last night that I had left the charger for my computer back in Exmouth, so I would need to find a PC World, or similar, to replace it. I thought that Portsmouth rather than the Isle of Wight would be the best place to do this, so an early arrival would give me the time to buy a charger and keep to schedule. The journey to the ferry was short but was notable for a sign outside The Fleming Arms Pub. Now quirky sayings outside British pubs are becoming very common, I suppose it is a way of saying – "don't look at our scruffy exterior, we're friendly people inside". However, I think the Landlord at the Fleming Arms must have had a bit of a mental glitch when he put up this sign. *"Come in for a drink and a shave – and bring your husband!"* Probably intended to be funny, but not sure this Landlord has a wife or she might have told him why women reading this sign might not want to come into his Pub.

I did get the earlier ferry and it was a sunny journey with a great view across to Portsmouth. Before you get to Portsmouth there are a number of large, round, black structures in the water. These date back to the end of the nineteenth century when they were constructed as forts to protect Portsmouth harbour from an anticipated French invasion. Today they are obsolete and some of these forts have now been turned into rather exclusive and isolated private residences. Indeed daily ferries to and from France run right past them without any shots being fired!

I had not realised, until I looked up the history, but Portsmouth is actually built on an island, Portsea Island and is Britain's only island city. There are so many roads and bridges into the City that I had not appreciated this before and you do not at all get a feel of being on an island. Along with the harbour forts there are numerous other forts around the City and it was at one time the most heavily fortified place in Britain. However, the forts were constructed before the aeroplane was envisaged and the city was heavily bombed during the Second World War with the loss of almost 1000 civilian lives.

On my first visit to Portsmouth I can remember seeing it as a rather bleak place with black, weeping and crumbling concrete structures, built in a hurry after the war. This is not the case today. It is a bright, clean, lively city, which makes the most of its waterfront and its maritime heritage. It is the home of Nelson's flagship, HMS Victory, which remains as the oldest naval ship in the world still in commission, though it no longer sets out to sea. It was on the Victory that I learned the meaning behind the saying "It's cold enough to freeze the balls off a brass monkey"! If you didn't already know, the brass monkey was a brass frame that would hold a pile of iron cannon balls, ready for firing by the guns. When it got very cold the iron of the cannon balls would shrink at a different rate to that of the brass. This meant that the cannon balls became slightly smaller and then did not fit the frame, so they would roll off across the gun deck.

As well as the Victory there is also the remains of the Mary Rose. The Mary Rose was Henry VIII's flagship. It had had an illustrious service, however, it was modified to carry larger and heavier guns, which potentially meant that it rode lower in the water. In July 1545 French ships tried to enter Portsmouth harbour and attack the English fleet. There was little wind so the French expected the British to be unable to maneuver. However the wind did get up and the Mary Rose sailed into battle. What happened is still disputed but it would appear that as she made a hard turn about, there was an increase in the force of the wind and the ship heeled over and water entered the open gun ports. The amount of water that came in was such that the stability of the ship was immediately changed and she quickly capsized and sank. Out of a crew of 400, only 35 managed to escape the sudden sinking. The wreck was eventually brought to the surface in October 1982 and now lies in a special gallery, where it is continuously treated to prevent further decay of the wood. The newly constructed museum and display was not due to open to the public until a month from now so, though I did not have time anyway, I was unable to view it. I understand that it is something well worth seeing.

As the ferry enters the harbour there is a good view of the stern of a wooden sailing ship and also the striking Spinnaker Tower, one of the tallest constructions in Britain

The Spinnaker Tower, Portsmouth, Hampshire

On leaving the ferry, I set my GPS to find the nearest PC World, which the GPS said was about a twenty minute drive away. I drove away from the docks and down North End high street. Though Portsmouth has been revitalized with a great blend of historic and modern buildings, as with most of Britain, it is the high street that spoils it. The ambience and the architecture of almost all British high streets has been ruined by retail shops being allowed to front their buildings with large, loud and often hideously coloured logos. Town center shops have of course been seriously affected by out of town Superstores, but the high streets don't help themselves by being so ugly and the councils worsen the situation by making parking either impossible or expensive. I recall, from a visit a few years ago to the tourist mecca of Stratford on Avon, how this town had made good efforts to tackle the problem. In Stratford, shops are not allowed to display brand names or logos on the outside front of their shop, they can only have something in the window. The streets there, when I last visited at least, looked quality and the architecture appealing and mainly uniform, which encourages you to go there. If the high streets became attractive places to shop and socialize, with easy access, I am sure people would come back and shop there. North America has a similar problem. Generally there are no English style high streets in North America, but in their place are horrendous strip malls of square boxes, with equally garish colours. Do we really need a golden arch to tell us where MacDonald's is located?

My GPS took me to PC World (easy to see as it had a big sign outside!) and I purchased a new Apple charger for the horrendous price of at £65 pounds. That'll teach me to check I have everything before I leave on a trip! I then returned to the City and drove along the very drivable sea front following signs to Southsea. Southsea is more the resort end of Portsmouth and has a two-mile long ocean esplanade. It looked clean and inviting.

Leaving Southsea, I drove through Eastney and noticed a sign outside Café Beano offering all day breakfasts, plus there just happened to be the convenience of a vacant parking spot right outside the door that confirmed I should stop. The proprietor was very friendly and asked me did I want a large cup for my tea or a mug. I opted for the large cup, but when I saw him put a tea bag in this and make a move to add hot water I had to stop him. "I live in North America" I said "where no one knows how to make tea and it is served not in a tea pot, but with lukewarm water in a cup and a very poor quality tea bag on the side. As I am now in England I would have hoped to have good tea, in a pot, with boiling water poured on it."

"Well you certainly can have that my friend" he replied "I've got a lot of teapots, but no one asks for tea in a pot these days. You're the first for ages". Surely England must be going to the dogs if it now does not even serve tea properly! I must say I thoroughly enjoyed my excellent and not expensive breakfast and of course the pot of tea. So Café Beano, if you have lots of teapots, use them. Buck the trend and get your customers used to tea made, as it should be!

After breakfast I headed on making for Selsey. The road from Eastney actually heads inland but follows the water around the natural Langstone Harbour. After about a twelve-mile drive you end up only about half a mile from Southsea, but facing it across the water from Hayling Island. This is a popular spot for day trippers and especially wind surfers.

49

Indeed the man who invented and patented the wind surfer came from Hayling Island. The beach here is a mix of sand and shingle, the latter having been brought in to prevent erosion. A lot of the seaside cottages here are rustic, but fetch a high price when they come onto the market. Overall though, the place feels quite shabby.

To the west side of Hayling Island are the waters of Chichester Harbour. Again you have to drive back up, about five miles, to reach the A259, which follows a number of fingers of water from the harbour. Just before Chichester I came across one of the prettiest villages that I have so far seen, Bosham. This is the quintessential English village, facing onto one of the many fingers of Chichester Harbour. Bosham Quay is hugely attractive and I was able to park right on the hard beach, though you can only do this when the tide is out! The houses and buildings all around the quay are old and quaint and the rest of the village similarly.

Bosham Quay, West Sussex

Bosham has strong links to the history of England. King Canut had a palace here, though nothing of it now remains. He is perhaps best known as the King who tried to command the tides, and it is here, at Bosham that this is said to have taken place. The story is often portrayed of a King who thought that he was so powerful even the tides would obey him. However, it is probably a wrong interpretation and was more likely Canut endeavoring to show to his sycophantic courtiers that he was but human and his power was limited. Amazing to think that I am sitting in my car, parked on the tidal beach, in possibly the exact same spot that King Canut once sat!

Canut was Danish and the son of Sweyn Forkbeard, the first Norse King of England. The history of the Norse Kings and the Vikings and their rule over Britain is an intriguing and fascinating one. In 978 King Aethelred had taken over the throne from his murdered half-brother Edward the Martyr. Though Anglo Saxon, he paid loyalty to the Danish King. His first wife was Danish, Aelgifu of York with whom he had 9 children. One of these children was Edmond who would later become King Edmond II (Ironside).

Aethelred's second wife was Emma the daughter of Richard, then Duke of Normandy. It is possible that this was a marriage of convenience to prevent Viking raids on England that emanated from Normandy. Aethelred and Emma had three children, two of them sons, Alfred the eldest and Edward, who would later become King Edward the Confessor.

Aethelred, though at first submitting to the King of Denmark, in 1002 carried out a massacre of Danish men living in England, due to his fear that there were plots to overthrow him. This later resulted in an invasion of England in 1013 by Sweyn Forkbeard, King of the Danes and Aethelred was forced to flee to Normandy. Sweyn had raided England on a number of occasions, but this time mounted a full invasion and seizure of the crown. Sweyn though died after just one year on the throne in 1014 and so Aethelred returned from exile and reigned again as King until 1016.

In 1015 Canut began to attack England to try to take the throne that had been held by his father. When Aethelred died in April 1016 Edmond Ironside, became King. However by October of that year, Canut had defeated him. Canut spared his life and Edmond was allowed to keep Wessex as his realm. He lived though only one more month, so Canut was now unopposed as King of England.

The next fascinating part of this story is that of Emma, previously the wife of Aethelred and the mother of Alfred and Edward. She married Canut, becoming Queen not only of England but also Denmark and Norway. Her marriage to Canut was probably to spare Alfred and Edward from being killed by Canut, who would likely have wanted to remove rivals. The brothers both moved to Denmark to be out of harms way. Emma then had a son by Canut, called Harthacnut.

Canut already had one other son, Harold Harefoot, by his first wife. When Canut died in 1035, Harold Harefoot became King of England and reigned for five years, but over a divided Kingdom. During his time, Emma's sons Alfred and Edward returned to England, but Alfred was captured by Godwin, Earl of Wessex, blinded and he later died of his injuries. Godwin at this time supported Harold Harefoot and it is very possible that when Edward came to the throne he held him responsible for his brother's death.

Emma believed that her son Harthacanut was the rightful heir, but he was in Denmark protecting it from attacks by both Sweden and Norway. Emma was a forceful woman and acted as Regent in Harthacanut's absence, ruling the lands south of the Thames, while allowing the lands north of the Thames to be ruled by her stepson Harold. Harold died in 1040 and Harthacanut then became King of England. Harthacanut is said to have had Harold's body dug up and thrown into a sewer as a sign that he had usurped him. As further evidence of how strong a woman she was, Emma made Harthacanut share the throne of England with his older half brother Edward. This lasted for only two years, when Harthacanut died, aged 24, while attending a wedding. History states that he consumed an excessive amount of alcohol and died of a sudden stroke. He was buried in Winchester Cathedral.

So in 1042 the throne of all of England became Edwards. Thus began the reign of Edward, the Confessor, son of an English King, Aethelred and of his wife, Emma, a French woman of Viking descent, who became Queen to two Kings of England and was also Queen of Denmark and Norway and who had done all that she could to ensure that one of her sons would survive and sit on the English throne. Hers is the story of a brave and powerful woman who certainly significantly influenced the throne and the realm of Britain, yet she is not perhaps given her rightful place in it's history.

In Bosham Church is reputed to be the grave of Canut's daughter who is thought to have drowned in the river. It is also suggested that in the church lie the bones of King Harold, after having been famously been killed at the Battle of Hastings in 1066. An Anglo-Saxon coffin was found buried in the Church in 1954 and the remains were consistent with wounds said to have been incurred by Harold, whose body was hacked in pieces after the battle. However, the Diocese of Chichester, when later asked in 2003 could the bones be examined to see if they were those of Harold, refused to allow this, ruling that the chances of the remains proving anything were too slim for the grave to be disturbed.

Here begins much of the fascinating history and connection to the ancient monarchs that I will find on my journey around the coast and we shall learn more of Harold and of the Battle of Hastings later today.

I skirted Chichester itself and drove once again down the side of the harbour, without too much sea view, until I came to the Witterings. The two villages of East and West Wittering remain popular with tourists and surfers. A notable resident of West Wittering is apparently Keith Richard of the Rolling Stones. I wonder if he is any good on a surfboard?

I then had to drive almost back up to Chichester, before driving down again to Selsey. Chichester is another ancient city with strong Roman and Anglo Saxon connections. It has a Cathedral with, unusually, the bell tower built separately from it. Chichester, I had found out in the past twelve months, was the area from which my Mother's relatives, the Fogdens, came. Through ancestry research I have been able to trace my roots back to 1457 and the village of Fittleworth, about twenty miles north of Chichester. I determined to find time to visit it later in the day.

Unfortunately Selsey has little going for it. It is not an unpleasant place, but the southern point, Selsey Bill, was chewed up and uninteresting. I spoke to some frustrated bird watchers who said they had wasted their time going there. What is interesting here though is the lifeboat station that is built at the end of a long pier out into the water with a ramp down which the boat is launched. (Not sure how they get it back up again).

The narrow roads in Selsey were heavy with lorries (trucks) but I had no idea why, there was no industry that I could see. Somebody later suggested to me that there are a lot of greenhouses here growing produce and so possibly the lorries were collecting fruit and vegetables for the superstores. There were two big rigs parked at the Bill having their lunch. Perhaps that's what they really all go there for – the sea air and a quiet place to have a nap in their cabs.

A real surprise though on driving away was the tiny hamlet of Church Norton. Here there is a most wonderful and pretty church and graveyard, built on the remains of what was once an ancient castle. It overlooks Pagham Harbour, which appears to be mainly silted up with grass and reeds offering a good home for birds.

My next coastal destination was to be the ancient seaside town of Bognor Regis, seemingly most well known for King George V who having been advised to go there for his heath, allegedly retorted, "Bugger Bognor". The journey required yet a further drive back up towards Chichester, before turning off through a series of small villages and finding my way to the point, at the village of Pagham, the other side of the marsh land from Church Norton.

Despite the name and King George V's comment, Bognor Regis seems a very nice place and as it was a sunny afternoon, I stopped on the Esplanade and had an ice cream. The young lady who served me from the hut on the beach had "assisting" her a young baby in a pram, whose face showed that she clearly had also been partaking of the ice cream; chocolate it looked like!

At this point I decided to break off from my coastal journey and drive inland to find evidence of my relatives in Fittleworth. Just before I arrived in Fittleworth the road crossed the South Downs Way, with a number of signs warning to look out for walkers crossing the road. As I reached the point where the road met the Way I swear that I could smell the chalk. There was a sudden very fresh (and chalky) smell that entered the car. It was actually quite energizing. No doubt if you are looking for good air, walking the chalky downs is a place to find it.

I found my way to Fittleworth Church and thanks to a detailed grave map in the church, I located seven Fogden family graves. However, the oldest only went back to 1774, so there must be others not identified. This is the first time that I have ever found graves of any of my relatives, so it was quite moving. The graves were grouped together with the largest being the significant square upright tomb close to the main door of one Richard Fogden, Grocer of London, who died in 1774 aged 84.

After paying my respects, I motored back as fast as I was able to the coast again but due to road works was diverted through the town of Arundel. This has a fantastic castle and unexpectedly, a lovely cathedral. (Having a cathedral I think makes it a city not a town). The Castle is the home of the Duke of Norfolk. I find it odd that the Duke of Norfolk has his castle in Sussex and similarly the Duke of Devonshire has his in Derbyshire. In British nobility a Duke is the highest of the nobles after the monarch. William & Kate are the Duke and Duchess of Cambridge, yet William was born in London, Kate in Reading and both went to University at St. Andrews in Scotland; so, no Cambridge connection. Similarly the Prince of Wales (Charles) is not Welsh; perhaps it does not matter what the Queen makes them Dukes and Duchesses of, but it is confusing for tourists I'm sure.

Arundel Castle, West Sussex

I arrived back at the coast close to Littlehampton and Worthing. All of these places and the little towns in between have row upon row of beach huts on their sea fronts. As the beaches are pebbly and the towns have a bias to elderly residents, I suppose there is a high demand for these huts where you can brew a cup of tea and look at the sea, but keep out of the wind. Sleeping in them though is forbidden. If you could do so I expect they would garner beachfront prices. I read that a privately owned one near to Bournemouth was sold fairly recently for well over £300,000. It must have been gold plated or someone had just too much money. In most cases though you cannot purchase the huts, only rent them from the Council.

I next reached Shoreham, the scene of an air disaster last year when 13 motorists on a nearby road were killed by a crashing jet plane doing a loop too close to the ground at an air display. What fascinated me were the houseboats and large barges, some converted from mine sweepers, lying on the far shore of the estuary of the River Adur; there must be 40 or 50 of them, presumably all lived in. The tide was out and they were all beached, but I saw no one using this opportunity to clean their bottoms! Shoreham has a working commercial harbour, whereas the harbours of most of the neighbouring towns along the south coast are today almost entirely yachting marinas.

The commercial harbour appears to continue into Portslade, which is very much the industrial face of the area with a number of large cargo vessels loading up with various cargoes. This is a working town unlike most of its neighbours, immediately of which is Hove. Hove is now conjoined with Brighton one of the most elegant towns on this coast. Brunswick Square with its yellow painted Georgian houses comes almost to the ocean and is outstanding in its architecture, which must equal the famous crescent in Bath. Almost completely restored with most being expensive homes and apartments rather than hotels or offices.

Brunswick Terrace, Brighton, East Sussex

Ironically the Pier facing the lovely square is an ugly twisted mass of metal following a fire a couple of years ago, just after it was purchased and set to be restored. It is fit now only to be pulled down, but nothing seems to be happening to it. I suspect the owner is still fighting with the Insurance company. Our daughter went to University in Brighton so it has a special place in our family memories.

Leaving Brighton by the cliff road started wonderfully, but then turned into a nightmare. If it wasn't for the fact that my journey plan required me to follow the coastal route I would have turned back and gone inland. You leave Brighton, past the famous Roedean Girls School on a dual carriageway road, which then filters into a single carriageway. As this was now about going home time for workers, there was a queue of at least a quarter mile ahead as traffic filtered in. What I did not know was that this queue actually stretched for nine miles all the way into Newhaven. I eventually discovered that a new Land Rover Discovery had broken down right at the junction of three roads merging into one at a narrow roundabout. It took ninety minutes of stop-go traffic to travel just nine miles. Land Rover are now owned by the Indian company TaTa. It seems ironic that whenever we have any breakdown of any piece of equipment today, no matter who makes it, the 'phone help line finds you talking to someone in India. As this vehicle had clearly been there, unmoved and blocking the road for at least 90 minutes, I had to assume that the breakdown truck was being sent from India to remove it!

At last released, but frustrated, from the jam, I headed around the ferry town of Newhaven and then through Seaford toward Eastbourne. Just before Eastbourne are the famous cliffs and point of land known as Beachy Head.

The countryside here is stunning with rolling chalk downs. Beachy Head is a very tall (531 feet) cliff of white chalk. It is unfortunately most famous as a place where, tragically, many people choose to commit suicide. As I drove up to it, a car with the wording "Chaplain" on its door was just leaving. I believe that there is someone here every day, on hand, for anyone who is thinking of taking his or her life. What amazed me though is that you can walk right up to the cliff edge. There is no barrier, and the edge looks as if it would crumble if you stood on it. I stood back about two feet and took photos. It would be horrendous to visit here with young children; anxiety levels would be off the scale for fear of them going over the edge.

Eastbourne Pier, East Sussex

Dropping down into Eastbourne, I found another town that has really improved. It always was genteel, but now it has to be called impressive. Its esplanade is a joy to drive down with elegant and well-maintained buildings. To the east of

Eastbourne, is Pevensey Bay the landing site for William the Conqueror. I did not stop, as I was still anxious to get to my planned stop for the night in Dover. On reviewing my map at Bexhill the next quiet retirement town on the coast, I realised that this was just too much of a stretch and I could feel tiredness creeping up. I decided that Hastings should be my place for the night, so I started to 'phone guesthouses and small hotels. "How much?" I found myself exasperatedly saying. There used to be a time when a late booking could get you a good discount rather than the hotel have an empty room. It now appears to be a ransom price for you to get a room. At this point I made up my mind that I would try and sleep in the car, after all it was an SUV so there should be plenty of room.

Hastings is of course most famous for it's "Battle" which took place on the 14th October 1066 between King Harold Godwinson of England and William the Conqueror. As most schoolboys will tell you, King Harold, was killed when an arrow pierced his eye. Recent research though says that this was not so and he was actually hacked to death, with his remains, as mentioned earlier, possibly being in Bosham church. The "Conqueror" was of course William of Normandy. William, who was Edward's cousin, had come to claim the throne that he said had been offered to him by the childless Edward.

Harold Godwinson was actually the brother-in-law of Edward and although with no bloodline to the throne, claimed that Edward, on his deathbed, gave him the throne. So being in the right place at the right time he was crowned as King Harold.

It should be noted that there were actually six kings of England called Edward. It wasn't until the fourth Edward that the nomenclature of "the first" was used. So Edward the Confessor was actually the third King Edward and Edward III was actually the sixth King Edward! The first Edward was Edward the Elder (reigning 899 – 924) who was the son of Alfred the Great, King of Wessex and the first Anglo-Saxon king. The second King Edward had a short reign from 975 to 978. He was the son of Edgar and a half-brother to Aethelred, before he was murdered at Corfe castle and Aethelred took the throne. He became known as Edward the Martyr. The third Edward was Edward the Confessor, who we now meet here at Hastings. It was actually the fourth King Edward who was called King Edward I. He was known as Edward Longshanks the Hammer of the Scots and he reigned from 1272 to 1307.

William the Conqueror was the great, great, great grandson of a Viking leader, Rollo. One hundred and forty years earlier Rollo was given land, what is now Normandy, in return for a promise to no longer raid Paris. He allegedly converted to Christianity and married a French Princess and is buried in Rouen Cathedral. Normandy got its name for being the land of the North (or Norse) men.

Edward the Confessor had married Edith, the daughter of the most powerful Lord in the land, Earl Godwin of Wessex, but their marriage was without issue, which became the trigger for the war. Earl Godwin had three sons, Harold, Gyrth and Tostig, who were all brothers-in-law to Edward. When Earl Godwin died in 1053 his eldest son Harold took over as Earl of Wessex. Gyrth became Earl of Anglia and Tostig, in 1055, became Earl of Northumbria, on the death of Siward the previous Earl.

When it was clear that Edith and Edward would have no children, Edward visited France in 1051 and promised the throne to his cousin William of Normandy. Harold Godwinson was apparently present at this meeting and gave recognition to William that he would be the King. However, at the time of Edward's death on 6th January 1066, Harold claimed that Edward had changed his mind and given the throne to him. Edward was attended at his deathbed by his wife Edith and by her brother Harold Godwinson, along with Archbishop Stigand and Robert FitzWimarc, a Norman Lord related to both Edward and William. These present at the deathbed attested to Edward nominating Harold as his successor.

There was actually one blood relative of Edwards that could possibly have been made King, Edgar Aethling, grandson of Edmond Ironside and nephew of Edward the Confessor. However, the Barons and Lords of England considered him to be too weak. Harold was undoubtedly the strongest person in the land and thus the Lords accepted him as the heir, although he had no bloodline relationship to the throne.

Even though Harold expected an attack from William, there was another, unexpected enemy that he had to face first, King Harald Hardrada III of Norway, who had recognised a chance to put a Viking back on the throne. Harold's brother, Tostig, had in 1065 been banished from England by Edward, due to his bad leadership of Northumbria, which had fomented insurrection. Recognising an opportunity, the banished Tostig offered his services to both William and then Harald Hardrada to fight with either of them to overthrow his brother. Tostig felt that William was too cautious and would take too long to invade, so he went to King Harald Hardrada, who, instigated by Tostig, began to believe and plan that he could depose Harold. Tostig though was impatient and attempted his own invasion, landing with a small army on the

Isle of Wight, before he was chased out and fled to Scotland. Here he waited for the invasion by Harald Hardrada. When this came, in September 1066, Harald Hardrada, along with Tostig quickly captured the ancient Viking city of York. However as soon as King Harold heard this he marched his army swiftly from London and in the ensuing Battle of Stamford Bridge both Harald Hardrada and Tostig were killed. Thus ended the power of the Vikings in England, but, not even a month later, the rule of the Anglo Saxon Kings would be ended as well.

While Harold was fighting his brother and the invading Norwegians in the north, William and his army, previously delayed by bad weather in the Channel, landed at Pevensey and began to make defensive positions. King Harold with a tired and weakened army was now forced to rush back to the south of England to defend against the invasion of William. This was to prove crucial in the subsequent battle between the two armies. Harold and the English army held the high ground against the Normans and for a good part of the battle were able to fend off the Norman attacks by forming defensive shield walls. However, after one attack the Normans turned and appeared to run. The English troops sensing victory broke the wall and ran after them, only for the Normans now to turn and fight them in open ground. This changed the course of the battle and the Normans, also using cavalry, overwhelmed the English and as we know, King Harold was defeated and killed along with his brother Gyrth. William then marched on London to claim his throne.

Under Edward, the royal seat and thus the capital of England, had moved from Winchester, the traditional home of the Kings of Wessex, to London. Here Edward had called for the building of a Church at Westminster, where his body eventually was interred. This building in the reign of Henry III was enlarged and became the magnificent Westminster Abbey,

At first the Barons and Earls thought that they could hold off William and so went ahead and elected Edgar Aethling as King, although he was not crowned. Edgar, who had been brought up in exile in Hungary, was only a teenager and unable to command an army, so rather than fight, he agreed to give up his claim to the throne and along with the Barons they agreed to recognise and be subject to William. Thus on Christmas Day 1066 in Westminster, William was crowned King William I of England.

In 1068 an older and more emboldened Edgar rebelled against William, but was forced to flee to Scotland and the protection of King Malcolm.

It is Edgar's sister, Margaret that we will come across much more on my trip around Britain. Margaret, later known as Saint Margaret of Scotland, had married King Malcolm III of Scotland. One of their daughters, Matilda, would later, in 1100 marry William's son, Henry I and become Queen Consort of England. Their daughter, also called Matilda, would later herself be involved in a violent dispute over the throne and her son, Margaret's great grandson, would eventually become King Henry II.

It was Margaret's husband, King Malcolm III of Scotland, who with Siward, the then Earl of Northumbria, seized the throne of Scotland by killing my ancestor, King MacBeth in 1057; so I clearly have an interest in the monarchy of Britain! Today, having earlier found a connection to my Mother's side of the family, I am now in a place with hints to my Father's lineage.

Now back to present day Hastings. Hastings is one of the five "Cinque Ports". The history of these is quite fascinating. The original five ports were Hastings, New Romney, Hythe, Dover and Sandwich. They were established in 1155 and in return for providing the King with "57 ships for 15 days" each year were granted significant tax relief. No duty was payable on goods brought into the country at these ports (the original free trade port) but this led to considerable levels of smuggling. Over time some of the ports silted up and could no longer be used and replacements were found. For example New Romney silted up and Rye became a Cinque port in its place. Other local ports were also added as "limbs" attached to a Cinque Port. The Cinque Ports still exist, but now only in ceremonial form. The title Lord Warden of the Cinque Ports is an honorary one bestowed by the Queen and notables from recent years are Winston Churchill and the Queen Mother.

Despite being a Cinque Port, Hastings has no natural harbour and has often been inundated by the sea. Today apparently it has the largest beach based fishing fleet in Europe, though I did not see any vessels on my drive along Hastings sea front. The front is again a mix of hotels and guesthouses and I found a welcoming car park by the ocean. Having my camping stove I was able to cook myself a good hot meal and then set about sorting out the car to make my bed. Unfortunately, despite this being an SUV, I could not get the seats into any position in which I could lie out flat and so I spent a restless night, listening to the ocean.

It is amazing that even throughout the night, cars still drive into and out of the car park. No doubt various liaisons take place, or is it the burglars switching cars? It's incredible what scenarios your mind looks at when you are trying, fruitlessly, to sleep!

Hastings to Southend

Miles 204

Dover Castle, Kent

At four in the morning, while still wishing that I could sleep, I saw my first jogger, a woman. Now I know that jogging can be good for you and that many people get evangelical about it, however 4.00am does seem a bit too enthusiastic. As she passed in front of the car, I could see that she was quite thin; possibly a young banker, up early before the markets opened I thought. Maybe I should be inspired and get out of the car and take a jog, or at least a walk along the seafront. After all I am doing a lot of driving. But I decided no, I should continue to try and sleep as I felt this would aid my driving more than the jog.

About fifteen minutes later and still awake, I noticed the thin lady jogging back in the opposite direction, but this time I saw her face. It was extremely wrinkled and she looked very haggard and I guessed that her age was probably close to 90. But still, what an inspiration to us all. I hope that I am still able to jog when I get to ninety. As you get older so sleep patterns change and older people don't sleep as well as teenagers, so perhaps she used this time just to stay healthy and keep osteoporosis at bay.

I then began to wonder whether perhaps she is not 90 after all. I've noticed that many joggers, despite the lycra and expensive trainers, often look very pained and haggard while they are running. Certainly this would be more so at 4.00am in the morning when your body tells you it should be asleep. This was what my body was telling me; it was just that my brain didn't seem to agree with it. My final conclusion was that the sight of this lady confirmed to me that I had been right not to take up jogging, and certainly not at 4.00am in the morning. Sure I want to get to ninety and be able to jog, indeed at least be able to still walk, but I don't want to look that haggard. So, moment of inspiration passed and rationality, at least in my mind, took over

When the other outdoor sleepers emerged at around 4.30am and began going through the bins looking for breakfast, I decided that sleep was definitely not within my mind and I would head out and set off for the Kent marshes and the road to Dover.

What a contrast from one day to the next; from the beauty of yesterday to the bleakness of today. The county of Kent begins just after you leave Hastings. This area is one of flat marsh lands, untended properties and buildings that seem to have been built without architect's input or planning permission and the whole area appears seedy and lacking in any character. I can perhaps get away with these comments as my ancestry searching has shown I have two relatives who came from this area (two hundred years ago).

In the untidy place of Camber Sands there are two holiday camps: Pontins which has a large hideous blue and pink building and Camber Sands Holiday Park, about which I know little other than it is caravans, caravans and caravans. The sands here though are very good and I saw a couple unloading two horses from a horsebox and then set out for a ride along the sands.

Further along from Pontins I came across another holiday camp, consisting of chalets and bungalows, but with an absolutely gigantic electricity pylon towering right over the main gate. You had to drive under it to enter your "holiday destination". The pylon was one of hundreds marching out from the Dungeness nuclear power station, which is visible out on the marshes a mile or so away. Why would anyone want to have a holiday here I asked myself and especially right under a set of electricity pylons.

On looking again at my notes, I find that I have written prominently, three words: bleak, bleak, bleak.

The small houses and bungalows here all face the sea, but yet do not have a view of the sea as all along the coast a wall, a banking, has been built up to keep the sea from inundating the area. Indeed, though I was driving the road closest to the ocean I could not see it. When it was visible it looked very grey and uninviting, so perhaps the sea wall had a double role.

Lydd Caravan Park, Kent (under the pylons)

Later in my journey, I was to hear about a group of illegal immigrants who had been rescued from an inflatable boat a few miles of this coast. They had set out from France under the control of people smugglers and the story was that the smuggler's boat broke down in the Channel and they thought they were going to sink. Thus they rang friends in Calais and asked them to send help. The UK coastguard and the RNLI both set out to assist and rescue them. I surmise, though have no proof for this, that the smugglers told them that they were going to be landed on the Kent marshes close to Dungeness; on hearing this they decided it was better to get arrested than have to land on this bleak and depressing place.

Following the road from Hythe, close to Folkestone, there runs a narrow gauge railway, the Romney, Hythe and Dymchurch Railway. This is popular with tourists and runs all the way past the power station and into the village of

Dymchurch. I saw evidence of it and followed the rail track for some of the journey, but I must say having seen the view, I'm not sure that I would want to take the rail journey. I love these sorts of engines and unusual carriages, but this would be one journey where I think it would be better to stand at the station and enjoy the rolling stock, rather than take the trip. OK, the day was grey and overcast, which is not the best time to view a place, but the weather just seemed to sum up what the Kent marshes are and seemed fitting for the topography.

Driving on you come to Folkestone. Folkestone is a ferry town rather than a holiday resort and unfortunately there appears to have been no attempt to smarten it up to attract tourists. As I entered the town and drove down the hill towards the beach I saw a very large white structure that I thought was an engineering works, mill or old factory. I was actually looking at the rear of a building. Imagine my surprise when I came to the front and saw that the building was actually a hotel, calling itself "The Grand Burstin." There were lots of coaches outside so presumably it gets most of its trade from ferry passengers staying overnight. Its architecture is such that I can only assume that it was once a factory that has been converted into a hotel. If not, it was a transplant of a communist era building from somewhere behind the iron curtain. Perhaps if you cater for coach parties who stay only one night, creating an ambience to make people want to come again does not matter.

The next town up the coast is also a ferry town, Dover, famous for its white cliffs. At this point I have to take a diversion and correct something written by Bill Bryson. I hesitate to do so, but having read his write up on Dover just last night, I noticed that in this section, he described Britain (with Dover as a main gateway) as being the 8th largest island in the world and listed Vancouver Island as being larger at number seven. Now I know that this is not correct as I look out onto Vancouver Island from my house every day. I decided to check in the fount of all knowledge, Wikipedia, which states that Britain (not including Northern Ireland) covers an area of 229,000 square kilometers. Vancouver Island is just 32,000 square kilometers, so sorry Bill you have that wrong! Vancouver Island is actually about the length of England (Truro to Carlisle) and has a population of 1 million as compared to England's 55 million. However, it does have a larger bear and wolf population than England!

Dover is a major coastal port for Europe, in particular France. Many a British caravanner will have his first experience of Dover waiting in line to board a ferry from here. Similarly many an illegal immigrant having stowed away aboard a lorry in Calais and passed through the docks undetected, will have his or her first memory of England as being Dover, even if they don't actually see it and leave the lorry at a motorway service station many miles away.

Driving into the town there is a major dual carriageway but it is restricted to 50 mph on the final four or so miles section. Despite there being virtually no other traffic at all, I kept to the speed limit, though I was the only one of the few other vehicles around that did. At certain times, such as Public Holidays, this stretch of road can be a car park, with long queues to get to the ferries, and then even 50mph would be an impossibility.

As it was only 6.00am, unfortunately nothing was open. I would have liked to have visited the magnificent Dover castle and especially seen the miles of passages that it has in the rocks beneath, carved out by the military, but it would have been too long a wait and I needed to move on, realizing already that my journey planning was perhaps too ambitious.

Dover castle was built, or at least rebuilt to what it is today, by Henry II. Henry II was the son of Matilda, the daughter of Henry I. As we learned yesterday, Matilda's grandmother was Queen Margaret of Scotland, of the lineage of Anglo Saxon Kings of Wessex. Matilda's brother William Athelin was heir to the throne so Matilda was married off to Henry, King of Germany who was also the last Emperor of Rome.

William Athelin unfortunately was drowned in 1120 and Henry I, having no male successors, wanted Matilda to succeed him. When Matilda's husband, Henry of Germany, died in 1125, Matilda, then aged 25, was recalled to Normandy by her father and made to marry Geoffrey of Anjou who was aged only 13. Matilda was unhappy with the marriage, especially as she had now been forced to marry, not only a boy, but also someone beneath her previous station as a Queen and Empress. Henry I persuaded his court to recognise her as his heir. However, this was not popular with the Norman Barons who had been given great power and lands when William the Conqueror divided up the Kingdom. They preferred a male on the throne and they favoured Henry's nephew, cousin to Matilda, Stephen of Blois. As a grandson of William the Conqueror, Stephen was already prominent in Henry 's court and had strong support from the English Church.

Matilda abandoned Geoffrey shortly after the marriage and went to England, but Henry I persuaded her to return and in 1131 she gave birth to a son, also called Henry, who later would become Henry II.

Henry I died in 1135 and with Matilda in France, the Barons were influential in having Stephen crowned as King. But Stephen's reign was not peaceful and he had to battle invasion from Scotland by Matilda's uncle, King David and rebellions in

73

both Wales and the south west of England. In 1138 Matilda's half-brother, Robert, Duke of Gloucester, who was the illegitimate son of Henry I, also rebelled and the country slid into civil war. In 1139 Matilda, left her husband in control of Normandy and invaded England to press her right to the throne and to remove Stephen. She first stayed at Arundel Castle and was besieged by Stephen, but, he pressed a truce and she was allowed to leave and join her brother in Gloucester. In February 1141, due to others rebelling against him, the tide turned against Stephen and he was captured by Matilda's forces at the Battle of Lincoln. Matilda, then sought her coronation, but she was not crowned, as London mobs, incited by Stephen's wife, rioted and caused it to be abandoned. She was never formally declared as Queen.

Loyalties of the Barons and gentry in England to Matilda or Stephen went back and forth, but in November of 1141 an army led by Stephen's wife (also called Matilda) besieged Winchester (the old capital of England) where Matilda and Robert both were. Matilda escaped but Robert was captured. In order to save her brother's life Matilda was forced to release Stephen in exchange for the release of Robert and in December Stephen and his wife Matilda had a second coronation.

In 1148 Matilda returned to Normandy leaving her then 17-year-old son Henry to continue the fight.

Henry and Stephen, continued to battle, but neither could gain the upper hand and a stalemate ensued. In 1153, Stephen's only son Eustace died. Having no heir Stephen sought a settlement with Matilda. So at a meeting in Winchester a compromise, brokered by the Church, was agreed. In this Matilda would give up her claim to the throne based upon Stephen's acceptance that her son, Henry, would succeed Stephen. This ended the fighting. Within just one year

Stephen died and so in 1154 Henry II ascended to the throne of England, along with his wife, Eleanor of Aquitaine, who was the annulled wife of Louis VII of France.

Henry II was energetic in his determination to rule and restore the riches and lands of his grandfather Henry I that had been lost during the years of fighting. He ended up controlling all of England and Wales, the eastern side of Ireland and the western side of France. In 1160 he determined also to reduce the legal powers of the Church and this put him in conflict with his previous close friend Thomas Beckett, who Henry had appointed as Archbishop of Canterbury. Henry II may not have ordered Beckett's subsequent murder in Canterbury Cathedral in 1170, but he was implicated and the thousands of people who came on pilgrimage to his tomb in the Cathedral, irked him intensely. A lot of these pilgrims came from France and landed at Dover, so he determined that Dover would, along with other castles in England, be strengthened so as to impress and demonstrate and warn of his power. By modeling them after other great Norman castles, such as the Tower of London, he sought to confirm that he was a powerful descendent of his Norman great grandfather, William.

William, the Conqueror had brought the concept of castle building with him to England. Indeed the Bayeaux tapestry and historical records show that his invasion fleet carried timber to quickly erect a castle after his landing so that he would have a fortress to protect him. The typical Norman fortress was of the Motte and Bailey design. A wooden Motte or tower built on raised ground surrounded by a Bailey ditch. Once in control of England, William strengthened his defenses by having the castles built of stone and each of his Barons who supported him was given land in England where they were allowed to build a stone castle in order to control their domain. William's first stone castle was built at Exeter, Devon in 1067 after the subjugation of the city there. It is known as Rougemont Castle as it was built out of the local red sandstone.

Henry II reigned over what became known as the Angevin Empire, but family disputes as to who would inherit his wealth and lands put him in conflict with his three eldest sons: Henry the younger, his immediate heir, who had unusually been given a coronation to confirm him as the heir apparent; Richard, later Richard I, the Lionheart; and Geoffrey who became Archbishop of York. Henry had two further, younger sons: John, later King John and William, who became Earl of Salisbury. In 1173 King Henry put down a rebellion by his eldest son Henry who was frustrated and wanted to become King before his father died. King and son were reconciled, but Henry revolted again in 1183. Unfortunately the young Henry contracted dysentery during the course of his campaign and he died, leaving his brother Richard as heir.

In 1189, Philip of France made Richard believe that Henry was going to make his younger brother John his heir instead of him. Richard rose up against his father and this time Henry II was defeated, dying shortly afterwards. Richard I then took the throne. Richard was hardly ever in England, fighting in the Crusades or held in captivity. In his absence his younger brother John acted as regent but usurped his authority, though Richard later forgave him. John is perhaps best known during the time that Richard was absent through the legendary stories of Robin Hood. He became King on the death of Richard in 1199.

Richard's death was unusual in that he was accidently struck by a crossbow bolt fired by one of his own men who was showing him how to use a shield to parry a bolt. Richard forgave the young man who had fired it, but his wound become infected and Richard died of septicemia. On his death the young man who had injured him, though forgiven by the King, was savagely slaughtered.

My journey on from Dover found nothing pretty along the coast until I got to Walmer and Deal. These are quaint, but again, there are more and more beach huts. Deal is an old Cinque Port and as such exercised its right to import goods freely from the Continent. In January 1784, the Prime Minister, William Pitt the Younger, angered at the apparent level of smuggling by the Deal fishermen, waited for a night when weather had all of the fishing boats pulled up on the beach and then sent in soldiers to burn them all.

Deal has a fairly modern pier, built in 1957, replacing others that had collapsed due to weather and ship collisions.

Deal Castle is at Walmer to the south of the town and is still very much intact. It was built by Henry VIII as one of many gun bastions along the English coast to protect against French invasion.

Ramsgate a few miles on, though a cross channel ferry port, has a large and charming harbour full of pleasure boats. No doubt a lot are moored here for their owners to gain easy access to France. These ferry ports may be severely hit if Britain votes to leave the EU later in June. No quick day trips to France, coming back with vans (over) loaded with cheap wine and beer, all for personal consumption of course! The UK Customs & Excise people have seen a huge drop in alcohol taxes particularly from Kent and nearby areas. I suppose it is modern day smuggling in a different guise.

Turn the corner at Margate and it is now the Thames estuary that dominates the coast. Margate and the nearby places of Whitstable and Herne Bay, with its long sea front and hundreds of B&Bs, had their heydays when Londoners came here for oysters and winkles. Now the beach hut residents prefer fish and chips and curries as they look out on to the muddy foreshore where the tide has gone out.

Margate is another town to which I can trace relatives. My 2nd great to my 5th great grandfathers, on my Mother's paternal side, all lived in Margate. Until today I had never been to the town. Their surnames were Davis, so possibly further Welsh connections. I have no information as to where they are buried so I had no graves to visit, or indeed time to explore all of the many churchyards that there must be in Margate.

Margate is associated with the painter John Turner and nearby Broadstairs with Charles Dickens, who describes very well the bleakness of the Kent marshes in a number of his books, perhaps the most famous being Great Expectations. It is also said that Bleak House, in David Copperfield, is named after a house he stayed in in Broadstairs. Broadstairs still retains a lot of its original fishing village type of charm, but it was once known as breezy Broadstairs and this was certainly true on the day of my visit.

Turner, known through his paintings as the Father of Light, was sent to Margate at age 11 after his Mother was admitted to hospital for a mental illness. He returned to the town many times in later life and is said to have had a long running affair here with his landlady, Sophia Booth. The site of her house is now the Turner Gallery.

Margate has been trying to revitalize itself and in recent years opened "Dreamland" as a Pleasure Park with rides and amusements. Compare this with "Dismaland" a temporary artistic project built in Weston Super Mare, in Somerset in

2015, by the artist Banksy, which parodied the English seaside towns "amusement parks".

I continued to feel the bleakness and even the sadness of lost glory days as I drove along the sea fronts and saw the arcades, pubs and "tourist tat" shops.

I motored on along the south side of the Thames Estuary and then turned outward to the Isle of Sheppey. I ventured along the boring road out to Leysdown on Sea. Leysdown has the historical claim of being the place in Britain that John Moore-Brabazon made the first heavier than air flight. Leysdown today is overrun with chalets, caravans and too many arcades. A nearby place called Mud Row is appropriately named and adequately describes what life is like on a flat, partly industrialised, island in the middle of the Thames estuary.

Sheerness is a major commercial port and as such, unless you are a ship's captain or a lorry driver, there would be no need to visit it, other than if you have to make it part of the coastal drive!

One thing I did find time to do and enjoyed in this area, was a visit to the historic dockyards at Chatham. The docks have seen the building of many a British warship, from the times of Henry VIII through to this century. There are a number of ships and a submarine, HMS Ocelot, available to view. The Ocelot is an Oberon class submarine of which 6 were built, 3 for the Royal Navy and 3 for the Canadian Navy. There is also a splendid display of old and historic RNLI lifeboats. Once you have paid to get in, your ticket is good for numerous visits for the next 12 months and you probably need to come more than once to really appreciate it. Unfortunately it is too far for me to come again this year.

Historic Lifeboat in RNLI Collection at Chatham Docks

My GPS seems to be programed to take me through every traffic jam and traffic light in Kent, so I decided to ignore it and navigate myself in order to drive over the Thames at the Dartford Crossing. I only got lost twice, but was more disappointed to find that traveling north, vehicles still use the old tunnel rather than the splendid new bridge that I was looking forward to traveling on. It would seem that you have to be going south to use this. The crossing requires you to pay a toll, which fortuitously I had found out about the night before and paid in advance on line.

Over the bridge you enter Essex. The coastal area here is very similar to that of Kent on the opposite bank of the Thames; lots of chimneys, industry and gas distribution facilities. The Thames Estuary is of course a major port area. The high tidal difference similarly makes the small seaside resorts here as muddy, when the tide is out, as their counterparts on the Kent side. Earlier this century, these towns were where the workers from London would come for a day out or an inexpensive short holiday. Cheap flights and ferries took this business away and the resorts have never recovered. No doubt this is why I saw so many Brexit "Leave" posters here, encouraging people to vote to leave the EU and take a "staycation" on the Kent and Essex coasts instead!

It was a fairly straightforward journey into Southend. I missed out on the opportunity to go down to Canvey Island (which I once visited as a child) and then back up again, deeming it an estuary town with mud and fun fares little different from that on the Kent side, just over the Thames. Canvey Island was the fastest growing seaside resort in England in the early part of the 20th century, but severe flooding in 1953 brought this to an end and now large sea defence walls block most sight of the estuarine Thames.

Tomorrow I am looking forward to being joined by my friend Jim. I have known Jim since we both lived in Gloucestershire. He and his wife recently moved from Devon, to Kings Lynn in Norfolk. It will be great to have a friend along for the ride, especially one with such a great sense of humour as he has. I am due to pick him up at the railway station at Clacton-On-Sea (a name almost as romantic as Bognor!) at 12.43pm tomorrow. I have only been "going coastal" for three days but already I am feeling tired by the amount of driving and a bit depressed by the most recent coastline. What have I taken on? Jim will no doubt cheer me up and provide good companionship.

Southend to Lowestoft

Miles 218

Lug Wormer, Southend Pier, Essex

I woke up this morning in "Sarfend" (as the natives call it) to bright sunshine. Today I am due to meet my friend Jim at 12.44pm at Clacton-On-Sea, 50 miles away, so at last I will have a companion who I can have a proper conversation with. My companion to date has been the lovely lady who lives inside my GPS, however her conversation is limited to telling me what to do and I would ideally like to experience more varied conversation. Jim retired from his job as a medical lecturer at the University of Exeter when he moved to Kings Lynn, in Norfolk, with his wife Jean last year. As the east coast is a relatively new area to Jim, he jumped at the chance to join me on my trip, to get to know his new part of the country better and to stay with me all the way up to Edinburgh. He called to tell me that he was on the train and also give me the good news that the weather report had said that this region of the UK would be the only place that would be sunny today. I must be truly righteous after all!

I was last in Southend aged 11 years old, when I was taken as a day treat from London by a much older (20+ years) cousin. We traveled out of London on the train and the return was by boat to Tower Bridge. I remember going to the funfair, which is still there on the beach. However, the only other thing I remember is the journey back on the boat and throwing bottles into the water. Unfortunately one of the ship's crew took hold of me by the scruff of the neck and marched me up to the Captain. The Captain was more understanding of the actions of an 11 year old, especially when he saw me crying and shaking. He said don't do it again and let me go. I never told my cousin, but she could not understand why I was so quiet for the rest of the journey.

Southend has the world's longest pier at 1.3 miles. I think that they had to build it this long to allow holiday-makers to at least see the sea. The tide goes out a very long way and this morning was no exception. I stopped to take a photo and a young woman in another car did the same. "It's so unbelievable this place. You just have to take a picture of it don't you" she said.

The mud is not all bad. There was a man with a rake, spade and bucket, close to the pier, digging for lugworms as fishing bait. I wonder if they will be shriveled up by the time the tide comes back in and he is able to fish?

Close to the Pier I saw something called a "Genting Club". Now I know that Americans make up words all the time, but I had not come across this word in England. I tried to imagine what such a club would be for. It said Casino and entertainment, but I imagined the emphasis more on the entertainment rather than the casino. I did not see a "Ladying Club", but I dare say that in the name of equality and fair play there must be one in Southend, probably just a bit further down the road I expect.

Going eastward along the esplanade you run into Shoebury and Shoeburyness. This is the posh end of town, just the sort of place that you would expect to find a Ladying Club (but I still did not see one). This is also where the Beach Huts start. The other posh area is West Cliff. I did not actually explore this, so perhaps the Ladying Club is located there. If "Sarfend" were by the Mediterranean rather than the Thames Estuary it would be a mecca for all gentlemen and ladies. One lady that hails from Southend is the actress Helen Mirren, who of course has even played the role of the Queen of England, but without a Sarfend accent.

I then had to travel back inland quite aways to go around the estuary of the River Crouch and over to Burnham-On-Crouch. Burnham Yacht Club is very select and up market. I used to know two of its members and they told me this, so it has to be true.

Before I got to Burnham, I stopped briefly at the Co-op in South Woodham Ferrers to buy some fresh milk for a cup of tea. As I paid, I asked the cashier "is there a toilet in the store". She answered quickly, "Yes, just behind the next aisle, up against the wall!" This brought a hail of laughter from everyone else in the line-up. "Isn't that a bit too public and will I be arrested if I use it" I replied. She also laughed and said, "I always tell people that. If you go behind the next aisle you will see it. You can't miss it. The door in the wall that is, not the wall itself." With continued laughter and the rest of the line-up watching me, I went behind the next aisle and sure enough there was a wall with a door in it. Thankfully the sign on the door said toilet. I noted with some irony that the products for sale on the shelf right by this door were baby and adult nappies (diapers)! Obviously these were what you were expected to purchase before the door was built – or if someone was in there too long and you couldn't wait!

Burnham-On-Crouch Yacht Club, Essex

I drove on and came to the much vaunted Burnham Yacht Club. It looked very nice with lots of mainly sailboats of all shapes, sizes and levels of luxury. Unfortunately they were not able to sail anywhere as the tide was out! I sat in the car park and brewed a cup of tea – in a teapot of course. I had purchased my butane stove and kettle before I left Devon just so that I would not miss out on a good cuppa. I bought the stove just over a week ago in Budleigh Salterton in a camping shop that was having a sale. I got it for £14.99, 50% off the list price. I was chuffed with this, but they were out of the butane gas canisters. Two days later I purchased some canisters at Darts Farm Shop in Topsham, which has a camping section. After buying them a man came up to me and said he had just purchased a butane stove and what did I think of them. I said they were brilliant and he would find them really handy. I then made the mistake of asking him how much he paid for his. "Oh, £12." They must have been on sale then" I replied. "No" he said "that's apparently the regular price"! This quite spoiled my weekend!

Anyway back to my cuppa. My kettle on the stove boiled quickly, but just as I was pouring it, a workman with a blower came along. He began blowing the grass cuttings that he and his colleagues must have just mown earlier from the bank around the car park. He then decided to turn the blower on himself in an attempt to blow off the grass that had stuck to his clothes. His mates clearly thought this was a good idea so they all lined up to have a blow down. What they did not appreciate was that although the blower blew away the grass, the dusty gravel and mud of the car park also got blown up and it made a huge dust cloud that enveloped them. I only just got back into the car with my cup of tea before it passed over me as well. They got into their vehicle grass free, but now covered head to foot with dust!

I did not get to discover whether the Yacht Club was indeed select and exclusive. There was the usual mix of smart and swanky boats alongside older fixer-uppers. Also, with the tide out, as it was now, I wondered how much sailing the members did anyway, so probably the Clubhouse is where most of the action is. If it is only possible to get a boat out at high tide, I did wonder whether local employers might have noticed if a higher rate of absenteeism from work coincided on days with particularly high tides!

After my tea I set off to meet Jim at our agreed point, the station in Clacton–On-Sea. This meant yet another big journey inland to go around the estuary of the River Blackwater. At its head is the town of Maldon. Here I was amazed to find as I drove over the bridge, lying on the mud banks, three old Thames barges that looked in good order. These were once prolific on the Thames and carried many different goods, both on the river and along the coast. Years ago the boatmen used to have races with them. Few now remain, but these no doubt are some enthusiast's pride and joy. Maldon is famous for the production of sea salt, which has continued here since the nineteenth century.

After Maldon I had to drive on to Colchester in order to get around further estuaries and get to the Clacton road. Colchester is the oldest recorded Roman town in Britain and as such therefore lays claim to being Britain's oldest town, though its origins are clearly older than Roman. It became a Roman town in AD43 but was destroyed by Boudica (Queen Bodicea) in AD61and the Romans then made London their capital. The Romans later rebuilt Colchester with the city walls completed in AD80. There is a lovely castle here, built by William the Conqueror on top of the ruins of a Roman temple, which can still be viewed under the castle. The castle Keep is the largest ever built in Europe and is fifty percent larger than the keep at the Tower of London.

I left Colchester and came off the main highway as soon as I could and drove a narrow B road to keep me on the road closest to the ocean. Suddenly, as I came around a bend, I saw a field of bright blue stretching into the distance. This was flax, which in ancient times was used to make cloth, as its fibers are three times stronger than cotton. It is probably grown today as a Linseed oil crop. It certainly lights ups the countryside. I pulled off onto a narrow rutted track to take a picture and had only just done so when of course the local farmer and his tractor decided they wanted to drive down the track as well. With many apologies I reversed back onto the road, but I had got the photo I wanted. We are used to seeing swathes of yellow across the countryside from the fields of oil seed rape, but to now have this mixed with fields of blue flax, green grass and plowed fields of red soil would make a wonderful tapestry. A great aerial shot I would imagine.

I got to Clacton in good time so decided to drive along the front to the end and the village of Jaywick. This seemed to be a very odd place with a strange "feel" about it that I could not quite explain. Driving on the high street were a number of people in thin motorized mobility scooters, almost entirely covered in black plastic, despite the hot day. I would imagine that the elderly death rate in Jaywick is quite high, as they seemed oblivious of the traffic or to any rules of the road. At the beach car park at the end of the street, a car boot sale was taking place, so I stopped to have a look. It was a sad affair. The items on sale all looked as if they might have been salvaged from the local tip. Even the cans of beer and bars of chocolate on sale looked distinctly dodgy.

It was only later that I found out that Jaywick tops the list of the most socially deprived neighbourhoods in the country. I assume that many of its residents, being unable to afford a car, have been able to persuade a doctor that they have some form of disability and thus qualify for one of these mobility scooters. Perhaps if life here is so bad, they don't care if they do get run over. The beach though I discovered to have excellent sand and there was a woman, with young children, playing on it making sand castles.

Jim's train was due to arrive precisely 12.44pm. Not 12.45pm, but precisely one minute before that. From my recent journeys to Britain one thing that has improved is the timing of the trains. Today they are usually no more than 15 to 30 minutes late, unless it is on a Sunday, when "track repairs" seem to take over the lines like traffic cones on the motorway. This is a great improvement from 20 years ago when I lived in England. However, Britain has a long way to go to catch up with the timekeeping of the trains on the Continent, especially those in Germany and Switzerland. I don't know which came first, the Swiss train timetable or the Swiss watch; both can be set by reference to the other.

In Britain of course, in search of competition (so it was said) that would improve customer service, the megalith of British Rail was sold off piece meal, in the 1990s, to a number of companies; the owners of which then got rich by quickly selling them on to someone else. But the oddity of the arrangement is that the company operating the trains is never the same as the company owning the rail tracks. So this is great when the train runs late you can always blame someone else. The old Music Hall song about the unreliability of the railways is probably still true today "Oh Mr. Porter, what can I do? I wanted to go to Birmingham but they took me on to Crewe". Anyway, on this trip I won't be finding out if they take you on to Crew when trying to get to Birmingham, as Birmingham is noted as being the place in Britain that is furthest away from any coastline. However I am expecting trains in Clacton-On-Sea to be as advertised in the timetable!

Ticket prices on British trains are also as varied as the number of train companies. There are peak and off-peak prices; there are savers and super-savers; there are discounts for seniors and students, but you have to purchase a special pass to prove it before you can get the discount. Indeed most misunderstandable of all, it is often possible to purchase two single tickets more cheaply than it is to purchase a return ticket.

Well, Jim's train arrived at precisely 12.44pm, at least according to my watch (though it was not made in Switzerland). Spot on time and contrary to my negative expectations! At least this part of the rail network functions well.

It was good to meet up with Jim again as he is always a cheery person to be around with a unique sense of humour. We quickly toured Clacton driving along its lovely sea front, sunny and charming. It of course has a pier, which was built essentially to land day-trippers traveling from London by steamer. The steamer no longer runs.

The residents of Clacton can see not only the waves but also a forest of wind turbines, about a mile out to sea. There must have been fifty of them, but despite being a breezy day, not one of them was turning. Why would someone go to the huge expense of building a wind turbine farm if they were not going to turn them on? Perhaps they already had enough electricity for the day.

Jim related to me that where he lives in Norfolk the new entertainment, which the locals apparently spend hours doing, is watching the wind turbines. They stand so that two or three structures are in alignment and then they wait and wait and wait for that one moment when all of the blades are in perfect symmetry. It is just a split moment in time, but for a Norfolk lad this is ecstasy! Apparently it makes them feel that their lives are worthwhile and is now the latest "big thing to do" in Norfolk! Indeed if they can get five wind turbines with their blades all in a row I am told it is positively orgasmic!

One thing that I did not see in Clacton was beach huts (maybe they were hiding them) but continue along to Frinton-on-Sea and Walton-on-the-Naze and they return in droves. Both these places were exceptionally clean and inviting, apart from the rather ugly looking, but obligatory, pier at Walton-on-the Naze.

Beach Huts, Walton-On-The-Naze, Essex

Frinton is known as a retirement town. In 1890 the area was mainly farmland, until a property developer bought the land and built the town, but with restrictions; they're could be no pier and no pubs! Indeed the first pub in Frinton did not open until 2000. It has an up market reputation and was visited by the Prince of Wales. Even Winston Churchill rented a house here. Frinton was the last town in England to be bombed during the Second World War – perhaps they were looking for Churchill's house!

We traveled by narrow roads around Pennyhole Bay to Harwich, a major ferry port to Holland; quite a small town for such a large ferry jumping off point. There are an interesting series of old navigation lighthouses (now not in service) once used to guide ships sailing in and out of the port.

From Harwich the journey is back in-land again to round the estuary of the River Stour. We crossed the river at the pretty town of Mistley, but as Jim had come equipped with a full set of Ordnance Survey maps (from Clacton to Edinburgh!) he identified Tattingstone as a suitable place to take afternoon tea and eat the rather large teacake we had purchased in Walton-on-the-Naze. We stopped by the lake here, brewed fresh tea and then shared our over-sized teacake with a friendly Muscovy duck. Rather his waistline than ours!

We then drive on to Felixstowe, which meant a seven-mile journey down the bank of the River Stour and then back up again. Felixstowe is Britain's largest container port and reminded me somewhat of Vancouver and the container ships we see from our house. Felixstowe is located less then a mile across the river mouth from Harwich and there is a ferry between the two, but not one that takes cars. So, we had made a drive of thirty five miles, just to get one mile as the crow flies.

Felixstowe has an ancient history going back to Anglo Saxon times. It also has had its share of war. In 1667 it was the scene of the last opposed armed landing on mainland British soil, halting a Dutch attack. It was bombed in the first word war by a German Zeppelin and then again in the second world war by the Italian air force using old biplanes. Its pier is now considerably shorter than it once was, again due to the war. It was once almost a mile long and had a train running on it, but it was shortened during the war to stop it being used as a German invasion point. Unfortunately it was never rebuilt to its original length.

Felixstowe is in the ancient and beautiful county of Suffolk and certainly the rest of our drive was through amazing countryside with picture book villages. As I have mentioned before, although we are driving the road closest to the ocean, it does not necessarily mean that you can at all times see the sea. But we did appreciate the countryside and all of the blossom and hedgerow flowers. The May blossom this year is particularly stunning. It really did confirm to me that I am in England.

From Felixstowe we drove around Woodbridge, which is very pretty and a major sailing town, but it is not coastal, being 10 miles inland. Unfortunately it was now 5.00pm and we were not able to go to nearby Sutton Hoo, the site of a Saxon burial. Here a king, or at least a person of very high status, had been buried with his long ship. The ship had long since rotted away though the imprint of it in the earth still remained. The gravesite gave up lots of jewels and a fantastic helmet, which is now in the British Museum and I saw it there just two weeks ago when I was in London.

We drove back to the coast to Orford, which provides a passenger ferry crossing to Orford Ness, a world famous bird watching site. The Ness is a shingle spit that reaches all the way along the coast to Aldeburgh and is divided from the mainland by the River Alde. Orford has a wonderfully preserved Castle Keep dating back to the time of Henry II.

Lanes out of Orford take you to the Snape Maltings, made famous by the composer Benjamin Britten and now an arts and concert venue. The Maltings are at the head of the lake formed by the River Alde, which then flows down to Orford. Seven miles further on, on the coast, is Aldeburgh a majestic town with a timeless quality. It is an ancient port and Sir Francis Drake's famous ship, the Golden Hind, was built here.

Driving out of the town we discovered Thorpeness. This was an absolutely charming little village with a large Mere around which lovely homes were spaced.

Inland again and then we returned back to the coast at Dunwich, where we had an excellent dinner of fish and chips in the local Inn, The Ship. Dunwich was once one of the largest ports in England with a residency of over 4000 people and had 10 churches and a Priory. Unfortunately in the 14th century the whole town and port were overwhelmed by the sea and now nothing remains but a small village of only 100 souls, a long shingly beach and crumbly cliffs. It is said that on certain low tides, at night, you can hear the old church bells ringing under the ocean. There are some who suggest that the destruction of the town in one great flood is just a myth and that silting up of the harbour over time meant that the town lost its purpose and was eventually abandoned and left to erode. However, I think I prefer the sudden destruction and sounding church bells story – much more romantic.

Having eaten well and feeling tired we then drove through the equally charming town of Southwold. Southwold harbour benefitted from the downfall of Dunwich, however a shifting shingle bar across its entrance meant that it never became a major port. A group of puritans who founded the Massachusetts Bay Colony came from here. The writer George Orwell, who wrote the famous novel Animal Farm, also lived here in the 1920s and 1930s, after his parents had settled in the town. Southwold today is a small holiday town with an RNLI lifeboat station and the obligatory pier and beach huts.

Pier & Beach Huts, Southwold, Suffolk

After Southwold we made our way, via the minor road to Wrentham and then the A12, directly to Lowestoft and the Travel Lodge, our overnight stop. We had booked an "accessible room" as this is the only way to ensure twin beds when staying at a Travel Lodge. The room was adjacent to the reception and we got to know the receptionist rather well. This was due to the positioning of an alarm button on the headboard of the bed. If you sat up in bed to read and leant back against the headboard, or turned over in the night and touched it, an alarm would go off at the desk and the receptionist would then have to rush into the room, unannounced, to check that we were alright!

Lowestoft to Kings Lynn

Miles 133

Windmill, Cley-Next-The-Sea, Norfolk

Today we went to California, climbed windmills and traveled on a steam train – all on our coastal route.

Having arrived late last night we toured Lowestoft this morning. Although Lowestoft is said to be the driest town in Britain, it presumably does not necessarily mean that it is the sunniest. Although not raining, our day here started grey and overcast.

Lowestoft is a pleasant enough town, but I was secretly disappointed that it was not my imagined picturesque harbour with lots of fishing boats. I know that the British fishing fleet has been decimated, but I was still hopeful that I might see some trawlers in the harbour. It's a shame really as Lowestoft fisherman played major roles in both the first and second world wars, taking an active part in patrolling for U-Boats. As it was Europe that contributed in large part to the British fisheries decline I daresay the good folk here will be voting "Leave" in the upcoming Brexit election.

Lowestoft is divided in two by Lake Lothing, which forms the harbor and is the confluence of Oulton Broad, Oulton Dyke and the River Waveney, so is therefore technically part of the Norfolk Broads. Tourism seems to have taken over from fishing and this was quite evident as we drove along with the docks and old fishery buildings on one side of us and tourist attractions (arcades) on the other.

Lowestoft is the most easterly town in England and Lowestoft Ness its most easterly point. As I am aiming to visit all of the cardinal points of Britain, we of course had to drive to the Ness. This was quite easy to do and is close to the RNLI Lifeboat station on the seaward side.

We decided to move on to Great Yarmouth only a few miles north and stop for breakfast. You can follow the minor road along the coast through Corton and on to Hopton-On-Sea, where we unfortunately found five holiday camps all close together.

Great Yarmouth is a town of two halves, pleasant enough, but again not the place I had expected it to be. It is at the mouth of the River Yare, which divides the town in two. The harbor itself is industrial in appearance and is on the inside of a promontory, which stretches back as far as Gorleston-On-Sea on the mainland side. On the seaward side of the promontory, just two blocks away, in complete contrast to the industrial buildings is a pleasure beach. There is of course the obligatory pier but the fun fare seemed untidy and uninviting. Next to it we saw a sign saying "Free Parking for Paying Guests", which seemed incongruous that you had to pay to receive free parking!

We could not find a greasy spoon with parking outside, so decided to treat ourselves to a good breakfast at the Imperial Hotel. We were met by extremely friendly staff and given a lovely table in the conservatory facing the ocean. They even put on the heating for us, as, despite the weather forecast for sunshine over the whole of the UK, Great Yarmouth remained cloudy and chilly. The view was out onto another wind farm about a mile off the coast. We counted 30 windmills, which was confirmed by our Ordnance Survey map. Ordnance Survey must be the best maps in the world whether you are a walker or a driver. Accurate, detailed, colourful and inexpensive. They even offer a free app which you can use without Wi-Fi to show where you are if you feel lost. Ordnance Survey maps have their origins right back to 1791 when George III ordered high quality mapping of Britain to enable better military and defensive planning.

Our breakfast was superb and though there were only the two of us eating, we had all four of the staff attend to our needs. The waitresses enquired as to what we were doing and when we said "Driving all around the UK", one said "How fantastic, can I come?" We said "OK, but you have just two minutes to quit your job, pack your bag and meet us at the car, as we are about to leave." Needless to say, she felt that was too short notice!

The area west of Great Yarmouth and Lowestoft is the famous Norfolk Broads. Numerous waterways pass through fields and reed beds and are a mecca for people seeking a peaceful time on the water. Most of this is inland, so unfortunately we only saw glimpses. The Broads are actually the lakes, but the name has over time now become used to describe the whole of the area. They were formed by inundation of the sea into centuries old peat workings, where peat was excavated and sold by monks to the towns for fuel. Now it is a network of natural rivers, canals and large and small broads and remains a popular tourist area and nature sanctuary.

From Great Yarmouth things deteriorated and we began to see a plethora of caravan and chalet parks and they multiplied and multiplied all the way along the coast, well into Norfolk. Most incongruous of all were the chalet parks at California. If you ever book a holiday to California in America and it seems really cheap, check that it is to the California on the west coast of America, not to the one on the east coast of the UK. You could be very disappointed. There are a number of places named Sidney in Canada and frequently there are stories of people who think they got an unbelievable deal to Australia, but arrive in Nova Scotia where it is a lot colder than Australia and with no kangaroos. California in Norfolk is definitely not San Diego or Los Angeles! California, Norfolk is adjacent to the wonderfully named village of Scratby – you don't want to go there either, but then I can't imagine this name getting mixed up with somewhere more exotic!

The road takes you inland quite a bit, but whenever we could get back by the sea, chalet and caravan parks were still present. They spoil what is otherwise a lovely area. I ask myself what sort of towns and places do people live in for them to feel that a stay in an ugly, overcrowded chalet or caravan park is a holiday? There must obviously be a big demand or there wouldn't be so many of them. Apart from their presence though, the countryside in this area is generally very attractive.

The seaside itself remains very much the same along the whole of this coast. Beaches of shingle pushed up into steep banks with flat fens, marshes and muddy river outflows. The first really pretty place we came to was Horsey a National Trust property at the end of a Broad with a Wind Pump (mill).

The Broads at Horsey, Norfolk

Not much further on, at Stow, near to Mundesley, we found a windmill that we could enter and explore. This has been restored but is not operating. We paid our entrance fee into the honesty box and climbed to the top. Little to see by way of a view, but it was only as I was climbing, carefully, down the very narrow stairs from each of the four floors that I remembered that it was exactly a year ago today that I had an argument with the Vicar of Dibley's baptismal font (true!) that resulted in my breaking my right femur. This remembrance caused me to hang on tighter, but as my right wrist has also recently been under the surgeon's knife, I took it very carefully and reached the bottom without accident (phew). Jim filmed my descent in case we needed to show it to the insurance company!

The Stow windmill and house is currently up for sale with permission to use it as a holiday let. If you have £550,000 to spend this charmer could be yours! Caution though, before you buy a windmill in Norfolk you have to wonder whether Norfolk will still be here in fifty or a hundred years. Most of the east coast of England is being slowly eroded, but this seems particularly so in Norfolk, where it is either falling into the ocean or being submerged by the sea. Go and visit it now, before it's gone!

All of the small towns moving further up this coast have so much more to offer the traveler looking for peace and quiet than the larger resorts such as Great Yarmouth. We stopped for an ice cream (our lunch) at Overstrand beach and then went on to Cromer.

Cromer is another small and pretty town, which during our visit was quiet, certainly compared with Sheringham, which was our next stop. Cromer is world famous for its crab and we noticed it being advertised at a number of shops and stalls.

Cromer came to prominence after golfing visits in the nineteenth century by the future King Edward VII. This gave the stimulus for wealthy people from Norfolk and other large local towns to build seaside homes here. It has a fairly modern pier with a well-used theatre on it and the RNLI Lifeboat station at the end. The lifeboat is launched down a very steep ramp and presumably they have an efficient system to get it back up again. Cromer RNLI station is especially noted for a past Coxswain, Henry Blogg, who received the RNLI's highest bravery award, a gold medal, three times. He was also awarded a silver medal on four occasions. There are no natural harbours for about 30 miles in either direction, hence the lifeboat being launched from the pier. Blogg's heroic deeds and awards demonstrate how fierce can be the ocean at times along this coast.

In 1871 the government approved the Holiday's Act, which designated four Monday's in the year as Bank Holidays, when businesses shut down. This meant that these particular weekends would see a mass migration of workers to the coast. Cromer did not see much of this trade initially as the railway did not come to the town until 1877, but by 1893, thanks to the patronage of King Edward VII it became the place to see and be seen and remained fairly exclusive.

In 1883, Clement Scott, a writer for the Daily Telegraph was commissioned by the town council to write an article on Cromer; one of the earliest holiday guides. In writing his article he noted the poppies growing in abundance and coined the phrase "Poppy Land" to describe Cromer and the local area. This phrase then became the marketing tool, which brought Cromer to the attention of the country and so tourist numbers boomed. There were lots of Poppy Land souvenirs made, including a china tea service, which is today a sought after collector's item.

The late 1800s also saw manufacturers, who were often interdependent on each other, deciding to close their businesses for the same two weeks to give their staff and themselves a holiday. By tradition this was the last week of July and the first week in August and came to be known as "Factory Fortnight". It worked well, especially while the majority of people could travel by train. However by the 1960s and Mr. Beeching's closure of many railways and the rise in numbers of the motor car, serious congestion on the roads made driving on holiday to the seaside a real nightmare. As a child I can remember journeys in the car of ten or more hours from Cheltenham down to Devon as my parents took us on holiday. This journey can now be driven in two hours thanks to the motorway. Easy flights and cheap holidays to warmer foreign climes added to the pressure on the British holiday resort. Later, flexible working arrangements brought the factory fortnight tradition almost to an end. During this time though a lot of resorts felt a boom and bust phenomenon and it was in an attempt to extend the season that many seaside towns began to look at other attractions, the most notable being Blackpool with its illuminations.

Cromer maintained its compact size and somewhat exclusive position and remains a charming place today.

Sheringham, just four miles further up the coast is also charming and seems to offer the visitor everything they might wish for. From cutesy shops and places to eat, to lovely cottages by the ocean. It has been the setting for many a movie and the TV home of "Dad's Army" as Walmington-on-Sea. I did not see any chalets or caravans here, but maybe they were hidden away. What is very prominent as you enter the town is the steam railway. The smell of the coal smoke and the whistle of the steam engine called out invitingly to us such that our driving had to be halted for two hours to allow us to take a coastal rail journey.

It was magical and even allowed us to see parts of the coast that we could not see from the road. The journey was only 20 minutes each way, with a break mid-way, at the end of the line, in the village of Holt, to allow passengers to buy a cup of tea before returning. The golfers at the very smart Sheringham Golf Club stopped their games to give us a wave, both outbound and inbound.

Steam Locomotive, Sheringham, Norfolk

Before we left the town I tried to find and photograph a house that had belonged to the father of a friend in Vancouver. I had myself only seen the house from a photograph so I had to drive around trying to identify it from the image in my head. I think I did so. What was so special about this man, who I had the pleasure to meet on a number of occasions, was that he had managed to escape from the Japanese advance in Burma, by stealing a steam train in Rangoon. He went on to live to 103, dying only two years ago.

As well as caravans and chalets, Norfolk has windmills and large churches a plenty. Indeed Norfolk is said to have more than 650 churches, making it the highest concentration of churches anywhere in Europe. More than 125 date back to Saxon times and are notable by their circular towers. Most of the churches, even in the small villages, are large in size reflecting the wealth of Norfolk in past times. We did see three churches that have become derelict. One of these we noted had received a grant from the Lottery Heritage Fund to be rebuilt as a village cultural centre. Perhaps the good folk of Norfolk are losing their faith.

After Sheringham we followed the flat coastline through Cley-Next-The-Sea. Cley was once a trading port, second only to Kings Lynn and a major exporter of woolen cloth, but silting in the 17th century turned it into a small backwater, but the name "next-the-sea" still remains! The wonderful 18th century windmill here was owned for a number of years by the family of the singer James Blunt and run as a B&B.

Blakeney follows on and is at the mouth of the River Glaven, which carries a lot of mud and soil off the land. Once again the tide was out and boats were marooned on large mud flats. This used to be a busy seaport but the harbour, as was clearly in evidence, is now silted up. When the tide is in you can take a boat from here out to Blakeney Point, which shelters the harbour, and view the seals hauled up on the beach.

Norfolk has extensive bird life; particularly around the broads and dunes and all along the coastline there are extensive areas for bird watching. We saw oystercatchers on the mud flats by the boats at Blakeney and then just a little further, as we stopped to brew a cup of tea by the sea, we watched for twenty minutes as a pair of Avocets flew at every other bird that came near to their newborn chick. We also saw and heard Buntings, Meadow Larks and Warblers. The other creatures in abundance were of course the "twitchers".

The next place as you journey on is Wells-Next-The-Sea, with its most notable feature being the old granary with its gantry through which grain flowed into the ships in the harbour below. The building has now been divided into private flats. Wells is also no longer "next-the-sea". Significant silting up of the harbour means that the town is now one-mile inland. Wells is popular with holidaymakers having a nice beach that can be reached by taking the narrow gauge railway, which runs for 1200 yards from the town to the beach. Here there are sand dunes and some very cutely painted beach huts. There is also apparently a naturist beach, but we did not find it.

Wells-Next-The-Sea, Norfolk

Traveling on, the area from Holkham to Burnham Thorpe (the boyhood home of Lord Nelson) is known locally as Chelsea on Sea, due to the large number of smart homes. Many are second homes for wealthy Londoners. Certainly no holiday chalets are located here.

We finished off the "hump" of Norfolk at Old Hunstanton and "new" Hunstanton. The contrast here seemed to be a microcosm of so much of what we had seen along the Norfolk coast. Old Hunstanton was smart and quiet with fine architecture and old buildings. Just one mile later you enter "new" Hunstanton, coming over the brow of a small hill, on to what should be a lovely village green, but it was covered with lots of people eating fish and chips. Just below it, on the beachfront, was a gaudy fun palace. There were also more holiday parks here, but built just out of site of Old Hunstanton.

Across The Wash we could see Boston and Lincolnshire, our destinations for tomorrow.

Before leaving Norfolk I feel I have to say something about the Norfolk accent. This is very distinct, particularly in the country areas. Norfolk folk don't seem able to pronounce a word with "ew" in it, changing it to "oo". So they might tell you that they have a "noo tractor" or that they have visited "Koo Gardens". They also enunciate other words quite differently. I still remember the first time I knowingly met anyone from Norfolk. I was aged about eighteen and had gone on holiday with my friend Mike, to Jersey, one of the Channel Islands. Having both come from homes where we had full service Mothers, we found it impossible to cook a meal or even know what we should buy from the supermarket. So, each morning we would go to a local café where one of the waitresses took pity on us. We would order just a cup of tea, which when it arrived would have "on the side" a full English breakfast, courtesy of our friendly waitress. Our Norfolk interaction came one morning when the waitress greeted us and said "I've got a special treat for you this morning lads." We thought that we were going to get ice cream as well. However, her idea was to introduce us to two very attractive maidens, one blonde, one brunette, both about our own age.

Mike and I both looked at each other, pleased that it was not ice cream after all.

None of us spoke for a couple of minutes then I, bravely, used my favourite chat-up line, "So where are you two from"?

The blonde girl answered, "Us be frum Naarj".

"Sorry I didn't get that" I replied, and I genuinely could not understand her.

"Us be frum Naarj" she repeated.

"From Naarj" I responded, where about is that". "Naarj, yoom know. It's the main town in Narfuck".

Mike and I both looked at each other and decided it was time to go. Beauty really is only skin deep and it can disappear if you open your mouth! I think what she was actually trying to say was. "Thank you kindly for enquiring where we come from. My friend and I are from Norwich, the county town of Norfolk. We like you and your friend very much. Would you like to take us out on a date?"

From Hunstanton, Jim took me on a slight detour to meet his new neighbours. We toured Sandringham Estate, (the outside) the country home of the Queen. The whole of the exterior was hedged with beautiful purple (the colour of royalty) rhododendrons, fully in bloom. Shortly after Jim pointed out a road sign to Anmer, where William and Kate now live. Unfortunately Jim felt that, though they were his neighbours, knocking on their door to introduce himself might not be appreciated, so a drive-by was all that we achieved. This was the closest that we came to royalty all day! We soon arrived at Jim's house, just outside Kings Lynn, where his wife Jean had a meal ready for us and a very welcome glass of wine.

Tomorrow we set off for Lincolnshire and Yorkshire and some more very distinctive accents.

Kings Lynn to Hull

Miles 160

The Minster, Kings Lynn. Norfolk

Today nothing happened, or at least very little. After a very interesting tour of Kings Lynn, Jim's new hometown, we crossed into Lincolnshire where, nothing happened!

Jim took me to the old town of Kings Lynn, which is absolutely lovely, especially by the Minster. Unfortunately we did not have time to go inside. If we had done I am sure that we would have been there two hours at least as I do love exploring English churches and Cathedrals; so much history. Standing in front of the Minster I at first thought that I was not standing up straight, but then having assured myself that I was vertical to the ground, I realised that the right hand tower seems to be leaning inwards. Is this the (yet to be famous) leaning tower of Kings Lynn? Perhaps it was just as well we did not go in!

I took out my camera to take a photo of the Minster, but this proved slightly challenging, as, for what reason I do not know, other than he might have wanted to be in a photo, a man drove his car right between me and the Minster, got out and began to polish it! As he was dressed in shorts and smoking heavily, I didn't get the impression that he was a chauffer between pick-ups as. Having rubbed the car all over with a cloth for about five minutes he then drove off. Perhaps this is some strange religious ritual, polishing the car outside the cathedral. Or maybe, as Jim said, it might just be another Norfolk country ritual. Bizarre.

During the fourteenth century King's Lynn was Britain's most important port and a member of the Hanseatic League of trading ports. However, after the discovery of the Americas, most trade moved to the west coast of Britain in the fifteenth and sixteenth centuries and King's Lynn lost its importance. One black mark against this town is the horrific story of the public hanging in 1708 of a seven year old boy and his eleven year old sister for stealing a loaf of bread. In our new, enlightened age we might think this could never happen today. Probably not in Britain, but atrocities against children still do happen in countries across the world where medieval style rulers have power.

Living as I now do in Vancouver, British Columbia, we had to visit on the Quay, the statute of Captain Vancouver who was born in this city in 1757. The statue it is not as big as I would have expected for the founder of such a great city (indeed two cities) that are named after him. I think that Vancouver City Council (in BC) could perhaps pay for a much bigger monument to him as a token of friendship with Kings Lynn. It certainly would be cheaper and less self-indulgent than the ridiculous and expensive bike lanes that are in the process of being built that have now made Vancouver one of the hardest cities in the world to drive around. Don't get me started on that subject!

We drove out of King's Lynn and crossed over the River Ouse and into Lincolnshire, by the unfortunately named village of Clenchwarton.

Lincolnshire is the produce garden of England and according to Jim grows one third of all the vegetables eaten in the UK. Indeed Lincolnshire is especially known for potatoes. This therefore means that there must be lots of fields – there are. All the fields in Lincolnshire appear to be either recently ploughed and ridged, waiting for the potatoes to sprout, or, covered with hundreds of miles of white plastic mesh to keep the birds off. It also means that Lincolnshire is full of agricultural machinery, which when they travel on the roads results in slow, slow traffic. They are expected to pull over after one mile to let traffic that has built up, go past. This they do. However, they have created such a gap in the traffic ahead of them, that as the cars get past the first tractor, a second tractor is already waiting up the road, to pull out into the gap created by the first one. The cars released from behind the first tractor then catch up with and build up behind the second tractor and then, behind the third, the fourth the fifth and so on, right across Lincolnshire! We were fortunate as today was a Saturday of a Bank Holiday weekend so most farmers had taken the weekend off – apart from two, who each held us up for the obligatory one mile.

We stopped at Gedney Marshes as Jim had been told that you had a good view of The Wash from here. We wended our way down a very narrow lane running alongside a navigation channel. Interestingly they have a big sign here asking drivers to switch off their headlights if a ship is coming along the channel. I expect that either they don't want to dazzle the ship's master, or, the lights might be mistaken for navigation lights. However, I'm not sure what the poor car driver is expected to do if he has to drive next to a waterway at night with no lights on.

We drove a few miles down this lane, got to the end and walked to the high bank above what we thought was the Wash. However, when we got there the ocean was not to be seen. There was just a large expanse of nothing, grass and mud stretching as far as we could see! Jim was very disappointed. Indeed we hardly saw the ocean at any time we were in Lincolnshire. We were either in roadways lower than the banking built to hold back the ocean, or, the ocean was many miles away across the mud fields. Good for growing more potatoes no doubt. So basically we saw nothing, because there is nothing to see. One benefit of all of this though is that when we stood still we also heard nothing. Silence, broken only now and then by bird song. That in itself made the nothingness of Lincolnshire seem worthwhile.

One thing that we were surprised about was the absence of metal detectorists in the fields of the Wash, especially around Gedney and Fosdyke. It is here that legend states that King

John (he of Robin Hood fame) lost the crown jewels when the wagons carrying his treasure along a causeway moved too slowly and were overtaken by the incoming tide. No one has ever found this treasure and possibly, if we had had with us our own metal detectors, Jim and I might still be there now, searching. Perhaps I'll go back!

Lincolnshire Hare

Our next major destination was Skegness. Those of you who have read "The Road to Little Dribbling" will have seen the Jolly Sailor on the front cover of the book, which is the famous symbol of Skegness (or Skeggy as the locals call it). He was once part of an advertising campaign to encourage people to come to Skegness. The line for the advert was "Skegness is so Bracing". This is a marketing man's way of saying it is windy and cold!

Our first stop in the town was Morrisons Supermarket. Boy oh boy, I don't think I have ever seen so many unfit looking people wearing football shirts and track-suits gathered in one place since the World Cup finals. And the car park wow, there was certainly a lot of car park rage going on. We grabbed a salad (yes, honest we did) and fled as quickly as we could.

We then drove to Gibraltar Point a bird watching area on a promontory to the south of the town. Gibraltar Point and the road leading to it is clearly the up-market part of Skegness with nice homes facing onto the golf course. At the Point there is a good viewing area and cafe but you certainly needed binoculars, not only to see the birds but also the sea! The best thing all day happened here, there was a murmuration of starlings; a moving ballet in the sky. This is one of those wonders of nature that once seen is never forgotten. I have seen this about seven times now (always in England) and every time I see it I could watch it for hours. What makes them do it I don't know, but it is beautiful to watch. I have seen this begin as thousands of birds all took off together, seemingly in the same second and rose into the sky and created this incredible dark cloud. The end is also as sudden, with the birds halting their flight and landing in a field or trees, all at about the same moment.

We eventually drove into Skeggy town, which was true to its word – bracing. There is the obligatory pier, some nice sand, but in the far, far, far distance, across the mud banks, possibly, was the elusive sea. Few people were on the beach, but the chip shops looked full. Paul Theroux in his book, written in the 1980s, talked about the Mods (scooter riders) and Rockers (motorcyclists) who would meet at a seaside resort on a Bank Holiday, get drunk and then build up to a big fight on the Monday. Well de ja vue, or the wheel has turned full circle; there were groups of scooter riders and motorcyclists sitting outside the pubs and amusement arcades. All seemed quiet when we saw them, but we were glad we came here on a Saturday and would be somewhere else on Bank Holiday Monday, the traditional day for a rumble! We did notice a disability scooter on sale outside a "Kiss Me Quick" hat and souvenir shop. No doubt the owner thought he might have a good chance of selling it to an elderly Mod who wanted to remember his youth and join in the fun.

Driving on from here along the coast, eighteen miles to Mablethorpe, I swear that every mile of the road had caravan and chalet parks with the largest being a Butlins Holiday Camp and a nearby "Fantasy World".

We then took the main road to Cleethorpes, which interestingly (though it means nothing) is sited exactly on the Greenwich meridian. Our journey was thirty miles of not being able to see the ocean, only flat fields and of course caravan and chalet parks. At Cleethorpes we at last did get to see the sea, (or it might actually have been the River Humber) but it was perhaps a mile away. The beach by the esplanade had good sand on it and then it became mud for about a mile out to where the water was.

We brewed a cup of tea on the Esplanade and looked across to Spurn Head the starboard entrance to the River Humber. Just before Cleethorpes we spotted one of those signs that is official and also ridiculous. This was a public information sign that stated, "There are dangers associated with drowning". Duh – who wrote this, a lawyer working for Cleethorpes Council no doubt? Perhaps we should advise them that it might be more appropriate to say the dangers "are associated with swimming". By the time you get to drowning it is probably too late! (Yes I know it is not only in England that people put up dumb signs).

Cleethorpes, is the holiday end of Grimsby but has successfully remained independent, governance wise, from its big neighbour, Grimsby. Grimsby once had one of England's biggest fishing fleets. Sadly, like Lowestoft, this is no longer. Many say the EU killed the fishing industry; perhaps after the Brexit vote next month, it may come back again. No doubt the "Vote Leave" campaigners in Grimsby and Lowestoft are expecting this. There is still a Fish Dock in Grimsby, but all we could see were cold storage and closed buildings, no sign of any fishing fleet (that we could see). Despite this being a Bank Holiday weekend, the beach was, like the rest of Lincolnshire, surprisingly empty.

The empty beach at Cleethorpes, Lincolnshire

Our journey then took us along the Humber Estuary to the Humber Bridge and the crossing into Yorkshire. Tonight we are booked to stay at the Ibis Hotel in downtown Kingston Upon Hull. Though our preferred option is for small B&Bs by the sea, this was not possible. The only rooms available were in hotels in city centres where people did not want to spend their holiday weekend. However, having driven the coastline of Lincolnshire, there can't be many B&Bs actually by the sea. Certainly there are B&Bs on the coast, but the sea is so far out over the mud flats, they can hardly claim to be seaside B&Bs! We did try AirBnB once more. Hopeless.

After having checked in to our room, Jim Googled nearby restaurants and this led us to an excellent Indian restaurant, the Cinnamon, just a two-minute walk from the Ibis Hotel. We thus had a good evening. Surely there is no country in the world that compares with England for good Indian food!

Tomorrow we head up the Yorkshire coast to the resorts of Bridlington, Scarborough and Whitby. Hopefully, the sea will be in when we get there!

Kingston Upon Hull to Redcar

Miles 150

The Quay, Kingston-Upon-Hull, Yorkshire

Well I must say that Hull has improved enormously since I last came here, about 20 years ago. Then it was dreary and decaying. There is clearly a huge effort to make Hull a liveable city and congratulations to the Council for what they have achieved. We obviously have not seen everything, but the area around the Quay, although still under development, felt exciting. In 2017 Hull is taking on the mantle of European City of Culture, so no doubt a lot of the downtown and waterfront development is in preparation for this. Being a City of Culture has been the stimulus for a number of cities to regenerate and I'm sure the results will be positive for Hull also.

Hull is certainly a coastal city, despite actually being 25 miles up the Humber Estuary. The confluence of the Humber and the North Sea is at Spurn Head. Unfortunately being on an estuary it is not blessed with nice blue water, rather it being brown and muddy. Perhaps they can add a dye to it for the period that it is the European City of Culture!

Despite being assured by the BBC that today would be sunshine everywhere, Hull and the North Yorkshire coast is presumably not included when one talks about everywhere. We did get breaks of sun during the day, which was glorious, but much of the day was under damp sea mist and there was a cold wind. However, we found the Yorkshire coast to be an excellent part of the country.

Our first destination today was to the outer edge of the Yorkshire coast at Spurn Head. We passed a sign to the unbelievably named village of Thorngumball before taking the long road to Spurn Head. This would mean a return journey, but we had to do it to be true to the principle of a full coastal trip.

On our way we came across a surprising monument in a field near to Patrington. It was a metal cut-out of four of the gunpowder plotters. Guy Fawkes, Robert Catesby (who was the leader, not Guy) and two brothers, John and Christopher Wright, who lived locally at Plowlands Farm.

The famous Guy Fawkes plot took place in November 1605. It sought to blow up the Houses of Parliament when the protestant King James I was present. King James I of England was also King James VI of Scotland and son of Mary Queen of Scots. James, of the House of Stuart, had come to the throne on the death of Queen Elizabeth I. The plotters wanted to kill James and restore a Catholic monarchy by giving the throne to his nine-year-old daughter, Elizabeth Stuart.

Gunpowder Plot Memorial. Patrington, Yorkshire

Elizabeth was actually a protestant, but it was felt she could be influenced at this young age to become Catholic. Elizabeth was four years older than her brother Charles, but the plotters considered Charles too feeble to become King.

The Gunpowder Plot failed as certain catholic parliamentarians received letters tipping them off not to attend Parliament on the day James was to visit. The sender of the letters was unknown but it was thought to be one of the plotters, concerned that Catholics would be caught up in the blast. One of the recipients was so alarmed that a possible assassination plot was being planned that his letter was shown to the King.

James ordered the Houses of Parliament to be searched and Fawkes was discovered in the crypt watching over the explosives. He had been the one who had been tasked with lighting the fuse (and then running!). Under torture he gave up the names of his conspirators and all were sentenced to death. The executions took place in January 1606 alongside the Houses of Parliament in Westminster. The site was chosen to further humiliate the plotters and show them that their plans had come to naught. After watching his three companions mutilated, hung, then their bodies cut into quarters, either through fear or weakness, Fawkes fell from the scaffold and his neck was broken and he died. Though his death was not by hanging, his body was still cut up and quarters delivered to cities across the country. His head was put on a spike on Tower Bridge.

The punishment of hanging, drawing and quartering came into law in England in 1351 as a means of punishment and execution for high treason. Typically the condemned man would be fastened to a piece of wood and drawn naked through the streets to the place of execution. There he would be hanged by the neck until almost dead. He would then be strapped to a ladder so he could be seen by the crowd and while still alive would have his genitals cut off, before being disemboweled, watching while these parts were burnt in a fire. He would then be finished off by beheading. The body would be cut up into four pieces and put on display in various prominent places across the country. It's perhaps no wonder that Guy Fawkes chose to jump off the gallows to avoid this fate, after watching his co-accused die in such agony.

Hanging, drawing and quartering was the punishment for men. Women who were found guilty of treason were burned at the stake. It was not until 1870 that this law was removed from the statute books and it was only in 1998 that death as the punishment for treason was withdrawn.

The Gunpowder Plot memorial at Patrington was erected in July 2011 as a celebration of the fact that the plot failed and Parliament continued. It was not, as we first assumed, a comment on David Cameron's upcoming referendum on the EU.

Charles did become King on the death of his father James I/VI. Although a protestant, Charles I married a Catholic, Henrietta Maria, daughter of Henry IV of France. Marriage to a Catholic and of the royal house of France meant that Charles was deeply mistrusted by Parliament. This mistrust of the King culminated in a major dispute with Parliament over taxation, which directly resulted in the rise of the Catholic hating Oliver Cromwell and the English Civil War.

Oliver Cromwell is a significant figure in British history, having been a commoner who rose to power, overthrowing a King and becoming Lord Protector of Britain, effectively acting as a King.

Cromwell was born in 1599 in Huntingdon (not a coastal town) in what is now Cambridgeshire. He was a middle class farmer and landowner who became a fervent Puritan in the 1630s while he was a Member of Parliament. It was Puritanism that was the driving force in his life and he was vehemently anti-Catholic, also hating the Scottish Covenanter Presbyterians. In 1642, the conflict between Charles I and Parliament began, which deteriorated into the First English Civil War. At this time Cromwell commanded a cavalry troop, but by 1644 he had been promoted to Lieutenant General and was second in command of what was called the new model army. He was vigorous in battle and in the sieges of royalist held castles. Charles I eventually surrendered, to the Scottish army, in 1646 and was handed over to Parliament. His young son, later Charles II, fled to Pendennis Castle near Falmouth and then on to France.

In 1647 it was proposed by a majority in Parliament that the armies in Scotland and England be disbanded and Charles could keep his throne if he consented to a Scottish style of Presbyterianism. Cromwell was bitterly against this. A group of disgruntled soldiers released Charles I from captivity and the King then tried to regain his power by force. Cromwell opposed him and the second English Civil War broke out in 1648.

Cromwell first led his army into Wales winning back the castles at Chepstow, Carmarthen, Tenby and Pembroke. Then he turned to Scotland soundly defeating their army in battle at the northern England town of Preston.

Cromwell's soldiers physically intimidated and prevented from sitting in Parliament those Members of Parliament who favoured restoring the King. The MPs who were allowed to sit were all loyal to Cromwell and became known as "the Rump". Thus it was that the Cromwell dominated Parliament determined that King Charles I should be tried for treason. He was found guilty and executed in January 1649.

Soon after the execution of the King, Cromwell invaded Ireland and war here continued for three more years. Cromwell was fighting against both Catholics and their Royalist allies and he was responsible for significant massacres. Indeed he ordered that any Catholic priest discovered was to be summarily executed. Later in 1652, under the Act of Settlement for Ireland, all land owned by Catholics was confiscated and given to English and Scottish settlers. Catholic ownership of land in Ireland dropped from 60% to just 6%.

Meanwhile the Scottish Presbyterian Parliament in May 1650 had already proclaimed Charles II as King of Scotland, but he was not allowed to enter Scotland until he agreed to Presbyterian government across both Scotland and England. At first he did not agree and even sent an army to the Orkneys under General Montrose to threaten Scotland with invasion unless they accepted him as King with no conditions. Montrose though was defeated and so Charles accepted the Scottish terms and came to Scotland in June 1650.

In January 1651 Charles II was crowned King of Scotland at the traditional site for enthronement of Scottish Kings at Scone Palace. An angry Cromwell then invaded Scotland, slaughtering many prisoners, both Catholic and Presbyterians alike. Charles endeavoured to avoid directly fighting Cromwell and led a Presbyterian Scottish army on an invasion of England. Cromwell caught up and defeated him at Worcester and Charles II barely escaped with his life, famously hiding in an oak tree. He fled to France, where he remained for nine years.

In April 1653 Cromwell fell out with the Rump Parliament so his troops commanded by Charles Worsley cleared the chamber. Though another attempt was made to form a stable Parliament, the leadership of the Realm was "settled" by Cromwell being appointed as Lord Protector of the Commonwealth of England, Scotland and Ireland.

Cromwell's rule was dominated by his Puritan views. He actively encouraged Jews, who had been banished by Edward I, to return to England to assist in restoring its economy. He also actively promoted conversion of them to Christianity.

Cromwell died of malaria and kidney disease in 1658 and was buried in Westminster Abbey. His son, Richard, known as Tumbledown Dick, took over from him but was ineffectual and removed in 1659 by Parliament, which then invited Charles II to take over as King of England and Scotland.

In 1661, on the anniversary of his father's execution, Charles II ordered Cromwell's body to be disinterred from Westminster Abbey and subjected to posthumous execution and hanging at Tyburn. The head was impaled on a spike on London Bridge. The empty vault at the Abbey was later used as a tomb for the illegitimate offspring of Charles II.

One modern day note is that the current Duchess of Kent, Katharine Worsley, is a direct descendent of Cromwell, through his daughter, but became a Catholic having converted in 1994. Her husband the Duke of Kent is a first cousin to Queen Elizabeth. So, Cromwell's blood remains close to the current royal family, but he is no doubt spinning in whatever place his distributed bones now lie.

When the Stuart dynasty later lost the throne in 1714, it was the Hanoverian grandson of Elizabeth Stuart who became King, as George I. It was this same Elizabeth Stuart (daughter of James I and sister of Charles I) that the gunpowder plotters had sought to put on the throne. Interestingly, our current Queen, Elizabeth II, is a tenth and eleventh direct descendent of Elizabeth Stuart from two different sides of her family.

So, to continue on our journey; there is not a lot to see when you get to Spurn Head, but the twitchers, all with long lenses, certainly seemed to think so. You can at certain times tour the lighthouse, but it was not open when we were there and anyway quite a long walk from the car park. We had had to go to Spurn Head as it was part of the coastal route, but left without taking any photographs. At Hedon on the road out, we drove past gas and energy plants, interestingly fenced by double rows of razor wire. The word Stalagluft was spoken in the car and we expected to see Alsatians running between the fences.

We continued on to the small seaside town of Withernsea. Here there was a Tesco supermarket, open of course. We purchased some cinnamon buns to eat now and pork pies for lunch later. I am sure from what I have experienced so far that it would be possible to do this journey and purchase fresh food every day from one or other "superstore" at a handy junction. We went to the sea front, had a brew and ate our buns. We watched the RNLI in-shore lifeboat go out, but probably only for training. They practiced running the boat at speed through the waves; it looked very cold. No doubt they were the weekend duty crew as this was after all a Bank Holiday weekend. We continued to notice the caravan and chalet parks. Some chalets here were brown wooden affairs, old and tired. One or two had windows covered with newspaper, but others had fresh flowers and one even had wisteria growing up the front. At another camp down the road, new static caravans were on offer for sale at £9,500; a bargain if you intended to use it regularly and wanted to only go to Withernsea for your holidays.

Further along the main road and ahead of the traffic, we came across some road signs warning of road resurfacing and loose chippings and asking drivers to slow down. There were also signs advising caution stating that there were no white line road markings. However, there were no chippings, the road was beautifully resurfaced and the white lines were present and beautifully painted. Was this a sign of the old work practices of the England of the 1960s when the Unions said you only did "your job" and nothing else? It would seem that the white line painters did not see it as there job to remove the "no white line" signs and another group of workmen needed to be employed to remove these. No doubt they were not scheduled until after the holiday weekend.

We also noticed a pole close to the road with strange equipment and aerials on it. A sign attached to it said, "these are weather instruments and not speed cameras". I don't know why they would feel it necessary to advise that they were not speed cameras. Perhaps it was to prevent them being vandalized, or, maybe, just to stop unnecessarily raising the anxiety of passing motorists who might feel the need to reduce their speed.

In Aldbrough we found the roadside verges beautifully cut and the hawthorn hedges had been rounded. We could have been in Surrey in the south of England. It certainly demonstrated a civic pride as few places must actually cut the roadside verges. They are obviously so regular in cutting the verges that there was need for a "Mrs. Mowers Mower Shop" that was advertising mowing machine repairs.

Driving on to Mappleton, a very nice place, where we could see the sea, there were more cabins, but this time upmarket ones, built in the Canadian log cabin style. There are so many caravan, chalet and cabin parks that competition is probably driving the provision of more upmarket properties. The best way to differentiate yourself in a crowded market is to increase the quality of your product.

Thank goodness for Tesco. I had woken up this morning with a slight infection in my right eye (the one nearest the sea!). Now, a few hours later it had become very sore and I was concerned about driving. The only pharmacy open on Sundays in this area is at Tesco and the nearby town of Hornsea had one. The Pharmacist helpfully sold me some antibiotic eye drops and said that it would be better in the morning. Hopefully he is right, as Jim is not insured to drive the car, so it is down to me. I tried driving with my right eye closed, but my depth of field was severely impacted!

At the same time as the antibiotic began to work, so the sun came out. We drove into the very pretty village of Atwick with its lovely village green. However, on leaving to head towards Bridlington, we came across a horrendous traffic jam. The traffic was stationary as far as the eye could see. Rather than sit it out, we diverted in-land along some very narrow roads. This proved to be a good decision. It was an extremely pleasant drive, with once again, even though away from main roads, the verges beautifully manicured. The fields were glorious with either yellow oil seed rape or green shoots of wheat. To cap it all when we rejoined the main road it was well ahead of the traffic jam.

Our next destination was Bridlington, a small town, again seemingly trying to make its income from tourism. Amusement arcades, fish and chip and ice cream shops dominate its small sea front. Just outside the town is Flamborough Head with its chalk tower lighthouse, built in 1669 and chalk sea cliffs famous for nesting sea birds, especially puffins and gannets.

We passed briefly through Filey. Many years ago I attended a convention in Filey where the Butlin's Holiday Camp was the venue. I remember that we booked ourselves into a B&B, as the holiday camp accommodation was so rustic. We also visited Filey sea front and ate fish and chips on the esplanade in a freezing cold wind. Butlin's Filey has now long since been closed, but our memory of this bleak place remained strong in my mind.

We continued on to Scarborough. This proved to be one of the stand-out surprises of the trip. Scarborough is a glorious, stylish and bustling town. Both Jim and I had a preconceived view of what Scarborough would be like, mine based on my Filey experience. However, we found an extremely attractive town to which we gave the descriptor of "Harrogate on Sea". Those who know Harrogate may see the similarities, a lovely Georgian/Victorian town with prominent architecture and a timeless quality.

Scarborough has both south and north beaches, separated by a promontory dominated by the ruins of Scarborough castle. On this bright and sunny holiday Sunday the roads to the beaches were exceedingly busy.

Scarborough's stone castle was built by Henry II in 1159. Later King John expanded it and made it more comfortable. It later fell into some disrepair but was restored again by King Edward II, whose favourite, Piers Gaveston sought sanctuary here when pursued by the Barons in 1311. The Barons felt that Piers was too friendly and had too much influence over Edward II. It was Edwards father, Edward I, who, having met Piers when a boy, determined that he would be a good companion for his son, so Piers and Edward grew up together. Because of this Edward II gave Piers great riches and power, even making him Earl of Cornwall, thus kindling the hatred of him by the other Barons. It was rumoured that Edward II and Piers were lovers, but this cannot be proved and Edward II's wife, Queen Isabella, who felt that Edward wanted to spend more time with Piers than with her, may well have instigated the story. Certainly Edward II's murder at Berkley Castle in Gloucestershire has always been attached to the story that he was killed by a red hot poker being inserted into his backside as a reminder of his homosexuality. Pier's surrendered at Scarborough to the besieging Barons and though numerous promises were made and broken, the Earls of Warwick and Lancaster eventually killed him.

Though the castle went through periods of decay and rebuilding it never really recovered from the ravages of the English Civil War, changing hands between Royalists and Parliamentarians, seven times between 1642 and 1648 and later being used as a prison. Shelling from German warships in 1914 even further damaged it. English Heritage now manages it.

Scarborough, North Yorkshire, from the gorge bridge

There is a high road that joins both halves of the town spanning across a gorge. The bridge has attractive inward curving high barriers that are presumably to prevent people jumping off the bridge, but they actually improve the look of the bridge and the environs, rather than make it ugly or a depressing sight. (Vancouver take note for the Lions Gate Bridge). The bridge offers dramatic views down into park gardens with the sea behind. The buildings around are Victorian architecture, smart and striking. This is certainly a place that we both said that we would love to come back and visit. The English seaside town is certainly alive and very healthy in Scarborough.

At one time Scarborough was famous for Tuna fishing and fish up to 800lbs in weight have been caught by rod and line from boats off Scarborough. However this died out after the Second World War, thought mainly due to over fishing of herring and mackerel, the food fish for the tuna.

The only downside we found to Scarborough was the thirty-minute queue to get into the town, all due to some temporary roadwork traffic lights and bollards. When we reached them, the bollards appeared to be surrounding nothing, no holes in the road, nothing. No doubt their removal was down to the same crew who were due to remove the "no white lines" signage we had seen earlier. You would have thought that on a busy holiday weekend someone would have recognised the chaos that would ensue by leaving such impediments to free flow of traffic. ('Not my job Mate').

From superb Scarborough the road took us up onto the North Yorkshire Moors National Park. The views were magnificent and it reminded me a lot of Dartmoor in Devon. Our next destination was Robin Hood's Bay. We drove to it, saw it (it's lovely) but did not stay. Indeed we were completely unable to stay, as there were no parking places at all in the town and drivers were getting frustrated. Another place to visit for the future, but not on a holiday weekend.

For most of my life I have wanted to visit Whitby. You see it so often in photos showing the best places in Britain. It also features regularly in TV programs. This was planned to be the highlight of my day and I was excited to be going there. Our first stop was the ruins of Whitby Abbey that sits high up overlooking the town providing lovely views down into Whitby and the River Esk running into the harbor and out to sea. Next to the Abbey, but we did not visit it, is the Church that featured in the story of Dracula (which was written here). It is a mecca for "Goths" but we only saw one on her way there. How is it that both the stories of Dracula and Frankenstein were written in lovely English towns far from any dark and demonic surroundings? (Frankenstein was written by Mary Shelley in the lovely Thames side town of Marlow in Buckinghamshire).

Whitby Abbey, North Yorkshire

Whitby Abbey is today a ruin having been destroyed in 1539 in Henry VIII's dissolution of the monasteries. The ruin is a very prominent and dramatic feature on the hilltop overlooking the town. What you see now is the remains of the second Abbey, built on this site in the late 11th century by Benedictine monks from Evesham in Worcestershire. The original Abbey was established in 657 in the Celtic religious tradition with its first Abbess being Hilda, later St. Hilda. She was invited to head it up by Bishop Aidan from Lindisfarne, Holy Island, which we will be visiting tomorrow.

Hilda was born in 614 into a royal family being the great niece of the pagan Anglo Saxon King, Edwin of Northumbria. Edwin married a Christian princess from Kent and her influence on him and also later that of Paulinus a Roman missionary and Bishop, greatly helped in his conversion to Christianity. In battling with the King of Wessex, Edwin had promised that if he prevailed he would adopt Christianity. And so it was that in 627 he and his court, which included 13-year-old Hilda, were baptized. In 633 the King of Mercia killed Edwin and his Queen fled with Paulinus and Hilda to Kent, where the Queen founded a convent and where Hilda lived and became a nun.

Hilda was later asked by Bishop Aidan to come back to Northumbria and she established and ran a convent close to Hartlepool. Under Aidan's teaching, she took up the Celtic traditions of Christianity. Aidan later promoted her to be Abbess of Hartlepool Abbey, the remains of which are no longer in evidence. In 657 she became the founding abbess of Whitby Abbey. She was famed for her wisdom and would be consulted by Kings. The King of Northumbria at this time was Oswiu (Oswold), also a Celtic Christian. He had been raised in exile in Argyll on the west coast of Scotland after his father had been killed by Edwin. He returned to Northumbria in 633 after the death of Edwin and eventually took over from his brother in 642 as King of Northumbria. He was very devout and supported Aidan in the establishment of Whitby Abbey.

In 664 under the influence of Oswald and Hilda, Whitby Abbey was chosen as the site for the first Christian Synod in England and it was here that the Celtic Christians, urged by King Oswald, agreed to accept the Roman form of Christianity, with its liturgy and dating of holy times, such as Easter.

St. Cuthbert, who was at this time Abbott at Lindisfarne, led the Celtic monks in this, but many of them disagreed with the decision and returned back to the Island of Iona, off the west coast of Scotland, not wanting to follow the Roman traditions. The Roman church had much more structured liturgy than the looser form of worship common with the Celtic Christians. As monks, there were also striking differences; the Celtic monks having long hair, with shaved high foreheads, whilst the Roman monks had short hair and the centre of their head was shaved leaving a ring of hair supposedly representing Christ's crown of thorns.

St. Hilda died in 680. Whitby Abbey remained influential until its destruction by the Vikings in 870. No trace of that Celtic abbey remains, but the later Norman abbey was built on the same ground and is the ruin that you see today.

We had not chosen the best day to visit Whitby. It was heaving with people. I think that almost one half of Yorkshire was in Scarborough and almost another half was in Whitby, with those left over being in Robin Hoods Bay. After an incident of car park rage with a women being prepared to lie down in a car space rather than let us park in it, we got lucky and found another car departing. Jim's charm got them to give us their parking ticket, which still had two hours left on it. The "savings" meant that our afternoon tea was free!

I had one bizarre moment earlier when returning to the car, which was then in a limited time parking zone on the road. As I got to it I pressed the button, but the door would not open. After repeatedly pressing the button to no avail, I looked through the window into the vehicle and realised that it was not mine! It was the twin of mine; exactly the same model and colour and also rented from Hertz. The registration number of the vehicle was actually only one letter different so this one was the next in the registration series. What were the odds of that! It would have been interesting to speak to the driver and find out where it was hired from, probably not Exeter where mine came from, or perhaps it was.

Whitby has an unusual swinging bridge in the centre of the town, which turns outward to allow vessels to pass. The same company that built the famous Blackpool Tower built this in 1906. We had to drive across the bridge to leave the town. There were so many pedestrians on the bridge that they were walking all over the road thus we had to crawl slowly across, making every effort not to hit anyone. As we drove onto the bridge we saw a sign with the warning "weak bridge". I don't know whether they have ever determined the maximum weight of pedestrians and cars at one time together on the bridge, but we could feel the bridge "bounce" and so were happy when we reached the other side.

Because of the crush of people we felt that we did not want to stay any longer in Whitby and so drove out of the town and on to the small fishing village of Staithes. We had to park up the top and walk down the hill to reach the village.

Staithes is absolutely charming and built within a steep gorge leading down to the sea. Staithes as a word, describes a structure, like a jetty, where ships can load and unload

Though a small place now, it has a big history. At one time it had the largest herring fleet in England. It is also where Captain Cook grew up as a child. He apparently worked here as a grocer's apprentice, but was so fascinated by the tales of the sea told by the fisherman at the wharf that he one day ran away to Whitby and signed on a ship as a cabin boy.

Staithes, North Yorkshire

Close by, to the north of the village, is Boulby Head, which is the highest point (at 666 feet) on the east coast of England. Of particular significance today though is Boulby potash mine, which is the deepest mine in England and extends right out under the North Sea.

We decided to have dinner in Staithes and found the Crab and Lobster pub on the beach. The steak and ale pie was both delicious and huge. It was cooked in proper short crust pastry, not the awful cap of flaky pastry on top of a reheated, pre-prepared dish of meat that so many pubs now serve, falsely claiming it to be a pie.

Our journey to Redcar, the destination for tonight, was via Saltburn-by-the-Sea. I have old friends from Wargrave, who now live in a majestic house on the sea front at Saltburn-by-the-Sea and who had kindly offered me a room. Unfortunately they were in Ghana not due to return until the next day, so we had to find our own accommodation and Jim had got us a good deal in Redcar. Saltburn has a number of grand buildings built in a reddish stone. Saltburn also lays claim to having one of the world's oldest water powered funicular cliff railways, having been built in 1883 to transport people down the cliff to the pier.

We had ignored Samantha our GPS "lady" a lot today. We decided we ought to listen to her as we did not know exactly where our hotel was in Redcar. It should have been straightforward along the sea front, but we decided that to be sure we would let Samantha guide us. She used this to get her own back for our having ignored her! She directed us off the sea front, backwards and forwards (and a complete circle at one time) through lots of housing areas, until we reached the hotel – on the seafront!

The hotel turned out to be the most disappointing (but cheapest) so far. It was very old fashioned in its décor having heavy red patterned carpets, dark wood panels and rose patterned wallpaper. Parking at the back was only achieved by my pushing the large garbage container to one side to make a space. On looking at the bedding in the glow given off by the dim 60-watt light bulb, it looked to me to be stained. I mentioned this to the receptionist Ashley, who was horrified and called in the owner. They were able to demonstrate to me that the stains were actually part of the pattern on the sheets, but because they were old and the light bulbs in the room so dim, one could imagine that the pattern was indeed stains. However, to their credit, they pulled out all of the stops to make me happy and put crisp white sheets on the bed just to assure me. They said that they were in the midst of upgrading. If they do finish it and continue to show this willingness to make the customer happy, I'm sure they will do well. The responsiveness and customer attitude shown by Ashley I think could give have a great career with one of the major hotel chains if she wanted.

Tomorrow we expect to reach the borders of Scotland and the land of my Fathers.

Redcar to Lindisfarne

Miles 150

Lindisfarne, Holy Island, Northumberland

Today was a day of two halves. The morning was spent in the industrial northeast in grey, murky, misty, claggy weather and the afternoon mostly in sunshine along the glorious Northumberland coast.

We left our hotel in Redcar at around 9.30am. One thing that I noticed as we left was a building plot alongside the hotel, full of rubble and weeds. Not in itself remarkable, other than that the main weed plant growing there appeared to be oilseed rape. This plant lights up the countryside in bright yellow swathes at this time of year, however, the fact that it now grows in most cities, on any available piece of land, indicates just how much of it has been grown across the country and how it has now spread so far and wide that it is has become a prolific weed.

Redcar seems a sorry town, completely in contrast to others on this coast. One of its main employers, the steel works at nearby Warrenby has recently been closed. Redcar probably gets very little of the holiday trade. The fishing boats are drawn up onto the streets one block away from the quay, each with its own tractor. Is this for reasons of space on the beach or reflective of the wild weather on this coast?

The beaches are sandy and seem quite long. On the sea front there is what I at first thought was a huge helter skelter, but it turns out this is what they are terming an "Upright Pier". Rather than go out to sea it goes up in the air! In 2013 it was nominated for the Building Design Council's Carbuncle Cup, awarded to the ugliest new building built each year. The good news for the people of Redcar is that, though it was a contender, it did not win. The dubious award going instead to student accommodation built at University College London.

As we drove towards Middlesborough there was a distinct smell in the air. It seemed to be a cross between a fatty fried breakfast being cooked and acrid chemicals. Certainly it was pervasive in the car and I imagine that the locals have to endure this every day. The area was one of docklands with large cranes. We crossed the Tees Bridge and entered Billingham, a large chemical city. Huge factories and chemical plants and big buildings without any windows. One place was called Oxygen Corner. It was at this point that we realised that we had been holding our breath! Presumably this is where the locals come to breathe oxygen and refresh when they can! No doubt such industrial places are built on the coast because the land is available. As the sea here is uninviting and with a plethora of good resorts, no one wants to come to these parts, so a chemical plant can be sited here. Unfortunately whoever built such places did not appreciate, or perhaps care, that the wind is mainly off the ocean and onto the land. Indeed in these parts it originates in the frigid Ural Mountains before crossing the North Sea and hitting the east coast of Britain.

At Seaton Carew, which we felt had similarities to Redcar, new 3 and 4 bedroomed houses were being advertised for sale from £139,500, which is half of the current UK national average of £288,000. Seaton Carew's northern end is posher, with a golf club and dunes, but has on its sea front a large Indian restaurant called the Sheesh Mahal. Apart from spoiling the view, it supports the story that curry is now the national dish of England!

Here begins the Durham Heritage Coast road offering good sea views as the road is close to the ocean, which is now devoid of mud flats.

Entering Hartlepool we saw the masts of a tall sailing ship. Trying to get close to it proved difficult. We followed the occasional sign, but the road we were looking for into the Tees & Hartlepool Dockyard Museum was actually marked to a Yacht Club. Message to Councils, if you want visitors to come to your expensively built museums, please make sure that the signage is clear and complete! The great surprise to me was that this ship was the HMS Trincomalee. This vessel was instrumental in charting the Pacific North West where I now live. Indeed my daughter lived in a road named after this ship. The ship was built in India and launched in 1817 and was in the Pacific in 1852. She is the oldest ex naval vessel still afloat. HMS Victory is 50 years older, but in dry dock, so not floating.

Hartlepool is a town that has certainly had its ups and downs, mostly tied to the economic impact of the rise and fall of various industries, including shipbuilding and coal mining. It also suffered shelling by the German Navy during the First World War, along with Whitby and Scarborough and over 100 citizens were killed.

People from Hartlepool are often pejoratively known as Monkey Hangers due to a legend that a French ship foundered off the coast during the Napoleonic Wars and the only survivor washed ashore was a monkey. It was said that he was dressed in a miniature French military uniform and, so the legend goes, the townsfolk, who did not know what a Frenchman looked like, tried him as a spy. The poor creature was sentenced to death and hung. There is no evidence to support this as being true but in 2003 a man in a monkey costume stood for election as Mayor of Hartlepool, promising to give free bananas to school children – and he won with over 50% of the vote. To cap this he was re-elected for a second term in 2005! Either this means that the folks of Hartlepool have a low view of politicians, or can't tell the difference between them and a monkey (or both!). Probably though it's because he was good at his job – as well as having a good sense of humour.

Leaving Hartlepool to continue along the Durham coast Jim taught me the "Durham song". Basically you "sing"

Durham over and over again to the tune of the Pink Panther. Try it, it works!

We entered the villages of Blackhall Colliery and then Easington, both ex mining towns, which "died" on the closure of the pits and indeed of the whole mining industry in the early 1990s. The British coal industry had as many as 1000 mines at the beginning of the century, but by 1984 only 173 remained open. The miner's strike of 1984-85 was a defining moment in British industrial history. British Coal mining was not competitive on a world scale and demand for it was significantly reducing as a means of powering industry and heating homes. The strike was held to protest and prevent pit closures. It was very acrimonious with significant encounters between the miners and the police. The leader of the Mineworker's Union, Arthur Scargill, was pitted against the Prime Minister Margaret Thatcher and everything about them was a picture of opposites. Not just that one was male and one female, but background, education, up bringing, accents and politics, all were in sharp contrast. The only thing they had in common was seemingly stubbornness and a determination not to give in. Scargill was a communist and it was later found out that he had received money from the Mineworkers Union of Russia. Eventually though, the government won and the result was the closure of many of the pits. From this point on there was a significant weakening in the power of the Trade Unions in Britain. By 2009 there were only six pits still in operation.

My father and grandfather were both coal miners in Scotland, so I feel affinity with what these people went through. My father at age 14, for a period of time, was the only member of his family working as others were either sick or injured or had been laid off. Although proud of what he did, he said that it was a terrible job and you did it because it was the only work available. He was "saved" by the war and his meeting my Mother, which meant that when married he lived in an area, the Cotswolds, that was a long way away from the pits and there were other types of work. My father also became very disillusioned with the Unions and their representatives. This was very surprising to him as growing up as a lad in Lochgelly, Scotland his schoolteacher had been Jennie Lee. She was an ardent union Socialist and became the wife of Aneurin Bevan, a prominent Labour politician, who became Deputy Leader of the Labour Party. My father eventually came to feel that the union leaders were more concerned with keeping their own jobs and their political aspirations and had lost touch with the workers who they claimed to represent.

Easington was the scene of one of the worst mining disasters when in May 1951 an explosion killed 83 men. Neither town appears to be prospering or showing much sign of having recovered from the closure of the pits. New houses are advertised as being available for £114,000 or £98,000 with government "help to buy" which clearly illustrates that this is an area that has still yet to be regenerated.

Seaham, not much further up the coast, is a pleasant place, despite the very sinister looking Masonic Lodge on the sea front. It was around here that we learned that a sign advertising "WC" actually meant "no toilets here". Having found no toilets, despite the advertising, we were dissuaded from entering Tonya's Café as there was risk of castration (or something similar) if we dared to use her toilets without buying breakfast. We contemplated eating here, but the inhospitable signage encouraged us to keep our money in our pockets rather than give it to Tonya.

The bridge into Sunderland reminded us of the Tyne Bridge in Newcastle. The prettier part of the town is Roker where there are attractive houses facing a nice bay. Once again, like Seaton Carew, a large Indian restaurant "The Buddha" dominates and seriously lowers the tone of the town.

Sunderland was once claimed to be the "biggest ship-building city in the world" and this was a mainstay of its industry through until the 1980s when it collapsed. At this time Nissan, the Japanese car maker, opened a manufacturing plant here and I swear that the engine of my car, a Nissan Qashqai, skipped a couple of beats when it found that it was back in the town where it had been born!

Sunderland has a famous football team who now play in the "Stadium of Lights" at Monkwearmouth, built upon the sight of an old colliery. Monkwearmouth is said to be the place where glass making was introduced to Britain by French glaziers in the seventh century, who were employed to put glass into a new St. Peter's Monastery, hence the name of the stadium.

Moving on up the coast at Whitburn rurality became more evident. There were small farms now in evidence, an old stone windmill and indeed people riding on horses. There is a lighthouse here and a nice view up the coast.

South Shields is an Edwardian town that once flourished through shipbuilding, coal mining and glass making. It is situated at the mouth of the River Tyne, on its south shore. We were pleasantly surprised by the number of nice beaches close to the town along with large limestone cliffs, mainly National trust protected.

Thank goodness, again, for Tesco. Not only did they provide us with some nice cinnamon buns but also information as to the cost of the Tyne Tunnel toll fee. We needed to have the exact change to throw into the basket to allow us through the barrier – and there are no signs advising how much you would need to pay until you get to the toll gates! Once over the bridge you are in North Shields, which itself is part of Tynemouth. A ferry operates from here to South Shields and there is also a RoRo ferry operating across to the Netherlands.

Tynemouth runs into the seaside resort of Whitley Bay. Entering the town reminded me of the Captain of the Seabourn Legend who I had got to know on a cruise we had taken to Central America and the Panama Canal. He had moved from Norway to Whitley Bay on the advice of Sir Cliff Richard who had once been a passenger on board his ship. Cliff had told him of a wonderful place to live in the North East of England. All he could remember was that the name began with "Whit". He drove to the North East and asked around as to which town it might be. A women in a service station said it might be Whitley Bay. That sounded right so he went there. He saw little of it but it seemed pleasant enough so he asked his wife to find them a house there while he was away travelling. It was only about a year later, when Cliff was again a passenger, that he found out Cliff had said Whitby, not Whitley Bay! He wasn't too upset though as Whitley Bay is actually a very nice place, with a good sea front and a splendid lighthouse at St. Marys, visible from Whitley Bay, but located close to Hartley.

Just up from Hartley is the oddly named Seaton Sluice. The name dates from when Seaton was a natural harbour but the continuous silting up restricted its operation. The local landowners were the Delavals, whose ancestor, Hubert de LaVal was given the land by his Uncle (in marriage) William the Conqueror. In the 1660s a system of sluice gates was constructed which allowed the silt to be washed (or sluiced) out at low tide. One hundred years later a new harbour entrance was built and the main exports were coal, glass bottles and salt. Salt exports came to an end in 1798 due to imposition of heavy taxes (which also hit the Cornish fishing villages and gave rise to smuggling). A mine disaster in 1862 at the nearby New Hartley mine put an end to coal shipping. The main beam of the pumping engine broke and fell down the mineshaft, blocking it and 204 men and boys perished. Ten years later bottle manufacturing, which had been extensive, also ended.

Blyth, further up the coast, could be as nice as Whitley Bay but does not quite seem to have made it. It was once a major shipbuilding port and exporter of coal. Now much reduced it is a center for the import of timber and paper for the newspaper industry. With the rapid decline of newsprint in favour of electronic media this would not seem to be a long-term sustainable industry. There is a twice-weekly ferry connection to the continent. It would appear that the town itself has decided to give itself over to a big funfair. We did not stop.

We drove through Newbiggin-by-the-Sea, which seemed surprisingly busy. Here, driving by, we noticed an advert for a "family boxing club". Perhaps they choose to fight it out with gloves on in this part of the world rather than with kitchen utensils!

Druridge Bay, just past Cresswell power station is the start of the glorious Northumberland Heritage Coast and the end of the industrial and mining towns. This was the second half of our day; we had now entered "Vera" country. For the next 30 miles we were bowled over by the beauty of the coast and its pretty towns and villages.

Warkworth Castle, Northumberland

The small harbour village of Amble has seen better days. It has an RNLI station here with one of the new Shannon, beach-landing lifeboats. Just past Amble, the imposing castle at Warkworth hoves into view. You just have to stop and reach for your camera. This castle, possibly dating back to Henry 1 and owned at one time by Malcolm King of Scotland, is most associated with the Percy family, the Dukes of Northumberland, who took ownership of the castle in the fourteenth century. Henry Percy, Shakespeare's famous Harry Hotspur, was born her in 1364. Over the centuries the Percys both supported and resisted the various monarchs and though having the castle confiscated at various times, always succeeded in getting it back. In the 1920s the castle was given over to the care of English Heritage.

The current Duke of Northumberland lives at Alnwick Castle (pronounce Ann Nick) about ten miles away and

148

inland. I would have liked to visit Alnwick Castle, which looks magnificent in the photos. It is apparently the second most visited castle in Britain after Windsor Castle and featured in Downton Abbey. One "attraction" at Alnwick relates to an award won by the Duchess in 2014. She entered a national competition and won the "prestigious" title of "2014 Best Loo In Britain" award, run by the British Toilet Association. The Duchess is apparently a stickler for cleanliness and believes that you can tell the quality of a person and place by the way the toilets are kept. Good for her. You may think that I am making this up, but no it is true there is a British Toilet Association and having made this journey, I shall forever be a supporter of them. Maybe the BTA (toilets) could become amalgamated with the other BTA (the British Tourist Association). Both have similar aims in making Britain a great place to spend your pennies!

As I have mentioned before, the road closest to the ocean is not always the best place to view the coastline but our road map had handily marked, in green, the most scenic route. In the main this was the route we were on, but Boolmer, Howick and Craster required diversions to keep us on the coastal route.

Between Craster and Embleton stands the ruins of Dunstanburgh Castle. The castle was built by Thomas Earl of Lancaster and completed in 1322. He was the leader of the Barons opposed to Edward II but was captured in battle with the King's forces in the same year and beheaded. The castle was passed to the Earl of Lancaster in 1380s and in the 15th century featured strongly in the Wars of the Roses changing hands several times between the Yorkist and Lancastrian forces. Due to the damage caused by the sieges the castle never recovered and fell into a ruin in the 16th century.

Just before reaching Bamburgh you come to Seahouses, the largest harbour on the Northumberland coast. It is famed for the exploits of Grace Darling the daughter of the lighthouse keeper on Longstone Rock, part of the Farne Islands offshore from Seahouses. In 1838 she and her father used a rowing boat in very rough seas to rescue eight of the survivors of the "Forfarshire" that had foundered on the rocks with the loss of almost 50 souls. The weather had been considered too rough for the lifeboat to go out from Seahouses, but Grace and her father carried out the rescue in a rowing boat. Following the rescue the Duke of Northumberland took on the role of guardian of her and the Duchess assisted in nursing her when three years later she took ill and then unfortunately died from tuberculosis. Grace spent her last days in the town of Bamburgh where she had been born.

Bamburgh Castle, Northumberland

Bamburgh is dominated by its mighty castle. A castle has stood on this spot since 420AD, but the Bamburgh castle that you see today, dates back to the time of the Normans. It has been altered many times and also been attacked by both Scots and English monarchs. During the War of the Roses in the fifteenth century it was defeated by artillery fire, the first castle ever to have been so. For 400 years the Forster family owned it, but after falling into disrepair, it was eventually purchased by William Armstrong, a Victorian industrialist, whose family owns it to this day. From the castle you can look out across the glorious wide expanse of beach at Budie Bay towards Holy Island and Lindisfarne Castle.

Holy Island Abbey

151

Holy Island with its ruined priory and the castle of Lindisfarne was to be our final destination for today. We were fortunate in that the tide was out and we were able to drive across the Causeway to the island. If you mistime it you have to abandon your car to the sea and take to a refuge tower. As the notice warning you as you begin the journey says "the responsibility is yours"! It was here that the sun came out and dramatically highlighted the beauty of this place.

Holy Island was originally the home of St. Aidan a monk from St Columba's Abbey on the Island of Iona (which I will be visiting in about one week) in Scotland. He was invited to build a Priory on Holy Island by Oswiu (Oswold) King of Northumbria who had been converted to Christianity. On the day Aidan died in 651 a youth of seventeen, named Cuthbert, living in Dunbar, Scotland, claimed to have had a vision of Aidan telling him that he should train as a monk and take on his work. Cuthbert had been a Knight but gave this up to become a monk. After a number of years of training at Montrose Abbey in Scotland, near to his home, he became the Prior at Lindisfarne in 662.

Cuthbert was of the Celtic Christian persuasion with its strong emphasis upon humility and self-sacrifice. Celtic Christianity did not have a hierarchy or edicts, unlike the Roman Christian church, which itself was trying to evangelize Britain, its movement coming up from the South. The matter came to a head in 664 at the Synod of Whitby, where, influenced by King Oswold, it was decided to take on the Roman form. Cuthbert acted as an arbitrator attempting to smooth the waters seeking to ensure that there was only one common face of Christianity to those they were trying to evangelise. However, a number of the monks on Lindisfarne were not prepared to accept this and returned to Iona. In 684 Cuthbert became Prior of Lindisfarne, but within two years, fearing his near death, he took a small boat over to the nearby island of Inner Farne, where he lived in almost total isolation until he died in 686.

He was highly revered for his piety and good works among the poor and after his death he was buried on Holy Island. After ten or so years, as was the custom, his body was exhumed. The idea being that his flesh would have decayed and his bones could be accessed and used as reliquaries and sent to many churches. However, on digging him up they found that his flesh had not decayed and his joints were as pliable as if he were still alive. This proved to everyone that he was truly a saint. Many years later, because of the continued threats of Viking invasions, his body was moved. After a journey of around nine years, moving around the north of England and Scotland he was laid to rest in what became Durham Cathedral, built to venerate his resting place.

Lindisfarne, Holy Island, Northumberland

Lindisfarne Castle on Holy Island was built in 1550 at the same time that the Priory was abandoned and many of the Priory stones were used in building the castle. Between 1906 and 1912 Edwin Lutyens remodeled the castle with the gardens designed by Gertrude Jekyll, on behalf of the publisher of Country Life magazine who then owned it. The castle passed into the hands of the National Trust in 1944.

We spent three hours walking around the island and village and ended our day by participating in the service of Evening Prayer in St Mary's Church adjacent to the ruined priory. The Church has within it a huge and magnificent carving, made from tree trunks, of six monks carrying the coffin of St Cuthburt.

We had no accommodation booked for the night, but fortunately managed to book the last room at the Lindisfarne Inn just off the island.

Tomorrow we enter Scotland.

Carving of St. Cuthburt's coffin on its journeys.
St. Mary's Church, Holy Island

Holy Island to Dunfermline

Miles 108

Berwick-On-Tweed, Northumberland

Today we entered another country – twice! Weather went from cloudy to spectacular, better than Jim's home in Norfolk where his wife said that they had received 1½ inches of rain overnight!

Berwick on Tweed was our first destination after leaving Holy Island. This is the last town in England before you enter Scotland. In 1018 the Scots took control of Berwick from the Anglo-Saxon kingdom of Northumbria. Over the next 500 years it was raided and besieged many times. Ownership moved thirteen times between Scotland and England, through war and by gift, but since 1482, under Edward IV it has remained in English hands. When James I of England (and VI of Scotland) came to the throne in 1567 after the death of Elizabeth I, the two countries were united under one crown and Berwick then was confirmed as being in England.

Berwick played another important part in the unification of Scotland and England in that it was here that the railway bridge built across the Tweed by Robert Stephenson, in 1850, joined together the railway systems of England and Scotland. Up until this time both railways had been built independently. It was the greater access provided by the railway that was the launch pad to allow world wide availability and marketing of one of Scotland's biggest exports, Scotch whiskey. Robert Stephenson was the son of George Stephenson, often known as the father of the railways.

Albeit it was cloudy most of the time we were there, Berwick still presented as a magnificent town. It has the oldest intact defensive walls still in existence in England. They are just over 1 mile long and cover three quarters of the town. They are mainly high stone and mud bankings with some stone built gun emplacements. We had a bracing walk on top of them. They started to be built under Bloody Queen Mary and then continued under her sister Queen Elizabeth and were reputedly the most expensive thing that was built during her reign. Total cost over 12 years was £137,000 about £40 million in today's money. Elizabeth was almost bankrupted over this.

We found the people to be extremely friendly and helpful. They are so welcoming that parking in the town is free of charge, though you do need to purchase a parking disc for $1. This allows you to park anywhere for up to three hours and lasts for a year. The only surprise was that you had to pay 20 pence to use the loo. We heard yesterday on the BBC that the majority of towns in England are now getting rid of their public toilets altogether. Apparently as Tescos (and a few other supermarkets) have them, many Councils have decided to save money and leave it to the supermarkets.

At one place on the walls we looked down on probably the neatest allotments in Britain. All the plots looked beautifully planted or dug in preparation for planting. The soil is black and rich, almost like peat. Not a weed in sight. From one allotment hut we could hear Mozart being played. Clearly the gardeners in Berwick have sophisticated tastes!

After a cup of hot chocolate in a small café we both decided that our hair was getting too long and looked for a hairdresser. The first was full up, the second closed and the third could only take one of us. As there was a guitar shop close by, Jim opted to forgo his haircut and play with the guitars. I did get mine cut and am now feeling very tidy.

After Berwick we set off for Eyemouth, over the border into Scotland. Just before arriving in this little fishing village, panic struck. I had decided to text my wife but, putting my hand in my pocket, discovered that my mobile phone was missing. I checked the car, not there, so wondered whether I had left it back at the Lindisfarne Hotel. I could not continue my journey without a mobile phone, so, using Jim's phone, I called them. Indeed I had lost it at the hotel and the maid had found it down the side of the sofa cushion in the room. We then had to make the obvious, but painful, decision to return and get it. It meant an extra 30-mile round trip and about

45 minutes added to our journey. Anita at the hotel (who called me "Pet", which I thought was lovely) had found it and returned it to me. She had also, earlier, told me of places that I must visit when I get to the Orkneys. So Anita thank you for not only saving my trip, but also adding to it with good advice. I think it also speaks volumes about the effort they make in cleaning the rooms at the Lindisfarne Inn, even removing the sofa cushions to clean!

We crossed back into Scotland for the second time within the space of an hour and journeyed on to Eyemouth. Eyemouth is a bustling place with an active fishing industry as evidenced by the trucks departing with fresh fish. Eyemouth collects its fresh fish on a daily basis from all over the north of England and Scotland, as I was to discover later while awaiting the ferry across to the Isle of Mull. The main fish processing building is built to look like a large wooden ship.

As we started to drive out of the town we found ourselves behind a funeral cortege with lots of people walking behind the coffin and on to the graveside. We did not know who the deceased was, but he or she was clearly well liked and respected as borne out by the number of people who were present. Rather than wait, or worse still drive behind them, we decided to allow Samantha to direct us through the back streets and out of the town, which she did successfully.

St Abbs Head and its village was our next destination and what a wonderful little place this is. There is a steep road down into the little harbour, which can only be described as charming. The sea was blue but the surf was up and the waves were crashing over the rocks. There is a poignant memorial on the point overlooking the village remembering three fishermen from St Abbs who perished in a great storm in March 1881.

This storm claimed in one night, a total of 189 fishermen from all along the Scottish east coast. We could have had lunch in either of the two cafes in the village, but instead, still somewhat full from our cooked breakfast, decided to heat up on the stove a lunch of pea and ham soup. This proved sufficient for the rest of the day (only needing to be topped up later by a bag of jelly babies from the RNLI shop in Dunbar!).

St. Abbs Head, Berwickshire; The Borders

The whole of the east coast of Scotland is dramatic and beautiful. The sun shone brightly and the sea remained blue all the way towards Edinburgh. The roadsides still had gorse in bloom but the hawthorn, unlike further south, was only just beginning to blossom. We felt that Scotland was about 3 weeks later in blooming than the south of England.

The A1107 towards Cocksburnspath is wind turbine alley with rows and rows of blades spinning gracefully. I wonder if in 100 years time these turbines will be as revered as much as the windmills of 100 years ago are today.

Dunbar is a fine town with excellent sandy beaches and is the start of the "Golf Course Coast". Here we visited the RNLI shop. The RNLI do such a great job. It is striking just how many RNLI stations there are. Almost every bay, village and seaside town I have passed through, have an RNLI station with boats large and small. Volunteers man every vessel and the RNLI is funded only by donations. There are many sailors alive to day who have to give thanks to the RNLI for their rescue. Tragically there are also many lifeboat men who have lost their lives trying to save mariners.

Just before North Berwick we stopped to photograph the Bass Rock and Tantallon Castle, which looked magnificent across a field of oilseed rape and against a backdrop of the blue water.

The Bass Rock was at one time home for a group of hermit Irish monks, one of whom became venerated as St. Baldred. There are also the remains of a castle, dating to at least the 13th century and owned by the Lauder family.

In 1406 the 12 year old, soon to be James I of Scotland, great, great grandson of Robert the Bruce, took refuge on the Bass Rock while being hurried to France for safety over fears of plots to assassinate him. However, when he did set sail from here to France, English pirates captured his ship and he was delivered to Henry IV. Within a couple of weeks James father, Robert III died and James thus became King of Scotland, but in absentia in England, as a prisoner of Henry. His time in England was a good one and he even served in Henry V's army and fought for him in France. After 18 years in England he was ransomed and returned to Scotland, taking revenge on his Uncle's family who had governed in his absence and whom he thought responsible for his father's death. Having been brought up in England and fought for Henry V, he was never fully trusted in Scotland and was assassinated in 1437 during a failed coup by his Uncle the Duke of Atholl. James' wife escaped with their 6 year old son, who became James II.

Tantallon Castle & Bass Rock, East Lothian

James II became an effective and popular King in Scotland. An interesting fact about him is that in 1457 he banned what are today two of the most popular games played in Scotland, golf and football. Apparently he was concerned that men were playing these games at the expense of military training and in particular the skill of archery and the use of artillery. If he was King today and banned the playing of these games he would very quickly lose his popularity. James strong interest in all things military and especially artillery became the cause of his death. Whilst besieging Roxburgh Castle, near Kelso, then in English hands, he was fascinated by the power of a large artillery piece nicknamed the Lion. Unfortunately something went wrong and the cannon exploded and took off his right leg, an injury from which he quickly died.

On the Bass Rock today stands one of David Stevenson's lighthouses, built in 1902. He was responsible for building 26 lighthouses on the Scottish coast. He came from an illustrious family of lighthouse builders, his brother Charles, his Uncle Thomas and his grandfather Robert, all were lighthouse designers and builders. Charles built 23 lighthouses, Thomas in excess of 30 and grandfather Robert more than 16, with some of these being in the most difficult and challenging of locations. He was also a cousin to author Robert Louis Stevenson.

Tantallon Castle was built in the 14th century, but was slighted by Cromwell and is now a ruin. It was owned by the Douglas clan, the Earls of Angus, who for many years were allies of the Stewarts, the royal house. However in 1490 Archibald, the 5th Earl, sided with Henry VII against James IV and the castle was besieged until he surrendered. In 1493 the Earl regained the favour of James IV and was made Chancellor of Scotland. In 1502 James signed the "Treaty of Perpetual Peace" with Henry VII and married his daughter Margaret Tudor so as to unite the two thrones. Again another case of a possibly unwilling royal daughter being used as a political pawn. James had also made a peace treaty with the French and when in 1513 Henry VIII went to battle with the French, James, though in a quandary as to which ally to support, decided to seize the opportunity and invade England. He unfortunately only got as far as Northumbria where he was defeated in the Battle of Flodden Field.

Within a year his widow, Margaret, married the 6th Earl of Angus who became Regent to the now 2-year-old King James V. In 1525, the Earl, with the support of Henry VIII, staged a coup and captured the young King. James escaped in 1528 and besieged the Earl in Tantallon castle. The Earl fled to England, but returned to the castle in 1542 when James V died. James' one-year-old daughter Mary (later Queen of Scots) was James only surviving heir and though Henry VIII wanted her to marry his son Edward, she was taken to France for safety. The 6th Earl died in 1545 and Mary's Mother, the French Mary of Guise, acted as Queen Regent and took over the castle. The Earls of Angus, being Catholic, supported Charles I and thus it was that the castle was besieged and then eventually slighted by Oliver Cromwell in 1651.

On entering into North Berwick we found another lovely Scottish town. Scottish towns seem to have an air of solidity, orderliness and perhaps also a certain somberness. They are generally smart and without an over abundance of awful garish high street signs that I have seen on my journey through England.

We drove through Muirfield Golf Course where a US Boys golf tournament was taking place. Muirfield has recently been in the news for having been denied the opportunity to host the British Open because it does not allow women as members. I am stunned that they can even continue to take this stance and I hope that the "loss" of potential income and prestige they will incur for not hosting the Open is at least a kick to their snobbish backsides and that changes happen soon. I was particularly shocked to hear Peter Allis, the main TV commentator for golf tournaments say, that "If women want to play at Muirfield all they have to do is marry a member". I am glad that my hobby is not golf and that I don't have to mix with such people.

One other annoyance was that Muirfield is allowed to put up temporary traffic lights to allow golfers to cross the road. These are "golfer controlled". I certainly am all for road safety, but for some misogynistic person chasing a little white ball, to be allowed to hold up main road traffic seems crazy. (How many points for running over a golfer?). Perhaps if James II had lived longer, the course would be in better use as an archery club or, even perhaps a cannon firing range!

We entered Edinburgh at Musselburgh and continued on to Leith to try and get to see the Royal Yacht Britannia before it closed to visitors. We were too late but did manage to get some pictures from within the magnificent shopping mall that is built alongside. The presence of the Royal Yacht has certainly dramatically changed Leith from poor and run down docklands to a very upmarket place.

I visited Britannia soon after it was brought to Leith. At that time the area was one of dismal old harbour buildings, but no longer. The Royal Yacht then also seemed drab, as virtually anything of interest had been removed from it. I do recall the cabin in which Charles and Dianna spent their honeymoon. It was very plain, with a Queen sized bed (aptly named I thought) with a ghastly brown bedspread on it. I also recall in the galley a photo of Dianna mixing with the galley staff. She apparently spent a lot of her time with the crew while on the ship; perhaps an early sign that this marriage might not last.

Moving on, we fought the Edinburgh homebound traffic through to the Forth Road Bridge. This is very congested, but in 2017 a new bridge will open right alongside it. The construction of this is tremendous and it will be a work of art when it is completed. It will come close, but not surpass, the original Forth rail bridge which still stands as an icon for Edinburgh and British engineering. The old necessity of having to constantly keep painting the bridge ("when you get to one end you go back to the beginning and start again") is now no longer true. Modern paints allow them at least a few years break before repainting is necessary.

The road bridge took over in 1964 from a ferry that ran from South Queensferry across the Firth of Forth to North Queensferry. The origins and names of these two villages go back to the time of Queen Margaret (later Saint Margaret). She was noted for her piety and had supported the building of a Benedictine Abbey at Dunfermline. To enable pilgrims to travel to the Abbey from Edinburgh, she paid for a ferry to be put in place across the Firth of Forth. This ferry service ran for 900 years, from the 11th century right up until the "new" road bridge opened.

Margaret's story as we found out in Hastings, is linked to the earliest times of the English monarchs. When only a small child, Margaret's family fled from England to Hungary, after the invasion of Canut in 1016. She was the great granddaughter of King Aethelred (the Unready) and the granddaughter of King Edmund II (Ironside), who was King for less than a year. She was also the niece of Edward the Confessor, who took over in 1042 from Canut and the two sons, who had succeeded him. Margaret and her brother, Edgar Aethling, later came to Scotland. Edgar Aethling had been proclaimed King on the death of King Harold in 1066, but he was never crowned. He submitted to William (the Conqueror), but eventually fled to Scotland after resisting William. Margaret had by then married King Malcolm III (who was the one who had taken the crown from my ancestor King Macbeth!). She had 8 children by him. Three of her sons became Kings of Scotland and one daughter, Matilda, married Henry 1 of England, son of William the Conqueror and their son, Matilda's grandson, became Henry II. Margaret died in1083, three days after King Malcolm and her eldest son were killed in battle.

One strange but interesting fact about Margaret is that in 1560, Mary Queen of Scots, ordered the opening of Margaret's tomb and the removal of her head, which was brought to her in Edinburgh to provide saintly protection for her during childbirth. Mary's son was safely delivered and went on to be James VI of Scotland and to unite the Scottish and English thrones as James I of England. Margaret's head was passed by Mary to the Jesuits in Douai in France, but lost during the French Revolution. Her remaining bones were later given to Philip II of Spain and moved to Escorial, but have also since been lost.

Unfortunately Samantha got confused by all of the construction at the end of the bridge, where new roads will soon merge. Trying to be nice to her today and follow her instructions we got hopelessly lost for about five minutes, but we can't blame her as the road works have not yet been "charted".

Jim and I spent the evening with two of my cousins, who greeted us with waving flags when we arrived – just like royalty. A good meal, lots of chat and an eight-week-old kitten to play with ended a fine day's driving.

Tomorrow Jim returns back to Norfolk and I continue on, on my own, towards Aberdeen. I will once again have to get used to my own company.

Dunfermline to Aberdeen

Miles 160

Today was an exceptionally beautiful day. The weather was warm (22 degrees) and sunny. The journey, well signposted as the Coastal Tourist Route, took me through the loveliest of countryside, with the sea almost at all times visible on my right side. Today was also the day that I returned to being my own scribe and my own company as I dropped Jim off at Inverkeithing station for him to catch a train back to Norfolk. Today is

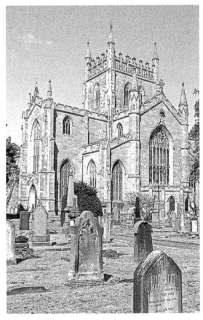

Dunfermline Abbey, Fife

also the day that I am staying at my first Air BnB!

Dunfermline is the capital of what is called the Kingdom of Fife and used to be the capital of Scotland until the

167

seventeenth century. It has played a major role not only in Scottish but also English history. The Abbey, built by the support of St. Margaret, the wife of King Malcolm III, was very powerful. It is second only to the Island of Iona in the number of Scottish Kings buried here. Robert the Bruce, who reigned from 1306 to 1329, is buried here; well, that is, all of him except his heart is buried here. This was interred in Melrose Abbey. Alongside the Abbey is the ruins of Dunfermline Palace where in 1600 was born Charles I, second son of James I of England and VI of Scotland and grandson of Mary Queen of Scots.

I'm already missing having a companion in the car. Samantha does not have much by way of conversation and this is usually limited to "turn right" or "take the second exit at the roundabout". At least I can be grateful that when I decide to take a different route than she directs, she does not shout at me. Programing her has proved frustrating at times as she can only tell you one of three options: Shortest Route; Quickest Route or Eco Route. I have not yet found what the "Eco Route" actually means. No matter which one I have programed in, if I follow the official Coastal Tourist route as laid down by Fife or Angus, she still tries to take me a different way. I am trusting the map and my own instincts more. Samantha has already today twice tried to send me down streets that have barriers across them. Just as well she does not operate more important equipment such as the GPS or radar on my boat.

I worked my way along from Dunfermline to Anstruther, passing through Burntisland and Kinghorn to Kirkcaldy. All places were charming and welcoming. This region is known as the East Neuk of Fife and runs from Burntisland, right around the coast almost to St. Andrews. It basically encompasses all of the small fishing villages from Lower Largo to Crail. These villages are all picturesque with stone harbours and fishing boats.

The east coast of Scotland generally is rolling gentle hills and farmland and the seashore is in the main sandy and the sea blue. I did not see one town or village today that I could dislike. Like the north east of England, Fife had been a major coal mining area and similarly went through the traumas of the closing of the pits. But the vitality of this area seems in sharp contrast to the north east of England where some of the mining communities do not yet seem to have moved on from their pain over the closure of the pits.

My father was born and grew up close to Kirkcaldy and worked here as a miner. He came to England during the war, via the beaches of Dunkirk and met my Mother whilst stationed in Devon. He married in England and never returned again to live in Scotland. Expecting a post mining, industrial town, I was pleasantly surprised to find that Kirkcaldy, like the other towns and villages in this area, is smart, well kept and inviting, with a lovely beach fronting onto the Firth of Forth. I had to keep reminding myself that today was "perfect weather" and I was not seeing it in the rain, but "smart and well kept" does not change in rain.

There is no mining in the area now but I noticed a mill for the famous Carr's biscuits, so they have obviously moved from mining to milling. One other, now ended, major industry that I only today became aware of, was the manufacture of linoleum floor covering. Apparently Kirkcaldy was the world's major producer from the late 1800s through to the end of the 1960s. Apart from my father one other notable person born in the town was Adam Smith, the economist, who wrote the influential book, "The Wealth of Nations".

After Kirkcaldy is Wemyss (East and West). Between East and West Wemyss lies Wemyss Castle. This is now a private house but the gardens are a feature and open to the public.

Wemyss Castle is famous as the place where Mary Queen of Scots met her second husband Darnley. Darnley was also her first cousin as both he and Mary were grandchildren of Margaret Tudor, sister of Henry VIII. Darnley was also a grandson of Henry VII and fourth in line to the English throne. At eight months old in 1543 Mary had been crowned Queen of Scotland on the death of her Father James V of Scotland. Henry VIII had proposed the future marriage of the infant Mary to his 5-year-old son Edward (later Edward VI) when she reached the age of 10, so uniting both nations. However, Henry's rejection of the Catholic Church caused those in Scotland acting as Regents for the infant Mary to have her sent to France. Mary's mother, Mary of Guise, was of course French and there was a close connection between both countries.

Henry angered by this rejection and the infant Mary being sent to catholic France, invaded Scotland demanding Mary's return. His troops sacked Edinburgh and the time became known as "the rough wooing". However the Scots stood firm and Mary did not return.

Henry VIII now wrote into his will that no Stuart could ever inherit his crown. When his only son Edward, by his third wife Jane Seymour, succeeded him as King Edward VI in 1547 Edward was aged just nine years old. Edward though died in 1553 and was succeeded by his sister Mary, daughter of Catherine of Aragon, Henry VIII's first wife (and previously wife of his brother Arthur who had died). Mary became the first reigning Queen of England.

When he was dying Edward, who like his father, was a protestant, tried to stop his sister Mary, a Roman Catholic, becoming Queen by naming their cousin Lady Jane Grey as his successor. Unfortunately, for Jane, Mary put together an army and deposed Jane, eventually having her beheaded.

Queen Mary I was fervent in her hatred for Protestants and had hundreds burnt at the stake for refusing to accept the restoration of Roman Catholicism. History has dubbed her "Bloody Mary" because of the atrocities she committed. She married Philip of Spain in 1534. Both her and Philip were direct descendants of John of Gaunt and thus claimed further legitimacy to the crown of England. She had no children despite two false pregnancies.

On her death in 1558, the throne then passed to her half-sister Elizabeth, daughter of Henry VIIIs second wife, Anne Boleyn. Mary hated Elizabeth, as she was not only a protestant, but saw Elizabeth as illegitimate and Anne Boleyn, as being the reason why her Mother, Catherine, was deposed as Queen. Henry VIII had sought annulment of his marriage to Catherine when it was clear that she could not bear him a son. The Pope had refused and thus Henry had the marriage annulled by his own Archbishop, Thomas Cranmer, using the excuse that as Catherine had previously been married to his brother Arthur, his marriage to her was not legitimate. Henry then declared himself Head of the Church of England and Protestantism displaced Roman Catholicism in England. Elizabeth became the second Queen of England and ruled for 45 years.

Throughout this time, Mary Queen of Scots was brought up in the royal household and at age 17 married the King of France's son, becoming the Queen Consort of the King of France when he succeeded to the throne in 1559. Unfortunately he died just one year later and so in 1561 the widowed Mary returned to Scotland and her other throne. By this time on the throne of England was now the protestant Elizabeth I.

Mary Queen of Scots had a claim to the throne of England through her grandmother, the sister of Henry VIII. Thus Elizabeth was always concerned that there would be an uprising to put Mary, a catholic, onto the throne and return England once again to influence from Rome and the Pope.

After meeting Darnley in Wemyss in 1565 Mary quickly married him. Mary was certainly impressed by the handsome Darnley and it is said that she proposed to him. However, there was probably also recognition by her that any child she had with Darnley would have a strong claim to the English crown, as Elizabeth was unmarried and childless. It seems though she regretted the marriage almost as quickly as she had proposed to him, finding him to be a philanderer and a violent drunkard. He did father her only child, James, who would eventually succeed to the English throne as James VI of Scotland and I of England, on the death of Elizabeth.

Darnley was responsible for the murder of Mary's Private Secretary, David Rizzio, who Darnley jealously suspected of being the real father of James. Darnley was then himself murdered eight months later, in February 1567, in an explosion, with the main suspects in his death being Mary and James Hepburn, Earl of Bothwell. Bothwell had known Mary for some years from when she lived in France and he was a favourite of hers.

He was tried for Darnley's murder in Edinburgh in April 1567, but acquitted. Just four days later, Mary displayed her support of him by getting him to accompany her to the opening of Parliament. Three weeks after this Mary married Bothwell, fueling people's suspicions that Mary had colluded with Bothwell in the murder of Darnley. Their marriage took place only 8 days after Bothwell was divorced by his second wife for adultery with her servant.

Their marriage caused an outcry in Scotland and was the eventual downfall of Mary. One month after the marriage, 26 Scottish Peers formed an army to remove Mary and Bothwell. The two opposing forces met, but men on both sides were reluctant to kill fellow Scotsmen so no battle ensued. Bothwell was allowed to leave the field and Mary was taken to Edinburgh where crowds turned out to denounce her as an adulteress. One day later she was taken prisoner, by her half-brother the Earl of Moray. (An earlier Earl of Moray had been MacBeth). He took her to Loch Leven Castle where she agreed to abdicate and give the throne to her infant son James, with Moray acting as Regent. Whilst at Loch Leven Castle she miscarried twins, fathered by Bothwell.

After nine months in Loch Leven, on May 2nd, 1568, Mary escaped with the help of Sir William Douglas, the brother of the castle's owner. Two weeks later, having raised an army of 6000 men she met a smaller army led by the Earl of Moray. However, Moray defeated her and she fled, first to Dundrennan Abbey and then crossed the border into England.

Bothwell attempted to get to Denmark and possibly raise an army to support Mary. However a sea battle with a pursuing ship caused his vessel to be damaged and he was subsequently wrecked off the coast of Norway. Unfortunately for him, Norway just happened to be the home of his first wife, Anna. He had treated her badly and stolen her money. She caused him to be imprisoned and demanded he repay her dowry. He was later transferred to Denmark (which at this time ruled Norway) where the King also had him imprisoned.

Bothwell is said to have died after being chained for 10 years to a pillar in a dungeon.

Although Mary fled from Scotland, in the hope that she would receive the safety and support of her cousin, Elizabeth I feared that Mary had eyes on her throne. She used Mary's alleged collusion in the death of Darnley as part of the reason for imprisoning her.

Mary never saw her son again, or regained the throne of Scotland, or of England, being executed by Elizabeth in 1587. Her son though did inherit the throne of England upon Elizabeth's death and as James I of England and VI of Scotland became the unifying monarch of both England and Scotland. So despite Henry VIII's command that no Stuart should take the throne of England, this is what happened.

As the son of a Scottish father and English mother I have a huge interest in the history of the two nations and their unification. Even today the issue of Catholicism and Protestantism is still strong especially in Scotland. It is evident in things such as football with the two Glasgow teams of Rangers and Celtic having respectively their origins as Protestant and Catholic teams. This has though also been true in England with teams such as Manchester City and Manchester United, and Everton and Liverpool all having their origins and identities in one or other denomination. In Scotland this still remains a big issue for some even today. With the establishment of a Scottish Parliament a few years ago and the recent rise in Scottish Nationalism, one can see that the issue of the Union and if it will survive is once again a major topic of conversation.

Now back to my journey! Moving on from East Wemyss you come to Buckhaven, then Methil and Leven. Buckhaven at one time was one of the largest fishing villages on the Fife coast, but later relied upon coal for its income and now is in regeneration after the closure of the pits. Nearby Methil and its docks are also still recovering from the closure of the mines and the fairly recent closure of its coal fired power station.

From Methil the coast road follows through Leven and then on to Lundin Links. As I drove into Lundin Links I was surprised to see a notice stating that the town was twinned with "Robinson Crusoe Island" in Chile. Apparently Lundin Links was the birthplace of Alexander Selkirk a mariner who was shipwrecked off the coast of Chile and became the inspiration for Robert Louis Stevenson's story, Robinson Crusoe.

After Lundin Links I entered Largo. Just off the coast were three oilrigs. Presumably not drilling but "resting", waiting for the upturn in the oil industry.

My next stop was to look at the small harbour in the lovely named village of Pittenweem. Here I recalled a few years ago sitting on a wall with my cousin and eating one of the best fish and chip suppers that I have ever had.

So many of these small places have a lifeboat station, but when I got to Anstruther I had to go and find the Station Leader there. I wanted to enquire as to the whereabouts of a model of the Anstruther lifeboat made about 30 years ago by my cousin, an expert model maker who is sadly now dead. They had three models there, of different lifeboats, but none by him and no one at the station today recognised his name. I tried to contact my cousin's wife to find out what she knew, but was unable to reach her. The Station Leader at Anstruther, Roger, looked so like the Station Leader in West Vancouver, Dugal, that I thought it might be his brother, so I took Roger's photo to send to Dugal so that he could see his "twin". I also purchased an Anstruther RNLI sweater in case the weather in Scotland turns to that of Norfolk and I need the extra warmth!!

The Anstruther lifeboat went out on 40 calls last year, which is about half of what our lifeboat in West Vancouver gets called out on. But with so many RNLI stations so close together I suppose that the average call out per station will be less. They post all of their callouts on a board outside the station, so the public can recognise the work that they do in saving lives at sea. They had been out over the previous week-end to rescue a person who fell down a cliff and broke a leg.

Anstruther, East Neuk of Fife

My journey continued on around the Neuk without my seeing anything but prettiness. Actually not quite true I did see two men walking down the street with their shirts off. Neither were an Adonis, but no tattoos either. There is a saying in Scotland "Cast not a clout 'til May be out." A clout is an old word for a coat. As today was June 1st I think they took the saying literally, casting off their shirts and vests as well. On the beach is OK, but along the High Street, it can put you off your latte!

One other common sight on this lovely day was learner drivers under instruction. They seem to be taught to drive at 5 miles per hour below the speed limit. Much of Scotland has now instituted speed limits of 20mph in towns, along with a plethora of speed bumps and traffic cameras. Jim and I noticed yesterday a driving instruction vehicle advertising lessons for £9 per hour. Seeing as the driver has to purchase or lease a vehicle, have it adapted for extra pedals and then pay the fuel and make a living wage, I can't understand how anyone can give lessons for £9 per hour. Perhaps that's why they get the learner to drive so slowly so that they can at least use less fuel and keep their costs down!

You next enter the lovely University town of St. Andrews (where William and Kate met) via the famous golf course, "The Royal and Ancient". I noticed that Fairmont had their name at the outer gate so I assume that they have purchased it and it is now part of their worldwide resorts.

Almost directly across the water from St Andrews is another famous golf course, Carnoustie. So many world class courses are in this area, which I suppose is only right as the Scots claim that Golf (or Goff as it is called here) was invented in Scotland. James II banning of golf and football in 1457 does not appear to have succeeded in the long term as both golf and football today have fanatical followings in Scotland, but of archery clubs, there are nary a sign.

I must admit that I don't know if women are allowed to play at Carnoustie and St Andrews, but I dare say if Kate returned to her Alma Mater and wanted to play a round, there would be no one who would refuse her.

St. Andrews, East Fife

St Andrews was named after the apostle Andrew. It was said that Constantine, fearing Islamic raiders would destroy Christian relics, had the bones of St Andrew separated and sent to different parts of the Christian world. Legend has it that the ship carrying some of these bones was wrecked off the Scottish coast and the bones brought ashore at what is now called St. Andrews. St. Andrew also usurped St. Columba (and St. Margaret) as the patron saint of Scotland because being an apostle he had direct contact with Christ.

St. Andrews became the ecclesiastical capital of Scotland and its cathedral, built in 1158, supposedly housed the bones of the saint and was the largest building in Scotland. Wherever there are saintly relics there are pilgrims who travel to the shrine and pay money for miracles to happen or sins be forgiven. The cathedral here was thus a wealthy place. However, the reformation of 1559 removing Roman Catholicism in favour of Protestantism, caused the cathedral to be stripped of what were considered to be idolatrous images and altars and over time it fell into ruin and was abandoned to the elements.

The ruins still dominate the town. Whatever happened to the bones of St. Andrew, if indeed they ever were lodged here, nobody knows.

The University of St Andrews is the oldest in Scotland and said to be number three in Britain after Oxford and Cambridge. It has very smart buildings just on the western edge of the town.

The town has a superb sandy beach being used by children and kayakers when I passed by.

The Coastal Tourist route then took me to the lovely town of Tayport, close to the Tay Bridge. The land here and on over into Angus reminded me very much of Devon with its rolling hills and farms.

Tay Road Bridge to Dundee

The Tay Road Bridge is celebrating its 50th year this year (younger than me). The Tay Rail Bridge close by was the scene of a terrible tragedy in December 1879 when in a great storm the Bridge collapsed while a train was crossing it killing all 75 souls on board. A new bridge was built, but the footings of the old bridge can still be seen alongside it.

Over the bridge is the City of Dundee, which I did no more than skirt as it would take me away from the coastal route. Dundee is the fourth largest city in Scotland and has two Universities. At Discovery point is now located the RSS Discovery. The ship, built in Dundee, was the one that took Captain Scott on his ill-fated voyage to the Antarctic and the race to be first to reach the South Pole. The Coastal Route was clearly signed to take me to the right, as I crossed over the bridge, with the main part of the City off to my left.

I was now in the county of Angus. The first towns, Broughty Ferry and Monifieth are at least as pretty as their counterparts in Fife. In Monifieth I called in to Tesco where I purchased a "meal deal". I got a freshly made chicken and bacon pasta (good sized bowl) a bottle of orange juice and a Kit Kat, all for £2. Unbelievable value. Why can't the supermarkets in Canada be as good as this? I sat on the sandy beach to eat my meal and looked across the Firth to North Berwick where we were yesterday. I decided to call Jim to see how he was getting on. He was on a train moving south in grey and overcast skies. His wife Jean had called him to say it was still raining in Norfolk. I suggested he turn around and come back and join me!

The next place along the trail is Carnoustie, with its famous golf course. Carnoustie is mainly a dormitory town for Dundee. It still has its nice sea front for tourists to enjoy, but I suspect that most tourists come for the golf.

After Carnoustie is the ancient town of Arbroath, famous for it smokies, a type of smoked haddock. A shop selling them as I entered the town seemed to be doing a roaring trade as evidenced by the number of people queuing to get in. Arbroath is a town built of red sandstone. The Abbey, mostly ruins, is built of the same stone and is prominent in the town.

Arbroath Abbey, Angus

I have since discovered that my cousin Gordon's model was of the Arbroath lifeboat not the Anstruther one that I had thought it was. The RNLI have since sent me a picture of it. It is now in their Heritage Collection.

Arbroath is famous for the 1320 Declaration of Arbroath. This was a letter to the Pope from Robert the Bruce and 51 Scottish nobles seeking the Pope's confirmation that Scotland was and always had been an independent nation and its people free to choose their own King and that Robert was their rightful King, chosen and supported by the people of Scotland. At that time John Balliol (King John I of Scotland) was living in exile under Papal custody, having been forced to flee Scotland and also having fallen out with King Edward I. When King John was deposed a Guardian Council of 12 ruled Scotland and signed an alliance with France, known as the Auld Alliance. This greatly angered Edward I as Scotland was now allied to Edward's enemy.

The Declaration of Arbroath hoped also to get the Pope to lift the excommunication of Robert the Bruce, who had murdered John Comyn, one of the 12 Guardians, before the altar of Greyfriars Church in Dumfries. John Comyn was himself a potential competitor to the throne of Scotland, being descended from Donald III. His Mother was a sister of John Balliol and his wife was a cousin of Edward I.

The Pope at first acknowledged the Declaration, but then a year later supported the English over the Scots. However it was not until 1328 when Edward III was King and renounced all claims over Scotland, that the Pope rescinded Robert the Bruce's excommunication.

Interestingly in 1997 the US Senate passed a resolution stating that the American Declaration of Independence was modeled on the Declaration of Arbroath.

The coastal road out of Arbroath provides wonderful views over Lunan Bay, before reaching Montrose. You enter Montrose over a bridge across the River South Esk, which drains out of the Montrose Basin and into the sea. The Basin is a major nature reserve and the largest inland salt-water basin in the UK. When the tide is in this forms a large lake. Unfortunately the tide was out when I crossed the bridge and it looked to be mainly mud flats, great for bird life.

I had noticed that the Caledonian Railway was about five miles out of the town so I thought that I would go and take a look. I drove to Bridge of Dun, which is a halt for the train. This station was also a halt for Queen Victoria's royal train. She would spend the night here, in a siding, en route to her castle at Balmoral. Unfortunately there is little here now with only five miles of track in existence. The preservation society that runs the trains does so only occasionally.

Disappointed, I drove back to Montrose and back onto the coastal route.

The view continued to be wonderful. I stopped to brew a cup of tea at a parking area and look-out point, with a view across to the ocean on one side and a field of very bright yellow oilseed rape on my other side. The colours were so striking and complementary that it had caused me to stop. However, the smell of the rape was so overpowering that I had to sit in the car so that it did not mask the taste of the tea.

Dunnottar Castle, Angus

Just before you reach Stonehaven, on a headland, sits Dunnottar Castle. This is now a partly restored ruin, but its past has seen its involvement in much of the history of Scotland. Legend has it that its beginnings lie in a chapel founded by St. Ninian in the 5th century, but its origins as a castle date from the 12th century. Around 1400 the castle came into the Keith family who maintained connections and ownership of it right up until the end of the 19th century. The Keiths were the Marischals of Scotland, a somewhat honorary title charging them with responsibility for the Scottish Royal Honours (crown jewels). The family's allegiances changed over time. In 1639 William Keith sided with the Covenanters, who were opposed to Charles I and his religious views. However in 1651 after the coronation of Charles II as King of Scotland at Scone Palace in Fifeshire, the Honours were hidden at Dunnottar to prevent Oliver Cromwell capturing them. Though Cromwell besieged the castle the Honours were secretly moved out and hidden 10 miles south under the floor of Kinneff Old Kirk. In 1715, George Keith supported the Jacobite rebels and the castle and lands became forfeit to the Crown. The Keiths bought back the castle in 1761 and it remained in their family until being sold in 1873.

Stonehaven, Aberdeenshire

On entering Stonehaven from the south you are at a high point when you get your first view you of the town and its harbour. It is stunning. A notice proudly proclaims that

Stonehaven was the birthplace of Robert Thomson the inventor of the pneumatic tyre. Without him I probably would not have been making this journey, so thank you Robert. Stonehaven also lays claim to having the first heated outdoor swimming pool in Scotland and it still exists and is in use today.

From Stonehaven it was only fifteen miles into Aberdeen and my first experience of Air BnB. I had booked it on line the night before using my computer. I had tried using the App but it was hopeless and kept kicking me out as soon as I wanted to book. Samantha took me to my hosts who provided an upstairs room in a small house close to the old docks. Very clean and my hosts were helpful and charming, making me tea and offering me the run of the kitchen in the morning. I shall shortly be trying to book a similar place in Inverness for tomorrow night. Hope it works twice.

I drove into Aberdeen for dinner, very much a concrete jungle. Lots of big ships in the harbour, most of which seemed to have a connection to the oil industry. I found a Thai restaurant (not very Scottish I know) in the shopping mall and had a reasonable, but over priced meal. My last visit to Aberdeen had been many years ago when I landed at Aberdeen Airport. I went to use the toilet in the Arrivals area and as I faced the wall, on either side of me came two men who continued a conversation across me, while of course continuing to look at the wall. I couldn't understand one word of what they were saying, so assumed that these were the famed Norwegian oil workers. Know my surprise therefore when I went outside to find that one of them was to become my taxi driver. They were both Aberdonians.

My B&B hosts both came from Glasgow; the waitress who took my order in the restaurant came from Edinburgh and the person who served my food possibly came from Thailand.

I therefore did not knowingly hear or speak to anyone that came from Aberdeen. If I had, I wonder whether I would have understood them. Perhaps given the growth and internationalization of the city the Aberdonian accent has become modified and is possibly now more understandable. However, at the same time, I somewhat hope that it has not changed at all.

Tomorrow I turn across the top of Scotland and so my northernward journey is almost done. On Friday I expect to be at John O'Groats my northerly cardinal point. One day after that I will reach Cape Wrath, my north westernmost cardinal point and then my journey southward will begin.

Aberdeen to Inverness

Miles 183

Wild Seas, Fraserburgh, Aberdeenshire

Well even though the saying is 'Cast not a clout til' May be out' and many people did so yesterday, today was a very different story. 'Now where did I put my clout, I need it again?' This morning broke wild, windy and grey, but fortunately not wet. Yesterday temperatures reached 22 degrees; today the highest was 11 degrees!

Anyway, today (with my clout) I have seen angry seas, visited a boyhood haunt, considered trying to claim my ancestors' castle, seen the site of the last battle between the Scots and the English and gone looking (briefly) for the Loch Ness monster.

The journey north out of Aberdeen takes you into very different countryside than that south of Aberdeen. OK so I saw this in grey rather than sunshine and neat & tidy still remains neat & tidy, but there is a definite difference in the look and feel of the countryside. It seems more like moorland right up the coast and across to around Banff. There are no colourful fields of crops. Indeed I only saw one field of oilseed rape all day and that closer to Elgin. The fields were mainly sheep and the occasional cattle, but nothing looked very productive. Interestingly, I have only seen two small herds of Aberdeen Angus cattle while in this area. I imagined that I would have seen lots of them. Perhaps they only have a few for postcards and tourists.

My first stop was at Crudens Bay and the little harbor at Port Errol. The sand here looked to be 'good digging sand'. There were three motor homes parked here, looking as if they had been there all night. The road out came near to a huge gas plant, at St. Fergus. I suppose for us to have easy access to energy in our homes you have to pay the price of industrial ugliness somewhere.

Peterhead seemed quiet and I surmised that the fishing boats had decided to stay home because of the weather. However when I got to Fraserburgh, it was a very different story with large boats going out and others coming in and rows and rows of fish sheds. Having set off at 7.30am with only a banana for breakfast I decided to stop here and have a cooked breakfast and then I could skip lunch. I had breakfast at Angela's café on the fish dock. Her "quick" breakfast was a huge fry up (and I can assure you I only ate half of it) with a mug of tea, all for £4!

In Fraserburgh there is also what looks to be a great museum, the Scottish Lighthouses Museum. I regrettably did not feel that I had time to look at it, but it was housed in a nice building so I am sure it is done well inside. It is built adjacent to the Fraserburgh lighthouse and also the very large (now inoperative) foghorn. The sea looked very cold and uninviting with large waves, whipped up by the wind, smashing onto the rocks. There is an RNLI station here and 14 members of its members have lost their lives in service in these seas between 1919 and 1970.

The well signposted tourist coastal route took me on a winding road to MacDuff where I at last began to see colour other than green or grey. I hummed the tune from the Wizard if Oz as I drove along one road that I dubbed the "Yellow Gorse Road" and for miles I seemed to be driving almost through tunnels of prolific yellow gorse as they covered the banks and hillsides. Despite the cold and windy weather there were golfers out on the links at MacDuff. Rather them than me.

On the opposite side of the Bay from MacDuff is the very small town of Banff. The harbour was fairly empty of boats apart from a Sargo, which is a boat that I am currently interested in. It comes from Finland and is happy in the North Sea! As I left Banff there was of course a Banff Springs Hotel, definitely not as large or attractive as its namesake in Alberta. Another notable thing in this area are the very prominent graveyards. They all have large gravestones or monuments, built just outside of the town, often on a hill and having walls or metal fences around them. They seem more reminiscent of those in Italy than the "typical" graveyard in the UK built alongside a church.

As I motored on towards Portsay the country became definitely softer in appearance and the wind dropped. The little town of Cullen proudly states that it is the 'home of the skink' and a local hotel won the 2015 world championships. I daresay the 'Skink World Championship is a bit like the baseball 'World Series' in the US. It's open to the world, but the world doesn't turn up! Cullen skink is a thick soup made from haddock (ideally Finan haddock) potatoes and onions. If it had been just a bit later and I had not had my cooked breakfast at Angela's, I would have stopped and had some, as today was perfect skink eating weather.

Portknockie, Moray

At Portknockie I began to notice the very distinctive architecture of the houses, typical of the area. Around the windows and door are large stone blocks, which make them stand out from the rest of the building material. These blocks may be left plain in the contrasting stone or, may be painted which makes them stand out even more. Mostly they are painted white, with the rest of the building left plain, but some are painted in bright colours. Indeed some have the inner brick painted in a colour as well. One I saw as I entered Buckie had the walls painted in lilac with the window and door stones pained white.

In a number of the small fishing villages I passed through, I noticed that the terraced cottages were built in rows, side on to the ocean. Quite common apparently for this part of the world and probably meaning that less of the house is open to the weather.

I continue to be drawn to the RNLI stations and like to look at all of the different classes of lifeboats. There are 349 operational lifeboats in the UK and Ireland operating from 237 stations with 4,700 crew members, all of them volunteers and from all walks of life. The lifeboat in Buckie is a large 17-meter Severn class boat, which costs around £3m. The latest vessel in the fleet, the Shannon (which they have in Exmouth) costs £2.1m and its launching system another £1.5m. These numbers are just for the boat purchase and do not include the operating costs. The board outside the station indicated that it had last been called out on May 17th when it assisted a trawler with a broken engine and towed it into Burghead. These are large and very expensive boats to purchase and to maintain. The RNLI receives around £150m per annum to maintain its operations. A small sum if this was paid by the Government, but in fact the majority of it all comes from public donations. It seems a huge expense to have one of these vessels sitting, unused, for much of the time. However, in these waters, this type of vessel is essential to keep crews safe and allow them to go out in all weathers to assist mariners in distress. Just one life saved is surely worth all of the cost. In 2014, over 8,700 people were rescued by the RNLI, which is an average of 24 per day. Of these 368 would have died if it were not for the actions of the lifeboat crews. Interestingly, 40% of these call outs were at night, which in a storm makes the job harder and more dangerous than ever.

Severn Class RNLI Lifeboat at Buckie

My next stop was at Lossiemouth, with its major air force base. Here they fly intercept missions against Russian aircraft that test out Britain's defences and reaction times by deliberately flying into British air space. RAF crew also support air sea rescue operations when required.

After Lossiemouth I went on to Burghead. Burghead holds special memories for me as at 18 years old I attended an Outward Bound School here for a month from mid January to mid February. I swear it was warmer then than it is today. The OB experience was wonderful, at least I thought so afterwards. They would get us up at 5.00am and we had to have a mile run before taking a very cold shower. We also went climbing in the snow-covered mountains and sailing on the frigid ocean. I very well recall sailing a dipping lug cutter from Burghead to Findhorn.

Regrettably nothing remains of the school. I went to the information center, set in a pretty round white painted stone building on a lookout point. Here they had some photos and records, but all for years either earlier or later than when I was there. The only thing my memory was able to place was the spot in the harbor where, on trying to get into a sailboat with another boy, he pulled the bow line as I was getting on the stern. The stern moved away from me as I stepped forward and I fell in up to my waist. As it was February I had to go home and change, but then I was too late to sail.

I also recall us going to Gordonstoun School (where Prince Charles had been). This was 5 miles away and we travelled there in an old army truck. Once there we had to jump in the pool and pull ourselves out twenty times, then swim four lengths backstroke, four lengths breaststroke, four lengths butterfly and then four lengths crawl. After getting out, exhausted and drying off, we went outside to find no truck. 'Sorry lads you have to run back' said the instructor with a great deal of glee! Actually I found that I really enjoyed the run.

From Burghead I drove around the bay to Findhorn and made myself a cup of tea. This still has an "alternative living" community dating back to the 1960s. The road then led me on towards Nairn and Inverness. On this road I noticed a sign for Cawdor Castle.

You may know in Shakespeare's MacBeth that he is described as Thane (or Earl) of Cawdor. There is no evidence at all that he ever had anything to do with any castle in Cawdor and the one there now was built a few centuries after he had died. It was due to close at 5.00pm and as it was now 4.00pm I decided not to pay the £10 entrance fee, so I took a sneaky picture of the house from over a hedge.

On leaving Cawdor I saw a sign for Culloden, the site of the final battle of the last Jacobite uprising of 1746. I had to go there.

Charles II had been restored to the throne of England in 1660 and died in 1685. Having no legitimate heirs, the throne passed to his brother James, who became James II of England and VII of Scotland. James II was a protestant and by his first wife he had a daughter, Mary. Mary, like her Aunt before her (James' sister) married into the Dutch House of Orange. She married her protestant cousin, William, who had become the Prince of Orange at birth, his father having died one week before he was born. Mary and William were thus closely related, Mary's father and Williams' mother being brother and sister.

Opposition to James II turned into action in June 1668. His second wife, Mary of Modena, was a Catholic and she gave birth to a son, James Francis Stuart (later known as the Old Pretender). This raised fears in England that the baby might be named as heir, meaning a Catholic King would once again be on the throne. This fear was further heightened as James had repealed the Test Act that had blocked Catholics from holding any significant office. Influential political and religious leaders in England therefore decided to approach Mary and her Dutch husband, William and invite them to invade England and take over the throne from her father. The letter of invitation to William and Mary was prepared and written in Lady Place at Hurley on Thames, about five miles from where I lived at Wargrave. In truth William had been looking for just such an opportunity and had even connived to have the invitation sent to him. He was staunchly anti-Catholic and loathed his neighbour King Louis XIV of France who he saw getting stronger and who could potentially restore all of Europe, including Holland and England to Catholicism. If William were to be King in England he would have the English navy at his disposal to counter and indeed threaten King Louis. Arthur Herbert, a politician and ex-Admiral, delivered the invitation to William. James II had earlier dismissed Herbert from his post, for opposing his repealing of the Test Act.

William accepted the invitation and with Mary, sailed for England in November 1688, giving command of his fleet of 300 ships to Arthur Herbert. As a show of strength to both James II and Louis XIV, he instructed that the ships sail down the English Channel in line abreast of 25 ships to create as much evidence of their presence and power as possible.

William and Mary landed at Brixham in Devon on November 5th 1688, ironically the same day as the Gunpowder plotters had tried to blow up James I in 1605, but with opposite objectives. He first marched to Exeter, in full armour and astride a white horse. There, in the Cathedral, he had read out a proclamation that explained to the English people that he was coming as their saviour from Catholicism. He and his army of 35,000 soldiers marched on to London. Notable protestant officers in James' army left and joined William and James quickly knew he could not succeed in a fight with William and so fled to France.

William and Mary became joint monarchs. Mary legitimized the accession to the throne, being both a Stuart and an heir as daughter of James II. William of Orange's mother as sister of James II also gave William a claim to the throne. The following year, in 1689, the Bill of Rights was signed that said no future Monarch of England could be a Catholic or marry a Catholic and that Parliament had sovereignty over the King. The Act, which was read out at their Coronation, is still in force today. When Mary died in 1694, William ruled alone as William II of Scotland and III of England. It is a point of interest to me that this invader King should also be called William, like the Conqueror, 600 years before.

James tried to take his throne back in 1689 with the help of the Irish but was defeated by William at the Battle of the Boyne. One year later, in 1690, at the Battle of Aughrim the remnants of the Irish Jacobite army was virtually annihilated and William took full control of the north of Ireland, being known by the Protestants there as "King Billy". These battles gave rise to the Orange day celebrations that still, controversially, take place in Northern Ireland to this day.

William died in 1702 and as he and Mary had no children, the throne passed to Mary's younger sister, Anne, who had supported Mary's taking over the throne from their father James II. Of Annes' seventeen children, all either died at birth, in infancy or before she herself died. She therefore died without natural heirs in May 1707. The Act of Settlement, signed in 1701, was passed after the death of her son William at age 11, when it was considered that no child of Anne would be available to take the throne. The Act determined that if she were to die without heirs, the throne would pass to the descendants of Elizabeth Stuart, daughter of James I/VI and the one that the Gunpowder plotters had planned to put on the throne. Elizabeth had married a German, Frederick Prince of Bohemia. At the time of Anne's death in 1714, Elizabeth's eldest descendent was her grandson, the German speaking George of Hanover, who thus inherited the English throne as George I and whose son later succeeded him as George II in 1727.

Meanwhile, James Francis Stuart, "the Old Pretender" son of James II, had a son Charles Edward Stuart born in 1720. He became known as the "Young Pretender", or Bonnie Prince Charlie. In 1745 another uprising among the Jacobite Catholics saw Charles Stuart arriving in Scotland to try and take the throne from George II. The armies of England led by William, Duke of Cumberland, youngest son of King George II and the Jacobite rebels met at Culloden on 16th April 1746.

Culloden Monument

The Jacobites were made up mainly of Scots but also included some English troops from Manchester and a number of both French and Irish troops. Due to disorganization, poor ground and lack of strategy, the Jacobites were routed, indeed slaughtered. Fifteen hundred Jacobites were killed, to only fifty government troops. Bonnie Prince Charlie fled the battle and though hunted, escaped to Skye and then to France and never again became a threat. This battle signaled the violent beginning of the Highland clearances and the mass migration of many Scots. No Catholic has since sat on the British throne and the Act of Settlement still remains on the statute books of England.

The Culloden battle site today is run by the National Trust for Scotland and I discovered that membership of the NT for Scotland gives you entrance privileges to NT for England properties. However, the joining fee for two people is considerably less – £60 in Scotland rather than £107 in England, so I took out membership. My wife and I are in the UK frequently so it makes sense, given the cost of entrance to the various properties and the car parks.

Before going to my accommodation for the night I decided I had to take a short trip down Loch Ness. How could I be in Scotland and not at least look at it and hope that I might be the next person to espy Nessie the monster? I drove to the wonderfully named Drumnadrochit, but Nessie was not showing herself today. I then turned around and headed back to Inverness.

My accommodation tonight is in another AirBnB booked house. It turned out to be the home of a lovely older couple, Jim and Jean and I had a sink and refrigerator in my room with tea, coffee and cereal, plus a private bathroom, all for half the cost of a Travel Lodge (indeed one third of the price they were charging here in Inverness tonight!).

Inverness is the traditional ancestral home of MacBeth, though in his time his name would have been spelt in Gaelic, which today is translated as MacBeadth MacFindlaech. He was the son of Findlaech who according to Irish history was described as King of Scotland and later killed by his nephews Malcolm II and Giles Coemgain. MacBeth is alleged by some historians to have later avenged his father's death and killed Giles Coemgain, marrying his wife, Gruoch, the fabled Lady MacBeth.

Tomorrow I drive up the Black Isle and along the coast to John O'Groats. I intend to stay two nights at Gills Bay and take the ferry across to the Orkneys on Saturday to view the 4500-year-old settlements. Perhaps, perhaps, perhaps the sun will shine once more.

Inverness to Gills Bay

Miles 156

Duncansby Sea Stacks, John O'Groats

Today was a pretty straightforward driving day – eventually. At the start I was hindered by ferries that weren't there and grey skies and rain. But the day got better.

Inverness is a fine city, bridging between Loch Ness to the southwest and the Moray Firth to the northeast. These two waters are joined by the northern end of the Caledonian Canal. At the southern end of Loch Ness, a further part of the Caledonian Canal joins it to Loch Lochy, from where it runs into the River Lochy and then accesses the sea at Loch

Linnhe. Effectively Scotland is dissected by water. It is possible to take a boat from the Irish Sea on the west coast, right through Loch Ness and out into the North Sea on the north east coast. Someday I should like to hire a boat and do this trip

To the west of Inverness is an area known as The Aird, which is allegedly the site of a battle between King Malcolm III of Scotland (the successor to King MacBeth) and Thorfinn the Mighty, likely a cousin of both MacBeth and Malcolm.

Red stoned Inverness Castle only dates from 1836 but is reputedly built on the site of old fortifications, going back to 1057 when Malcolm III is said to have built a structure here after his killing of MacBeth. I will explore more of the history of MacBeth when I get to Iona, where he is buried, in a few days time.

Leaving Inverness by the bridge with Beauly Firth to your left and the Moray Firth to the right I followed the A9 going north. My objective was to turn off onto the Black Isle and take the ferry from Cromarty to Nigg. This would keep me on the coast and save twenty miles of the A9. The Black Isle is as beautiful as I expected it to be. It is rural farming land with wonderful views. My drive was from Munlochy, to Rosemarkie and then on to Cromarty. This is the point where the Cromarty Firth empties into the North Sea, with Nigg approximately 1 mile across the water. On arriving in the village I asked a friendly gentleman I saw leaving the newsagents as to how I could get to the ferry dock. 'Well the ferry ramp is straight down the road, you can't miss it. However, I don't think the ferry is running just yet.' 'But their web site says they are operating from the first week of June.' I replied. 'Och, that maybe is what it says, but I think they have decided to wait another week.' Well whenever it is they are deciding to start, it certainly was not today.

The Cromarty Firth has a number of oil rigs "resting" so maybe with the downturn in that industry, business is slower for the ferry. However, with no advertised ferry operating, I would have to generate some extra business for the oil industry by now having to take a thirty mile diversion – perhaps that is the aim, to help resurrect the oil business!

I drove back along the southern shore of the Cromarty Firth aiming to join the A9 at the bridge that crosses the southern end of the Firth. Now I've commented before about some of the funny names that I have been noticing on my drive. Today on the Black Isle I passed a place called Jemimaville, an unexpected name for deepest Scotland. Jemimaville, although definitely on land was the site of a naval engagement in October 1914. Two British warships the Lion and the Queen Mary, spooked into believing that there were U-Boats in the area fired on what they thought was a German submarine. No one knows exactly what they saw, it might have been a dolphin, but the shells landed on Jemimaville, causing extensive damage and wounding a child.

Having crossed the bridge I was now on the A9 and I stayed on this until I branched off to the Tarbet Peninsular and Nigg, where the ferry was supposed to go to. The cloud base had fallen dramatically and rain was threatening, so there was little to see and pictures were not worth taking

I eventually arrived at Tain and the bridge over the Dornoch Firth. There are some wonderful beaches here and the famous Glenmorangie whiskey distillery. As it was now raining hard, I had driven thirty unanticipated extra miles and I don't really like whiskey anyway, I decided not stop. I am planning to try some at other distilleries later. "You can't be a real Scotsman" I hear you cry, but my Father and most of his family also did not like Scotch. I am determined to try and find out though why other people rave about it.

The rain now started to fall very heavily and all the cars had on their fog lights. We were definitely on the coast road as I could see occasional glimpses of the North Sea a few yards away on my right. The only colour once again was from the very prolific and abundant gorse. In some places the bluebells were also in full bloom – finished already in the south of England.

Wick, Caithness

The coast road was a journey of 60 miles to Wick, with little to see because of the rain and low cloud. I made a brief pit stop at Helmsdale, but pressed on until I eventually arrived in Wick. I decided to stop here in the harbour and have some lunch. Within ten minutes of parking, the clouds lifted, the sun came out and the temperature began to rise quickly. As

I made a cup of tea an elderly couple came up and talked to me. They now lived close to Wick but had previously lived in Devon. She was Scottish and he was a Devonian. They were fascinated at the journey I was doing and especially interested that I had started from Devon.

I stopped again a little further on to take a picture of the coast and found myself alongside another of the very prominent cemetery's that appear to be common in this area. Looking at some of the grave markers, so many of them were for children and where there were family plots, most of them had names of children who died in infancy, or while still young, some just teenagers. We have only had antibiotics for about sixty years so it makes you appreciate how many of these children might have lived productive and fruitful lives if antibiotics had been available in their day.

%

This reminded me of a story from my wife's family, who at the end of the 19th century had emigrated to Canada. A second-generation daughter decided to leave Canada during the dust bowl era and with her husband and children moved to Ashreigny in Devon, where her parents had originally come from. Within a year of being in England all eight of her children died, in a three-month period, due to a diphtheria epidemic. I can't imagine their grief or how anyone could get over the loss of all of ones children. How times have changed, thanks to pharmaceuticals and improvements in the health care system. However, today, there are now concerns being expressed that we may be facing new epidemics from bacteria that are resistant to most antibiotics. Potentially we could be moving back to those days when infections are feared.

Milepost at John O'Groats, Caithness

At last I reached the top of the world, or at least what was claimed to be the top of Britain, John O' Groats. There is actually very little here, only the famous signpost and a few merchants. Just on the edge of the village is a collection of purpose built wooden chalets that seem to be offering a place for retreats. There is also a passenger ferry that will take you to the Orkneys and provide what looks to be an extensive bus tour of the Islands and sites of interest. I have booked to go on it tomorrow. I had planned to take my car on the ferry from Gills Bay, but it was already fully booked and even though I could get on the wait list, there was no guarantee of my getting on the ferry. This then decided me that I would have a day without the car and give myself a break from driving.

The milepost is the famous marker and points to a few places around Britain and the world with the mileage distances indicated. I was fascinated to see that the post showed Lands

End as being 874 miles and Orkney at 8 miles. A second marker on the wall of the harbour, no more than fifty yards away, showed Lands End as 876 miles and Orkney, 6 miles. I think I will take the post as being the most accurate – if only because it is the more famous. However, checking with Google Maps they give the distance between Lands End and JOG as 837 miles. Maybe it just feels longer if you are cycling the route!

The milepost also shows the distance to the North Pole as 2200 miles. JOG is at Latitude 58.6 degrees and the North Pole at 90 degrees. Therefore the difference is 31.4 degrees. As each degree of Latitude equates to 60 nautical miles, the distance to the true North Pole is therefore 1884 nautical miles. As a nautical mile is 10% greater than a statute mile the distance to the North Pole is actually 2072 miles.

The discordant second sign

Over the next hour a number of people arrived by bicycle, sports car and motorbike and all went up to "claim" their arrival at the post. Only the cyclists though had travelled from Lands End. I was distinctly humbled by two young doctors from North Petherton near Taunton, Mark and Ian, who had completed a ride from Land's End on behalf of the Alzheimer's Society, of which Marks's mother-in-law was a sufferer.

They had done the journey in only seven days. Incredible. I am on day twelve of my journey, I started 250 miles further north of Lands End and I am in a car. Of course I am taking the longer route around every nook and cranny, however, to cycle that far in only seven days is a tremendous feat. Over 100 miles per day, starting at 4.00am each day. They had been sleeping in bivvy bags (a bit like a body bag!), behind hedgerows and one night apparently in a graveyard. I gave them a donation because of their achievement.

Past John O'Groats is Duncansby Head lighthouse and just beyond three huge sea stacks, which are a three quarter mile hike but well worth seeing. These are famous for their bird colony. This is the most northeasterly point of Scotland.

My B&B for the next two nights is excellent and considerably better than a hotel. It is smart and very clean, with a separate sitting room and my Hostess, Ethel, promises me a good English breakfast in the morning. My AirBnB places for the last 2 nights have also been good.

I am concerned about finding places to stay on my three nights in the highlands, as these are fairly remote places. I may yet still end up sleeping in the car. At least I have a stove and food if necessity strikes!

Food tonight was at the Seaview Hotel in John O'Groats. I can only call it just passable, but with a huge failing grade on presentation. I ordered chicken curry. What I received was three long strips of chicken breast placed on top of rice and chips with a bright yellow curry sauce (allegedly) poured over it. I don't think that there had been any attempt to cook the chicken with the sauce. The room had a snooker table in the middle around which very loud, local youths would play while shouting at each other. Unfortunately it seems to be the "only place in town". I'll bring sandwiches next time I come to John O'Groats.

Tomorrow will be a day of history (pre-history even, back to 4,000BC).

The Orkneys

Miles 10

Skara Brae, Neolithic Village, Orkney

W ell, apart from the journey to and from my B&B to the ferry at John O' Groats, I did not do any driving today, although, apparently, the coach I journeyed on traveled 80 miles on the islands.

The Orkneys have always been somewhere that I have wanted to visit, both to see the Neolithic remains and also Scapa Flow, which played such a significant role in both World Wars.

My ferry left John O'Groats at 9.30am. It had a very unusual way of docking in that it puts its bow into the dock and partly ties off. Then it goes into reverse and pivots around the bow line, which is slowly let out and the ship slides around and along rubber tyres on the sea wall until it comes in alongside. Seems to work OK, but I'm sure that they have to repaint the side of the boat at the end of the season to remove the black tyre marks!

JOG to Orkney Passenger Ferry

The ferry takes 40 minutes to make the 6 miles crossing to Orkney (so it is very slow). There are other ferries that run from Gills Bay and Scrabster, both of which also take cars. You can even travel from Aberdeen, over night, and that ferry then goes on to the Hebrides. The ferry was cold and they are missing a trick by not serving coffee on board. As we crossed the Pentland Firth we got to the point where the current from the North Sea meets the current from the Atlantic Ocean. Quite wild waters and the boat rocked a good deal. I definitely would not like to make this trip in the winter. The Pentland Firth is apparently the most treacherous water crossing in the British Isles.

For 500+ years the Orkneys and the Shetlands belonged to Norway (875 to 1472) and still to this day, Norway Constitution Day (in May) is a holiday on the islands. Apparently the King of Norway wanted his daughter to marry James III, King of Scotland. She must have been fairly ugly as James asked for such a big dowry that the King of Norway could not pay it all, so pledged the islands as security while he found the money. He never did make up the sum so the islands became Scottish. The Orkney flag is very much like the Norwegian flag apart from the addition of yellow around the cross.

There are 70 islands, big and small that make up the Orkneys and they have a population of 70,000. Only 20 of the islands are inhibited. The area they cover could apparently fit easily within the M25 motorway ring around London. They are at latitude 59 degrees north, which is the same as Churchill in Canada (which has polar bears) and St Petersburg in Russia (where the sea freezes in the winter). The winters in the Orkneys though are becoming milder and they rarely ever now get snow or frost. Their summers are cool, the highest temperature ever recorded was 27 degrees, but generally 17 degrees is the warmest they get to. They get a lot of rain, especially in the winter. In winter the sun does not rise until 10.00am and sets at 3.00pm. In the summer they get 21 hours of daylight, with the sun rising at 3.00am and not setting until 11.30pm. The one saving grace of only 5 hours winter daylight is that they frequently get a good display of the Northern Lights between October and March. It lifts their depression I'm told.

Our first piece of history was the Churchill barriers. There are four, with roads running across them and they join up the main islands. As Britain prepared for war in 1939, ships were deliberately sunk between the small islands to prevent U Boats from entering and attacking the fleet in Scapa Flow. Unfortunately even with these sunken wrecks in place a U Boat did get through in October 1939 and sunk the battleship Royal Oak with the loss of 824 lives (only 12 sailors survived the sinking). Churchill ordered the building of concrete barriers and Italian prisoners of war were brought onto the island to build them, though they were not fully completed until almost the end of the war. At this time local fisherman lobbied for them to be removed, but, as they now provided easy access between the islands they remained. Driving across them you can still see the remains of some of the sunken wrecks that they replaced.

At first the Orcadians were not at all friendly to the British troops and sailors stationed on the island at the beginning of the war, resenting their presence. It was seen as an awful place to be posted to. However a junior officer wrote a poem about the "bloody islands and the bloody islanders" that was published in the local newspaper.

Here is the first verse:

"This bloody town's a bloody cuss
No bloody trains, no bloody bus,
And no one cares for bloody us
In bloody Orkney"

There are eight verses in total.' You can find the whole poem on the web.

After being "shamed" at the way they were acting, the Orcadians decided to change their ways and began making the sailors and soldiers more welcome.

One notable feature of the Orkneys is the almost complete absence of any trees. They were cut down many centuries ago. We were shown a small plantation in a protected valley that the local primary school children are taken to, so as to let them see what a wood looks like! I saw daffodils still in bloom, bluebells and also primroses. They say they are about 6 weeks behind the south, but their weather is changing. They are on the Gulf Stream.

The cathedral in Kirkwall the capital is a very interesting red stoned building. It was built by the Norwegians and later, during the reformation was destined to be destroyed, but King Henry VIII relented as long as no catholic services were held there. At one time Oliver Cromwell used it as stables. It is also the only cathedral in Britain to have a jail within it. There is a pit, right by the pulpit, where recalcitrants were incarcerated so that they could hear the sermon and mend their ways. It was also a place of hangings and a number of women were hung from the rafters for allegedly being witches. Now it is a completely open religious building and can be used by any faith.

Today when I visited there was a "weeping window" display of ceramic red poppies, which had come from the 2015 Tower of London Remembrance Day display. This was in memory of the Battle of Jutland, which took place one hundred years ago on May 31st. One of my wife's great-uncles, Bob Young, took part in the Battle of Jutland. He was an adventurer and later went on to work as a diver assisting in constructing the Sidney Harbour Bridge and then to be member of the two Admiral Byrd expeditions to the South Pole.

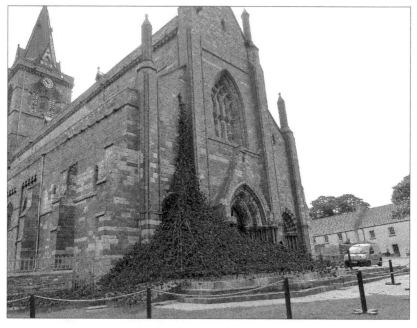

Kirkwall Cathedral, Orkney

David Cameron, the German President, Princess Ann and other dignitaries attended a service here on Tuesday. Tomorrow, Sunday, there is also to be a commemoration of the sinking of HMS Hampshire, which hit a mine in 1916, with the loss of 737 lives, including Lord Kitchener who was leading the British war effort at that time.

Kirkwall is very small by mainland standards and feels almost like a small country town in England, but with few people or cars. All the shops shut promptly at 5.00pm. I did notice an out of town Tesco, so no doubt this is where most shopping now takes place.

My main reason for visiting was to see the Neolithic remains which are abundant on the island, with almost certainly lots more still to be unearthed. The most fascinating was the 5000-year-old village at Skara Brae. This was only discovered in the late 1920s when a windstorm took away sand dunes and the village underneath was exposed. The buildings are older than the pyramids and archeologists know that more buildings are probably near by, still buried under the surrounding fields.

After this we drove to the Ring of Brodgar, standing stones about 1000 years older than Stonehenge. These form the third largest henge in Britain. I had not appreciated that there are over 1000 known henges in Britain, with Stonehenge being the most complete and well known.

We next saw the Standing Stones of Stennes; a much smaller henge, but with stones up to 6 metres high.

Close to the henges is the fairly recently discovered, Ness of Brodgar. There are at least 12 extremely large buildings, of unknown function, which are still being unearthed. Unfortunately there was nothing to be seen today as the buildings were covered with black plastic. They only have money to excavate during July and August when volunteers are available! I was particularly disappointed as this was what I had most wanted to see.

Equally disappointing was the fact that we could only drive by, but not stop, at Maese Howe a Neolithic burial tomb. This is so small that coaches are not allowed to take groups here, only cars with few occupants are allowed any one time. The opening of the tomb is such that at both the summer and winter solstices the sun shines right down the entrance and lights up the inside of the tomb. This same feature has been found in many of the stone tombs and barrows found in southern England, so certainly, like the henges, this practice was "exported" to other places as people moved.

All of these sites had their hey day during Neolithic times, but it is likely that they lost their position in society when iron and especially bronze came along. We see similar things today, as old industries give way to new ones and new towns or societies take over from earlier ones (think of coal and steel, computing and the economic rise of China and India). The difference today is that it happens at a much more rapid rate.

Scientists also believe that at some time the climate became much colder, which thus made the north less habitable; so the population eventually abandoned the islands and moved further south. Certainly there is now evidence emerging that the abandonment of the Ness of Brodgar was a deliberate and conscious one, with the cattle being slaughtered all at the same time, potentially for a feast or even because they could not take them with them across the Pentland Firth. The Orcadian influence is certainly seen at places such as Stonehenge. If, as we were told, the Orkneys now get winters without snow, perhaps a millennia from now, the islands will be warm enough to sustain a significant population once again.

We also visited Stromness, the second largest town. It is very small and has only 1 main street with little by way of shops along it. There was a cruise ship in port, the Silver Seas Explorer. I was surprised to learn that the Orkneys are in fact the second biggest cruise liner destination in the UK. I would imagine that the passengers from the ship would be put on buses and given a tour of the Island, similar to what I am on, as you can see all there is to see in Stromness in thirty minutes.

On the funny names front, there is a good-sized village on Orkney called Twatt. My British friends will understand this. I saw the sign to it but did not visit.

The Italian Chapel, Orkney

Our final visit was to the Italian Chapel. This was a wonderful find. It is an ersatz church "built" by the Italian prisoners of war within their prison camp. In 1942, five hundred and fifty Italian prisoners were brought to the uninhabited Lamb Holm Island to begin the work of constructing the Churchill Barriers. The prisoners had an Italian Padre who persuaded the Camp Commander that they be allowed to build a place of worship on the island to support them during their stay. They were given two Nissen huts, which they joined end to end. To brighten them and make them more like a place of worship they lined them out with various pieces of scrap material and began painting and decorating. One of their number was a master decorator, Domenico Chioccetti and he painted the interior, over time, in such

217

exquisite detail that unless you actually touch it you would think that the painted boards are really stone blocks and plaster frescos.

Outside the building is covered with concrete, also elaborately painted and it is quite remarkable how much like a real Church it looks in its setting. It is also amazing how ordinary items were redrafted. Light fittings were made from old corned beef tins and the baptismal font from a car exhaust, covered with concrete. The Chapel was not quite finished when the Italians were taken off the island and repatriated, but Chioccetti stayed on for a while to complete the project.

The Chapel became a symbol of unity between the Orkneys and Scotland and in 1960 Domenico returned to assist in the restoration of the Chapel. He came again in 1964 with his wife, but was too ill to attend the 50-year celebration in 1992. In 2012 for the 70th anniversary his daughter came and sang in the Chapel. The Chapel is now a grade 1 listed monument, meaning that it is to be preserved for generations.

There is a sad love story connected with the Chapel. At the sanctuary end of the chapel are a pair of low gates. Where they join in the middle there is set in the floor a metal heart. Apparently the prisoners became friendly with a number of the islanders while in Orkney and one, very much so, with a young women and they fell in love. He promised to marry her when the war was over, but before he left the island he revealed that he was already married with a wife and family in Italy. He told her that he had left his heart for her in the chapel, which is the one at the joining point of the gates. He never returned to the island and the young women never married.

The heart on the floor

The journey back to JOG on the ferry was slow and cold and I was glad to get back to my B&B. I stopped on the way to cook a meal in the car, parking close to the JOG cemetery, an old ancient one with large monuments and surrounded by metal fencing like so many others that I had seen in this part of the world. Alongside it was a modern cemetery behind a low wall and with much more modest memorial stones.

Weather today was generally sunny and is forecast to get better as I travel west tomorrow. I have managed to secure a Bed & Breakfast booking in Lochinver. I hope the drive there is OK, as I will be joining the famous "North Coast 500 mile drive". This is almost only on single-track roads and it may take me longer than I have planned. As I leave JOG and turn west I feel somewhat that I am now on the downward leg of my homeward journey, although I realise that I am not yet at the halfway point!

Gills Bay to Lochinver

Miles 186

Dunnett Head, Britain's most northerly point

T oday has been a journey of jaw dropping, eye watering, splendour, along with a touch of disappointment, one caused by nature and the other by (possibly) the Kirk.

I set off this morning to drive the 90 miles to the village of Keoldale in order to catch the 11.00am ferry across the neck of the Kyle of Durness to join the road to Cape Wrath.

Once across you board a mini-bus that bounces along a track for one and a half hours to get you to Cape Wrath, the most northwesterly point of Britain.

When I left Gills Bay it was still cloudy and I heard on the radio that the east coast was to remain cloudy all day. Eerily, when I reached the village of Reay, where the Dounreay nuclear power station is located, it suddenly warmed up! The clouds parted, the sun began to shine and then shone all day, touching 19 degrees. Was this as the result of a radioactive leak?

Before reaching Reay another of my misconceptions was revealed. John O'Groats is not the most northerly point of the British mainland, this is Dunnet Head about 10 miles east of JOG. So why then does everyone say that it is JOG and then trek from Lands end to JOG, when they should be going to Dunnet Head? In fact Lands End is not even the most southerly point either. It's Lizard Point and I will be going there.

Through Thurso, where the shape of its bay helps create one of the world's best surfing beaches (provided you are wearing a wet suit!) and Scrabster, the coastline remains little changed. The countryside is fairly bleak, the drabness broken up only by odd patches of brightly flowering gorse. However, as soon as you enter the County of Sutherland, magical things happen. The gorse becomes prolific and is a brilliant yellow and covers the roadways and hillsides. At one time, as I drove along, the purple rhododendron bushes arched high either side of me right over the road. The very bright gorse on the hillside at the end, lit by the now full sunshine, made it feel as if I was driving towards the light at the end of the tunnel!

There are now lots of sheep around, many wandering into the road. The beauty continues to build mile by mile. There are breathtaking views across moorland to lovely hills and even mountains that are like the Rockies, so high that nothing grows on the top of them. The road narrows again and you are provided with well signposted passing places. This is unlike Devon, where they hide the passing places to make your drive more "interesting". The narrow roads in Devon are all well below hedge height so you can't see what is coming. In Sutherland you can see for miles so it is a calmer place for drivers.

It is the wonders of nature that have totally bowled me over today. My journey has been constantly interrupted by the need to stop to take photos. It is almost a case of around every corner the view is better than the last.

The road rises and falls and you drive past lots of vivid blue lochens (the name for small lochs) and views of gorgeous white sand beaches. From Tongue onwards even the sea changes colour to a wonderful greenish blue. I think they call it Tongue because this is your organ most affected and it may drop out when you see the beauty that awaits you!

Tongue, Sutherland (Highland)

However, when I got to Keoldale, although the beauty continued, nature determined that my arrival would coincide with the time of an exceptionally low tide such that the ferry across to Cape Wrath was unable to pass over a sand bank and would not be able to run before 2.00pm. I was disappointed in not being able to make the ferry journey, although the minibus journey is apparently tortuous and I really was not up to many more narrow roads, especially full of potholes. Even though Cape Wrath is the northwesterly point of Scotland, it not one of the "cardinal points" of Britain. The west cardinal point is Ardnamurchan Point, further south. With some regret, I decided to motor on rather than wait three hours, plus at least another three hour round trip to the Cape and back. Nature had decided that I should continue my drive.

Having had to miss Cape Wrath, I drove on for another fifty miles almost entirely on a single-track road. All drivers on the route are very good and everyone adjusts their speed so that you both arrive at a passing point at the same time. The camper vans, of which there were quite a number, also pull over to let other traffic pass. I found myself pulling over to let pass four very high-powered sports cars: a Lamborghini, a Ferrari, a McLaren and a Porsche. I discovered yesterday at JOG that there are a couple of Scottish firms that hire out these cars for three days of a driving experience. "Petrol heads" are very much the target market for these firms. The companies do send along accompanying drivers and support vehicles, but over three days customers get to experience driving three or four very high-powered vehicles. On such narrow roads the excitement is intense, especially for the oncoming traffic. These vehicles are being driven at speeds of up to 90 miles an hour on a road where anything over 40 seems insane.

Just as well their brakes are as good as their engines! The two doctors who had cycled to JOG told me that it was frightening when one of these vehicles suddenly opened up and swept past them with a huge roar from their engines. They said that the lorries were much less scary.

You also see on these roads, vintage cars (today open topped ones), packs of high-powered modern motorcycles and smaller packs of vintage motorcycles. I even saw a group of vehicles dressed up with signs and balloons apparently for "Pete's 40th bash". There are of course lots of cyclists.

The Scottish Tourist Board established "The North Coast 500" in 2014 offering a 516 mile circuit of the most splendid areas of the Highlands. It starts and ends at Inverness Castle. It is certainly proving to be a success. The route is said to be named after a song by the Proclaimers, two Scottish brothers whose song was, "I would walk 500 miles ...." The song is one of those where the singing is awful (I think) but it has a certain charm and a rhythm that annoyingly gets you humming it all day!

On driving the road closest to the ocean, I will always follow the road if it is a loop, but I have not always followed those roads that are just there and back. So with time to spare, as I was not going to Cape Wrath, I decided that I would take a "there and back" road and turned off to Tarbet with the sign advertising a seafood restaurant, "The Seahouse". As it was Sunday I thought that I would treat myself to a nice healthy fish Sunday lunch. My stomach has been crying out for some good healthy food. This road was definitely single track and even some of the passing places were very tight, but again an incredibly beautiful drive. It almost took my breath away as I saw the location of the little beach and the restaurant. The restaurant was raised up on a hillside overlooking the blue water. There is also a little ferry here to Handa Island a short way away, which is a bird sanctuary and there were plenty of twitchers in evidence with their binoculars and long lenses.

Unfortunately, and I'm sure that you are ahead of me here, the restaurant was shut and the ferry not operating because this was a Sunday! Well I am sure that everyone deserves a day of rest, but, unless the Kirk has insisted, why would you do this on Sunday when most people are not at work and looking for lunch and a day out to a bird sanctuary? I had my lunch anyway, out of a can and cooked on my stove in the trunk of a car. At least I had saved a good bit of money I consoled myself. There were quite a number of twitchers in the car park with their telephoto lenses pointed across to Handa Island, trying to console themselves with long distance views.

I followed the narrow road back to the only slightly wider single-track "main road" I had originally turned off. I looked again at the sign for the restaurant and noticed that it did state "Closed on Sundays". Oh well if I had read it more closely I could have saved myself the journey, but, then again, I would not have experienced the wonderful view of Tarbet and Handa Island.

After approximately twelve slow miles (slow because I had to keep stopping to take photographs!) I turned off again on another loop to Drumbeg and the Old Man of Stoer. Once again this was an adventure in wonderland but my dash cam chose this point to give out as I had worn out the battery. I took my life in my hands a number of times as I just had to stop and take a photo and hope that someone was not coming the other way, or even up behind me. On the map this road is edged with green shading marking a road of exceptional beauty. They were not wrong. If you buy a road atlas in Britain and it has roads edged in green, go on them, you will not be disappointed.

This particular road had gulleys either side of it, which you definitely would not want to get your wheels into. It also had one or two blind hillcrests. They warn you to go slow, but even slowly you have no idea if there is another vehicle coming at you from the other direction. You are committed to driving over the top and for just a moment all you can actually see is the sky; then the front of the car drops down as you go over the crest and you are relieved (hopefully) to see that the road is empty.

I had to stop at the "Secret Tea Room" in Drumbeg and take an ice cream break. At this point there were certainly more sheep and lambs on the road than vehicles. Later on along this road there was a sheep, standing in the roadside gulley. She waited until I was about 10 feet away and then jumped out in front of me. I stopped in time but the contents of the passenger seat (camera, maps etc) did not! Lambs are beautiful and cuddly but they grow up into what must be the dumbest of all animals. (I learned at the Devon County Show which I visited before I started my journey from Devon, that lambs go to the great green pasture in the sky at about 12 to 15 weeks). At this precise moment I did not care. Older sheep though only turn into mutton and I don't think anyone eats that these days so any road kill would not be picked up.

My last trip of the day was via Achnacarnin and onto Stoer Head with its lighthouse; again a rough track road. The car park at Stoer Head is called the walkers car park and there certainly seemed to be a lot of them, with hiking boots, walking sticks, headscarves, silly hats, shorts and maps. Most seemed to be steaming gently in the sunshine; one or two were even lying in the grass taking a snooze.

Achnacarnin, Sutherland (Highland)

Samantha took over for the last twelve miles of my journey and directed me through what I thought was someone's farmyard and then a second one. It would appear that this is crofting country and there are numerous small farms making a living from the sheep and whatever they can grow on the moorland soil. One part of the road had actually disappeared under sand that had blown across from a lovely white beach, where it seemed it was only enjoyed by sheep. Indeed all of the beaches I saw today were hardly used, but if these were anywhere else in the country, especially in the south of England, I'm sure that you would not be able to walk on them as they would be too crowded. These must be the best beaches in the whole of Britain, but no one uses them.

Having not gone to Cape Wrath I was able to arrive at my B&B in Lochinver very early. I wanted to get on top of my emails and also send my blog from yesterday. Last night's B&B had a good WiFi expander but a not very efficient router and so it was almost impossible to get and keep a connection. However, when I reached the house where I was staying, I found a notice on the door to say that the owner had gone shopping to Ullapool, the nearest town 37 miles away and would not be back until 5.00pm!

The battery was dead in my computer, so there was nothing for it but to have a cup of tea at a small café in the village and see if I could plug in. There was no Wi-Fi at the café so I decided to sit outside and enjoy the sun. Here I met a German girl who, entirely on her own, had decided to take a cycling holiday in Scotland. She had a tent and a fairly heavily loaded bike, but said that she did not find the hills too bad. She was now on the west coast of Scotland and was due to take a ferry home from the east coast in only four days time. I have never been much of a cyclist, the road surface always looked too hard if I were to fall off, which I probably would. I'm sure though that today my legs, my lungs and indeed my bottom would not be up to the task. I did wonder later whether any Dutch cyclists ever came to Scotland. I saw lots of Dutch registered camper vans, but I would think that hills, even small ones, might be off-putting for someone from the Netherlands.

I returned to the B&B at 4.30pm and eventually there were seven of us sitting on the front step waiting for our host to arrive. When he did get there, I was given a lovely single room overlooking the water, but it was hot, hot, hot. Temperature at 8.00pm was 22 degrees and no wind. The room was stifling. I took dinner in a local restaurant. I had Teuchter chicken. I had no idea what a Teuchter was, but thought it must be meaningful as the next door B&B had the same name. I later looked it up and it is apparently an old, somewhat offensive, Gaelic word used by lowland Scots to describe the

Highlanders. It means something like the English equivalent of an uncouthed country yokel or bumpkin. As a dish, it was chicken stuffed with whiskey infused haggis and covered with pancetta. Very nice and definitely a Scottish dish and I did not care whether it was from high or low lands.

Lochinver is a very small village prettily situated at the top of Loch Inver. It is apparently the second largest fishing port in Scotland with most boats being French or Spanish, though there were few boats in port when I visited.

For what reason I cannot tell, they had two Severn Class RNLI lifeboats, tied together in the harbour. Possibly one is en route to somewhere else, or maybe one is broken and the other is a replacement. Certainly I could not see any other real justification for having two £3 million boats sitting idly together in a quiet sea Loch.

Tomorrow I hope to get away early and reach the Kyle of Lochalsh from where I then expect to drive over the sea to Skye.

Lochinver, Sutherland (Highland)

Lochinver to Kyle of Lochalsh

Miles 214

The Summer Isles from Reiff, Ross-shire

Today proved to be a long day of some fairly tough driving, through incredibly beautiful scenery. I traveled on roads that really should have quotation marks around the word "road". Weather has been perfect once again. It was 18 degrees centigrade at 7.00am and reached 27 degrees by lunchtime. The scenery continued to be jaw dropping and at the same time varied, from moorland and mountain to sea and islands. I today found an animal even dumber than a sheep!

Though I had a nice room and a nice view and a terrific breakfast, I did not get a good night's sleep as my B&B was too hot. Actually at breakfast time I found that the radiators were on and the owner, Cathel, had not realised this. Still on winter setting! In times past Scottish houses only focused on how to heat them. Global warming is happening in Lochinver!

On paying my bill I was asked for a price higher than quoted to me over the phone when I booked it. I spoke up and Cathel immediately gave me the quoted price. He said that he has begun asking more when only one guest is in a room – but I was in a single anyway. Interestingly the previous day the same thing happened when I went to pay, but there the lady of the house insisted that she had quoted me the price she was charging. Perhaps her Scottish accent had fooled me, or is it just the canny Scots! She had very kindly allowed me to put dirty laundry in her washing machine and then she dried it and put it into my room. She said she would have to charge for this, so no doubt that was "the extra" in the bill.

The road out of Lochinver to Ullapool is a single track with passing places, but I was able to make good time when I left this morning. I soon passed into the County of Wester Ross and again there was good signage for the coastal route. Initially the road was in a treed valley, but then it became moorland and high hills, though still with views of the ocean and the islands.

I continued on around the coast coming eventually to the final point at Reiff. Here there is the most beautiful view across to the Summer Islands and being full summer, they did not disappoint.

Ullapool and Loch Broom, Ross-shire

I had to backtrack to return to the Ullapool road. Ullapool is really a village rather than a town. It is not very old being founded only in 1788 as a herring port. It is now a major tourist place due to its generally good weather, courtesy of the Gulf Stream. I stopped and had a look in the camping shop here and considered buying a tent and sleeping mat, however their stock was all very serious stuff and I did not feel that the expense of buying this gear for perhaps only a couple of nights of camping was going to be worth it.

After Ullapool I continued on towards Gairloch. The road follows the east bank of Loch Broom before coming into wooded areas at the bottom of the Loch and then taking a right to travel behind a low mountain and on to Little Loch Broom. After this Loch you come to Gruinard Bay, with Gruinard Island ahead of you and the ocean. The road then follows over a small peninsula and on to Loch Ewe at the small village of Aultbea. Though not a large place Aultbea has both a distillery and a NATO base, with the occasional warship coming in here to refuel. A hotel in the village once won the award of the best Whiskey Hotel in the World, because of the wide range it stocked.

The little village of Poolewe at the head of Loch Ewe was delightful. It seemed to be built along the stream running into the Loch rather than facing the Loch itself. It reminded me of a Dartmoor village. It had an excellent looking campsite. It also has a hotel and I understand an indoor heated swimming pool. Nearby are the sub-tropical gardens of Inverewe, potentially indicating that this area has a very mild climate.

I continued on to Gairloch. A distance of only about five miles, but across what I would describe as a peninsular dividing Loch Ewe from Loch Gairloch.

Gairloch is also on the Gulf Stream, which positively impacts its climate. I noticed quite a few jellyfish in the water here. Gairloch is again a small town, but like them all, neat, clean and tidy. It looked lovely in the sunlight but I have to wonder what these places are like in the winter because they are all quite remote. I understand that the winters are mild, which is a way of saying it rains a lot. They get little snow. It has a smart Tourist Information Office that was hosting a local craft day when I was there. They also had very clean free toilets and a notice board with a list of B&Bs in the town. I wish all towns had these.

My temperature gauge was now reading 25 degrees and there was hardly a cloud in the sky. I continued along an inland road for about twenty miles, which followed the southern side of Loch Maree. Loch Maree empties, via the small river at Poolewe into Loch Ewe and the sea. Loch Maree was itself at one time also called Loch Ewe, hence the name of the town at the head of the Loch being Kinlochewe. Here I turned right and followed the road back towards the coast again, driving through Glen Torridon, with spectacular mountains, and on to Loch Torridon and then to Shieldaig.

Shieldaig is a tiny place. Its' name comes from the Vikings and means Loch of Herrings. Loch Sheildaig is quite a protected Loch, almost a nook off Loch Torridon. No doubt it is a great place to spawn (if you are a herring of course).

Just past Shieldaig you turn off on to the coastal road to Applecross, 25 miles away. A guest at the B&B in Lochinver told me that the road into Applecross is the most difficult in Scotland and she would not dare drive on it, but I had no choice if I was to complete my coastal journey.

Applecross is a small settlement, in an idyllic setting on the coast facing the Isles of Skye. It has become famous in recent years because of a BBC television program following Monty Hall, an outdoorsman, as he lived here for six months and tried to adapt to a crofting life.

The road certainly proved challenging and was the narrowest that I had yet been on. It twisted and turned and went up steeply and down equally as steeply, usually with two or three bends at a time. It looked as if it had been tarmacked at some time, but it must have been in the days of very small cars because you run with your wheels very close to coming off the road on either side, onto rocks or gravel – or nothing! The few vehicles I met all were driven very carefully and politely but one of us had to pull off the road to let the other pass.

Despite the difficulties of the drive the scenery is breathtaking and if you have gotten the courage to journey this road, then the sheer beauty of the place will reward your bravery as you drive along the southern boundary of Loch Torridon.

Kenmore, Loch Torridon

Looking down onto Loch Torridon you can see a number of aquatic farms close to Arrina. Some are obviously for salmon, but others look like shell fish farms. We have these of course in BC, however there is an ill informed outcry against them, with a lot of emotion that says farming is damaging to the natural environment. Here in Scotland people are much more sensible, or is it that they are just more pragmatic.

Clearly it is only brave travelers who use this road. If you were a driver from North America your heart would be in your mouth for the next twenty miles. I wondered whether the motor home drivers knew what this road would be like before driving their vehicles here? Once committed though, you can't change your mind as there is nowhere to turn around. Many a time an oncoming vehicle and I had to maneuver, as the passing places were not always wide enough. I also wondered how the locals got on with shopping, living out here in the wilds, as they would have to face this road on a regular basis. Around a corner the answer became clear. There was a Tesco home delivery van (parked off the road in one of the few wide areas, having a coffee). "Just click and we'll deliver" it said on the side of the van. Do the Tesco delivery drivers get paid extra for having to drive these hazardous roads? If they don't I hope the inhabitants give them a good tip. I'm sure the people in Applecross at least all say "Thank God for Tesco".

It was on a flatter section of this road, high up and looking across to Skye, when I came across the animals that are dumber than sheep – Highland cattle! There were about a dozen of them milling around the road with two of them standing in the middle of the road and incredibly three of them actually lying down in the road, no doubt soaking up the heat from the road surface. There were about three cars stopped in each direction, all wanting to get past, but in the end most of us got out and took pictures of them. Revving the engine did no good but one driver, oblivious of his paint work slowly drove up to them and nudged them out of the way, helped by his wife, walking in front, trying to shoo them. I actually remember years ago when I used to help a friend in Gloucestershire with his farm that, in bad weather, we would drive the cows home from the field for milking with the Land Rover rather than on foot. Ah the old ways are still the best!

Dropping down into Applecross provides a spectacular view across to Skye. There is also a fantastic beach on which people were walking. Noticeable was that this beach had sand blown half way up the cliff and was being piled up as if dunes were starting to form. I think this shows the power of the sea here when a storm comes through and how the waves must crash, driving the sand with it.

Highland Cattle sunning themselves, Applecross

The next beach strangely enough appeared to be all rock, but the one in the village centre was again sand, this time pink in colour. The tide was a long way out and the beach seemed huge. I stopped in the car park and used their very clean unisex toilets putting a donation in the box. I then brewed a cup of tea, enjoyed a slice of ginger cake (an earlier Tesco purchase) and sent a selfie to my wife to show her that I was still alive.

Then, oh boy, the drive out of Applecross! Very nervous drivers should not attempt the road that I took in, but even very bold drivers can be reduced to a quivering wreck by the road out. It is much narrower than the other road, has very steep inclines and also steep gradients, with switch back bends and blind corners. It also has incredible drop-offs which seem to want to "pull you" towards them. It is signposted as not being passable in the winter, but it is only just passable in the summer! I thought back to the lady in my Lochinver B&B who had talked about the awful road into Applecross. I thought that it must have been the one I drove in on, but now I think this is the one she meant! However I did it, along with perhaps 50 other vehicles (all going the other way) who must have been as naïve as me when they set out. I saw no accidents, or even dead cars in the deep gulleys, so perhaps it is much safer than it looks.

The road out of Applecross, Wester Ross

There were lots of motorbikes on the road. Motorcyclists seem to enjoy these sorts of roads and all of them were driving sedately. There was one MG sports car that had boiled on one of the steep hills. And of course there were the white van drivers (3 of them) plus 2 Porsche drivers who under no circumstances were willing to pull over at the passing places. They were all traveling in the same direction, so nothing happened as far as I am aware, but if Porsche driver had met white van man coming the other way, I wonder who would have won the stand off. Apart from these idiots, everyone seemed very jolly as people often do when sharing the same dangerous experience. I got down the mountain safely and felt very proud of myself. Just as I got to the wider road at the bottom I met, coming toward me, a large tractor with a mechanical excavator attached at the front, plus an even larger furniture removal truck following behind the tractor. How they would ever get to Applecross I do not know? Certainly I don't think anyone else coming down the mountain would be able to get past them. I obviously made it out just in time.

I then followed the road towards my destination at Kyle of Lochalsh about 30 miles further on, following for about half the distance alongside the southern edge of Loch Carron.

Having come from Applecross you are fooled into thinking this is now an easy road, but strangely it has areas where the two lanes suddenly go into a single track for about 100 yards and there is little warning of this. It must catch drivers out. The worst point is a tunnel that seems wide enough for only one car and you are blind, until right onto it, as to what might be coming through the other way.

Just 5 minutes out from Kyle of Lochalsh (at 5.00pm) I received a text from my B&B host to say that her husband was delayed and would not be at the B&B until 7.15pm. As I had planned to be there by 5.30pm to write my notes and sort my photos, I was more than a bit miffed. If this had not been past the AirBnB deadline for cancelling and there were other options, I would have driven on. But, 214 miles on narrow roads is enough for me today

About five miles out of Kyle of Lochalsh, at the junction where I was to turn right, I saw a sign for Eilean Donan castle to the left. Eilean Donan castle is considered an icon of Scotland. This is the castle that often appears in those wonderful moody shots of the Scottish Highlands, sitting on a small island in a Loch. I had not realised it was in this area and so it provided me with an excellent distraction.

Unfortunately once again the tide was out when I arrived, which would have made for a better photograph and though an island at certain times, today it seemed joined to the mainland. The ticket office had just closed but it was possible to walk around the walls.

The castle was the seat of the MacCrae clan but was destroyed by British ships in 1719 in putting down a failed Jacobite uprising, involving also the Spanish. It remained as a ruin until 1919 when Lt. Col. John MacCrae-Gilstrap began to restore it, completing it in 1932. It now contains, on the outside, a shrine to all of the soldiers named MacCrae (of all spelling variations) from Britain, Canada, Australia and New Zealand who died in the First World War. There are a lot of names.

Ruined castles are such a feature of Britain, but here you find what can be done with them if they are restored to their former glory. I am all for history and love visiting the ruins but would prefer to see many of them restored as much as possible and brought back into daily use and open to the public. There have been numerous occasions when an appeal has gone out for multiple millions to save a piece of artwork from being sold overseas. I think the money could sometimes be better spent on restoring a historic castle and thus provide wider public access and appeal. I know that it is not as simple as that, but it would be great to see many of Britain's castles restored or at least brought up to somewhat of a habitable state.

Eilean Donan Castle, Kyle-of-Lochalsh

I went to a pub in the local village to have an early supper while waiting for the B&B to be available. Scotland beats England hands down on spectacular scenery and neat and tidy towns, however, England definitely has the edge in respect of cosy, good food pubs. Of the four pubs that I have been to so far in Scotland, all were dark and dreary inside and hark back to the days when they were men only places to drink. The one I went to tonight, like the one in John O' Groats, had a pool table in the middle. Drinking is still a big thing here in Scotland (and sadly is becoming an increasing problem in England, especially binge drinking). An NHS report issued just last week stated that the average person in Scotland drinks each year the equivalent of 41 bottles of vodka, or 166 bottles of wine or 477 pints of beer. That's almost one bottle of vodka a week or 3 bottles of wine or 9 pints of beer per week. Considering that this is the

241

average across all persons in Scotland, it must mean that some individuals are drinking way more than this!

At the pub and also at the car park for the castle, were a lot of assorted vehicles of the RAF Mountain Rescue Service. The names on the sides of the vehicles suggested that they had come from all over Scotland. I assumed that they were gathering for a conference or a training exercise. It might seem odd to some that the RAF provide mountain rescue teams, rather than the army or local civilian groups. However, the organisation goes back to the beginning of aviation when teams were formed to go into the mountains to try and rescue pilots who had crashed. Today they continue as the main mountain rescue organisation, particularly where aircraft are involved. The Scottish teams were heavily involved in the search for victims of PanAm 103, which was blown out of the sky over Lockerbie in 1988 by a terrorist bomb.

I arrived at my AirBnB booked house at 7.15pm and found a young German couple also waiting. The husband at the B&B, who would be looking after things, was still not there. He eventually arrived at 7.45pm, just as I was thinking of leaving. Frankly the house was old, musty, dirty and decaying. AirBnB always ask for feedback on the property and the host, however in this case no such request was sent to me, but I would have had lots of comments to give them. One being, remarkably, that the house in the photograph looked nothing like the one we are staying in!

Out of the mouth of babes comes the truth. The young daughter let out to me that she had been out on a birthday treat with her father and they were having a meal and not held up by traffic or other reasons. Why then the need to lie and why also only notify me at 5.00pm that he was delayed? I think that this is the difference between a "proper" B&B and an AirBnB property. In the case of the former it is their business and they (generally) care about it. In the case of the latter it is just a way of making extra money. My host for tonight stated that they own an adventure business in Sri Lanka and are only in Scotland for 6 months. Hence no doubt the reason for the dilapidated and dirty home they had offered for people to stay in.

Tomorrow I am set to tour Skye, of which the relatively new bridge across to the island is only about five minutes from where I am staying. I will spend tomorrow circumnavigating the island and then will take a ferry across to Mallaig in the afternoon, though I have yet to find accommodation for the night.

I today passed 2300 miles. My journey plan says that I will be traveling 4600 miles in total so I am now exactly half way (possibly)!

Kyle of Lochalsh to Strontian (via Isle of Skye)

Miles 204

Over the Sea to Skye

I had never before been to the Isle of Skye so I chose to make this part of my outer coast drive and miss of some of the inner coast that the Island covers. I could also have gone to the Outer Hebrides, but this would have added a further 2 days at least and also did not really cover off any of the mainland. It would be an indulgence too far on a trip of this length.

I was glad to leave my musty B&B, who contacted me later to say that according to AirBnB I was booked for a second night and they realised that I was not staying. This probably happened when trying to book over the internet using the AirBnB app at the previous B&B. The internet crashed while I was trying to book and I started again, but it must have picked up both bookings. However, I would have thought it would have been two bookings for the same night rather than for a second night. I will need to find a café on Skye with WiFi and go on line and cancel the booking, but I am not sure that AirBnB will give me a refund. If they do not then they can take a hike as far as any future business from me!

Anyway, on to Skye. The (fairly) new bridge was a lot shorter in length than I had imagined, I was across in a couple of minutes. The previous ferry journey from Kyle could not have taken more than five minutes. I had always assumed that Skye was quite some distance from the mainland. It still is of course if you travel from other parts of Scotland by ferry but somehow, this short bridge took away a lot of the magic that I had been expecting. I would imagine that the bridge has made a huge difference to the economy on Skye, especially tourism and also house prices close to the bridge. Commuting should be possible though I'm not sure where you would commute to for a job as Inverness is about 80 miles from the bridge.

The first thing I noticed on coming onto the island was the high number of B&Bs with their signs outside. With internet bookings these signs are quickly becoming a thing of the past. Anyway I did not see one all day that had "vacancies" on their sign, so business is clearly booming. If I had pressed on last night, as I was tempted to do when my host did not turn up on time, I would have had a bleak time trying to find a bed.

The view from Skye back to the mainland and over to the islands of Scalpay and Raasay, was incredible. Unfortunately there was quite a haze over the ocean (it was 21 degrees at 9.00am) that photos were not especially dramatic.

My objective was to do a loop around the north of the island, to the furthest point, and then drop down and cross over to the western spur of the island, circle this and then go on to Armadale and catch the ferry over to Mallaig a distance of around 130 miles.

The road to Portree, the main town on the island, takes you up through a wide pass with very large mountains ahead. Once again these mountains are high and are just rock faced for their final third. The ground below is mainly moorland.

Old Man Of Storr, Isle of Skye

Eventually I arrived at Portree, which is a really pretty little harbour town. This has B&Bs and small hotels overlooking the working harbour. All had no vacancy signs and I could see why; it is beautiful. I took a walk along the harbor and saw a man unloading an old red Royal Mail van (though it had been painted you could still see the Royal Mail livery underneath). He was handing creels of some sort down to a colleague standing in a fishing boat. This person was throwing in some bait, plus breaking up an unidentified shellfish and adding this as well. Then the creel was stacked at the back of the boat. All were tied together so he was careful how he stacked them. When they would be thrown over the side of the boat they would pay out one after the other so they should not tangle. It seemed unusual though that these were being taken, already tied together, out of the back of a van. I asked the first guy how many creels they had. "Don't know" he said. "However many I could get in the van." "What are you fishing for" I then asked. "Wrass" he said, although I had to ask him twice as his accent was difficult to attune to. I then asked his partner, in the boat, "How long do you leave them out, once set". He looked up at me and laughed. "Haven't a clue" he replied. "We've never done this before. It'll be our first time out." I wished them luck!

Looking back after having toured the whole island I think that Portree is probably the prettiest place on Skye; a little bit like a Cornish fishing village.

My next stop was at Staffin, as I needed to find WiFi so I could contact AirBnB and cancel the room booked in error. I saw a café sign and found myself in the Columba 1400 Centre. This is a charitable organisation that seeks to help youth at the crossroads time of their lives, late teens, early twenties. They particularly focus on young people who have dropped out of education or had difficult backgrounds. They come to Skye, or their other site at Loch Lomond and spend a week in the classroom and then outdoors building their confidence and being helped to understand that they can achieve more than they might have believed they could.

Portree, Isle of Skye

As I mentioned earlier at age 18, I went on an Outward Bound course at Burghead This was more militaristic and outdoorsy focused, or so it seems, than Columba 1400. However at Columba 1400, after attending the one week course, there is then regular follow up, which Outward Bound did not do. At the time I felt glad only that I had survived, but I certainly realised (after I got home) how much I had enjoyed it and indeed over the years I'm certain that I have benefitted from it. I hope these youngsters who attend Columba 1400 do so too. I'm glad that my coffee money is being used for a good cause. The WiFi worked and AirBnB did let me cancel the erroneous booking.

As I left Staffin, for the top point of the island, some of the romance and "Scottishness" of Skye was rubbed off! I passed a nice looking bungalow named Graceland. Outside there were two large, green, professionally made signs. One was made to look as if it was a street sign and said 'Elvis Presley Boulevard' and the other stated in very large letters 'We will always love you'. This all seemed very much out of place on the Isle of Skye. I really wanted to go and knock on the door and see who answered it. Would the person be dressed in a silver sequined jump suit opened down to the waist and talk with a pseudo southern drawl? I wonder if they knew that Elvis had died sitting on the toilet, his heart giving out as he was straining due to constipation through overuse of narcotics. Not quite so romantic an image!

This must have really had an effect on me because I later found myself singing an Elvis song, but with a Scottish accent. This then changed to an impression of Elvis singing 'Donald Where's Your Trusers'. This was a very old old song (of my Father's era!) by an artist called Andy Stewart, about a man from the Isle of Skye who went to London and the girls laughed at him for wearing a kilt rather than trousers!

At the top of the island I walked to view a cairn that had been erected to memorialise the MacCrimmon pipers who were the hereditary pipers to the chiefs of the MacLeod Clan. Shame there was no one there actually playing the pipes. I do love their haunting sound.

Having photographed the northern tip of the Island and obviously feeling lonely just singing to myself, I noticed a young man with a backpack who was hitching a lift. When he spoke I thought he was French, but it turned out that he was a student of architecture visiting from Quebec. Those Canadians get everywhere (and not just the geese). He was hitching to a campsite at Uig about 15 miles further along my loop.

This should have been a quick journey, but once again we had cattle in the road, this time being herded by a farmer. He seemed happy to allow the cattle to graze the grass on the side of the road and you can therefore imagine the traffic build up that occurred either side of this moving road bloc. As this was again a single-track road with passing places and the passing places were now all full up with cars, I was concerned as to how traffic would be able to pass and clear itself once the cattle had been put into a new field. We were car number two from our side and were only just able, mirrors folded, to squeeze by when the cattle had gone.

After dropping my hitchhiker off at Uig where his campsite was located, I followed the coastal trail and started on my final loop of the western spur of Skye. Unfortunately it now started to rain quite heavily and blurred any view, which was mainly of moor and mountain. To amuse myself I tried out my Scottish accents and I think I made a discovery about how the different accents vary across Scotland. I found that, at least the way I spoke the words, the east coast accent is caused by speaking from the top and back of the mouth near the nasal passage, with the tongue arched up. Whereas the softer western accent is spoken by keeping the upper lip still and annunciating the words from the bottom of the mouth at the front inside the lower jaw with the tongue in a u shape. It seems to work for me!

I began my final loop in Skye at Borvie turning up towards Dunvegan. The castle here has for over 800 years been the ancestral home of MacLeod of the MacLeods the chief of the Macleod Clan. It is the oldest continuously inhabited castle in Scotland. As it was raining and I wanted to get to the ferry, I decided not to stop. As I drove past, a car beeped his horn at me and it turned out to be the young German couple from the B&B. They had just come out of the castle, which they described as fantastic. It is apparently full of memorabilia of Bonnie Prince Charlie who took refuge on the Island after the defeat at Culloden. Although dating from the 13th century the castle was remodeled in the 19th century as a (mock) medieval castle, which it really isn't.

The road from Dunvegan runs alongside a sea loch until turning back across the island at Drynoch. At Sligachan I returned to the road from Kyle along Raasay Sound, before turning south toward Ardvasar and Armadale and the ferry. This part of the journey was quite uninteresting.

When I got closer to the ferry terminal at Armadale, so the sun came out again. With the sun came my luck as well. I was booked on a 4.30pm ferry but when I got there, the 2.30pm had not yet left due to exceptionally low tides at the moment. They agreed to let me on (I was the last car) so I got to Mallaig around 3.00pm rather than the 5.00pm I was expecting. The ferry journey is only half an hour but this ferry has a bar, a simple restaurant and a shop.

Mallaig is not an old town and dates back only to 1840 when the local Laird encouraged his tenants to move west and take up fishing. When the railway arrived in 1901 it expanded rapidly and in the 1960s became the biggest herring port in Europe. It is now mainly a ferry terminal and tourist town. The train journey from Mallaig to Fort William and Oban was voted the best train journey in the world in 2009.

From Mallaig the journey to my B&B at Strontian was about 50 miles. I chose this place simply because it was the only vacancy I could find that was close enough for me to visit Ardnamurchan Point in the morning and then catch a ferry to the Isle of Mull, where I will stay tomorrow night.

Immediately outside of Mallaig I found a lovely beach and so stopped and made myself a cup of tea. For those of you who know me you will realize that just because I am traveling does not mean I should not drink tea properly. I have a stove for boiling fresh water, a kettle (with a whistle), a china teapot and a china cup. The water boils in less than four minutes so it is all very quick. I even had a piece of ginger bread with it (bought at Tescos 2 days ago).

Eigg and Rum from Arisaig, Inverness-shire

The road on from here became another coastal route and at one stage, for a few miles, I was driving right alongside the beach. There was a great view across to Skye and the islands with the wonderful names of Eigg and Rum. There is a third island, not visible from here, called Muck. The Isle of Muck is currently advertising for a teacher for its school, which has only seven pupils; a good job for someone who might like life off the beaten track.

The main road out of Mallaig, though classified as an A road, is once again, single track with passing places. It is a bit wider than others I have traveled, so as long as I kept a good look out, I made good time.

I stopped once at a small community café at Glenuig where I read on their notice board that the locals had formed a Development Corporation, (based on their post code) so as to access government funding and grants, plus raise other monies, in order to buy up local land when available and build low cost housing. This was being done expressly to allow young people to be able to remain in the area. At the moment, due to the plethora of houses being bought for B&Bs, the housing stock is becoming limited and expensive. I thought that this was an enterprising way of maintaining their community and helping to ensure its longer-term survival.

One joy on being back on the mainland, indeed being back in Britain, is BBC Radio 4. The news and comment is so good, the programs are varied from current affairs, to plays and there are good quiz and comedy programs. Today I began to enjoy the program "A Good Read" where the guests were two ex-television newsreaders talking about their favourite books. One of them said that his favourite book was Bill Bryson's "Notes From A Small Island". Great I thought, let's hear what they think about someone traveling around the UK and making comments on the British people. At that precise moment the radio went silent! Most radio in Britain is now broadcast digitally and my car is fitted with a digital radio. Unfortunately the mountainous terrain spoils the signal. It does not just crackle, as it did in the old days when you could still hear the program through the crackle, now it just goes to silence. As sod's law operates, when the signal came back, the program was just wrapping up and they were thanking the guests for their comments. Anyway we all know that Bill wrote (now two) excellent books and mine is not intended to compete with his.

Finally after a lot of twists and turns and searching in hills and woods I found my B&B for the night, a very nice place, deep in the country. The couple who have taken it over have only owned it for 3 weeks and their internet has broken so it could be a quiet night. I went out to dinner at the local Community Centre, which served meals in the evening and breakfast and lunch in the day. How enterprising and what tremendous community spirit. They also had good WiFi.

Tomorrow I hit the west cardinal point at Ardnamur-chan Point and then it is on to Mull to look up my royal ancestor on the adjacent island of Iona.

Strontian to Isle of Mull

Miles 204

Mist over Loch Sunnart, Highlands

Today I had hoped to achieve two of my objectives for the trip. First was to visit my (third) cardinal point at Ardnamurchan Point, the most westerly point of the UK mainland. Of special importance to me though was the second objective, to travel to the Island of Iona, a very spiritual place and find the grave of a notable ancestor, King Macbeth! The day did not go quite as planned.

My B&B in Strontian was the best so far on this trip. The young couple who are running it moved from Edinburgh just three weeks ago to fulfill their life long dream. I woke up to a glorious sunny morning with wonderful views across lovely countryside to the hills. My breakfast was excellent with fresh duck eggs. I had actually never tasted duck's eggs before, but they were rich and mouthwatering. If given the choice I would not go back to chicken's eggs, though no doubt I will have to.

I think this B&B and one of the others I have stayed in, shows up the difference between those people who are committed to running a good business and know how important it is to make guests feel welcome, and those people who advertise a room via AirBnB. The latter are often just doing it as an opportunity to make extra money rather than intending it be a way of life. This means that an Air B&B booking will always be a bit hit & miss for me to use it regularly. The older couple I stayed with in Inverness probably came from a generation that really made a fuss of visitors to a home and sought to make them feel comfortable, so I had a pleasant stay. My AirBnB experience in Kyle of Lochalsh was, by contrast, awful. In this case the couple lived out of the country for 6 months of the year and this was their way of giving themselves an income while in the UK. They had a musty, damp house and probably saw their guests as a one off so what did it matter.

As I am writing this, quite coincidentally, an email has just come into my Inbox from AirBnB. It is urging me to see AirBnB as a way to 'earn extra money during the busy holiday season'. Exactly my point, so, very good timing. This is what people respond to; the chance to make some extra money, but the experience for the traveller is not necessarily a good one if the focus is only on making money from them.

I left my hosts at around 8.30am, closing the gate at the end of the drive to keep out the deer that will eat their garden, and other animals that might take a liking to their ducks and hens. The road was the narrow one that I came in on last night. The view across Loch Sunnart with the mist rising was beautiful, but I did not realise that this was a portent of what was to come. I had to turn off onto another road to now make my way to Ardnamurchan Point and then to the ferry at Kilchoan across to Mull. This road was quite literally a coastal road about 25 miles long. I followed the edge of the Loch for quite a long way and then the coast. Drive this road on an icy winter's day and you could possibly end up in the Loch if you are not careful!

The new road was designated a B road as opposed to the previous A road. This meant it was about 2 inches narrower. It was also a beautiful drive and both sides of the road were covered in gorgeous flowering rhododendrons.

I stopped to take a photograph of Glen Borrodale castle. A lovely red bricked building. The gates were closed and had a sign saying "Private, Trespassers do so at their own risk". I had to wonder whether this was a legal get out in case somebody impaled themselves on the railings surrounding the grounds, or, was it more of a threat that an angry Laird or his gamekeeper might claim they mistook the trespasser for a wild stag and shot them!

One thing that did strike me was the number of properties with For Sale signs along this road. No doubt people find these idyllic places on a warm summer day, but then discover how bad the winters are and that friends and family possibly wont visit at these times. If you are a gregarious person then these properties are certainly not for you. You have to be a very private person like the Laird at Glen Borrodale castle.

About 5 miles from Kilchoan you move out again into mountain and moorland. On entering the village I went to the Visitors Information Centre to enquire of the lady at the desk as to how long would I need to be at the ferry dock to be sure of catching a ferry. "Well normally only about 20 minutes, but today you have all these other people ahead of you". She pointed to the coffee area where there must have been about 30 people waiting. "The ferry is not running just now because of the fog".

I sighed, but was not too bothered, as I still had to go to Ardnamurchan Point and therefore expected the fog to have burned off when I returned. I drove on to the lighthouse, which is about a five-mile drive on a very poor road. The sun was out and it was 19 degrees so I relaxed and enjoyed the drive with the window open.

Road to Ardnamurchan, Highlands

Just before you get to the lighthouse there is a traffic light that permits traffic to safely traverse the 400 or so yards along a narrow, tight, walled road that hugs the cliff edge. It is a long red light, no doubt to give time to those people on bicycles or foot to pass safely. The light turned green and off I set.

At the end was a café but no lighthouse! It was obscured in the fog. I decided to have a coffee and see if the fog cleared. It continued to swirl around but there was a small break sufficient for me to take a photo in the murk just to prove I was there. However, I then purchased a post card and photographed that so I could see what it would look like if there were no fog! My sister had told me about the fabulous beach at Sunna Bay just past the lighthouse. Unfortunately nothing could be seen of it, but I will accept her word that in the sunshine it is beautiful.

I hurried back to the ferry in the hope that I might just about make it for the 11.45am run. No doubt you are ahead of me at this point. No ferry, just thick sea fog on the water.

At 1.00pm the ferry from Mull, arrived at the dock, so we all got excited. However, they then determined that the fog was still thick in mid channel and announced that we would wait until 2.30pm to see if it cleared. I asked the Purser, who was advising us, as to why, with radar, they don't just sail, especially as the docks on either side are clear. He said that they are worried about hitting any rubber boats in the channel that do not have radar reflectors. They want full visibility. I think BC Ferries do a better job in this respect. Though our local collision regulations require all vessels to have radar reflectors fitted a rubber boat might not have space to fit one. But BC ferries run anyway!

I began talking to a couple from Yorkshire who were driving a vintage Jaguar XK120. They were touring the Highlands, but the car broke down in Elgin and they thought that their holiday was over. They checked into their B&B and enquired about a breakdown truck or something that could take the car back to Yorkshire, while they caught the train. Their hostess said "Let's ask Hamish (or some such Scottish name). He's just a few doors away and into old cars and he might be able to help you". They went to see Hamish to find that he was a vintage car nut and had 4 E types in his garage! They wheeled in his XK120 and Hamish diagnosed a blown exhaust valve in one cylinder. The Yorkshire couple thanked him for his diagnosis and said they would arrange to have the car recovered and they would need to order the parts. "Wheesh" (a Scottish expression) said Hamish, "I've got a valve kit up in my loft and the gaskets. Your engine is the same as in the E type so I keep some spares. If you help me out we can get it fixed and have you back on the road." Together they spent a day and a half repairing the engine and they were then off again on their vacation. What are the chances of breaking down in a rare vintage car, right where there is someone with a full set of spares and the ability to fix it? The man was still in amazement as he told me the story.

Lochaline to Mull Ferry arrives

On the subject of cars, the ferry dock at Lochaline has an electric car charging point. I was surprised to see this as I have not seen one electric car during the whole of my trip and also this ferry dock is literally in the middle of nowhere. I dare say it was what one might call "political expenditure" to show the world just how green Caledonian MacBrayne ferries are!

At 2.30pm the decision was made to wait until 3.30pm! We continued to sit in the sun and could see Mull quite clearly. A different crewmember told me that the ferry does not have a rudder so it steers by a propeller on each corner. He said it can turn on a dime, but the skipper does not want to enter the fog bank without a rudder. Me thinks they have decided to have a crafty afternoon off and sit and top up their sun tans! The alternative is to drive back for 51 miles along the single-track roads and take a different ferry across to Mull. I was not though in the mind set to make that decision and retrace my steps on that narrow road.

I had noticed a white van drive onto the dock a little earlier and the driver was passing boxes too and fro with a fishing boat that had come in to the wharf. I went up to see what they were doing and chatted to them. Apparently the white van driver was collecting fresh caught Langoustines from the fishing boat crew. He was then going to drive 240 miles to Eyemouth, near to Berwick On Tweed, where they then ship them to Spain and France. Indeed if you eat Lobster or Langoustines anywhere in the Mediterranean you are almost certainly eating ones from Scotland. Ironically I noticed two restaurants later that both had a sign saying 'Sorry no Lobsters today'. No doubt the fisherman were getting better prices selling them to the Spanish. After Lochaline the driver was then going to two other small harbours to collect shellfish before returning back to Eyemouth. He said that he made this trip every 2 days! I found him to be a very pleasant chap, but some would find his appearance fairly aggressive and off-putting. He had a shaved head, covered in tattoos and at least twelve pieces of metal in various places on his head. Every credit to him if he wants to be an individual. He said that he did not get on with his family or have a wife and this job suited him down to the ground. He seemed a happy guy though and had clearly found his niche. I bet there are a lot of people who are more conformist that are not as happy as he seems to be.

"Gentlemen, start your engines"! Not quite a Le Mans start, but at 3.45pm we were given the go-ahead to start loading and with loud cheers from around the car park, everyone got into their cars and we boarded. There were only 9 cars to go on the ferry (which can hold 10) so there was skepticism expressed by some drivers that the delays might have been for economic reasons, waiting for a full load, as well as the fog. What I found surprising was that they made all passengers get out of the cars and walk on, with only the driver allowed to be in the vehicle as it was parked. I thought that it might be in case the car fell off the ramp, but actually it is because the ferry is quite narrow and it would be difficult for all the car doors to be opened. Once on board the driver also has to leave the vehicle. Again different procedure to the small vehicle ferries in BC.

There was a little bit of fog on the journey but he only sounded his horn twice. Under international Maritime Collision Regulations, you are supposed to make one long blast of the horn every two minutes when under way in fog. You can tell from this therefore that the fog bank was probably not very thick.

We pulled into Tobermory. A delightful little town with coloured buildings facing the water. Based on what I had been told by a cyclist on the ferry, I decided to take the northern coastal loop rather than go directly to my B&B by following the southern road. He had said it was quite short and not a difficult road. Well, it was another one of "those" roads. Though the view was wonderful and the sun very warm, I began to regret my decision as I soon began to feel tired.

West Side of Isle of Mull

The journey was around forty miles in total and at one point I had to drive along a cliff road with a huge drop off and tight bends. I began to pray that I would meet no other vehicle on this section of road. My prayers were fortunately answered. I had met an American couple at the ferry dock, with an unfortunate scrape on their hire car, who were also cursing the narrow roads. I think if anyone showed a video of these roads to people living in North America, none of them would come to Scotland.

The View from my B&B at Pennyghael, Mull

By the time I got to my B&B I was beat. To get Dinner I was told I would have to drive to the only pub, which was 9 miles away. I nearly decided to starve, but as I had had nothing since breakfast, I went there. My comments of yesterday about Scottish pubs were more than amplified by the Argyle Arms at Bunessen; a big old barn of a place, which looked as if it might have been built in the 50s and still had the original paint and wallpaper. The men's loo was probably the foulest one I have seen anywhere on my trip. It looked as if a fight had taken place in there (it probably had) and the remains of one urinal was hanging off the wall. Another man came in and decided he would use the open drain as I was using the only other serviceable piece of porcelain. I mentioned to him how awful I thought this was. He said "Och, it's no so bad. I've seen worse." Apart from French hole in the ground toilets, I think this was the worst toilet I had ever seen.

My B&B looks directly onto the Loch but I have been advised to keep my windows shut as the midges are out in force at the moment. Tomorrow I will go directly to Iona, about 15 miles away. My ferry off the island to Oban is not until early evening so I should have a fairly relaxing day tomorrow. I'm now glad I got the steep and narrow roads done today and don't have to do any tomorrow other than the one of about 15 miles to the ferry dock. Hope I sleep soundly tonight and the midges don't bite.

Isle of Mull to Oban

Miles 60

The Island of Iona

Well today is St. Columba Day, which is a complete coincidence as this is also the day that I go to the Island of Iona where Columba established his monastery. Today has also been somewhat of a day of rest; partly due to ferry bookings and partly as I am feeling fairly frazzled with all of the driving that I decided I needed a day off. I have also decided to abandon my plans of visiting Islay. All of these islands are incredibly beautiful, but there are only so many mountains, sea lochs, single-track roads and sheep that you can take. This will not impact my objective of traveling around Britain by the road closest to the ocean as I will be driving the Mull of Kintyre, the mainland route rather than taking Islay as an outer route.

My B&B last night provided a lovely view across the Loch and breakfast was fresh eggs from the hens wandering around the property. The couple who run this B&B come from the North East of England, with relatives in areas that I have recently visited. They have been on Mull for 16 years, with my hostess originally working as a nurse and a carer for terminally ill patients. Her current job she said is much less emotionally draining.

My B&B for tonight in Oban is another one booked through Air BnB. It looks and sounds very nice, but as I arrived on Iona I had a text saying would I mind moving into a single bed in another room as their current guests wanted to stay for an extra night in the double. On the basis that I thought that this was a cheek and unprofessional and I had paid in advance and that I was needing a good night's sleep and did not want to change, I said no let me have the room I'd booked. I later relented and sent a message to say OK let the other couple have the room. The message I got back was they did not mind moving after all, so, it seems as if we will all be happy, but did they really need to ask me to change and by so doing, irritate me?

On my way to Iona I had to stop for fuel. I drove past the petrol station first time as it did not appear to have any bright signage, or indeed pumps. But, second time around I found a pump, close to a pile of old cars that looked as if they were up for scrap. A friendly man and his even more friendly dog served me. I had a conversation with him, or at least I nodded and smiled as I genuinely could not understand a word he was saying. Maybe his was the local country accent of Mull. I expect all day long he was wondering why this Sassenach just smiled at him and kept nodding his head.

The Abbey on Iona

The Island of Iona is certainly a very peaceful place. It is quiet in that few people live there and there are no cars. Of course four coach loads of tourists all descending by ferry at once does make an impact on the peace of the place. I wandered around slowly and went first of all to St. Oran's Chapel, which is the burial ground alongside the Abbey. I thought that this would give time for the coach parties to view the Abbey and disperse and return for the next ferry and in the gap between I could see the Abbey in peace with few people around.

The history books say that Macbeth is buried in St. Oran's churchyard, which is adjacent to the Abbey. It is said that he lies here with 47 other Kings of Scotland. Unfortunately there are no signs of him or any of the other Kings of Scotland in the cemetery. Over hundreds of years it has been allowed to decay and for any old graves the burial markers have long since disappeared. (Macbeth died in 1057 so almost one thousand years ago). Indeed it is only speculation that royalty is buried here. It is known that noble men of the isles were buried here and it has always been seen as a place of spirituality from the days of St. Columba, with pilgrimages being made, so perhaps it was the Westminster Abbey of its time. However no proof remains, and many of the 48 "Kings" may only have been local nobles rather than full Kings of Scotland. Indeed, from King Kenneth MacAlpin, today recognised as the first King of all of Scotland in 843, to Macbeth, there were only 18 true Kings of Scotland, though others came afterwards. But, whether those buried here were local Kings or rulers of the whole of Scotland, I don't know, but I still would like to think that I had walked where King MacBeth was lying.

I went to the information office and said I was looking for a grave and could they help. "Ah you must be looking for John Smith's grave" the young woman replied.

"Well no, MacBeth actually, he's an ancestor of mine."

"Wow that's great, but I don't know where he is, only that he's in there somewhere."

I searched all over, but the cemetery and gravestones give no clue.

John Smith's grave was prominent though. John Smith was a Labour Party Politician who became Leader of the Labour Party back in the 1980s. He was considered a very honourable and honest man by everyone. He was serving as Chancellor of the Exchequer under the leadership of Neil Kinnock, who all the polls predicted would win the General Election and replace John Major's Conservative government. John Smith was so honest that on the night before the election he gave a speech as to what Labour would do when they came into power. One of things he said they would do would be to raise income tax by 2%. Overnight the electorate reacted to this news and did not vote Labour into power. I suppose this is an example of why politicians are less than frank and are, what is said to be, "economical with the truth".

Sometimes politicians make promises they just cannot keep, but their pledge at election time, to do certain popular things, gets them elected. In the recent Canadian elections, Justin Trudeau was elected, based on who his father was and what he promised to do. However, his first three big promises have all been pulled back on and failed to materialize. So now he has, early into his government, a real credibility problem that may come back to haunt him.

The grave of John Smith is certainly well visited and almost looks as if it is a pilgrimage site. The gravestone lies flat on the ground and is covered with pebbles, coins, flowers etc. and a number of cards. I expect to hear a request for sainthood coming shortly!

I feel that here on Iona, where MacBeth is said to lie, I have need to put a more truer account of my ancestor than that portrayed by Shakespeare. According to Shakespeare, MacBeth was a person driven by a lust for power and urged on by his evil wife, was prepared to kill to take the throne of Scotland. The reality of the history that we now know is very different. Shakespeare is thought to have written the "Scottish Play" in around 1606, just after the Gun Powder Plot. It is thought that it was specifically written to please King James I/VI, who was the Patron of Shakespeare's company and it is said that the introduction of the three witches reflects James' interest in witchcraft. Certainly in 1590 at the Berwick Witch Trials the accused were said to have conducted rituals and cast spells in an attempt to have a storm sink the ship carrying King James and his wife returning on a trip from Denmark. These rituals are similar to those Shakespeare puts in his play.

To fully understand the story of MacBeth, you have to know a little of the history of the Scottish Kings. Kenneth MacAlpin, the first King of Scotland (or Alba) had two sons; Constantine, who succeeded Kenneth and when he died, his brother Aed came to the throne. It is the heirs of both of these men from whence originated the various rivalries that played out over the years that followed.

The succession of Kings at this time was by Tanistry, wherein the heir was not necessarily the eldest son in line but was elected by the Lords from all of the claimants, which could be uncles or cousins. Thus the sons of both Constantine I and Aed had claims of potential succession.

The throne went back and forth between the two brother's lines over the next two hundred years. In 995 Kenneth II, from Constantine's line, tried to move away from tanistry and make his eldest male son the rightful heir. However, he was opposed in this and killed by Cuillen and Amlaib, descendents of Aed who would see their right to the throne being lost. The line from Aed though died out with Constantine II in 1005 when Malcolm II (from the line of Constantine I) came to the throne and he put an end to tanistry. However, he had no sons to inherit from him, so the throne passed down to Duncan I, his grandson, whose mother was the eldest of his three daughters, Bethoc. His two other daughters were Olif and Donada. Olif was married off to Sigurd, Earl of Orkney and their son was Thorfinn, who succeeded his father as Earl of Orkney. Donada was married to Findlaich, Mormaer of Moray and their son was MacBeth.

If this genealogy is correct, not only were MacBeth and Thorfinn both grandsons of Malcolm II but so was King Duncan I, thus all three were cousins.

Most of what is known about Thorfinn comes from the *Orkneyinga Saga*, a history of the Orkneys under Norwegian rule from the ninth century to around 1200. It was written by an unknown Icelander and its historical accuracy is open to question, as the events noted occurred at least two hundred years earlier. Otherwise, written history is almost non-existent and so is open to wide interpretation and confusion of names and places. However, the Saga names Thorfinn the Mighty as Thorfinn Sigurdsson a Christian 11th century Earl of Orkney and ruler of the western highlands. In the Saga he is said to be the grandson of Malcolm II of Scotland, which ties in with the other historical accounts.

Scotland at this time was certainly not, geographically, the nation that we know today and it is likely that the Earls who ruled the west did not see themselves as necessarily subject to one King of Scotland. Indeed Thorfinn paid homage to and recognised King Olaf of Norway as having power over the Orkneys. There are also reports that Thorfinn possibly fought in Fife in support of his grandfather Malcolm II. In 1031 King Canut was in Fife, receiving the submission of King Malcolm II. MacBeth (then Earl of Moray) and a third person "Lehmarc", who it is possible was Thorfinn, was there to confirm to Canut that there would be no threat from the Orkneys.

These were violent times and the various Earls of Scotland, potentially as many as seven of them, were constantly at war with each other and were often called Kings. This was also a time of alliances made and broken and brothers and cousins killing each other. Power struggles were constant and usually the protagonists were related in some way and so fighting could be seen as rooted in family jealousies and in deep-seated arguments, but on a much grander scale.

The story of MacBeth is very much one of these, involving his relatives in both Scotland and in Northumbria. MacBeth's first wife was probably Sybil Bjornsdotter (or Bjorn's daughter) the daughter, or possibly sister, of the King of Northumbia. He possibly married Sybil long before he became King and it may have been one of those marriages of convenience for the sake of uniting lands and retaining power. He does not appear to have had any children with her.

He ruled as an Earl (or Mormaer) in the north west of Scotland around the Moray Firth area and across to the western highlands. The northern areas of Scotland out to the western isles and the east coast of England, down through the Borders and into Northumberland, were ruled by descendants of the Norwegian and Danish Vikings. MacBeth was known as the Red King and it is likely that he had red hair, which is a strong genetic indicator of Viking heritage.

It is now thought that in 1040 MacBeth got into battle with his cousin, King Duncan when Duncan, aided by the Earl of Northumbria, tried to seize some of his lands. MacBeth fought them off and Duncan was killed. Some historians believe that Sybil may have been Duncan's wife and MacBeth took her as a prize after killing Duncan. She is thought to have died within a year of this, As MacBeth had both title and lineage, he took on the role of King, ruling until 1057, when he himself was killed by Duncan's son, Malcolm, who then became Malcolm III.

MacBeth's seventeen-year rule was apparently a time of peace and prosperity in Scotland. His ability to leave Scotland in 1050 and visit the Pope in Rome is suggested as indicative that he was confident that his kingdom would not be invaded in his absence. While in Rome he is said to have given out large sums of money to the poor as a penance for the death of Duncan.

MacBeth had a second wife, the infamous (but only according to Shakespeare) Lady MacBeth, whose name was Gruoch. She was also of royal descent, being a grand daughter of King Kenneth II. Gruoch was a widow when MacBeth married her and she already had a son, Lulach. Her husband had been Gille Coemgain, Mormaer of Moray and also cousin to MacBeth. He was killed in 1032 along with 50 of his men when the building they were in was set on fire. It is thought that this was done by Malcolm II, but some historians say it might even have been perpetrated by MacBeth himself. If the latter is true it could be understandable, as Gille Coemagain had allegedly killed MacBeth's father (thus his own Uncle) in 1020. MacBeth might therefore have married Gille's widow Gruoch, perhaps as a prize, but it is more likely that it was out of a duty of protection to his cousin's widow. This is indeed more probable if it was in fact Malcolm who had killed Gille.

Lady MacBeth was apparently a kind woman and she is credited with starting the first widow's pension. She is said to have offered to provide money and support to the family of any man who was killed in battle fighting for her husband. This also supports her favouring MacBeth as her protector rather than she being his prize.

In 1052 MacBeth was involved in the strife in England between Earl Godwin, Earl of Wessex and Edward the Confessor. From my visit to Hastings you may recall that Edward was married to the daughter of Earl Godwin and it was his son, Harold Godwinson who took the throne, briefly, when Edward died. MacBeth apparently had received a number of Norman exiles from England and this had angered Edward. It may have partly been because of this that Edward encouraged Siward, then Earl of Northumbria, to invade Scotland in 1057. Alongside Siward was Malcolm, the now grown up son of Duncan, who wanted to avenge the death of his father and take the throne that he felt was rightly his. At the time of Duncan's death, Malcolm was only a child. He had fled to Northumbria for safety. Now seventeen years later he was old enough to fight and he wanted the crown.

King MacBeth died after a battle against Malcolm and Siward at Lumphanin, in Aberdeenshire. It is now thought that MacBeth did not die on the battlefield but was seriously wounded and able to escape to his castle at Dunsinane in Fife, near to Scoon. It is here that he died and the remaining Earls gathered at Scoon Palace and quickly crowned his stepson, Lulach as King. Lulach was apparently a gentle soul without leadership abilities. History has dubbed him as "Lulach the Fool" and Malcolm killed him in battle only seven months later and took the throne of Scotland as Malcom III.

It is not clear when or how Thorfinn died, though around 1054 is thought to be the most likely time. On his death, his wife, Ingibiorg is said to have married King Malcolm III and it was their son, Duncan, who later succeeded Malcolm as King, although he died within a year of becoming King. Malcolm III then later married Margaret of Wessex, granddaughter of King Aethelred of England and she became Saint Margaret of Scotland and her grandson became Henry II of England.

So now back to the beautiful Island of Iona. The Abbey here was founded by St. Columba in 563 and the work that he did was instrumental in spreading Christianity across the British Isles. It was one of the monks from this community, St. Aidan, who went to Lindisfarne on Holy Island and founded the community there.

Columba was born in Donegal in Ireland in 521 and trained as a monk. In 563 he came to Scotland. There is some debate as to whether he came willingly or fled following a dispute over a Psalter that he had copied that ended up in a fight with

Celtic Cross, Iona Abbey

another Abbot. The west coast of Scotland at this time was very much an Irish domain and he was given the Island of Iona by an Irish noble. He founded the first Abbey; not the one standing today as his was made of wood and has disappeared. Columba was responsible for the magnificent illustrated Gospels, now known as the Book of Kells. It was made on Iona by the monks, but was taken to Kells for safe keeping from Viking raids in about 840. The Vikings on one occasion raided the Abbey and slaughtered all 68 monks who were there.

When Columba died in 597 his bones were interred in a grave over which a chapel was built. His body was later dug up, after the flesh had decayed and his bones placed in a decorated ossuary to which pilgrims would come and pray. In 849 his bones were removed to Ireland and now reside in Downpatrick. A chapel on the same site still exists.

It seems Ironic that the (one time) Patron Saint of Scotland, Columba, came from Ireland and the Patron Saint of Ireland, Patrick, some suggest, came from Scotland!

Jump a few hundred years and the Abbey is destroyed at the time of the reformation and becomes a ruin. It was the magnanimity of the Duke of Argyle who in the 1960s paid for the Abbey to be rebuilt on the ruins, which is what you see today.

Entry to the Abbey, grounds and museum is a reasonable charge and you get a digital player and head set that provides a very informative guide. On entering the Abbey building you do get an impression of history, although what you see is of course only about fifty years old. Iona is well known for its music and chants. When I entered the Abbey there was a young man playing the organ. Unfortunately he was playing with a headset on (clearly electric and not a pipe organ) and all I could hear was his feet thumping on the pedals. There is nothing quite like entering an Abbey or Cathedral and hearing the organ being played or a choir singing. I felt quite let down, as the music, which was obviously being played enthusiastically, could not be heard.

There is an ecumenical community living at the Abbey with groups of people (mainly young) who come and stay for periods of time. Their focus is on social justice. I was surprised to see a great deal of prominence given to the "Ban the Bomb" symbol, which I had not seen being used since about the 1970s. They have a public worship time at 9.00am and 9.00pm every day, with occasional daily services, such as today at 2.00pm when they had a fifteen-minute Justice and Peace service. I was surprised though that nothing special happened to celebrate St. Columba's Day. I sat quietly in the sunshine for an hour before then going into the 2.00pm service, which was a spoken service, taken by a middle-aged woman. Without music it seemed very flat and uninspiring, to me at any rate.

If you visit, make sure you do not miss the museum at the Abbey. This is especially interesting with a number of original Iona crosses on display.

There are a number of places providing tea and lunches on Iona, plus there are short walks to other parts of the island. I decided to find lunch and then not have a meal this evening. I was recommended a fish place at the dock, but when I got there, there was a line up and the ferry was just loading, so I jumped on it. On the dock on the Mull side is also a fish hut and I purchased fresh scallops and salad for £6. They were also offering fresh mussels and Langoustines as well. (Clearly all the Langoustines don't make it to Spain). Probably the healthiest meal I have eaten in 18 days!

One particular thing of note is the exceptional blue water around the island. With the white sand it could almost be mistaken for being in the Caribbean.

After my healthy lunch I decided that there was no more to see on Mull and I would drive to the ferry and try and take an earlier one than the 7.30pm, which was the only one I had been able to book. I got there at 4.45pm and was allocated a place in the stand-by line for the 5.05pm sailing. I got up to number two in the line before being told that the boat was full and I would have to wait for the next one at 6.10pm. Not a problem; across the road was a bar/café that had been heaving with people waiting to get on the ferry. As I sat down at an outside table in the sunshine, the owner came up and said "Sorry we close at 5.00pm" and cleared everyone out from the terrace, so I had to return to my hot car for an hour.

The Spar grocery shop next door to the café stays open, they say, until the last ferry departs. I was amazed that a café/bar that is clearly well used by ferry passengers would close at 5.00pm with more ferries still to run. OK its his business and he can do what he likes, but I bet he is also one of those who complains that business on Mull is hard, especially when it is out of season and no tourists are there. If I come again I wonder if he will have shut down; if so, serves him right.

There was nothing for it then but to buy some milk from the Spar grocer and go and make myself a cup of tea. While in the Spar I also purchased a prawn pasta salad for my supper tonight. So, I got all that I needed and the Spar got extra business.

Arriving into Oban was also in the glorious sunshine that I have had all day. Oban is a fine town that I had not been to for over 30 years. I had forgotten how attractive it was, especially coming in from the ocean. It is set beautifully in a horseshoe shaped Bay. We plowed through hundreds and hundreds of jelly fish as the boat approached the dock.

As a very keen Formula 1 motor racing fan I happened to know of one notable person who comes from Oban; Susie Wolff. She was a female racing driver, who very nearly made it into Formula 1 with Williams. She is married to Toto Wolff who is the head of the Mercedes Formula 1 team, who are the current world championship constructors.

Arriving into Oban, Argyll & Bute

Tomorrow I will be traveling the Mull of Kintyre and then will take the ferry to the Isle of Arran for another AirBnB; this time a vegetarian one, who particularly request on the web site that you bring no meat products with you into the house. Just as well I plan to eat at a local pub, though I hope it is better than the other pubs I have so far eaten at.

Oban to the Isle of Arran

Miles 188

Kintyre Countryside, Argyll & Bute

Today I traveled to the Mull of Kintyre, but there were no bagpipes playing or any sign of Paul McCartney. I finished today on the last island of my coastal trip.

My Air B&B overnight proved to be fine and coincidentally the couple running it are off to Vancouver in three weeks time so they were glad of some tourist advice. Their route to

Vancouver is via Halifax and Edmonton and then after visiting Vancouver and Vancouver Island they are going to San Francisco, San Diego and Las Vegas, all in a two-week trip. I think they are going to be fed up of traveling and as tired as me by the end of their holiday.

The couple who had wanted to remain in my room, were two young women, who I only saw fleetingly as they came out of the bathroom. The other guest was a lady from Southampton who was tackling the Munros. These are a collection of 282 mountains in Scotland, all over 3000 feet, that hill walkers have to climb to be able to "bag" a Munro. Apparently over 5000 walkers have bagged all 282. I think that it was climbing one of these that John Smith, the politician now buried on Iona, collapsed and died. This lady is also in the midst of trekking, a bit at a time, the South West Coastal Path around Devon and Cornwall. This is one that I feel I would also like to do. Perhaps that will be my next adventure!

I left Oban in 17 degrees with clear signs that the weather is beginning to turn after two weeks of almost uninterrupted sunshine. The day became grey, but with almost no rain. I took some photos, but coastal pictures were hardly worth taking as the light was not good enough to give sharp pictures. I realised that today was the first day for three days that I had driven on a road with a white line down the center! Though later in the day I did once again end up single track driving.

It's 37 miles from Oban to Lochgilphead, which is where the road shortly begins to run along the bottom end of Loch Fyne, famous for its fish and shellfish and a number of aquatic farms were visible in its waters. Loch Fyne empties into the Sound of Bute just above the Isle of Arran. The eastern edge of the Kintyre peninsula is Kilbrannan Sound.

Sounds can look very similar to Fjords, but there is a difference in origin. A Sound is formed by the ocean inundating low level land and valleys that abut the sea, whereas a Fjord is formed by glacial action that carves out the valley into which the ocean then enters. Either way the resultant geography is usually very beautiful.

Just before Ardrishaig I came up behind a truck transporting logs. It was just like being in BC. The driver kindly let me pass. I have found that virtually all of the truck and bus drivers here in Scotland are very aware of other road users and let vehicles pass and especially give lots of room to cyclists.

I turned off just after Brenfield and then began a looping road for about 30 miles that traveled out to the west and Loch Caolisport and the Sound of Jura. This was back to my old friend, the single-track road! The greyness certainly lowered the impact of any views. The looping road comes around to Tarbert. Tarbert is a Gaelic name by origin and means carrying place. Typically it is a small isthmus joining two places at which boats or goods would be portaged, or carried, across from one to the other. Tarbert links West Loch Tarbet and the Irish Sea to Loch Fyne and the Firth of Clyde. It is a pretty little harbour town.

I was able to get good Radio 4 reception about half way along this road and listened to the ceremony from St. Paul's Cathedral to mark the 90th birthday of the Queen (though she was actually born in April) and today was also the 95th birthday of the Duke of Edinburgh. I'm sure that this was a great spectacle if you were a tourist in London today as all of the Royal Family, most politicians and the Archbishop of Canterbury were all there. Britain really does do majesty and splendour in a magnificent way. As part of the celebrations, on Sunday, there is to be a picnic along the Mall for 10,000 people. I am assuming that this is only open to people with an invitation, though some good friends of ours, who own a dairy business, will be there, having supplied some of the food that will be in the picnic hampers. The audience, apparently, come from the 600 or so organisations that the Queen is a patron of.

In early July we are also going to have a celebration of my Mother-In-Law's 90th birthday (she was born in May). Her party though will be a somewhat smaller affair, with about 50 people present. I heard today that there are an estimated 500,000 people in Britain who are aged 90 and above. Assuming that in 1928 the population of Britain was about 50 million then this means that around 1% of people from this generation have lived to their 90th Birthday. On the BBC last year they said that because of improvements in pharmaceuticals and medical care, 25% of people born today would live to 100. That could really wreck the pension schemes.

From Tarbert I travelled along the western side of the Kintyre peninsula crossing over after about 30 miles to Cambeltown back on the eastern side. Just before I came to Campbeltown there was a strong smell of gas. I could not see any facilities that might be to blame for the smell, but I made sure that I did not light a match as it was very strong. I even stopped to check that my butane stove was not leaking.

Campbeltown, Argyll & Bute

Campbeltown was a tidy place but a bit of a disappointment. I had heard songs about it and stories of the ferry journeys from here, but it seemed fairly small and ordinary. Probably because it was a grey day and my mental image was too dreamlike.

I decided to drive down to the bottom and the famous Mull of Kintyre. I saw a sign for the lighthouse and then later another sign showing that it was only eight miles. It then began to rain heavily and visibility dropped. We even ran out of road and I was on no more than a dirt track with grass or hedgerow touching the car on either side. After about four miles I decided that I could get into serious difficulties with the car if I continued, but my problem was being able to turn around. I continued for about another mile and a half then stopped on a bend and I did a (probably) 20 point turn with the collision sensors going full blast all the time.

As I started back to Campbeltown the rain stopped. Indeed the sun threatened to come out. At Campbeltown I followed a different road, which took me up the east side of Kintyre with Campeltown Loch to my right. This was a much prettier journey. There was little traffic and almost every time I met someone there was a handy pull in.

About five miles before I got to Claonig and the ferry to the Isle of Arran I saw a sign warning of soft roadside verges. A mile after that a black van came at speed towards me and ignored the pull in. I stopped and he decided to pass me by going onto the verge. I heard the bump and in my rear view mirror saw the van settling gently and beginning to lean over into the ditch. I got out to see if I could help but his near side wheels were firmly in the ditch and his wheels on the road were so lightly touching the tarmac that all he could get was wheel spin and create a lot of smoke. The driver was aged about 19 and had come from Wales to work on a local construction project about two miles back up the road. There was no way I could assist him out of the ditch. His phone did not work either, so he borrowed mine and called his firm to send someone to rescue him. My only surprise is that he was driving a black van and not the notorious white one.

I got to the ferry dock with an hour to wait so did my usual and made a cup of tea. The ferry across to Arran was about 35 minutes and we landed at the small village with the lovely name of Lochranza. It has a small ruined castle and a whiskey distillery. I thought here was my chance to sample some whiskey, though I don't really like it, but wanted to find out why so many people rave about the different types. Unfortunately when I got there it was closing in half an hour and the last tour was already underway. I actually felt slightly relieved!

Lochranza Castle, Isle of Arran

Lochranza castle is not very big, but goes back to the 13th century. Robert the Bruce and James VI have all stayed here and also Oliver Cromwell in 1650. It was abandoned in the 18th century and became derelict.

Tomorrow I go across to Ardrossan on the mainland and my penultimate night in Scotland, probably in Troon or Turnberry, both famous golf towns.

The weather is forecast to get very wet on Sunday. This may impact what I do and where I stay. I will still drive by whatever road is closest to the ocean, but if photography opportunities are ruined by the weather I may just press on and pull back a day on my journey home.

And so now to find my Buddhist B&B. Unfortunately the WiFi is poor and cell phone coverage non-existent so I may have to locate it by looking at the pictures and guessing – it is a small island after all. My alternative is to find a pub (and hope that it is a nice one this time) and use their 'phone. A pub seems like a good idea right now!

Isle of Arran to Portpatrick, Galloway

Miles 120

Culzean Castle, Ayrshire

I set off this morning with no accommodation booked for tonight. This was again the fault of AirBnB. I tried to book somewhere, went through all of the process and then they asked me (again) for verification, which involves holding a piece of government ID up to the computer camera. I had already done this two weeks ago and have been booking normally since then, but, I could not proceed without doing it again. So I did it again. However it still would not let me proceed and kept repeating a request for verification.

I sent them an email, via their website, asking for assistance and explaining what was happening. I received a reply in five minutes saying (something like) 'Your business is important to us and we care about you very deeply and want to love you to bits so much so that you will only ever give your business to us and leave us all your money when you die. We love you so much that we are handling your problem and will be back to you at the speed of light.' I fell asleep waiting for a reply and still don't have one this morning, so, no place to stay tonight. AirBnB, let's hope you get competition very soon that is much more efficient and customer friendlier than you are!

My B&B last night was actually wonderful, not surprising really as the young women called her B&B "Alice's Wonderland." She is a Buddhist and had lived in a retreat on the adjacent small Holy Island for a few years, before moving to the larger island of Arran. Her hospitality and her welcome were warm and friendly. If only she were typical of all AirBnBs – and AirBnB the company was as customer friendly as she is! The room was clean and tidy and I slept well.

I declined the cooked breakfast as I had eaten well at the local inn, the Pierhead the night before. At last a Scottish Pub that is doing it right and providing good food and clean interior. I chose the muesli for breakfast for my stomach and my waistline's sake.

The Holy Isle next to Arran is ecumenical, but is apparently owned by a Buddhist Monastery based near Dumfries that have two centres on the island, one a 'closed order' and the other 'open'. Saint Lamlash, who gives his name to the Bay, was an Irish monk who was brought up in Scotland and lived as a young man in a cave on the Holy Isle in the 6th century. He later became a Bishop in Ireland. He is credited with introducing the Roman calculation for determining the date of Easter. This was later a point of dispute between the Celtic Christians and the Roman Christians which was settled at the Synod of Whitby in 664 when the Roman dating was agreed on by both.

The Vikings took over Arran in the 11th century and it became part of Norway before being integrated into the kingdom of Scotland in the 13th century. The highland emigration in the 18th and 19th century, brought about by a number of Enclosure Acts, saw the population decimated and the end of Gaelic culture and language on the island. A series of Enclosure Acts had resulted in the aristocratic landowners fencing off and restricting access to Common Land, turning it over to sheep farming instead of arable use. Farming jobs were thus significantly reduced. Unable to work or farm any land, or pay higher rents, families became destitute and many left Scotland for new lives in North America and Australia.

It was only when I got to the Pub last night that I realised that I had been on Arran (briefly) once before and possibly even had a drink at this pub. When living in Cheshire a number of years ago, we went sailing one weekend with the CEO of the advertising agency that my Company worked with. We anchored in Lamlash Bay overnight and went to the pub by dinghy. I recall going back to his sailboat and getting a very wet bottom as a lot of air had gone from the dinghy and it sagged where I was sitting!

My stay this time was also brief. I saw a fair bit of the island yesterday but as it was grey and drizzling this morning, I tried for and got an earlier ferry to Ardrossan on the mainland. My map pages are now going down in number as I turn them over, so I must be on the homeward stretch.

Ardrossan is clearly a holiday town with a very long sandy beach that stretches all the way to the next town of Saltcoats. On a sunny day no doubt this beach will be well used. At Saltcoats, rather than try again with AirBnB, I stopped to surf the web, to find a place to stay for tonight. I came across a small hotel called Harbour House in Portpatrick on the Rhins of Galloway, which is where I wanted to head today. As Harbour House is the name of my home in Vancouver, it had to be a sign. It was; they had one room left, so I booked it.

Irvine, Ayrshire

I continued on the coast road from Saltcoats and the next town was Irvine. This brought back memories of when I was early in my career at Beecham. I once visited our antibiotic

manufacturing plant there. It was then very much an expanding "new town". I could not tell which of the tall factory vents
that are there now (if any) was the Beecham plant. Certainly
Beecham no longer exists as a separate company; the assets are
today part of Glaxo SmithKline. I saw a sign for the Maritime
Museum and though I did not go in they had made the whole
area look very attractive. It seems as if the old buildings have
all been smartened up and it makes it a very attractive area,
with old vessels to view.

I next drove into Troon. Troon is famous as the home
of the "Royal Troon" Golf Club where the British Open has
been held eight times and is due to be held again this year.
It almost did not get to host it this year as the PGA refused
to allow The Open to be played on a course where the club
barred women members. To ensure that it was able to retain
the competition, the crusty old committee at the club took
a vote and decided that they would allow women members
after all. You could almost hear some of them harrumphing
into their scotch that this was "the thin end of the wedge".
However maintaining their status and especially receiving a
huge payday won the argument so women members are now
allowed and the Open will once again take place here in 2016.
I think I mentioned this before but Golf Clubs seem to me
more about keeping people out rather than letting people in
and I therefore applaud the fact that Troon and the other elitist
clubs have had this spotlight shone upon them.

The Open is the oldest major championship in golf. A
famous golfer with strong associations with Troon is Colin
Montgomery. His father was Secretary at Royal Troon for a
time. However, although winning the US Open in 1994, he
never won the British Open, even when held at Troon.

The entry into the town of Troon brings into view a long row of houses all faced with a brown coloured stucco, which unfortunately makes them look a bit depressing. If they were painted in different colours, or even all white, they would lift the look of the whole of the town. Troon seems surrounded by golf courses and I could not tell which was the Royal one. Last time I was in Troon was at the same time as our sailing trip to Arran. The day was a Sunday and the last day of the British Open. As we sailed into the harbor we were met, coming directly towards us, by the RAF Red Arrows aerobatic team. They had been performing over the golf course, but we liked to think that they were there specifically to greet us!

At the end of our sail we had thrown out some make-shift lines with hooks having pieces of aluminium foil as the only bait on them. Within 20 minutes we had caught about 30 mackerel. My Father used to say that 'you never catch mackerel, they just give themselves up!' This certainly seemed to be the case on this occasion. When we got to our berth in Troon Marina our Captain just happened to know the lady in the boat next to us, who was Dutch and a chef! She took the fish and we soon had mackerel, cooked seven different ways, with boiled potatoes and some very nice bottles of wine. A memorable fresh and tasty meal.

My next stop was the large town of Ayr with again an excellent and expansive beach. I stopped here at Asda (no Tesco in sight) but was met by a very strong smell as I got out of the car. It smelled like horse manure. I suppose this is what they call "Ayr pollution!"

Ayr is now very much a tourist town because of its fine beaches. In its past its industries have included shipbuilding and textiles and carpet making. Currently it is mainly a large retail shopping center for the area. It has a fine horse racing track, perhaps the source of the smell! This is the home of the Scottish Grand National. Ayr also has a premiership rugby union club.

It's most famous son is of course the poet Robert (Rabbie) Burns, born in nearby Alloway in 1759. New Year, or Hogmanay as it is called in Scotland, would not be the same without the singing of Burn's most famous composition, "Auld Lang Syne". Burns had an "interesting", but fairly short life. He was mainly home schooled by his farmer Father. At various times he worked as a farm labourer, a flax dresser, a volunteer soldier and a farmer in his own right. Due to his extreme financial hardships and possibly as a way to escape an angry father, he accepted a job as a bookkeeper on a slave plantation in Jamaica. However the sale, at the last minute, of a number of his poems, allowed him to cancel this. His increasing recognition as a poet saw him to move to Edinburgh where he did start to make enough money to support his ever growing family. He fathered twelve children, nine with his wife Jean Amour of which only three survived infancy, and three by other women. His first child was born to his Mother's servant while he was courting Jean Amour and who shortly after gave birth to twins. From his surviving children it is said that he has over 600 descendants living today. He died at age 37 after a tooth extraction adversely impacted his rheumatic fever damaged heart. His upbringing in poverty probably was the cause of his poor health, but others have associated it with his heavy drinking and wayward lifestyle.

Out of Ayr, the road continues right along the coast and I pulled off at the little harbor village of Dunure, with its ruined castle on the cliff edge. Apparently Mary Queen of Scots stayed here for three days in 1563.

Leaving Dunure I saw a sign for Culzean Castle (pronounced Cullane) and noted that it was in the care of the National Trust for Scotland. Having just taken out membership (while at Culloden) I thought I would get some value from my membership and stop and have a look at the castle. It is a magnificent building with beautiful grounds.

It is not an old castle, certainly in British terms at least, dating only from the late 18ᵗʰ Century. It was originally the home of the Chief of Clan Kennedy (my paternal Grandmother was a Kennedy) but was given to the National trust for Scotland in 1945 with the unusual caveat that General Eisenhower be given the apartment at the top of the castle for his personal use. This was in recognition and thanks for his role as Supreme Commander of the Allied Forces in World War II. Eisenhower subsequently stayed at the castle a number of times.

I have to congratulate the very pleasant, trusting and helpful staff who work here. At the entrance gate I said that I did not yet have my membership card only a receipt, which I had to get out of the back of the car. "That's alright, don't worry. It's raining so you just drive right on in sir". Later in the house I asked a young lady where a certain room was and she said "Let me show you" and walked me to it.

One outstanding display in the house is that of the armaments, old pistols and swords. They are displayed on the wall in huge round circles I was told that there are 716 pistols and over 300 swords. These would have been part of the arms for the private army that would be raised, if needed, by the Lord.

I didn't have time to stay too long at the castle as I still had miles to go, though I did have nice afternoon tea in the stables.

Culzean Castle Armaments display

I continued to follow the coast road and coming around a bend entered the village of Turnberry. Unlike Troon the row of houses that greet you here are all very smart. A hundred yards further on I found out why. The entrance to the famous Turnberry Hotel and golf course proudly displayed on smart signage that this was now Trump Turnberry!

I have stayed at the Turnberry hotel about 4 times, but never to play golf, always at a conference. My first time was soon after I joined Beecham and they held their national conference there. At age 23 I can remember feeling awed by the splendour of the place, I had never stayed at such a glamorous hotel.

I understand that Donald Trump is coming to Turnberry on June 23rd, which also happens to be the day of the UK referendum, the "Brexit vote" on whether or not to leave the EU. I have been asking a number of my B&B hosts which way they are thinking of voting. Apart from my host of last night, on Arran, all of them had said they are voting to leave. This is clearly not a fully representative poll, but I did find it surprising that I have only found one vote in favour of staying. The official polls are saying that it is very close, but is likely to be just in favour of staying in the EU. They say that older people are likely to vote leave and younger people to vote stay, which generally fits the age ranges of the people I have spoken to.

Trump Turnberry, Ayrshire

The US Presidential Election is set for November of this year, with Donald trump as a controversial character. The Republican Party has been very divided on whether Trump should be their party candidate. However just a few days ago his rivals for selection all pulled out so he has become the

Republican Party nominee. Despite many in his party being genuinely horrified that he has become their nominee, the Republicans want power more than anything else and if the voters turn towards Trump then the Republican hierarchy will support him. So both Brexit and the US Presidential election are in the hands of fickle voters, but this is what is called democracy, for good or bad.

There are a considerable number of undecided Brexit voters, who say that they just don't understand the arguments, or even trust what they are hearing in favour of staying in or leaving. Like so many voting situations, the last 24 hours will be decisive as to how people make up their minds. If a leave vote does win the day this could spell the break up the United Kingdom, which has existed since James VI of Scotland in 1603 became James I of England. Scottish nationalist politicians have said that they want to stay in Europe and if Britain opts out, then they will hold another referendum to decide whether Scotland should become independent. If this happens then perhaps the Welsh, who have a separate Parliament may also try to do the same, although they have only ever been a Principality rather than a separate nation state, which might limit their ability to break away. This worryingly could also signal a resumption of the troubles in Ireland once again. Though the stimulus will be very different the cause will be the same, a united Ireland, without border controls and moving to one government, based in Dublin.

Within the golf course and adjacent to Turnberry Lighthouse are the ruins of Turnberry Castle. Almost nothing of the castle remains, however this is the spot where, in 1274, was born Robert the Bruce, later King Robert the Bruce of Scotland and victor over the English at Bannockburn.

In February 1306 Robert murdered his rival to the throne John Comyn in Greyfriars Church in Dundee and was crowned King at Scone in March of that year. The Comyns, supported by Edward I, fought back and Robert was forced to go into hiding. Many of his family were slaughtered. In February 1307 the English held Turnberry Castle. Robert, who had been living in Ireland, landed with a small army at Turnberry and attacked and captured the castle that had been his birthplace. Two of his brothers landed further south at Loch Ryan, but were defeated by the Comyns and killed. Edward I, on his way to battle against Robert, died of dysentery at Burgh By Sands, just over the border in Cumbria in July 1307 and his son Edward II became King. Robert continued his fight across Scotland and gained popular support eventually defeating Edward II's army at Bannockburn in 1314. Ironically it was Robert who had ordered the destruction of Turnberry castle in 1310 to prevent it being used again by the English.

Edward II, as seen by his defeat at Bannockburn, was ineffective in fighting Robert. Robert remained King of Scotland, gaining the recognition by the Pope of his Kingship and Scotland's independence in 1324. In 1328 Edward and Robert signed a peace treaty, known as the Treaty of Northampton. Under the terms of this, Robert's son David, then aged 4 and Edward II's daughter Joan, aged 7, married so as to unite the thrones. Both Robert and Edward II died in 1329. Edward II was murdered in Berkley Castle in Gloucestershire. Some say that this was on the orders of his wife and that a red-hot poker was inserted into his bottom, a sign that his wife considered him a homosexual. This was a rumour that was not put out until 60 years after his death.

It is more likely that he was smothered to death. Edward III became King in England and David, at 5 years old, became King in Scotland. The marriage of David and Joan produced no heirs.

After leaving Turnberry I drove on to Girvan the next town on the coast. Again another neat and tidy town, but as you leave on the roundabout they have a big wooden sign, saying, "Haste ye Back" which on its own makes sense. But below this they have another set of words, which seems to counter the first ones. This says. "What's Yer Hurry,"? Well if they want you to hasten back, they shouldn't express surprise that you are hurrying.

Stranraer was my next objective on the coast. I passed through the small village of Ballantrae and then the road goes inland through a Glen coming back to the coast about a mile north of the village of Cairnryan. Not really a lot to see in either of these places. At Innermessan the road goes around the head of Loch Ryan and into Stranraer. This is a major ferry port for traffic to Ireland. It is actually also a very nice town and here the buildings facing the harbor are all painted in different pastel colours: blue, pink, green, yellow and white. (That is one colour per building, not all on the same building!). It all seems very much in keeping with a seaside town and I couldn't help thinking how much Troon would benefit from colouring itself up.

Stranraer is the start of the Rhins of Galloway an area of the coast that runs southeast and northwest and is very much given over to farming. I turned right and went up the coast to the top most point, Milleur Lighthouse, which is an entrance and exit point for the ferries from Stranraer. At this point the sun came out and the temperature climbed to 20 degrees. Further back where I had come from it still looked grey so I got the impression that the Rhins of Galloway had its own microclimate. The southernmost point is the Mull of Galloway and I will be visiting this tomorrow.

At Kirkcolm I turned off onto the minor roads and allowed Samantha to direct me to Portpatrick. As I entered the town I immediately saw my hotel. It was buzzing with people outside, sitting having a drink or a meal. Portpatrick is a charming place with a lovely well-protected harbour, and of course an RNLI lifeboat station. As evidenced by what I saw today, this is a popular place for people to come for the weekend. Portpatrick is said to be the place were St. Patrick set foot after his return to Britain. It is a journey of only twenty-one miles from here across to Ireland. At one time Portpatrick was a place that young Irish couples would elope to as the laws on marriage consent were much more lax in Scotland than in Ireland.

Portpatrick

No doubt influenced by my Buddhist B&B last night, I cooked myself a vegetarian pasta for my evening meal, sitting up on a point overlooking the town.

My room is nice and clean and had, I am glad to say, a TV so that I could sit and watch England play Russia in the first round of the Euro 2016 football tournament in France. I enjoy the international matches, but the TV news tonight showed the ugly side of football with rioting and fighting amongst English, French and Russian fans in Marseille. The benefit of England losing in the early stages of such a competition (which often happens) is that there are a lower number of casualties!

The outcome of the game was a one all draw, with Russia scoring a goal right at the end of full time. Unfortunately the aftermath was rioting, allegedly caused by Russian gangs, with at least two English fans critically injured. This used to be such a great game, but though having the best professional league in the world, England does not have the quality players it once had, probably because the major teams are so full of overseas players that English players have less chance to develop their skills.

I have to draw a contrast between the fans of Football and Rugby Union, a game I really enjoy. Someone once said that *'Football is a game played by gentlemen supported by a crowd of hooligans, whereas Rugby is a game played by hooligans, supported by a crowd of gentlemen!'* I used to play Rugby at school but was a keen Football supporter. However, I found that going to a football match was an awful experience due to the foul-mouthed fans, many of who had just gone for a fight. Today I know that things are much better, but there is still that element amongst the fan base that are genuine hooligans looking for a fight. Hence the problems that continue to be seen at the international matches. Contrast this with Rugby, which is now a very professional, all action game. When there is a penalty kick or a conversion attempt, a sign goes up asking the crowd to "respect the kicker". All shouting and whistling stops and the crowd go silent as the kick is taken. No one makes a noise to try and put the kicker off. Just imagine what this feels like in a stadium of 50,000 people when there is total silence! Gentlemen (and women) certainly are the followers of Rugby Union.

Portpatrick, Galloway to Annan, Dumfriesshire

Miles 185

Dundrennan Abbey

Today has been a very pleasant day of driving through mainly farming country. I finished off the Rhins and moved across to the Machars. The sun was with me all day and reached 23 degrees at one point, despite the dire weather forecast that I had heard.

Harbour House in Portpatrick proved to be quite a find and I had not only a nice comfortable room, but also an all too large breakfast, including both haggis and black pudding, of which I ate only a small amount. This was also one of the best value rooms I have stayed in.

I drove first thing down to the extremity of the Rhins to the Mull of Galloway. This has a lighthouse and is the southernmost part of Scotland. The lighthouse is another one designed and built by Robert Stevenson (grandfather of the author of Treasure Island, Robert Louis Stevenson). It began shining in 1830. Standing 99 metres above sea level its light can be seen for 28 miles.

Mull of Galloway Lighthouse

There is a small monument here to a plane crash that occurred in June 1944 when an aircraft delivery pilot in a Bristol Beaufighter, flying in low visibility, hit the boundary wall close the lighthouse, demolished a building alongside it and then went over the cliff. The two people on board were both killed. It is believed that the pilot was attempting to fly below the weather and thought that he was over the sea.

There are two botanical gardens at this end of the Rhins, but I did not have time to visit either of them. Returning up the A716, so as to take the road across to the Machars, I passed through Sandhead, which has a sandy beach that I estimate is at least 5 miles long and also a holiday home site. I was surprised to see a sign here advertising "3&4 bedroomed houses for sale. 4 bedroomed detached villas and 2 bedroom flats from £85,500 – assistance available." I am presuming that the price shown is for the flats, but either way it would appear that this is a fairly inexpensive place to live; yet it is less than 20 miles from Stranraer.

As I drove through the country lanes I began to see scarecrows, not in the fields, but outside farms and private houses. Some of them were exceedingly good. My favourite, for which I unfortunately did not take a picture, was of a farmer in his wellington boots and with a very realistic sheep dog. I assume that these are part of a competition, but they certainly add some fun and character to the area.

I moved on to the Machars and the road allowed me to follow the ocean, down one side and up the other. The Machers have a mix of rocky and sandy beaches. There was one static caravan and chalet site overlooking Luce Bay. Port William is a good sized village and nearby are neolithic standing stones and a stone ring. There are 5 neolithic sites marked on the map covering the Rhins and the Machars so clearly this was at one time another important site for ancient people. Indeed close to Drummore on the Rhins I had earlier noticed two small mounds that looked to me distinctly like barrows. I presume Historic Scotland have also noted these and investigated them.

At the end of the Machers is the Isle of Whithorn with a sign as you enter the village saying "Isle of Whithorn B.C." I've no idea what the B.C. stands for and cannot find any connection to British Columbia. There is a small harbour, suffering from the tide being out with the vessels lying on the mud. St Ninian's chapel is here and is a ruin. According to the history by Bede, St. Ninian was a monk who lived in either the 5th or 6th century and who worked amongst the Pictish tribes of southern Scotland converting them to Christianity. That he lived and was buried at Whithorn is about all that is known. Near to the ruined chapel is a small white tower that has apparently been a navigational beacon for hundreds of years.

There are also two memorials here; one in memory of the scallop fishing boat Solway Harvester that sank off the Isle of Man in January 2000 with the loss of all hands. The boat was brought up from the bottom of the ocean and all the crewmembers' bodies found. However, the boat sat in Ramsey Harbour on the Isle of Man for a number of years while an investigation and court case followed. Eventually the sinking was ruled as an accident but the owner of the vessel was heavily criticized over the seaworthiness of the vessel. It was broken up for scrap in 2014.

The other shrine has no details about it. It is a large cairn of stones and rocks and many of the stones have, hand-written on them, names of people (and of pets) who have died. There is also a wooden cross laid on top and Tibetan prayer flags. It is apparently called the Witness Cairn and was originally erected in 1997 to commemorate the arrival of St Ninian at this point.

As I walked back down the rough track from the white tower, my foot slipped on the sandy path and I fell over onto my bottom. My concern was for both my right wrist and right leg, which had at separate times been operated on in the last 12 months. I seemed to survive the tumble in once piece, but later discovered that I had indeed injured myself.

Witness Cairn, Whithorn, Galloway

Driving on from Whithorn you come to the village of Garlieston, which lays claim to being the birthplace of the Mulberry Harbour, large concrete barges that were towed across to France in 1944 to support the D Day Landings. As this place is on the east coast of Britain and France on the west coast, it would seem to be a long way to tow concrete barges! Wigtown about 10 miles further up the road makes the claim that it is Scotland's Book Town, the Hay on Wye of Scotland no doubt.

I drove on to Newton Stewart, but skirted the bottom of the town to keep on the coast road. A glimpse along the high street suggested flags and bunting, so it probably would be an interesting town to visit at some time.

The A75 at this point runs alongside the estuary of the River Cree and opens out into Wigtown Bay. It reminded me very much of the River Exe estuary at Exmouth when the tide is out, wide mud flats offering good feeding for birds, with a narrow river running between. There are also further Neolithic remains signposted along this road.

At Gatehouse of Fleet I decided to stop and have a break. This is a lovely little town but I was surprised that the Kilt weaving shop that I had thought I would visit and which is advertised on the edge of the town was not open. I only then realised that today was Sunday. Every day to me has become a bit of a blur. I suppose I should have realised this while listening to the omnibus edition of the Archers. It's amazing that having been in Vancouver so long, I can come back and turn on the radio and listen to the Archers and it seems as if I have never been away. The same characters are still doing almost the same old things (nostalgia is all that it is cracked up to be!).

I drove down a small promontory to keep next to the ocean and came through the pretty village of Borgue. I was not assimilated and never saw "7 of 9" (Star Trek fans will know what I mean) but it would be a pleasant enough place if I did have to spend an eternity of space-time here!

Just past Borgue I had to stop and take a photograph across the estuary to one of the prettiest little towns I have seen in this area, Kirkcudbright, which for the Sassenachs reading this is pronounced Kercoobree.

Kirkcudbright has a small harbor with a host of sailboats (the tide was out of course) and a fine ruined castle right in the centre of the town. Many of the houses here are also painted in bright colours, which I think makes many of these stone built towns so much warmer and brighter. If you wanted a holiday in this area, then this could be a nice place to base yourself. I again found here another connection with Holy Island in Northumbria.

The name Kirkcudbright is derived from Gaelic, which translates as the Chapel of Cuthbert. St. Cuthbert's remains were taken from Holy Island to protect them from the Viking invaders and his body travelled to many places, here being one of them, before being given a final resting place in Durham.

Kirkcudbright, Dumfries & Galloway

Just outside of Kirkcudbright are the ruins of Dundrennan Abbey, an old Cistercian monastery. It was here that Mary Queen of Scots spent her last night in Scotland before entering England and eventual imprisonment.

I drove on, going inland around the Urr Water estuary, then skirting the edge of Dalbeattie and back down to follow the coast road heading for Dumfries. Along this road there is a very long stretch of sandy beach at Sandyhills and the view from the road is right across the Solway Firth to Cumbria, where I will be tomorrow. I stopped outside a cottage to take a photo and talked to a gentleman with his dog who was sunning himself outside. He told me that the wooden posts in the sand (a long way out) were fish traps to catch salmon and trout as the tide recedes. Apparently these are being banned as from next year and only rod and line can be used from then on.

Sweetheart Abbey, New Abbey, Dumfries & Galloway

A few miles on I came to the village of New Abbey where there is another ruined abbey with the lovely name of Sweetheart Abbey. The Abbey was a sub Abbey to Dundrennan Abbey and takes it's name from the actions of Dervorguilla, the daughter of the Lord of Galloway. Her husband was Baron John de Balliol, who the College at Oxford University is named after. When he died she had his heart embalmed and placed into an ivory and silver casket and kept this with her at all times. She was buried in the Abbey along with his heart and the Abbey became known as the Abbey Dulce Coer, which means in Latin, "sweet heart".

The son of Balliol and Dervorguilla, also called John, became John 1st of Scotland in 1292 after Edward 1 found him to have greater claim to the throne than Robert de Brus, grandfather of Robert the Bruce, who later became King of Scotland.

When King Alexander III died in 1286, without any living children to succeed him, the next in line was Margaret, his granddaughter, aged three and daughter of King Eric of Norway and Alexander's daughter, also called Margaret, who had died in childbirth. Eric met with Edward I and a marriage between Edward's son (later Edward II) and Margaret was agreed, which angered the Scots. In 1290, at age seven, Margaret was sent by Eric to Scotland to claim her throne, but unfortunately due to severe seasickness was landed on the Orkneys, where she died.

John unfortunately fell out with Edward, who had demanded his homage, which would have recognised Edward's authority over Scotland. The Scottish leaders saw John as weak and thus deposed him, forming a Council of Twelve Guardians of Scotland. The Guardians then made an alliance with France, known as the Auld Alliance, by which each country agreed to support the other in the event of an attack by England. This angered Edward and in 1296 he did invade Scotland and John was taken prisoner and held in the Tower of London. France did not attempt to intervene.

In 1297 William Wallace raised the Scots against Edward I and initially pushed out the invading English army. John was released by Edward in 1299, but never returned to

Scotland, going to France where he lived until his death in 1314. As he prepared to depart for France, Edward had his baggage searched at Dover and it was found to contain, huge amounts of gold and the crown and royal seal of Scotland.

In 1304, William Wallace was betrayed and captured and brutally killed by Edward, but then Robert the Bruce rose up in 1306 and proclaimed himself as King. In 1307, on his way to do battle with Robert the Bruce, Edward I, as mentioned earlier, died of dysentery, ironically a crow's flight from this Abbey, just over the nearby Solway Firth, at Burgh By Sands, I had to stop and take a photograph and decided also to have afternoon tea in the garden of a small tearoom opposite the Abbey ruins. The car park was full of cars so I expected the café to also be full, but there were only three sets of couples there. I next thought the cars had to belong to walkers, as there was certainly no one in the Abbey. When I went back to my car I found out where everyone was; behind the hedge playing bowls in the local bowls club. There must have been a hundred people there, all enjoying the matches and the sunshine.

I skirted Dumfries and again followed the coastal road, stopping briefly at Kingholm Quay (tide was still out!) and made my way on to Annan, my stop for tonight. Annan is not as pleasant as its neighbours. It is mainly built of red brick and looks quite austere with a rather sad high street.

As I walked down the high street looking for somewhere to eat I noticed a small group of youngsters walk out of the back door of a pub and enter a betting shop, which was still open at 6.00pm on a Sunday. Clearly the Kirk has no influence here.

Another restaurant nearby was advertising its services, which included Birthday parties and Funeral breakfasts. I had not seen the latter offered before as a reason to go into a restaurant!

I ate my meal in what the sign said was an Italian restaurant, but it wasn't. Their food was just "ordinary" and pasta and pizza was the only ersatz Italian on offer. The waiter said that they had only recently reopened and were now a continental restaurant. I'm not sure what that is supposed to mean, other than they did not have fish & chips or steak pie on the menu, but did offer steak and salmon.

My B&B claims to be an old rectory. It is clean but the emphasis is certainly on the word old as the furniture in the room is definitely older than I am and must have been old even when my parents were young! Breakfast was hearty, but served by my unshaven host. Shame.

Tomorrow I am going to press on into the Lake District coastal area. If I have time I plan to ride the Ravenglass and Eskdale miniature steam railway (assuming the sun continues to shine on me). Ravenglass is allegedly the birthplace of St. Patrick who went on to become the Patron Saint of Ireland, though some historians say that he was born in Scotland. At one time these border areas moved back and forth and were not as we know them today. Certainly the Scots have held Cumbria on a number of occasions. If I do get as far as I hope tomorrow then I will certainly be almost one day ahead of my original schedule.

Annan to Grange Over Sands, Cumbria

Miles 173

Wind Turbines off Isle of Walney, Cumbria

Today I re-entered England, contemplated on the building of walls, rode on a train and found an island ruled by a King.

The day started grey and overcast, later turning to heavy rain, but ending the day with a dry and pleasant evening.

I set off from Annan and quickly entered Gretna, the border town with England. Gretna, the town, is now conjoined with the more famous village of Gretna Green. Gretna Green is world famous as the original place for "runaway marriages". When I was growing up this was the where young couples in England (under age 18) who wanted to defy their parents and get married without parental permission, would elope to.

From around the time of the Norse invasion through to the late 1600s there existed a ceremony known as "handfasting", wherein a couple, in front of witnesses, by joining of hands and stating that they "accepted each other as man and wife, till death do them part and thereby plighted their troth", became betrothed, or engaged to be married. Gifts were exchanged, which often included a ring. The Church recognised two forms of handfasting: one where it was like a non-binding engagement and would last for one year, at the end of which they could then marry or part; the second would be where it was accepted as a marriage. The church expected that any handfasting should be followed one week later by a Church ceremony, only after which intercourse could take place. However, if intercourse occurred during the time of engagement then the couple would be considered to have married. Handfasting was the most common form of marriage through until the seventeenth century, but was open to ambiguity and uncertainty as to marriage status. In 1753 the Marriage Act in England was introduced and stated that a Priest had to officiate or a magistrate had to be present at a ceremony.

The marriage laws in Scotland continued to be very different from those of England. In the 1700s a split in Scotland between the Kirk and the civil authorities occurred. The Kirk refused to recognise handfasting, or marriage by consent, whilst the civil authorities continued to do so. At this time in England a person under the age of 21 could not get married without parental consent, in Scotland however, boys aged 12 and over and girls aged 10 and over, could marry without parental permission. So, in the late 1700s young English couples, without parent's permission, would elope to Gretna Green, being the first place over the border, to get married.

In Scotland the law allowed for marriages to be legal if the vows were made before two witnesses, so almost anyone could perform a marriage ceremony. In Gretna Green the village blacksmith and his assistant took on this role and over the years the anvil became a symbol of an eloped marriage. The blacksmith was often the only person around and working in a village during the daytime.

In 1854 Scottish law was changed to require 21 day's residency for couples before they could get married in Scotland and this allowed time for anxious parents to try and find the young couple and either get them to change their minds, or possibly bring them home by force. It was not until 1929 though that Scotland moved the age for marriage to 16 for both men and women. In 1939 The Scottish Marriage Act no longer recognised handfasting and in 1940 a further change in the law required that witnesses at a wedding needed to be registered and could not be just any citizen. The 21-day residency requirement was scrapped in 1977. England and Wales now have the minimum age for marriage without parental consent at age 18 and with consent at 16.

These changes in the law, over time, meant that Gretna Green lost its "strategic purpose" and it fell back into being just another border town. However, it is claimed that over 5000 couples each year, approximately fifteen percent of all marriages in Scotland, still take place in Gretna Green. These now are in purpose built chapels and other halls, but with a traditional anvil still prominent at the ceremony. In North America, Las Vegas is the closest equivalent for "quickie" marriages. Gretna Green though has the history, although with no casinos and with much less sunshine!

Gretna is not an unpleasant little town, but it seems to have no other special appeal. On the English side of the town there is an Outlet Mall. This has a collection of well-known branded shops selling last year's designs or remaindered products, at prices, which you assume must be a bargain as you are buying them at an Outlet Mall. I didn't notice if there was a bridal gown shop selling new, or perhaps lightly used, ones.

I now took to the lanes so as to get to the Solway Firth coast. The road runs parallel for a little way with the M6 motorway and thus is a good place for a haulier to have a depot. I was interested to see a sign saying "Stobart Café." Eddie Stobart, has one of the largest haulage businesses in the UK, with distinctive red and green trucks, drivers in uniform and the reputation of being the "politest lorry drivers on the road". You can even buy models of his trucks in toyshops. I wondered whether the café is a one off at his own lorry depot, or, is it a new business venture open to all truck drivers and soon we will see it franchised along the motorway network, with waitresses in green and red uniforms.

※

At Bowness on Solway the road runs across low-lying meadows a few yards from the river estuary. I saw signs saying, "When the water reaches this point the depth is 2 feet" which I took to mean that the road would flood on certain tides. However, what is not clear is where is the "point" on the sign that indicates the height of the water. The sign actually stands four feet above the ground, so where then is the motorist expected to read the water depth from? Anyway the tide was well out when I was there and it was not raining so I felt it was OK to proceed.

The whole of this area felt very bleak under the grey skies and the open expanse across the Firth, which were mainly muddy flats as the tide was out. I personally could not live in a place such as this, but obviously it appeals to others. There were single properties looking out onto the estuary and also small farms and groups of homes. In the little village of Bowness, about a dozen hikers were waiting at a bus stop to catch a bus to somewhere. They had presumably stayed over-night in a local B&B.

This area is actually the western end of the Hadrian's Wall Trail. I was hoping to see some of the wall, but none of it is obvious (or possibly even existing at this point). The Roman Emperor Hadrian, in about AD50, had organized the building of a wall right across England, from East to West to keep the Scots from invading. This was the most northerly part of the

Roman Empire in Britain. Quite a bit of the wall remains to the east of Carlisle, but I could not see any of it where I was.

2000 years later and despite "civilization", people are still building walls, or fences, between countries and communities. The Berlin wall has now gone, but Israel is building a wall between itself and Palestine. There is a high fence between Mexico and the US, but if Donald Trump gets elected he promises to turn this into a wall. We even have Brits (jokingly on the Internet) "promising" to pay to build a wall between Canada and the US just to keep out all the Americans who want to come to Canada if Trump is elected!

At Cardurnock there are a large number of very tall aerials that I assume must be of military communications significance. In this day of cable TV they certainly can't be for television and based on the bad reception I was receiving they can't be for BBC Radio 4 either. It was close to this point that I saw the unusual sight of about fifty or so sheep all walking in single file. Possibly they were surrogate Roman soldiers marching along the top of Hadrian's Wall and it was there after all, but I just couldn't see it.

I continued on until I reached Silloth. This is quite a large town and was adjacent to a wartime airfield that is now an industrial park. The town was very pleasant with cobbled streets and a fine green fronting onto the waterside. The properties are large and of a style that suggested merchants' houses at one time. The other streets all appeared to be tree lined. I saw a coach from Edinburgh that no doubt had brought a party across to the town, presumably via the outlet mall at Gretna.

I continued to follow the coast road, and the beaches here became less bleak the further south I travelled, through tiny hamlets such as Beckfoot and Allonby eventually reaching

Maryport. Here there was a road sign pointing the way to "Tourist Attractions and Industrial Estate". Somehow the two don't seem to fit together. Maryport is the site of the major Roman fort called Alauna and some ruins still remain. It had a heyday in the nineteenth century as an industrial center and port, with coal from local mines as the main export; but at the end of the century it went into decline when the mine owners lowered wages stimulating a violent strike. With very high unemployment in the 1930s men from the town joined the Jarrow Marchers who walked to London to protest unemployment and poverty. One notable person, born close by, was Fletcher Christian who led the mutiny on the Bounty against Captain Bligh. No doubt the men from this area are prepared to stand up for injustice and their rights.

Just passed Maryport is Flimby and from here and on in to Workington things become very industrial. There are long rows of wind turbines on one side of the road and factories and tall chimneys on the other. There was also land advertised as available for building more, so clearly they're not finished yet. Workington was once a major coal and steel producing town, but no longer and regeneration is on-going.

By the time I got to Whitehaven the rain had returned and was pouring down. This has a small harbour, which is being rejuvenated. In its heyday Whitehaven was one of the most important ports for the importation of tobacco and in the late eighteenth century Whitehaven was second only to London as a port, but with the closure of the mines and loss of export of coal and steel it went into a steep decline.

There is a Tesco overlooking the harbour. I used the facilities in the store and purchased some more fuel (diesel) for the car. I am currently achieving 56 miles per gallon, which I think is excellent seeing as how I am on minor roads most of the time and rarely able to use the top two gears (this vehicle has 6).

From this industrial area I took the coastal road to the village of St Bees. St Bees head is the most northwesterly point of England and has a lighthouse, but it was too murky to see it clearly. This village is the only piece of designated Heritage Coast between Wales and Scotland and is a Site of Special Scientific Interest because of its large seabird colony. Although small, St Bees produced two Archbishops during the Reign of Elizabeth I: one of Canterbury, Edmund Grindal and one of York, Edwin Sandys. In 1981, an archeological dig at the old priory revealed a vault containing a lead coffin inside which was a very well preserved body of a knight, Sir Anthony de Lucy who died in 1368 on a crusade in Lithuania. The skin, nails and stomach contents were found to be in almost perfect condition.

St Bees is named after an Irish woman, Bega, who fled Ireland, probably in the mid 9th century, rather than marry the son of the King of Norway to whom she had been unwillingly betrothed. She felt that she should save her body only for God. She lived as a hermit on the beach at St Bees before traveling to Northumbria, where she entered into vows, and then later (possibly) returned and founded a convent here.

From St. Bees I continued on south to Seascale, which is the sight of a nuclear decommissioning center for the nuclear reactors from nearby Sellafield and Windscale. Nuclear material is also being sent here from the naval dockyards at Plymouth in Devon as various nuclear powered submarines are broken up. Just below here at Millom I was stopped at my first ever, manned level crossing. A man in a high visibility jacket stopped the traffic and closed the gates. Then a goods train came through at some speed. I presumed that it was going to Seascale and was involved with the decommissioning. No doubt this is a manned crossing to ensure that there are no accidents (or hijackings) involving nuclear materials, which would not look good on the national news and probably ruin the tourist trade.

Engine of the Ravenglass & Eskdale Railway

I had long heard about the Ravenglass and Eskdale narrow gauge railway and felt that I should go and see this as I was in the area. When I got to Ravenglass it had stooped raining and a train was due to depart within just two minutes, on its seven-mile journey. I wasn't sure that I wanted to go but with only two minutes to make up my mind and an hour before the next train, I hastily decided to go for it. I sat in a covered but otherwise open carriage. There were also open carriages (all empty) and some fully enclosed ones. I sat right at the very back of the train so could not see the engine, but would have a good view of the countryside. As we pulled out of the little station, the skies opened up again and the rain was torrential all the way up the track to Eskdale. Even the sheep, that were everywhere, were trying to get out of the rain by sheltering behind low walls or overhanging trees. I was glad when we got to the end of the line. I just had time for a cup of tea in the pleasant station café to warm me up before I caught the next train back.

I sat this time in a closed carriage, along with the guard, who was very interesting to talk to and learn about the railway. It was originally built to carry stone from the Eskdale quarries down to Ravenglass where it was loaded onto the main line trains to Barrow etc. The line went into disuse in the late 1800s but was purchased in 1903 and the new owner changed the track from 30 inch to 15 inch gauge in 1906. In 1988 a preservation society purchased the line and they own and operate it to this day. On a sunny day it would make a nice trip.

From Ravenglass I continued to follow the coast road through the small town of Millom. Millom was a village until the late eighteen hundreds when high-grade iron was found and mined to supply the local steel works. It grew into a fair sized town but fell into decline upon the closure of the mines in 1968. The largest local employer is now Her Majesty's Prison at nearby Haverigg.

I had to drive up the estuary to Broughton-In-Furness before descending again towards the sea and Barrow-In-Furness. Barrow once boasted some of the biggest shipbuilding yards in the country and built many of the Royal Navy's ships and nuclear submarines. When the yards closed the town went into a steep decline. Today however it is the home of BAE

Systems, whose business is armaments, aerospace and ships and from the size of the ginormous windowless towers that dominate the town and the dock area, it manufactures a lot of highly secret things here in Barrow.

BAE Weapons Factory at Barrow-In-Furness, Cumbria

Barrow faces onto and is joined to a large spit of land known as the Isle of Walney. This island is about 6 miles long. Approximately 2 miles offshore from Walney and running virtually the whole length of the island is another wind turbine farm. There were more than I could count. (It would no doubt drive a Norfolk man to heights of ecstasy). This is the largest wind farm that I have seen so far on my trip. So what with nuclear plants and wind farms, Barrow is very much an energy centre.

Between the Isle of Walney and the southern end of Barrow is Piel Island. This is one of those idiosyncrasies of British life. Barrow town owns the island and the council appoint a "King of Piel" who takes over the administrative duties of the island, (population four) as well as running the pub.

Piel Island, Barrow-In-Furness, Cumbria

The coronation of the latest "King" was televised on the BBC, not quite to the same extent as for a ruling British monarch, but it was featured on a TV series "Islands of Britain" hosted by Martin Clunes (a.k.a. Doc Martin). The King is "crowned" with a large quantity of beer being poured over his head!

Barrow Amateur Football Club plays in the Conference Division in English football and is apparently a very good team. They have aspirations to move into the professional English Football League, where they used to be until they were relegated in 1972. Of personal interest is that the brother of a good friend of ours, now living in the USA, recently purchased the Club with the intention of supporting them to achieve re-election to the League.

As I left Barrow I saw the only "Vote Remain" poster that I have seen on my entire trip so far. The referendum for Britain to vote to remain or to leave the EU will take place 10 days from now. I can understand at an emotional level the desire to have Britain fully under its own sovereignty and free of Brussels. But if Britain does vote to leave the EU, I fear that the outcome will be a significant economic downturn for Britain. The country has been in the EU far too long to be able to extricate itself and be immediately better off. The EU took a hard stance against David Cameron's threats to leave unless Britain was given significant concessions, so both are playing brinkmanship. However Cameron promised Britain a referendum and as the EU has offered no significant concessions, the danger now is that this will mean that the vote to leave wins the day. Everyone, including the EU, will likely be the worse for it.

Interesting times. I wonder, do those people who see themselves as singularly British, or English, realise that the population of these islands and their monarchs have all come from Europe: Danes, Norwegians, Germans, French, Dutch, Greek etc. Britain is actually a microcosm of Europe. It would be like a child wanting to reject and disown its family.

The journey from Barrow to my destination for today, Grange-Over-Sands, was a very pretty one. It had by now stopped raining and was a very pleasant early evening. As I came into Ulverston I noticed a very tall lighthouse on a hill, clearly a long way inland from the sea. On later checking I discovered that although designed to look like Smeaton's Eddystone Lighthouse, it is in fact just a monument built on top of Hoad Hill to commemorate Sir john Barrow, the founder of the Royal Geographic Society.

Again I had to drive inland around the estuary and then back down again to Holker and Flookburgh before getting to Grange-Over-Sands.

Grange is a nice little town. It has only 4000 residents but with shops providing everything someone would need.

There is a grocer, a baker, doctor, dentist, pharmacy, a pub, a church, an electrical shop, a furniture shop and those little craft and knick-knack shops so loved by tourists. The high street only has three or four visually "loud" signs, all food shops, apart from one, which is an estate agent. There are also two bank branches and a large Post Office here, which is unusual in that throughout England, many banks and post offices have closed down their smaller branches.

My B&B tonight is excellent and run by the Deputy Lord Mayor of the town, who tells me that the town's annual budget for local services is £130,000, which is soon to be reduced. He said that £18,000 pounds of this goes on maintaining the toilets, hence they are now charging for people to use them (like everywhere else). I suggested that they allow a Tesco to be built on the edge of town and they could then close the toilets and generate more tax revenue! As no doubt the council is made up of local shopkeepers I don't see a vote in favour of this any time soon

Tomorrow I head down the Lancashire coast and expect to spend the night in North Wales.

Grange-Over-Sands to Conwy, Wales

Miles 214

Conwy Castle, Clwyd, North Wales

I slept well last night, but woke at 5.00am, in the daylight and could not get back to sleep again. Breakfast was from 8.00am so I would have to wait three hours. Deciding that I could use the three hours to make further distance on my journey, I packed my suitcase and left as quietly as I could. I would 'phone my hosts later and let them know that I had left early. I had provided my credit card the night before so there should be no problem. Perhaps it was because I had not warmed up my muscles enough but as I swung my suitcase into the trunk of the car, I felt a twinge in my back. I knew that I had done something, but it did not hurt enough for me to want to stop: and so I drove on, heading for Wales. I only later realised that this was connected with my fall two days before. Much, much later I was diagnosed with damage to my sacro-iliac joint, which kept me in pain for many months!

Cumbria is famous for the Lake District, which is renowned as one of the loveliest areas of England. I felt a little disappointed that all I was seeing was the coastal area, which, though pretty, certainly does not share the splendour of the interior of the county. Indeed this can be so for many of the counties that I am passing through. In some cases the coastal area represents the county very well; in some cases it may be better than the county as a whole; in other cases the reverse may be true.

From Grange-Over-Sands I drove fifteen miles and reached Arnside, which is actually only just the opposite side of the estuary from Grange-Over-Sands. The two places are joined across the estuary, by a railway bridge, however, by road it is a long way to go around.

I drove on minor roads up and down the dales following the coast as best I could until I hit the A6 at Carnforth. Here I turned south until I reached Morecombe.

Morecombe is quite a sad town in that it has no cohesiveness about its architecture or sea front. There is an extremely large thin tower, the purpose of which I was not sure, but it was painted (presumably as an advert) as if it were a large packet of polo mints. There is also a fake wooden ranch house, painted orange that looked ghastly and I daresay is supposed to have a cowboy theme. Just over the sea wall, among the rocks there is a pool that fills with sea water when the tide comes in and makes a place to swim when the tide is out, which it was today. I remember as a child a pool like this at Burnham On Sea in Somerset. When not swimming in it we fished for eels, which seemed to like to live in this type of rocky, muddy pool.

The bay to which Morecombe gives it's name is the largest area of intertidal mud flats in the country. A number of rivers empty into the sea at Morecombe Bay, making it a super estuary. Most of the rainfall that falls on the mountains and hills of the Lake District and the Yorkshire Dales finds its way here. The Bay is noted for its bird life and especially shellfish, in particular cockles. It was the harvesting of these that ended in a tragedy in 2004 when 23 Chinese immigrants, who had been employed to collect cockles, were overcome by a fast incoming tide. The tides in the Bay are notorious and the water can come in faster than a horse can ride. There are also extensive areas of almost liquid sand, similar to quicksand that can trap the unwary walker.

As I drove out of Morecombe and on to Heysham, one resident was clearly a football fan and had a flag in his garden for each country currently playing in the Euro16 tournament that is on in France at the moment. The centerpiece was a very large football. He may like this, but do the neighbours?

At Heysham there is a large power station and commercial docks. The by now obligatory wind turbines were just off shore.

I had to then turn inland to go around the River Lun that flows through Lancaster. Lancaster had very heavy traffic, worsened by the large number of traffic lights that all seemed to go to red as we approached. When they did turn to green there would invariably be a pedestrian controlled traffic light about one hundred yards further up the road. Here there always seemed to be someone who would press the button, just as our light turned green. The pedestrian controlled light would then turn to red just as all of the traffic held up by the previous light got there. By the time the pedestrian controlled light changed to green the next light had turned to red. You would think that whoever designed the spacing and timing of these lights could have considered some form of synchronization. Perhaps they did but this represents part of a cunning plan to restrict traffic flow. Maybe this person is employed to spend his time going backwards and forwards across the road slowing down the traffic.

Just outside of Lancaster, Samantha sent me off down a country lane and showed me Glasson Basin, a section of the Lancaster canal. She clearly felt that I needed to be somewhere peaceful and idyllic after the traffic chaos of Lancaster. It was very lovely, so I stopped to make myself a cup of tea by a small bridge over the canal. In the field nearby, about 150 yards away, I saw a woman, facing away from me and seemingly staring out across the field. All of the twenty minutes I was stopped here, the woman continued to stand still looking across the field. I took the very British position of not interfering, but for the rest of the day I could not help but wonder whether or not I should have walked over and spoken to her. Perhaps she was sad, or lonely. Maybe even contemplating taking her life in the canal. But then again, perhaps there was nothing wrong at all and she just enjoyed standing staring out across the fields. I will never know, but I still have a conscience that maybe I should have gone and spoken to her, even if it did mean my being very un-British. I also tell myself that perhaps she was just a female scarecrow after all!

This road eventually led to a place called Knott End, which is just across the estuary of the River Wyre from Fleetwood. You get a good view of Fleetwood and the docks and harbour. The road is a dead end. There is a ferry here, but only for foot passengers and it did not appear to be operating anyway. They have a statue on the dock of a character taken from an L.S. Lowry painting.

L.S. Lowry statue at Knott End, Lancashire

To get to Fleetwood I had to return back up the road and travel ten miles inland. Fleetwood is still a major fishing port. Driving into the town I saw a large building signed as being the premises of an ice manufacturer. No doubt this ice is supplied, not for the gin and tonics of Fleetwood housewives, but instead for the fishing industry and specifically for the trawlers to pack their catch in ice while out at sea.

Fleetwood had very modern trams running down the center of the street, which travel too and from Blackpool about 15 miles south.

Here I saw evidence of one of the deleterious issues facing the British way of life resulting from membership of the European Union. In this case it was British farming and in particular dairy farming. A grocery store was advertising 4 litres of milk for £1.50. It's no wonder that the dairy farmers are finding it hard to stay in business. This milk almost certainly originated from outside of the UK. People will always go for the cheapest option, even if a better quality product is available and even if it means damaging a local supplier. What will our countryside look like with no cows in the fields? It seems ironic that in a fishing town like Fleetwood, where the industry has been decimated by European fishing regulations, that shops who rely for their existence on the expenditure of the income of people from the fishing industry, choose to sell cheap imported milk, which itself damages British farming. I suppose as their income is reduced, so they are forced to buy cheaper products, which in turn damages another industry.

I drove on down and into Blackpool following the ocean through Cleveleys, with its high wall along the esplanade blocking any view of the ocean. No doubt this has been constructed to prevent further damage from the sea as happened all along this coast in a severe storm two years ago. Just before Cleveleys I was interested to see a Boarding School with a sign stating that it took children from aged 2 to 18. Can you imagine anyone putting a two year old into a Boarding School? But clearly some do. These poor children must feel so lonely without a parent to cuddle them. The buildings that I saw looked more like old barracks closely resembling a modern day version of Dicken's "Dotheboys Hall".

Blackpool, well what can I say about this town? Apart from one or two new buildings, it has not changed much from when I last saw it about 10 years ago. It is a mix of smart buildings, scruffy B&Bs and too much tourist kitsch, all joined together by a mass of overhead electrical cables for the famous illuminations.

No doubt, once upon a time, many a person's retirement dream was to own a B&B in a seaside town. The changes in labour laws giving people longer holidays and flexibility as to when they could take them coincided with cheap airfares to Spain etc. Warm sunny beaches and cheap food and drink certainly trumped the cold and blustery Irish or North Seas and so the traditional English seaside town suffered and went into decline. Many have fought back by raising quality and focusing on providing gourmet food or different forms of entertainment and making attractive weekend breaks rather than a cheap fortnight. A lot of towns now focus on local geography and history rather than just the beach.

Blackpool, however, despite its seedy nature has always been at the forefront of trying to attract out of season vacationers. In the late nineteenth century, just before Edison had patented the light bulb, it installed some arc lights on its sea front, which it proudly described as *artificial sunlight*. Then in 1912, to coincide with a royal visit it expanded the light display along a new section of promenade, using thousands of Mr. Edison's light bulbs. This was so successful that the traders in the town asked the council to put on a similar display every September, which effectively extended the summer tourist season by a month. Apart from the years of the first and second world wars, the illuminations have shone out ever since, now running from late August to mid November. There have been times when more modern lighting such as lasers have been used, but Mr. Edison's light bulbs are still the main stay of the show.

Blackpool un-illuminations

Today many people come to Blackpool just to view the illuminations. However, it's a bit like Las Vegas, people go there once to see it and then are done –*"been there, seen that"*. Driving along the promenade in June, during the daytime, the structure of wires, metal frames in the shape of cartoon characters and empty bulb sockets, make a bit of a grim sight. It looks like the morning after a riotous party the night before in a marquee, where the marquee blew away and the light fittings were left dangling by their wires.

Blackpool was also innovative in constructing a large tower, akin to a small version of the Eiffel Tower. It has in it a theatre and at one time even a circus. Blackpool also built a large pleasure beach and fun fare, which still operates. The roller coaster is apparently the tallest one in Britain.

Apart from these, unless you are in to slot machines, fun palaces, drinking beer and eating fish and chips, there is not a lot that would bring you to Blackpool. Although the beach is broad and sandy, the English weather has to cooperate to make this worth going, especially as at low tide the sea is a long way out.

There is a large Hilton Hotel on the front, but as measured by the special offer signs outside many places, there is an overcapacity of rooms. It must be hard for many B&Bs to make money out of season. I saw one small hotel advertising en-suite family rooms for fifteen pounds a night. Further up the road, towards the fun park, there were even two fairly large hotels that had closed and all their windows were boarded up.

Despite it being grey and damp today the fun fare was operating with people on the rides and others milling around each of the three piers. I also saw another "Genting Club" like the one I had noticed in Southend. Though way more over the top you can't help but compare Blackpool with Southend. Southend is much more understated, but there is a similar "feel" about both towns. Both built to amuse and earn money from tourists from the local big cities.

Leaving the glitz of Blackpool, and driving south, you come quickly into Lytham St Annes. This is separated from the Blackpool sprawl by an area of sand dunes and is much more refined. Indeed it is the home of the very up-market

Royal Lytham golf course. It has a very nice and expansive area of open green fronting onto the ocean, where you can park your car, exercise your dog, or, like me, make a cup of tea and eat your lunch.

On the green is a lovely old windmill, which is now a museum with free entry. It was built in the early 1800s to grind corn, but when the large houses were being built across the road in 1860, the owners of the houses saw the windmill as an industrial eyesore and wanted to have it removed. In 1919 in a terrible gale the wind forced the sails to turn, despite being braked. This caused friction and sparks flew and the windmill caught on fire, completely gutting the inside. It remained derelict until the Council decided to repair it and open the mill to the public in 1989. Inside, on five floors, is a history of milling and of Lytham, ideal to visit with children. The owners of the houses opposite now no doubt see the restored windmill as an asset to the value of their properties.

After Lytham the drive is then back inland towards Preston, which I skirted in order to return to the coast at Southport. Many residential houses are built on the sea front at Southport, rather than B&Bs and tourist attractions, though further along there is Pleasureland and Ocean Plaza. Southport is the home of another very smart golf course, Royal Birkdale. Again you can't see the ocean as you drive along the esplanade due to the high sea defense wall. One glimpse of the shoreline though did suggest it is marshy grass close in leading out to a muddy shore. Between Southport and Formby is a Pontins Holiday Camp, painted purple, like the one in Kent, but with the addition of other even brighter and gaudier colours.

The road then continues all the way into Bootle and Liverpool. I aimed for the Mersey tunnel and the town of

Wallesey on the other side on the Wirrall. At one stage of the drive into Liverpool you go past modern-day docks with some big cargo vessels and lots of industrial buildings. It looked to be thriving. Liverpool was at one time Britain's most important industrial port being the major gateway to North America.

Thousands of emigrants would arrive here before journeying on to a new life in America. Indeed, like Hull on the east coast, the fact that there is a large Jewish population here is an echo back to European history. Jews from Europe and Russia fleeing persecution would arrive at the eastern town of Hull and then travel to the western city of Liverpool for onward passage to America. However, perhaps due to poverty forcing them to have to stay and work to earn enough to pay for onward passage, or, a sense of security on being in Britain, or just tiredness, many of them gave up on making the longer journey and remained settled in either Hull, or the second stop of Liverpool.

As patterns of trade and modes of transport changed and Britain's markets moved more towards Europe and east coast ports, so Liverpool went into many years of decline. The city has made great strides in seeking to reverse the decay, especially in its marvelous dockland area and though challenges still remain, it is a vibrant and lively city. The legacy of the Beatles and other bands that came out of Liverpool in the 1960s continue to this day to grow the cities reputation as a "happening place".

Just before entering the road tunnel under the River Mersey you come to a booth where, either you throw the correct fee of £1.70 into a basket, or, if you don't have the right amount of coins, you stop and they will change a £2 coin or a note and give you change and the correct money in coins so that you can then throw it into the basket. I handed in a $2 coin and the lady gave me sufficient change so that I had £1.70, with

£0.30 pence left over. I then threw this into the basket, but the barrier remained down, rejecting a five pence coin. This meant that the women who had given me the coins, had to come out of her booth and collect the five pence from the reject coin slot. After three attempts to get it to accept the coin, she used a key to override it and open the barrier. All the while she was chatting to the person from the adjacent booth that was doing the same thing for another motorist. It would seem to make sense that they do away with the baskets and just take your money. If they have to be there to give change then either take the £1.70 and open the barrier, or make it free (no chance!). I would suggest that if you have an automated system, but need people to be present to support it, then you need a new system.

On coming out of the tunnel you are then on the Wirral. Here, though only about a half mile from cloudy Liverpool, the sun was out. I once lived in the village of Prestbury, near Macclesfield in Cheshire, which gets a lot of rain; but the story was that no matter if it was raining in Cheshire, it would always be sunny at West Kirby on the Wirral. One day we tried it and left Macclesfield in the rain and it rained the whole of the journey, but when we got to West Kirby, the sun was out! So my now second experience has confirmed that the story must be correct!

I turned right and followed the road into New Brighton with its lighthouse. At one time New Brighton served as the main seaside resort for Liverpool. It has a lovely art deco style building, which unfortunately today houses amusement arcades. New Brighton merges into Wallasey. At Leasowe, which is part of Wallasey, the world's first hovercraft service operated in 1962 between here and Rhyll over on the North Wales coast. Unfortunately it only ran for one summer. As the then Member of Parliament for the Wirral, Ernest Marples, was Minister for

Transport, perhaps it was a trial operation. I don't know why it stopped after 3 months, but possibly the residents did not like the noise of the two large aero engines used to make it hover.

My son has flown a hovercraft as part of an expedition in Guatemala. He agrees that they are noisy, but great fun to fly and can provide transport across terrains that other vehicles cannot travel. Indeed many coastguards around the world now use them as rescue vessels for airfields that are built, as so many are, with their runways pointing to the sea. However, residential areas, where other options exist, are probably not the best places for this technology.

I next passed through Hoylake, where the Royal Liverpool golf course is situated and then on into West Kirby.

The coast here is the estuary of the River Dee and like that of the Mersey and the other estuaries on this coast, it means that there is a lot of mud when the tide is out. Again I had to turn inland a long way to get to Queensferry before I could then cross the river and return back to the coast. This now brought me in to North Wales.

My intention was to stay the night in the area around Flint. I knew nothing about Flint but somehow the name seemed eco friendly and attractive. This was when the torrential rain started again. I am not sure whether Flint would have looked any better in the sunshine but I found it to be very industrial, with my first sight being the large steel works at Shotton. I decided to head further into North Wales and see what I could find. I had deliberately not booked ahead any accommodation, as, even though I had Flint as an area in mind I was not exactly sure how far I would get today.

I drove on and came to Prestatyn. It was as awful as I had expected it to be with a large Pontin's holiday camp dominating the town. It does have long sandy beaches, which gives you a good vista of the extremely large offshore wind turbine farm. I counted at least a hundred before I gave up. Again a Norfolk lad would no doubt find this a great place to spend a vacation. Perhaps Pontins should make a feature of this and target their advertising on Norfolk!

Between Prestatyn and Rhyl there was another holiday village, this time with buildings painted, blue, grey, yellow and orange. Rhyl seems even more down market than Prestatyn with lots of amusement arcades. Rhyl has a small harbor with a Yacht Club, but as the tide was out and the boats were resting on the mud I suspect that this is a club where there is a lot of talk about sailing in the bar rather than sailing over the bar.

I stopped at Asda to buy something for supper and use their toilet. I was surprised to discover that unlike Tesco they have no toilets for customers. When I enquired where they were they said that I should go across the car park to Mac-Donalds. Needless to say I did not spend a penny in Asda. Thank God for Tesco.

At Colwyn Bay the area started to improve and everything became more up-market with what I would term as "Torbay style" houses. There is a nice sea front here with great digging sand and Rhoos-on-Sea at the west end being a particularly pleasant place.

I felt that I should now look for somewhere to stay. I consulted the map and saw that I was not far from Conwy, which I knew to be a walled town with an ancient castle. I Googled B&Bs in Conwy and up came a list with one that caught my eye. I phoned and was pleasantly told that they had a room and at a price again less than I was paying with

342

AirB&B, so I booked it. I now felt more at ease as I knew that I had a place to stay for the night.

One of my objectives, from looking at the map, was to drive around the Great Orme, which is above Llandudno. I thought therefore that I would do this before going to my B&B. I knew nothing about the Great Orme or Llandudno, but in my mind I had erroneously placed Llandudno on a par with Southend. I drove up and over the hill from Rhoos and on reaching the top was greeted with the most spectacular view of Llandudno. It was not at all as I had imagined it. The first impression was of the crescent at Bath transferred to the seaside. The buildings appeared to be Georgian in style and built in a crescent around the bay.

When I arrived down on the esplanade I was not disappointed. It was smart, clean, attractive and with a consistency of appearance that made it all very cohesive. Here the buildings were painted in attractive pastel colours. Certainly a place that I felt I would enjoy staying for a short holiday.

I took some photos, which did not do it justice and then drove along the front with its smart looking pier and took the Great Orme road.

The road around the Great Orme is quite narrow with a wall on the seaward side, but, as it is a circular route, it operates a one-way system, so you can enjoy the views without having to constantly look for oncoming traffic. There were a number of walkers and also places to stop the car. I noticed the old lighthouse, which is now open as a B&B. I was relieved to see that it had a sign saying no vacancies. If it had a vacancy I might have felt sorry that I had not seen it before I booked in Conwy. The Great Orme is wonderful and offers a very scenic "must do" drive.

Llandudno, North Wales

The road takes you right around the headland and then drops down towards Conwy itself. The first view of Conwy is magnificent, offering a fine view across to the castle and the three bridges (one rail, one road, one foot) leading into it. The setting is superb and I was glad that I had made the choice to stay here.

Conwy castle was built in 1289 by Edward I the "Hammer of the Scots". Edward built four massive castles as part of his conquest and control of the Welsh. The second one is at Caernarvon, not too far from Conwy. The third Beaumaris is on Anglesey, which I shall visit tomorrow and the fourth, about 30 miles further south at Harlech. All four have UNESCO World Heritage status. The English lived, barricaded behind the walls of the town and the Welsh lived outside. During the English Civil War Conwy castle was a holdout for troops loyal to Charles I. In 1645 it surrendered

344

to the government forces and to prevent its further use for resistance it was stripped out and eventually fell into ruin.

History is mixed on the accomplishments of Edward I's reign. He is noted for establishing Parliament as a permanent institution, but others suggest that this was done more as a way to enable him to better impose taxes. As well as subduing the Scots and the Welsh he is notorious for having executed the heads of 300 Jewish families in 1279 and then in 1290 expelling all Jews from England, confiscating their property when it was clear that they were no longer able to fund his many warring adventures.

There are three short bridges leading into the town of Conwy, all built alongside each other. The first is a suspension bridge built by the famous engineer Thomas Telford. This is now owned by the National Trust and used only by pedestrians. Unfortunately it was covered over with white plastic and undergoing repairs so the beauty of it that I had seen in photographs, was not on display. The other two bridges are a rail bridge and a vehicle bridge. Robert Stephenson, who also built the bridge at Berwick-On-Tweed, built the rail bridge. In building this bridge he invented the box girder construction method that was used for many years in building the bridges on the motorways of Britain, until a collapse of a structure in the 1970s took this design out of favour. The architect for this bridge was Francis Thompson, who designed the covers for the pylons at either end to make them look like barbicans, with crenellated turrets and arrow slits. This gave it a castle like feel and made it blend with the adjacent Conwy Castle.

The town of Conwy is very small and the roads restricted. I drove across the more modern road bridge and entered the town by the castle, but then Samantha directed me through a

345

different exit in the walls and to my B&B just outside the walls. To my surprise the couple running the B&B came from Woodley in Berkshire, a village only five miles from where I lived in Wargrave and where two of my nieces lived for a period of time.

On the recommendation of my hostess I walked back into the town, through a passage in the walls and ate at a superb Bistro. I don't think I would have found this place unless I had been told about it. It was in a small courtyard right under the walls. The meal was probably the best I have eaten so far on my trip. I wanted after dinner to walk the walls, but my back was now stiff and I had pain as I walked. I have been feeling my back all day as I got in and out of the car, which reduced my willingness to take lots of photographs

※

Tomorrow I leave this wonderful and historic town and head off further into Wales and the Isle of Anglesey and the search for another of Edward I's castles.

Conwy Castle

Conwy to Caernarfon (via Anglesey)

Miles 125

Menai Suspension Bridge, Anglesey

I drove 125 miles today, but ended up just 20 miles further down the coast. I also visited two more of Edward I's castles and the town with the longest name in Britain.

I had a late start this morning, not leaving my B&B until 10.00am. This was mainly because of the pain in my back. I had hoped to walk the walls of Conwy and visit the castle, but I decided not to do it as I thought it might aggravate it further. However, I did find that I was OK sitting down so felt that I could drive. I was stiff getting in and out of the car, but by early afternoon (and some ibuprofen) it felt a lot better and I was able to visit another great castle. I had also hoped to be able to take a photo of the Thomas Telford suspension bridge that used to be the main bridge into Conwy, but as it is currently covered in white plastic it was not possible.

The weather was sunny when I left my nice B&B and stayed with me all day. My objective was a circuit of the island of Anglesey and then on into mainland North Wales. There are actually three bridges across to Anglesey so it does not feel like it is an island. Samantha took me out through the old town of Conwy and I exited via a gateway in the city wall. On the other side of this was where I saw the only chalet park in Conwy. Out of the town and out of sight of the castle or from the castle.

As I neared the seaside town of Penmaenmawr the sea looked remarkably blue. Above the town was a mountain that had clearly been quarried and there were chutes or roads of some sort that had been used to channel the stone down to trains via special gantries, which I at first thought was a pier. Though quarrying is no longer very active, the whole top of the mountain and an ancient Neolithic fort have all been removed over the years. The town is now bypassed, but in building the new road a fine Georgian Esplanade was apparently removed. Because of the bypass the town is quiet and is still a popular holiday destination.

Out of Penmaenmawr the road passes through a very smart tunnel, emerging the other side of the mountain at

Llanfairfechen. This also has benefitted from the bypass and has nice coloured properties fronting the sea on the Promenade. I drove along the Promenade to take the road back to the bypass and passed through a short tunnel with a clearance of only six feet. Assuming that this was higher than the car (but not completely confident) I drove through slowly, and emerged unscathed on the other side.

The double "Ll" in Welsh is enunciated as "Cl", so Llanfairfechan is pronounced something like "Clan fair feck un". It is not quite said as "clan", but to make the sound you have to hollow your tongue and push the "clan" to the back and roof of your mouth. When some people say it, it resembles the noise made before they might spit. Make sure that you practice before saying it to anyone who lives here. Over 50% of the population in Llanfairfechan speaks Welsh so will expect you to pronounce it properly!

The bypass then took me towards Anglesey and I crossed the Britannia Bridge onto the island. Just over the bridge is the small town with the longest name of any place in Britain. The map shows it as Llanfair PG, but its full name, as written on the station signboard is:

Llanfairpwllgwyngyllgogogerychwyrndrobwllllantysiliogogogoch. Go on I dare you to try and say it! The English translation doesn't really help very much either. If you can't say it in Welsh you can always ask for a train ticket for the same place in English. Then you would need to ask for a ticket to: "The church of Mary in the hollow of the white hazel near the fierce whirlpool and the church of Tysilio by the red cave". Might be easier to learn to say it in Welsh! There is nothing especially attractive or distinguishing about the village, but I'm sure people go there just because of the name.

Llanfair PG Railway Station

Certainly of more significance than Llanfair PG and just two miles away, inland, is the village of Penmyndd. This was the home of one, Owen Tudor. He came from a wealthy and historic Welsh family whose offspring became one of the most noted of all British Royal houses.

Owen's father Maredudd was brought up with his two brothers, Rhys and Gwillam. The brothers were all first cousins to Owen Glendower, who in the 15th Century led a rebellion against the English and was crowned Prince of Wales. The Tudor brothers and Owen Glendower were allegedly all descendants of Llewellyn, who was Prince of Wales from 1216 to 1240. Llewellyn was a friend and supporter for many years of King John, but later joined with the Barons in getting John to sign the Magna Carta. The Tudor brothers supported Owen in his rebellion, but when the English managed to suppress this, most of the Tudor lands were confiscated; Rhys was executed, Gwilym later received a pardon and Maredudd disappeared, at least from history.

Maredudd's son, Owen Tudor, became a courtier at the palace of Henry V. When Henry V died, Owen married (though many said no actual marriage took place) his widow, Catherine de Valois, who herself was a daughter of a King, Charles VI of France. Catherine's first son, by Henry V, became Henry VI. She then had two further sons with Owen Tudor, Edmund and Jasper. Catherine died in 1446 following the birth of her fourth child, but Owen lived on.

Henry VI looked kindly on his half-brothers and supported Edmund and Jasper by making them Earls: Edmund of Richmond and Jasper of Pembroke. In 1455 Henry VI arranged for Edmund, now aged 24, to marry Margaret Beaufort, aged 12. She was a descendent of John of Gaunt, Duke of Lancaster and thus had Plantagenet blood, which gave her a potential claim to the throne.

The Wars of the Roses began in 1455 and continued on until 1487. It was a struggle between the supporters of the two branches of the Plantagenet royal house; one branch being the House of Lancaster (the red rose) and the other being the House of York (the white rose). Henry VI was considered weak and also suffered from bouts of madness. The opposition wanted to put Richard of York on the throne instead. Richard had been Regent for one year in 1454, ruling during a time of Henry's illness. When Richard died in 1460 the opposition then supported his son Edward (who would later became Edward IV).

Edmund, Earl of Richmond, leading Lancastrian troops, was captured early in the war and imprisoned at

351

Carmarthen Castle by Yorkist forces. He died there of the plague, in November 1456 and is now buried in St Davids' Cathedral, which I will be visiting in two days time. His 13 year old widow Margaret was 6 months pregnant when he died and Jasper, concerned for the safety and well being of his sister-in-law, took her for protection to Pembroke Castle. The birth was difficult and both Margaret and the child, a boy, also called Henry, almost died.

Edward was eventually successful and deposed Henry VI, becoming Edward IV. Henry VI was kept a prisoner in the Tower of London, but was briefly restored to the throne in 1470 by the Earl of Warwick, Richard Neville. However Edward IV defeated Neville and took back the throne in 1471 at the Battle of Tewkesbury. The battlefield here is on land once farmed by a friend of mine and was known as the Bloody Meadow due to the slaughter that took place there and in the nearby Tewkesbury Abbey. Shortly after, Henry VI, now back in the Tower, died.

Edward IV died peacefully in 1483 and the throne passed to his 12 year old son, Edward V, who was under the protection of his Uncle, Richard, Duke of Gloucester. Edward and his younger brother, also called Richard, were ordered to be taken to the Tower for their protection by their Uncle. There they disappeared, believed murdered and are today remembered as the Princes in the Tower. Uncle Richard took the throne as Richard III.

Two years later, in 1485, Henry, the son of Edmond Tudor, now aged 28, famously achieved retribution when he defeated Richard III, at the Battle of Bosworth Field, in Leicestershire. He is said to have taken the crown from the slain Richard on the battlefield and lifted it onto his head, proclaiming himself as King Henry VII.

One year later Henry VII brought an end to all of the fighting by marrying Elizabeth of York. She was the daughter of Edward IV and niece of Richard III, thus uniting once again the Plantagenet royal house. This gave rise to the symbol known as the Tudor Rose, a red rose with a white rose at its centre.

So, Henry VII, grandson of the Welsh Owen Tudor and his wife, the French consort of Henry V, became the first Tudor King. His dynasty continued until the death of his granddaughter, Queen Elizabeth I, dying without heirs in 1603. Here in Anglesey, in Wales, sprang one of the most well known of all British royal dynasties.

One thing that keeps being confirmed to me on this around Britain trip is that the throne of England has the genes of not just the English but also the Welsh and the Scots. But there remains to this day, a patriotism and independence amongst the Welsh and the Scots and even a desire by some for independence of each nation. Tony Blair, while Prime Minister, pandered to this view, or possibly sought to suppress resentment and keep support for his Labour Party, by allowing the establishment of separate governing bodies. In Scotland, which is seen as a separate nation there is now a Parliament. Wales, which is considered not to be a nation but a Principality, has established a Welsh Assembly. However, rather than retain support for the Labour Party, these separate governing bodies further stimulated the sense of nationalism. This was clearly seen in the 2015 general election in Britain when the Labour party in Scotland was virtually eliminated by the Scottish Nationalist Party, who swept the board winning all but one of the previous Labour held seats, with heavy defeats also for the Labour Party in Wales by the Welsh nationalist party, Plaid Cymru.

Having visited Llanfair PG, I turned round to follow an anti-clockwise route around the island and drove towards Beaumaris. This was a beautiful short drive and I stopped at a viewpoint where there was an excellent view of the Menai Bridge, which is the bridge I will cross when I leave Anglesey. You also get a good view here across the strait to Bangor with its attractive looking pier. There used to be a chain ferry at this point, prior to the bridge being built. You also look down upon Ines Gored Goch Island in the middle of the Strait. The word Gored means a stone fish trap used to catch fish that swim in but are left high and dry when the tide goes out.

Beaumaris is an exceptionally lovely little seaside town built around the now ruined Beaumaris Castle. The town has pretty painted houses, a small pier that seems to serve only the lifeboat station and lots of sailboats at anchor in the harbour.

Beaumaris Castle, Anglesey, North Wales

Beaumaris castle is another major touch point of British history like Conwy castle. Beaumaris Castle seems much smaller than Conwy, but at one time it was a mighty fortress with twelve towers on its outer walls and six on its inner wall. It was started in 1295 but work did not end until 1330. Indeed it was never fully completed as Edward I almost broke the exchequer in building this and at the same time fighting his many wars with the Scots and Welsh. The castle has the unusual feature of having concentric walls, such that defenders who are overrun at the first wall can retreat behind a second wall, leaving the enemy behind in a killing zone below the second wall. The castle had a dock to the ocean and a moat around three quarters of it, which is still evident today along with the large gatehouse. It was the last of Edward's castles to be built. I contemplated going in, but then two groups of schoolchildren, with around forty in each group, arrived and so I decided to give it a miss and just take photos from outside. I thought if time permitted, that I would later try and visit Caernarfon Castle, which is the most complete of the four.

Once again I found that the town toilets required a 20p coin to enter. One can no longer say that you are going to "spend a penny". It doesn't sound quite the same to say you are going to "spend twenty pence". I saw one elderly gentleman looking quite distressed as he did not have 20p, and neither did I so I could not assist him. He was hoping that someone was inside and he could go in when they came out. I think for coach parties or groups, you can all get in for the price of one person as each holds the door open in turn. I do understand a Council that says it costs them money to keep the toilets clean, but they also want visitors to visit their town and spend money there. Some of this tourist money goes to the Council through business taxes and can be used to maintain the toilets. If they want people to come and spend money in their town, then I think they should recognise that they need to be "hospitable" to their guests and provide basic facilities.

I continued on around the island passing through Amlwch and then Cemeas with its large power station (and on-land wind farm) near by. My destination was Holyhead the main ferry port to Ireland. As you enter Holyhead there is a turn off to the ferry, but keeping on to the town centre takes you to the large railway station from where numerous trains are ready to distribute passengers right across the UK.

I found Holyhead to be a pleasant enough place, certainly in the warm sunshine. I know that Paul Theroux did not like it when he came here. You have to take places as you find them and today my experience was of a nice place to stop and enjoy the view.

I drove out to the Esplanade and had a snack in the car. I decided to throw away some ham in the nearby garbage bin. I had purchased it two days before, but it had been sitting in the warm car. I also thought about throwing away some bread rolls, purchased only yesterday. I didn't really want to waste good food and decided to give at least one of the rolls to a gull standing looking hungry by the car. Big mistake. As soon as I threw some bread towards him others swooped in and a big gull fight broke out. In order to not allow further carnage to take place, I stopped. As I prepared to leave I saw a young man, who looked decidedly as if he was living on the street, put his hand into the garbage bin and take out my discarded ham and proceed to eat it. I couldn't stop him, however, as he was obviously hungry I gave him my bag of bread rolls. Rather him than the gulls.

I then continued on my round the island drive and headed for the village of Rhosneigr. This has the most fantastic beach and also an excellent view of the RAF Advanced Flying School at Valley where two jets were carrying out "touch and goes". It was here that Prince William was based as a helicopter pilot and carried out search and rescue operations on nearby Snowdonia. He, Kate and baby George lived somewhere in the area while he was stationed at RAF Valley.

Anglesey is very much a farming island and I saw little more of the sea as I headed back to the lovely old Menai Bridge. I crossed over it then followed the Menai Strait southwest to Caernarfon.

Caernarfon Castle, Gwynedd

As my back was feeling better I decided that I would take time to visit at least one of Edward I's castles so I parked up and went in to the magnificent Caernarfon Castle. The walls and towers of the Castle are still in good order though some areas of the castle inside, such as the Great Hall, are no longer there. The castle and the city walls were not fully completed until 1330, after Edward had died. After the English Civil War in 1651 the castle was allowed to decay and it was not until 1870 that the state decided to begin some repairs. In 1911 it was used as the site for the investiture of the future King Edward VIII as Prince of Wales and in 1969 the Queen used Caernarfon Castle to also invest Prince Charles as the current Prince of Wales.

Edward I had the castle built to a high standard and sought to make it as much a palace as a fortification. He wanted to spend time here and confirm his lordship over the Welsh. Indeed in 1284 he instructed that his heavily pregnant wife, Eleanor of Castille, travel to Caernarfon in a very late stage of pregnancy, so that if a son was born here in Wales he could rightly lay claim to being a prince of Wales as well as a future King of England. She indeed did give birth to a son, who would become Edward II. This child was actually Eleanor's sixteenth child by Edward. Four other sons had been born, but all had died. Eleanor herself died in 1290, some suggest of exhaustion.

Edward I's son, Edward II, who had briefly been betrothed to Margaret, granddaughter of both King Alexander III of Scotland and King Eric of Norway, eventually became King and married Isabella, daughter of the King of France. We learned something about him and his favourite, Piers Gaveston, while in Scarborough. Edward II was a poor King and was seen as a failure in England because of the defeat of the English army by the Scots at Bannockburn. Isabella had tried to support her husband who ignored her preferring his favourites, such as Piers. She eventually tired of Edward and returned to France on the pretext of negotiating a peace treaty with her brother, by now King of France, but secretly wanting to meet an enemy of her husband, Roger Mortimer. Mortimer had fled England after a failed uprising by several Barons that had tried to remove two other favourites of the King, Hugh Despenser and his father. The Despensers owned land in Wales around Cardiff and Newport and through their influence with Edward had cruelly killed people and usurped lands.

Mortimer had raised an army and seized their lands and assisted by the Earls of Hereford and Lancaster marched on London to demand that Edward get rid of them. Edward agreed to banish the Despensers, but within, a few months reneged on his promise and secretly brought them back. Fighting followed and Edward and the Despensers overcame the opposition of Mortimer and Lancaster. Lancaster was executed and Mortimer imprisoned in the Tower of London from where he later escaped and fled to France.

When Isabella went to France, the Despensers persuaded Edward that she should not take her sons with her in case she did not return and they took them into their care. Once the Peace Treaty had been agreed Edward was due to go to France to seal it, the Despensers fearing he would be captured, instead arranged for his 12 year old son and heir, Edward, to go in his place. This was their big mistake.

Isabella and Mortimer were now lovers. When her son arrived this meant that she now had with her the heir to the throne and was determined to play this trump card. She and Mortimer believed the Barons and the people were so tired of the Despensers and Edward II, that they would rally around them and remove Edward II in favour of his son. So she and Mortimer, with Edward the young heir, along with a small number of French mercenaries sailed back to England. Isabella and Mortimer were greeted warmly and the Barons gave support to her cause. Edward II was deposed and the Despensers executed, the younger being hung, drawn and quartered. Edward II was imprisoned at Berkley Castle in Gloucestershire but murdered soon after.

Isabella then ruled as Regent for her son Edward III who became King at age 14. At age 17 though, Edward became tired of being ruled by his Mother and feeling that Mortimer was himself acting as King, carried out a coup, killing Mortimer and taking over the throne in his own right. Edward III ruled for fifty years and stabilised the country and restored its military strength. His disputed claim to being the rightful heir of the throne of France led to the Hundred Years War.

Caernarfon castle today can be described as a glorious ruin. The walls and towers are still very much intact so you can get some of the feel what it must have been like to live there. The walls are thick and the towers have commanding positions from all sides. There are some very steep and worn steps up its main towers. I went up three of the towers but I must say I felt very nervous when descending. There is just a thick, slack rope and nothing else especially firm to hang onto. At the end of the visit my back was sore once again so I decided to find a B&B and stay in Caernarfon for the night.

My B&B was not as good as last night, even though it cost slightly more. It was clean, which is fine, but it is one of those places that have lots of "dos and don'ts" notices, which I find irritating. The owner met me in what I thought was a white overall as if he was a workman. I only later found out that it was his bee-keeping outfit, less the hat and mask.

Tomorrow I head further along the coast, firstly to the Lleyn peninsula, where I once holidayed many years ago and then on to Harlech (the site of the last of Edward I's great castles).

Caernarfon to Cardigan

Miles 205

Harlech Castle, Gwynedd

I set off early today from Caernarfon with the intention of seeing how far I could get and yet still enjoy all of the coastal views and villages. I saw more castles, drove miles up and down estuaries just to cross over to the other side, watched England beat Wales at football and ate an Indian meal on a boat on the river.

361

My first stop was at Morfa Nefyn on the Lleyn Peninsula. This was a place where we had vacationed a number of years ago as a family, with some friends. I tried to find the original beach but was not sure that I recognised it. At what I thought was the beach, I watched a woman assisting a man launch a dinghy. There was quite a wind blowing and the ocean was kicking up, but he was obviously going out. There were some sail boats anchored about a mile out so perhaps he was going out to one of these. He put on a rain jacket, but no life jacket. I did not say anything (but perhaps I should have). Having been in marine search and rescue for a number of years I am very aware that over 80% of boating fatalities are with people not wearing life jackets. His wife later passed me with the empty launch trailer so he was obviously going out on his own.

In the village I stopped to fill up with fuel and was surprised to find that not only was it cheaper on the Peninsula than on the "mainland" but the attached village store was superbly stocked, with lots of fresh local items; a gem of a place.

Aberdaron Village

From Morfa I drove to the end of the Peninsula to the pretty little village of Aberdaron, with its very nice beach. Indeed all the beaches on this Peninsula have very good sand.

I then had to drive along very narrow country lanes, mostly behind a tractor, to get to Abersoch, a well-known sailing town. When I lived in Cheshire, Abersoch was known as 'Wilmslow on Sea' as many people from this well to do town in Cheshire would have weekend homes here. I must say that Abersoch did not seem quite so thriving as I remembered it from 20 years ago.

I still remember the first time we went shopping in Sainsbury's in Wilmslow. There was no one in casual clothes and many of the women were not only dressed up, but actually were wearing their jewels! Also, the local department store in the town used to pride itself on serving only "our kind of people"! This was the north of England in the 1980s. In contrast, the south of England at the same time, was the opposite. People here, with money, tended to be the most casually dressed with old worn clothes, though usually designer labels.

I moved on to Pwllheli (pronounced, by the English, as "Puth Welly"), which was as I remembered it, a town dominated by a holiday camp and caravans. I did not stop, though it has to be said that it has another superb beach.

Further on I came to Criccieth, another town with a ruined castle, but a small one. Owen Glendower destroyed this castle during his revolt in 1404. Owen was the last Welshman to bear the title, Prince of Wales. He instigated an uprising against Henry IV in 1400. At first he was successful but his army was no match for the military might and especially the artillery of the English and by 1409 he had been defeated. He evaded capture and eventually disappeared entirely in 1412. He was said by a follower to have died in 1415.

I parked on the sea front in Criccieth next to a car identical to the one that I was driving. You might recall that in Whitby I saw the "twin" to my vehicle with the number plate being the next in the series. This vehicle was also close in its number, so I think Hertz must have received a large batch of them. This one the driver told me had been picked up in Birmingham.

The driver of the vehicle, along with others, was looking out to the ocean at something in the water. They thought it might be a whale in distress and they were thinking of calling for help. It was a black shape about a half-mile out, staying in the same spot but moving in a strange way. I could not make out what it was either but took a photo of it with my telephoto lens and then zoomed in on the image. It turned out to be a large grey seal that was obviously sitting on a rock that must have been just at surface level. I was surprised how clear the picture was with my camera and continue to be amazed at the power of digital cameras.

The next town was Porthmadog a cute place with a terminus of the Ffestiniog steam railway. Unfortunately I would have to wait for two hours for the next train and didn't feel that I could hang around for that length of time. However, the car park attendant very kindly allowed me to park, without charge, to use the facilities and also walk back into the town to take a couple of pictures. I later saw one of the trains passing me on a high track and as I pointed my camera out of the car the driver blew the whistle and gave a wave.

Close to Porthmadog is the fantasy village of Portmeirion. This is a pseudo Italianate style village built by the architect Sir Clough Williams-Ellis between 1925 and 1975. It is most famous for having featured in an old television series called "The Prisoner". It is also the home of Portmeirion Pottery, which many people collect. Having visited it a number of years ago, I did not feel the need to go again.

My next destination was Harlech but to get to it I first had to drive inland to go around the Traeth Estuary, a distance of 13 miles. Harlech Castle is the fourth of the UNESCO rated castles built by Edward I to suppress the Welsh and completed in 1289. Unlike the castle at Caernarfon, built as a palace, Harlech was built as a garrison to hold a force of soldiers.

The castle was captured and held by Owen Glendower from 1404 to 1409. During the Wars of the Roses, in 1481, the Lancastrians (red rose) captured it and they held out against the Yorkists (white rose) for seven years. This siege is remembered today in the proud Welsh song, Men of Harlech.

Harlech Castle, Gwynedd

The castle also has the distinction of being the last castle in Britain, to hold out against the Parliamentary forces of Oliver Cromwell, during the first English civil war, succumbing eventually in March 1647.

The castle has an interesting entrance built about half way up its walls and linked today by a modern walkway to the Visitor Centre. At one time the castle was right alongside the ocean and at high tides goods could be shipped in. The castle still has a water gate with steps leading down to where the ocean once was. However, today the castle sits proudly about a half mile from the sea, the shoreline having silted up and now being part of the Royal St. David's Golf Club.

※

The drive south from Harlech is particularly attractive as you follow the coast, from on high, with a good view of the ocean, which today was blue and sparkling. There were two caravan parks along this road, blotting the landscape, one I would estimate having perhaps as many as 1000 static vans.

The beaches along this coast continue to be large and sandy and I stayed close to the coast down to Barmouth, which as the name suggests is a large sandy bar that is almost right across the mouth of the Afon Mawddach River and its tributaries. These drain the waters from the Snowdonia range of mountains that are visible inland. Barmouth is quite a large town, but too many "tourist tat shops" for me. I had lunch at a café close to the Bar. Unfortunately I asked for a pot of tea. Big mistake. The girl serving me said they didn't have any teapots and did I want a large mug or a giant mug. I said I would have the smallest size. She then put a tea bag in the mug, added water from a tap and then mashed the tea bag as hard as she could with a spoon. Milk was then added and she asked did I want the teabag left in or taken out! This is unfortunately the state of Britain today. I should have brewed it myself with my stove.

Outside the café on the sands were a number of boats, one of them an old RNLI lifeboat that apparently had been there a long time. I would have thought that it should be in a museum not decaying on the beach. I later had correspondence with the RNLI Heritage Officer who said that this vessel had been sold some years ago to a private individual. It is allowed to remain in RNLI colours, but not carry their insignia. They already have a vessel of this class in the museum in Chatham, and being a charity, they do not have the money to keep and maintain all the old vessels and so they are sold on. This is understandable, but a shame that this boat was apparently being left to rot.

Barmouth from Fairbourne

To move on from Barmouth you once again have to drive up the estuary and down the other side, a distance of 22 miles. I was able to save 2 miles by using an old wooden toll bridge that cost 70 pence. I didn't save much time though as the toll keeper, who clearly wasn't busy, wanted to talk about the England, Wales football match that was to be played in a couple of hours time. We chatted for about five minutes with no other cars appearing. He was an Englishman and hearing my accent probably thought that he could safely share his views about the upcoming match.

I reached Fairbourne, the opposite bank from Barmouth and watched once again a train taking the "short cut". Perhaps one day there will also be a road bridge.

After Fairbourne I drove on with the sea on my right and then was forced to turn left once again up another estuary, this one of the River Dovey. The town of Aberdovey is a charming place with many coloured houses. I drove past the Outward Bound School. Though no longer having a place in Burghead, it still exists here in Aberdovey. Presumably the young people in canoes on the water were from here. Though the tide was out the river flows along the bank on this side so Aberdovey always has boat access.

One phenomenon of today was the weather. On the coast it was sunny, but as I turned inland to drive around the estuaries, so I came into rain. In each of the three estuaries the weather was the same. Dry on the coast, wet inland.

It was a 30-mile drive to Aberystwyth. This again proved to be a surprising and attractive town. It has the remains of an old castle but not much of it is left. This seems to divide the town with separate beaches on either side. The castle dates from the time of Llewellyn Prince of Wales in 1221. Edward I had it strengthened in 1277. It was captured from the English by Owen Glendower in 1404, but was recaptured again by the English four years later. In King John's day, in 1637, it was a Royal Mint producing silver shillings. Oliver Cromwell was its destroyer, having it slighted in 1649. Interestingly Britain's Royal Mint is still today in Wales, in the town of Llantrissant in Monmouthshire.

Aberystwyth is a large town, having a fine university. For tourists it has a pier and a cliff side railway, but it was eerily quiet with hardly anyone on the streets as I drove through. When I turned on the radio I realised why – the match had started!

New Quay, Ceredigion, North Wales

This part of the coast is particularly lovely with pretty little towns like Aberaeron and perhaps my favourite New Quay. This is a town I felt that I could enjoy staying in. Despite a very strong wind blowing, the harbor here kept the boats in calm waters. My original intention had been to stay in

New Quay but it was only 2.30pm so I decided to head further south and stay in Cardigan. I am meeting my friend Bob tomorrow in Tenby. Staying overnight in Cardigan will give me less miles to travel tomorrow as I am aiming to meet Bob from his train at 3.40pm.

Just outside Aberporth I saw a pub that was showing the match. I had heard on the radio that Wales had scored first and that England had eventually equalized. There was only 30 minutes left so I decided to go in and watch the last few minutes. The pub was full of very loud and excited Welsh fans. Although England scored in the last minute, it remained a friendly affair.

I found a B&B for the night in Cardigan. It is an OK sort of place but not as good as some I have been in. There are the remains of an old castle here, the origins of which go back to Norman times. It was severely damaged in the English Civil War and was later used as a prison. It then came into private hands and in 1940 was purchased by an heiress, but it fell into disrepair. The county council purchased it in 2003 and it was opened to the public just last year offering a heritage centre, a restaurant and bed and breakfast accommodation, though I did not find this out until I had booked my stay elsewhere.

I went out to find a place for an evening meal and came across a "Junk Food fest" where I was warmly invited to join them. A group that collects discarded supermarket foods and turns it into meals had organized this. At this event a meal was being prepared and you were asked to give whatever you felt the meal was worth. I thought that this was a great idea, but unfortunately I did not like the menu. It was all vegetarian, not necessarily a bad thing, but it did not sound very appetizing. One of the young women organising the evening told me about an unusual Indian restaurant on a boat on the river. It was tied up to a dock and actually did not look particularly seaworthy. But I went aboard, the food was excellent and it was still afloat when I left!

Tomorrow, my friend Bob from Wargrave joins me for two days. I again will have companionship and someone to make notes. Bob is Welsh and comes from South Wales and promises to show me 'his country.'

Cardigan to Tenby

Miles 106

St. Davids' Cathedral, Pembrokeshire, West Wales

Today I have driven through almost zero visibility in cloud and rain and also perfect visibility in beautiful sunshine. I have visited another castle and a Cathedral housing a shrine to a Saint lying beside the father of a King.

Leaving Cardigan early this morning I set off for Fishguard, another ferry town with ferries across to Ireland. Unfortunately as I crossed the border into Pembrokeshire, everything became grey and overcast with drizzly rain. I got a period of clearance so that I could see the small town of Fishguard. The beach close to the ferry dock seemed to have sand that was grey and uninviting, rather than the golden coloured sand that I had been seeing and was to see along the coast later in the day.

As I set out to get to Strumble Head the rain intensified and the cloud cover increased. The road on which I was driving was at a low level in relation to the fields and there were high hedges. This was the predominant feature of most of the roads today. So, unless the road actually ran along the edge of the beach, views were limited to grass banks and hedgerows. Even though I have to drive these roads to keep true to my objective of driving whatever road is closest to the ocean, there was little sign of the ocean and I could have been driving anywhere. No doubt you have to be sitting on a double decker bus here to get a good view!

I had never been to Pembrokeshire before so I was very much looking forward to it and viewing the much talked about coastline. Unfortunately the weather and the hedgerows did not play ball and I was limited in what I saw until later in the day.

Another one of my objectives was to visit the city of St. Davids and its cathedral. Until very recently to be called a city in the UK the town had to have a cathedral. A favourite pub quiz question has often been "What is the smallest City in the United Kingdom?" The answer was of course St. Davids, which has a cathedral, though the town itself is very small. Quite recently the 'need to have a cathedral to be a city' rule has changed and there are places now designated as Cities that do not have a cathedral, a retrograde step in my view, as well as eliminating a perfectly good quiz question!

St Davids is a lovely cathedral. Alongside it is the ruins of the Bishop's Palace, which appears to have been almost as large as the cathedral itself!

St. David lived from 500 to 589. He was born into royalty, with his father being Prince of Powys and his mother the daughter of a local chief. In medieval times they believed that he was the nephew of King Arthur. He became a monk and insisted that no personal property could be owned. It was also said, though cannot be proven, that he founded Glastonbury Abbey. There is certainly evidence that he was responsible at least for plans to expand the Abbey. He was canonised as a saint in 1120. He was buried in what is now the cathedral but in the 12th century it was sacked and burnt by the Vikings. Bones said to be those of St. David were carbon dated in 1996 but turned out to be bones from the 16th century, so clearly they are not those of David

In Medieval times Churches, monasteries and Cathedrals made a lot of money from pilgrims who would come to visit holy relics and pay for forgiveness of sins. There was thus a lot of temptation for places to claim to have an important relic so that visitors would come with their money. Indeed many monasteries could not have survived without the money to be made from a relic; sometimes the relics were genuine, many times they were fakes. This does not necessarily mean that relics were deliberately made up by monasteries so as to deceive, but there was also money to be made in selling "genuine" relics to gullible monks and this almost certainly meant some purchases made in good faith and with good assurances were in reality not true.

374

Pope Calixtus in the twelfth century supported pilgrimages to St Davids by decreeing that two pilgrimages to St Davids would equate to one pilgrimage to Rome and three pilgrimages would equate to one to Jerusalem. Of course each pilgrim visit gave money to the Cathedral and perhaps the size of the Bishop's Palace alongside the Cathedral was an indication of just how much money could be earned from the pilgrims.

Possibly the greatest pilgrimage "discovery" was that at Glastonbury. A fire in 1184 destroyed much of the Abbey and its income reduced greatly as visits by pilgrims dwindled. So it was that the alleged discovery in 1191 of a grave of a man and woman in an oak tree coffin, along with a grave stone that said that "buried here is King Arthur and his Queen Guinevere", changed its fortunes. This of course brought pilgrims flocking back to Glastonbury and within a hundred years it was the richest and most magnificent Abbey in England.

The amount of land and wealth held by the Monasteries was significant and so when Henry VIII broke away from the Roman Catholic Church in 1536 and made himself the Head of the Church in England, he dissolved the monasteries and claimed all of their land and wealth as belonging to the Crown. At that time there were over 850 monasteries in England. In 1539 Glastonbury was stripped and by 1541, no monasteries remained.

St. Davids' cathedral has some wonderful wooden bosses on its ceilings. It is not as elaborate as many other cathedrals, but is still a magnificent building. It remains today a place of pilgrimage and on every Friday at noon there is a short service to remember St. David.

The tomb of Edmund Tudor, Earl of Richmond and father of Henry VII dominates the area in front of the choir.

When he died in captivity in Carmarthen Castle in 1456, he was buried at a Franciscan Church in the town. However, when his grandson, Henry VIII dissolved the monasteries and took their wealth, he instructed that Edmund's body be removed and it was reinterred here at St. Davids in 1539.

Traveling through Wales the Welsh language is very much in evidence. The road signs are in Welsh (first) and then in English. In Caernarfon I heard many people in the streets and shops talking in Welsh. Wales is very much a land of two halves. The people of the north speak Welsh and use it in every day conversation, whereas the people in the south speak almost entirely in English. Until today I had not appreciated how much this was like Scotland where the highlanders of the north (especially on the islands) keep their Gaelic language alive, but the lowlanders of the south stick mainly to English.

In Scotland the highlanders have a Nordic ancestry whereas the lowlanders have more of an Irish origin. Recent DNA research has shown that there is a definite split in family origins between the people in North Wales and those in the south. Quite likely this is due to language, with people marrying only those who spoke the same language. When Edward I conquered Wales a number of English people were given land and power in south Pembrokeshire and the area became known as "Little England in Wales". Quite probably this influence impacted the use of the Welsh language and thus the divide seen today. Considering I was in Scotland only 5 days ago, this really highlights just how varied the British Isles are, two completely different languages only a few hundred miles apart.

After visiting the cathedral, I then drove along St Brides Bay. This took me right beside the water. There were wind surfers braving the elements, but not many other people on the beach.

Again I lost sight of the water as I drove through the lanes emerging eventually at the small village of Dale where the sun at last began to break through. Dale is another one of those places where rather drab looking buildings have been painted in bright blues, yellows, pinks and whites and the colours seem to harmonise so well with the colours of the landscape.

I next had to travel back through the lanes, again out of sight of the ocean, heading towards Milford Haven. Milford Haven is an industrial port mainly serving the oil and gas industry and my first sight of it was across a field of cows. The sight of the towers and chimneys seemed in sharp contrast to the rurality of the field of cows behind whom, in the distance, the towers and smoke and steam could easily be seen.

Rurality meets Industry

The waters of Milford Haven are a Ria and very deep so large ships can enter here. Milford Haven is now the main center for the importation of liquid natural gas from the Middle East. LNG is a cleaner fuel than coal or oil and the government is encouraging its usage as a means of moving further towards their "eco target". The gas when frozen reduces in volume down to 600 times its natural volume so keeping it in this state is efficient for transport and storage.

After crossing the toll bridge at Neyland and on towards Pembroke I drove over a high bridge, down below from which could be seen hundreds of boats moored and anchored in a large natural marina. This area was like that around St. Brides Bay, with lots of narrow lanes without a view of the ocean.

Pembroke Castle

Pembroke is another Welsh town with a fine castle. I determined that I had time to stop and visit. The castle was built in 1093 just 30 years after William beat Harold at Hastings and two hundred years before Edward I built his line of fortresses.

Pembroke Castle was built mainly as a fortified home, but over the year's it's ownership changed hands many times under various forfeitures or battles.

In 1452 the Earldom of Pembroke and the Castle passed to Jasper Tudor, brother of Edward (now buried in St. Davids' Cathedral). In 1457, when Edward died in captivity, Jasper brought his brother's young widow, Margaret Beaufort to Pembroke Castle and it was here, as we saw earlier, that she gave birth to Henry, who in 1485, after defeating Richard III at Bosworth Field took the throne as Henry VII.

In 1648 the English Civil War was raging. Pembroke was a Parliamentary stronghold, but after not being paid for a considerable period of time, soldiers in Wales rebelled, led by Colonel John Poyer, Governor of the Castle. Poyer had at one time led the Parliamentary forces that captured Carew Castle from the Royalists. After some early success against his previous brothers in arms the now Royalist rebels were forced back by Cromwell until all that remained was the stronghold at Pembroke. Cromwell lay siege to it in May 1648 and after failed attempts to scale the walls, or batter them down with siege artillery, the water supply to the Castle was discovered and Cromwell had this cut off. The defenders eventually were forced to surrender. Poyer was captured and taken to London along with two other rebel leaders, Major General Rowland Laugharne, who had been Poyers's Commander and Colonel Rice Powell who had tried to hold Tenby Castle. All were sentenced to death. However, the sentence was changed such that only one should die and the two others would be imprisoned. The three cast lots and Powell was the one who lost. He was executed by firing squad at London's Covent Garden. Cromwell ordered that the castle at Pembroke be slighted.

Laugharne spent almost a decade in prison, but after Charles II came to the throne, he was released and became Member of Parliament for Pembroke. Charles II awarded

Poyer's widow a large pension. There is no record as to whether Powell received anything by reward from the King.

It wasn't until 1928 that the ruined castle was purchased and partly restored by Major General Ivor Philipps. Today trustees of the Philipps' family and Pembroke Council manage the site.

Weather was now once again warm and sunny. My final destination for today was Tenby, where I was to meet my friend Bob at the railway station. I arrived about one minute before his train and it was good to meet up with him again and to share his company. Together we drove into Tenby to look for some afternoon tea.

Tenby, Pembrokeshire

Tenby revealed itself to be one of the most attractive places that I have come across so far on my trip around Britain. It was a wonderful sight looking down onto the boats bobbing around in the natural harbor and the water sparkling in the sunlight. I later discovered that there are at least four separate beaches in Tenby all with great sand and great views. This is a town that I would certainly like to return to and perhaps stay a while. My sister had told me how lovely Tenby is and she was not wrong.

Little remains of the castle at Tenby, which had been besieged by Cromwell during the civil war of 1648 and held, unsuccessfully, by Colonel Rice Powell.

Bob and I were kindly assisted by the Tourist Information Office in finding a lovely place to stay in nearby Lamphey. This meant a journey of about seven miles back towards Pembroke, but the small hotel proved to be extremely comfortable and their dining room excellent, though their internet connection was non existent.

Tomorrow we have a long drive through South Wales and back into England and Bob will leave me at Bristol. I will then be on my own again on Saturday evening in North Somerset and North Devon before being joined by another friend Pete, in Bude, on Sunday night.

Tenby to Weston-Super-Mare

Miles 268

Tenby City Walls

Today was the longest day of my journey so far. Too long really, though some of it, for only the second time on my trip, included motorway driving. We travelled through beautiful countryside and both ugly industrial and ugly seaside areas. We drove from one country into another. The final 80 miles of my journey equated to only 8 miles by seagull flight!

Our hotel overnight, at Lamphey, was excellent. We enjoyed not only a good night's sleep, but also an excellent dinner and a good quality breakfast this morning. For the rest of the day, we ate nothing but fruit. Lamphey contains a ruined 14th century palace known as the Bishops Palace. At one time it had extensive parklands and was said to be a favourite place to visit by the Bishops of St. Davids, who already had a beautiful palace adjacent to the Cathedral. Bishop Henry de Gower built both buildings around 1330. The Bishops were once described as "worldly men who enjoyed the privileges of wealth, power and status", probably all funded by the monies paid by the pilgrims for forgiveness of their sins!

We had to once again pass through the lovely little town of Tenby. This is certainly somewhere that I would like to come back to and spend more than just a few hours. There is a cottage close to the water in the harbour on which there is a blue plaque stating that Roald Dahl, the children's author used to holiday here with his mother and siblings, every Easter for sixteen years before the second world war. I can understand his family returning often to such a delightful place.

Just on from Tenby is Saundersfoot, small village, big beach. In Norman times the village was called St Issels, after a Welsh saint. Its church today is still called this. Before it became a holiday destination in the 20th Century, it was once a major shipment port for coal, iron and bricks.

A little way further on brought us to Wisemans Bridge beach where we saw an unusual sign stating *"Beware there have been reports of soft sand on this beach"*. Usually you don't feel concerned about soft sand on the beach, you welcome it. It's the best for making sand castles. Perhaps they meant something as sublime as "your wellies might get stuck in it", or, was it possibly a warning of quicksand? No doubt this is a "warning to the wise" so giving it the name Wiseman's Beach!

We also found ourselves in danger of getting run over here. There was an endless stream of joggers, some on their own, some with dogs, some in twos and threes and one where a man, on a bicycle, was urging on his wife, who was running! Clearly the beauty of this area encourages people to go out and get themselves beautiful also.

Our next target was the seven-mile long beach at Pendine. These sands have been the scene for numerous high-speed car trials, and land speed records. Malcolm Campbell in Bluebird was the first person to set a land speed record on these sands in 1924 when he reached 146 miles per hour. Over the next three years this record was beaten four times, twice more by himself and twice by J.G.Parry-Thomas. When Campbell set a new record of 174mph in February 1927, Parry-Thomas attempted to beat this one month later, but he crashed and was killed. His car, Babs, was buried in the sands after the accident, but was excavated in 1969, and restored by 1985. It is now displayed in the Museum of Speed and driven at Pendine in the summer months.

In June 2000 Malcolm Campbell's grandson, Don Wales, set the UK record on Pendine Sands for an electric car of 137mph. In 2010, also on Pendine Sands, he broke the world speed record for driving a lawn mower reaching a top speed of 87mph!

At the eastern end of Pendine sands is Laugharne where we came across another wonderful ruined castle. This was built at the estuary of the River Taf in 1116. It was the site of the signing of peace treaty between Henry II and Rhys Gruffudd, Prince of South Wales in 1171. The castle has played a part in a number of skirmishes and changes of ownership. In 1403 this was the place where Owen Glyndwr's rebellion stalled when he lost 700 men. His influence waned and he disappeared altogether in 1415. Perhaps the castle's most important owner was Sir John Perrott who was given the castle by Elizabeth 1 in 1584. Perrott was allegedly an illegitimate son of Henry VIII, so this was a gift to her half brother.

Laugharne Castle, Carmarthenshire

Once again during the Civil War, the castle's owners chose the wrong side and Parliamentary forces led, appropriately, by Major General Laugherne captured it. In 1644 Cromwell had it broken up. Major General Laughherne later, as mentioned under the Pembroke Castle history, rebelled against Cromwell and supported the Royalists. The famous Welsh author Dylan Thomas apparently loved this area and frequently visited the village and is said to have penned his novel "Portrait of the Artist as a Young Dog" while working in the castle.

We now moved on inland, up to St Clears, where only the mound of its once Norman Castle now remains, and then on to Carmarthen. This meant that we had to go around the two estuaries of the Rivers Taf and Towey. Carmarthen is not truly a coastal town being eight miles inland from the sea. It is said to be the oldest town in Wales, with a Roman heritage back to AD75 and a Roman amphitheater still in existence. One of the many legends about King Arthur is that he was born in a cave outside of the town.

From Carmarthen we followed the road to Kidwelly close to the mouth of the estuary. Unfortunately the area was made to look very scruffy and untidy by large amounts of litter scattered around.

Skirting the industrial areas of Llanelli and Gorseinon we crossed the bridge over the estuary of the River Loughor and entered the Gower.

The Gower Coast was Britain's first designated Area of Outstanding Natural Beauty (AONB). Again we drove through very narrow lanes with tall hedgerows blocking the view. We first stopped at Llanmadoc right at the far end of the Peninsula. There are a number of caravan sites here. I have no idea how anyone could drive a car and caravan down these very narrow lanes. You would almost need someone to go on ahead and stop any oncoming traffic, as there could be no possibility of reversing if two caravans meet head on. I wonder how they deal with this?

These small campsites are unobtrusive and clearly provide a good service to the traveller. What is a blot on the landscape though are the numerous static caravan and chalet parks. This is not just an eyesore in Wales, but as I have noted before, all around the country. I can understand councils seeing these places as a way to boost local tax revenue and I am sure that they create a few seasonal jobs in the area and the shopkeepers welcome them (often the council members are local shopkeepers anyway). However, they seem contrary to why many people come to the area. Have places for people to stay by all means, but don't allow them to be placed right alongside a lovely beach or up the sides of a prominent hill. This then detracts from the very beauty of the place people have come to see.

At the end of the Second World War, when Sir Billy Butlin started his Holiday Camps, they provided working people with holidays beside the sea at a price they could afford and people greatly benefited from this. The caravan and chalet parks today do a similar thing, but without the entertainment. However, having reviewed prices at one or two caravan/chalet sites, I can confirm that they are certainly not cheaper than many local B&Bs or houses to rent. I think people go to these places in the mistaken belief that they are the cheapest option and don't check out other choices. I once had an investor in a company I was involved with tell me that his income was so substantial, from just the one large caravan park he owned on the south coast, that he now had nothing to do with the management of the site as he was fully occupied with determining how to invest the income! He was quite open about how much money there is in caravan parks. Once the caravan/chalet sites are in place they form a new village and so they are accompanied by other "tourist services" such as shops, cafes and in many places, funfairs and bingo halls. They of course bring large quantities of people together at the same time and in the same place (with their money) but this can over burden the services and especially the beauty and tranquility of the local area.

Some of these places, such as the ones in Exmouth and Conwy, are built out of site of the town and fulfill their function without detracting from the beauty of the area. Others, like at Ingoldmells in Lincolnshire, are so dominant that any beauty of the coastline is completely spoiled and the areas can only be described as ugly.

We continued on further narrow lanes (I think Samantha was determined to give us a hard day) and eventually reached Rhossili.

Rhossili, Gower Peninsula, Wales

This is a charming cliff top and beach owned by the National Trust. It is listed as one of the world's top ten beaches and today it seemed that the world had come to view it! With my Scottish NT membership we entered the car park, a large field that was absolutely packed with cars. There were a lot of Japanese tourists here taking pictures with cameras on selfie sticks. This is the place to get out and walk to Worms Head, but you can only do this when the tide is right. Also you cannot walk to the end at certain times of the year when the birds are nesting. My purpose was to drive the coast so I did not make the walk, but at some time I would like to come back and do so.

After making a cup of tea and eating some fruit for lunch we drove back along the lanes and on to Port Eynon.

In the churchyard, right by the road, is a distinctive memorial to three lifeboat men who lost their lives during a rescue in 1916. The lifeboat twice capsized while trying to assist a vessel in distress. You cannot travel anywhere on the British coastline, tiny village or large town, without seeing an RNLI station. This memorial in this tiny village in West Wales is a good reminder of the fact that these men and women, all volunteers, put their lives in danger to save others. They will go out onto a stormy ocean in terrible weather to save the lives of boaters that the same bad weather has already brought into peril.

Not too far away was the little village of Oxwich, which gives its name to the Bay. Here there was a nice sandy beach and yet another ruined castle. Oxwich Castle was mainly a fortified Tudor house and has no major historical significance, other than a gold brooch, which was found here and is thought to possibly be part of Edward II's treasure.

We then drove around the Mumbles. The Mumbles allegedly gets its name from a corruption of the French *les mamelles* meaning "the breasts" which relate to the two small islets by the headland. In 1947 the Mumbles lifeboat, attempting a rescue, foundered in heavy seas and the whole crew of eight men were drowned. Close by is West's Beach, a mecca for kite surfers.

We continued along the coast until we came to the city of Swansea. This is where the prettiness and tidiness stopped. Whereas the Pembroke Coast and the Gower Peninsula looked cared for and were clean and tidy, for the next 30 miles we saw nothing on the coast that was attractive and the places were decidedly very down at heel and down market. Rubbish on the sides of the roads was very evident. Bob my native Welshman, who grew up not too far from here, was the one to comment how that these areas are in such sharp contrast to the prettiness of the countryside that we had been driving through.

Swansea once produced two thirds of all of the world's copper and was nicknamed *Copperopolis*. The Royal Navy were a big purchaser of Swansea copper which was used to line the bottoms of its warships to minimise barnacle and weed growth that restricted the speed of the ships. Indeed it is has been said that Nelson's victory over Napoleon at the Battle of Trafalgar was partly down to the fact that his copper bottomed ships were able to maneuver and travel faster than the French vessels.

The copper ore did not originate in Wales but rather came from Cornwall. However as 4 times the weight of coal was needed for the furnaces to smelt the copper ore it was cheaper to bring the ore to where the coal was rather than ship the large quantities of coal to where the copper was mined.

Further on from Swansea is Port Talbot, which was built to transport coal and in 1947 to import iron ore and manufacture steel. The town is dominated by the steel works. At one time this was the largest steel works in Europe and the biggest employer in Wales. It must be a very sad and difficult time for the people working and living in the area today, as the Indian company Tata, who now own the steelworks, are seeking to sell it. No family wants to live with uncertainty for the future and the dread that their income may come to an end. The cost of making steel in the UK is too expensive in relation to steel from China, which is effectively being dumped on the market. At this time no buyer has come forward.

We continued on and drove into Porthcawl. The sea looked uninviting and so did the town. At Porthcawl there is an enormous caravan park and funfair that dominates the town as you drive in. I remember coming here as a child on a Sunday School trip and playing on the sands. I could not see any beach today, only black rocks. No doubt the sand is the domain of the chalet/caravan park. I certainly would not want to take Sunday School children today to Porthcawl.

The next area is called the Glamorgan Heritage Coast, with the main town being Llantwit Major. In the sixth century a French monk, Saint Illtud established a monastery and centre of Christian learning here. It is thought to have been the first of its kind and it is said that St. Patrick, of Ireland and St. David, of Wales, were both schooled here. Legend has it that St. Illtud was at one time a Knight and the cousin of King Arthur. Some have even suggested that he is actually synonymous with Sir Galahad. The monastery was destroyed by the Vikings in 987 and then rebuilt again in 1111 under the control of Tewkesbury Abbey, in Gloucestershire, until it was destroyed again in 1539 during Henry VIII's dissolution of the monasteries. I have a slight connection with this place in that I lived in Tewkesbury for a few years when I got married.

In comparison with the Mumbles and the Gower coastlines, this coast seems to have little to offer by way of encouraging people to come here for a vacation – and then you get to Barry Island, which is just one big, ugly, fun fair. In its heyday trains used to run to here from the mining towns in the valleys and there could be up to 100,000 people on the beach on a Bank Holiday.

Barry Island, Glamorgan

Many years ago, on a Bank Holiday Monday, when I was about 19, four of us took a day out and drove to Barry Island as we had heard that it was an exciting place to visit. We parked our car in the main car park and went into the funfair.

We were quickly disillusioned and felt that it was an untidy, dirty and not very inviting place, so we decided to drive somewhere else. We returned to the car only to be stopped, along with other cars, from leaving the car park, by a policeman who stood blocking the exit. We waited and waited, but he would not leave. In the end after about 15 minutes, myself and two or three other drivers went and spoke to him and asked could we please be let out. He said that his sergeant had told him to stand there and not let anyone out until the traffic on the road had reduced. He was waiting for his sergeant to come back and tell him we could go. He would not budge and kept saying he had to wait for his sergeant. After almost an hour of increasing frustration with PC Ivor Nobrain we and two other drivers decided to declare UDI and take the law into our own hands and just ignore him and drive out.

Unfortunately the driver at the head of the queue was less bold and would not drive out. It took us about ten minutes to persuade him to back–up and move his car so that we could go for it. Eventually we maneuvered him out of the way and we and three other cars blew our horns and drove past the Policeman. He put his hand up to tell us to stop, but we ignored him and continued forward. He moved out of the way and we drove out. The traffic on the road gave way to us and then we were followed by most of the other cars in the car park. I'm not sure what this constable said to his sergeant by way of explanation as to why the car park was empty, I never heard. We also never heard anything further about having committed any traffic violation. Anyway, Bob and I decided not to park in case PC Nobrain was still on duty in Barry.

We confirmed that Barry Island continues to be just one big and gaudy fun fair. It was still busy, so clearly people enjoy it, but it was definitely not to our taste. Barry of course featured in the successful comedy TV program Gavin & Stacey, Stacey being from Barry and Gavin from Essex. The obvious similarities of Barry and Southend are therefore quite true. It is quite a go-ahead place in some respects in that it now offers free WiFi on the beach for the "discerning" holidaymaker.

Bob took me about two miles further on to Penarth, which is just around the point from Barry. Though close by, Penarth is the complete opposite of Barry. It is smart and clean, without any rubbish in evidence. Here houses are still houses in which people live and not turned into doughnut or fish and chip shops. Though close together they clearly serve different markets. At one time Penarth was an "overflow" dock for Cardiff and coal was loaded and shipped from here. Bob told me that there still remains a "secret" pedestrian tunnel under Cardiff Bay that allowed dockworkers to come back and forth between Cardiff and Penarth. It is now apparently boarded up, but still intact, and not many people know that it exists.

Cardiff from Penarth (Photo Jklo286 CC BY-SA4)

Cardiff is a modern day success story having reinvented itself from the downturn and demise of the coal industry and the decline of its docks. It is has rejuvenated itself into a tremendous commercial and cultural hub. It is an example to many other places in Britain as to what can happen if industry changes. This obviously did not happen overnight, but the energy and determination of the local people and council to attract investments and new businesses and rebirth the city has certainly paid off. There are similar success stories around the UK, such as Portsmouth, Glasgow and Newcastle, but there are also places that have yet to accept that change has to happen and make radical decisions to move on.

Interestingly Cardiff did not become the capital of Wales until 1955. Indeed Wales did not have any official capital until this time, although Cardiff had been treated as such for a few centuries. At the time of her Coronation, Queen Elizabeth II determined to visit all of the Capital cities in Britain. Only then was it realised that Wales had no official capital. So the Welsh people were given a ballot to choose between Cardiff, Caernarfon and Aberystwyth and Cardiff won.

In medieval times the capital was considered to be at Strata Florida, Ceredigion, where there was a Cistercian Abbey used as the seat of King Llewellyn from 1238. During the time of Owen Glyndwyr, in 1404 he based himself at Machynlleth (pronounced Ma-hunt-leth) so this effectively became the capital at that time and was thought of as such for some time afterwards. From the mid 15th to 17th century the Council of Wales sat at Ludlow a border town, now in Shropshire, England, but without a King in Wales and only an English Princes of Wales, the annexation of Wales by England effectively meant that no formal capital was established.

Cardiff Castle is in the centre of the City, but today looks nothing like the twelfth century stone castle originally built here. It has been involved in many conflicts including being stormed in 1404 by Owen Glyndwr. In 1318 this was the stronghold of Hugh Despenser, favourite of Edward II who carried out brutal suppression of the Welsh before himself being captured by Queen Isabella and Mortimer and ultimately hung, drawn and quartered, a punishment he had taken much joy in inflicting on others. In the English Civil War it was a Royalist stronghold, at one time taken by the Parliamentarians, but then recaptured. Cromwell, who wanted it to remain as a bullwork against Scottish invasion (though it is a very long way from Scotland!) did not have it slighted. In the mid eighteenth century the castle came into the hands of the Marquis of Bute (a Scot!) who began to change it significantly, removing much of its medieval structure. The only old part remaining is the ruined Keep. Others in his family continued the changes, paid for by their wealth from the Welsh mining industry. The third Marquis in the early nineteenth century had the castle remodeled in Gothic revival style. The Castle was given to the City of Cardiff in 1947 when the then Marquis died and is now a venue for events and a tourist attraction.

From Cardiff we left the water and missing out the B4239, which followed the Severn Estuary, took the M4 motorway and headed for Bristol and a train for Bob back to Wargrave.

We skirted the city of Newport, which is built on the estuary of the River Usk as it enters the Bristol Channel. This used to be another major coal exporting place. The first settlement here was at nearby Caerleon where the Romans built a fort, Isca Augusta, to defend the river crossing. Today at Caerleon can be seen the remains of a large amphitheater, hot baths and the Roman barracks.

The Normans started Newport in the 11th Century and built a castle a little way down river from Caerleon. Nothing remains of the castle they built but now very visible on the riverbank are the ruins of the 14th Century limestone castle built by the Earl of Gloucester. It has been visited by Henry II, Henry III and partially repaired by Edward I. It was sacked in 1402 by Owen Glyndwr and never fully restored. Owen Tudor was a prisoner here in 1460 and a few years later his son, Jasper Tudor, Uncle to Henry VII, occupied it. It was later owned by Henry VIII and then his short-lived young son, Edward VI. Cromwell captured the castle in 1648 and by 1743 it was almost a ruin. Today only its east side remains.

Driving the M4 meant that we would go over the "new" Severn Bridge, which crosses the River Severn and is built less than a mile from the "old" Severn Bridge, again demonstrating the commercial significance and growth of Cardiff and South Wales. There are no tolls on this bridge if travelling from west to east. It's free to leave Wales, but you have to pay to enter it. I think the Welsh joke that any Englishman should have to pay to come into Wales, but they are free to leave at any time!

Below the "old" Severn Bridge is the village of Aust from where for many years there ran a car ferry. Before the bridges, this was the only way to get across to South Wales, other than making a sixty-mile journey via Gloucester at the head of the Severn Estuary. The ferry made its last trip on September 8th 1966 when the Queen opened the first Severn

Bridge. I still remember very well playing hockey, while at College, against the army Junior Leaders Regiment whose camp was right underneath the bridge. I looked with awe at the men working right above us on the edge of the span which had not then been joined up. That's probably why we were so soundly beaten by twelve goals to one!

I said goodbye to Bob at Bristol Parkway station, back-tracked down the M4 and onto the southbound M5, leaving this quickly after the Avon bridge and driving into the town of Portishead. I must admit that I had not been to Portishead before but was genuinely impressed. It is another place that has had a rebirth, centred on the old docks. It is a complete new town that appears to have been designed and built almost as if it were an "old" town. It has a village green; many different styles and colours of houses and around the docks, which are full of modern yachts and power boats, there are new architecturally attractive blocks of flats. The area seemed to be thriving with young professionals and their families enjoying the marina.

From Portishead I followed the coastal road to Clevedon, where I stopped for dinner. Clevedon was a popular resort in times past before the railway came. Unfortunately the town council decided that they did not want dirty trains coming into Clevedon and refused to allow access to the railway companies. They therefore bypassed the town taking their railway and the holidaymakers to Weston Super Mare. Clevedon declined almost overnight as a holiday destination. It is now basically a pleasant dormitory town for both Weston and Bristol. I took a break here and stopped for a dinner in a modern steak house style pub built alongside the sea wall.

While having my lonely dinner I did some people watching. Usually when I am on my own I take a book to read, but I did not have one with me in the car, apart from my large road atlas, which is not really the sort of thing to have on the dining table. Samantha had gone to sleep, so there was no one for me to take to dinner or to talk with, so I ate my meal and did some people watching. I like looking at people and trying to imagine what their lives are like, what is their occupation and what had brought them to the restaurant tonight. One couple sitting near to my table had me intrigued. I surmised, though had absolutely no proof, that they were on an "internet date." She was attractive, aged about 40 I guessed, nicely dressed for a date, but probably too nicely dressed for this restaurant. He I guesstimated was much younger, probably late twenties or maybe thirty, but no real dress sense. I thought that she was possibly a clerical worker for the local council or an insurance company, while I put him down as working on a farm or possibly as a mechanic.

It seemed obvious by the way they both looked at the menu and he tried to find out what she might like to drink, that they did not know each other very well. They seemed to have very little conversation. He would ask a question that she would shyly answer with one or two words, then there would be long periods of silence, when they would look all around the room rather than at each other. Perhaps they were people watching like me and put me down as a lonely man, possibly an accountant, without any friends or family and out for a meal on his own. Indeed they might have been feeling very sorry for me! I would like to think though that they actually saw me as an intrepid adventurer on a quest to find his roots!

For their meal, she had a salad and he had ribs and fries. She ate hers with a knife and fork he ate his with his fingers.

She looked embarrassed, he seemed oblivious. If this was the "internet date" that I had guessed at, as nice as both of them were I'm sure, I don't think another date was on the cards. I paid and left the restaurant before they did so I don't know how the evening ended up. I certainly didn't have the courage, or the cheek, to put my theory to them and find out whether I, or indeed they, had guessed right!

Weston-Super-Mare, my final destination, is the town where I first saw the sea as a child and had many day trips here. I used to come here for Sunday school outings. It is the other side of the Severn Estuary from Barry Island, which is actually only eight miles away across the water.

My room was booked (at the last minute) at a hotel on the sea front right by the RNLI station. It turned out to be a hotel whose clientele were almost exclusively pensioners on coach tours. The hotel staff were pleasant and helpful, especially Olla the receptionist from Poland, who gave me her parking place when she went off duty. It was on double-yellow no-parking lines, but she assured me that the parking restrictions were not enforced. I certainly did not get a ticket.

My room though clean and functional and with a sea view over the RNLI station, was the smallest one I have ever stayed in. I measured it at seven feet by twelve feet with an even smaller bathroom! WiFi was non-existent in the bedrooms and I had to sit in the TV room to get any signal.

At breakfast in the morning I sat at a table that had a notice on it which said that "this table is required for breakfast service from 8.20am". As it was 7.45am I sat there. The waitress asked me for my room number. I was then told that I could not sit there and my table was somewhere else. Perhaps coach parties need to have their lives controlled and can't be left to make independent decisions about where to sit and eat their breakfast. Anyway this independent, non-coach party customer certainly felt that this was a stupid rule. I ate my (actually very good) breakfast and then left. My original table remained empty the whole time. Clearly the hotel management know how to make guests leave irritated, without a smile on their face and with a determination never to stay there again.

Tomorrow I enter Cornwall and will be joined by another good friend Pete, also from Wargrave, but now living in Cornwall.

Weston-Super-Mare to Bude

Miles 174

Baggy Point, Croyde, North Devon

Today is Father's Day. I visited old haunts with family memories. It also rained torrentially, my first really wet all day rain in the last 4 weeks.

I have a bit of a soft spot for Weston. As well as the Sunday school outings here, I have very happy memories from days on the beach with the family when my children were very small. It is also quite possible that I was conceived here, as I know my parents came on holiday to Weston, in a caravan, about nine months before I was born!

I had one sadness about having arrived last night in Weston; I missed the Red Arrows, the RAF aerobatic display team and by far and away the world's best, who had performed here just one day earlier!

I have not been to WSM in at least 20 years and not a lot has changed. It does have a nice sandy beach close in to the Esplanade, but being an estuary town of the River Severn it also has mud, lots of it when the tide is out. Indeed Weston Super Mare is often nick named Weston Super Mud!

Weston has three piers, or at least the remains of three piers. One is basically an aquarium and one, Birnbeck Pier, is now derelict. The third one, the Grand Pier is about a quarter of a mile long and is entirely a pleasure pier. It was badly damaged by fire in 2008 but repaired and reopened at the end of 2010. The owners of the pier successfully sued the fire alarm company for not servicing or monitoring the fire alarms, which proved to be faulty. They were awarded £30 million in compensation. However the alarm company went into administration three days before the verdict was announced and the pier owners are unlikely to see any of the money.

WSM became a cultural "hot spot" last summer when Banksy (the famous street artist who is still doing graffiti art) put on a "pop-up exhibition" inside an old swimming pool building. He called it "Dismaland" an anti-establishment "Bemusement Park". It contained quirky contributions from around forty major artists. It apparently generated £30 million in extra income for WSM. WSM is clearly going after the arty crowd as well as the pensioners on tour buses!

The Grand Pier, Weston-Super-Mare, Somerset

I drove along the Promenade and took the road into Uphill. The Manor here was offering B&B, shame I did not find them yesterday. This is the "Nob Hill" part of WSM.

I followed the quiet coastal road along to Brean, Berrow and Burnham on Sea. I remember having had a holiday here as a child, in a caravan, at Brean sands (where there is a nice sandy beach). This was then one of around 10 caravans in a field. Now the area is chalets, chalets and more chalets.

I did see two fields that the chalet developers have not yet moved on to, so if you're quick there is still space for you to start your own chalet park. These open fields are clearly farmed by an eco friendly farmer who does not plough or spray right to the edge of his fields, so as to allow wild flowers to grow. There were banks of wild red poppies. Set amongst the dreary caravan parks, crammed in either side, they provided bright and vivid colour to an otherwise grey and overcast morning.

Burnham on Sea a few miles further on feels older and quieter than Weston. There are no obvious caravan parks, but there is one holiday village tucked away at the end of the Esplanade and out of sight behind trees. Despite being "On Sea" there is no sea in Burnham. This is very much River Severn estuary water (and silt) and when I was there the tide was well out leaving the boats in the sailing club marooned on the mud banks.

The rain turned into a persistent drizzle and the winds increased. As I left the town I saw a sign for Exeter and very nearly turned off and took the road. Today is Father's Day in England and to spend it with my wife Marilyn would have been perfect. However, I was due to meet Pete in Bude and so turned away from this and headed towards another sign that said Hinkley Point.

Hinkley Point is a controversial nuclear power station that is being built on the estuary. It is not expected to produce any power until at least 2025, when the last of Britain's coal power stations are set to close. The area covered is enormous and at the moment new roads are going in to allow construction of the site. The plant is to be built by the French power company EDF. However, just two days ago senior managers at EDF told Members of Parliament that they feel that the go ahead should be delayed due to design flaws in two similar plants being built in France and China. If the people building the nuclear power plant tell you that there are design flaws then you should listen to them. Otherwise it may become a rather drastic way to get rid of the chalet parks!

I drove on in the murk to the pretty little town of Watchet with its old station, still in use as a terminus for the West Somerset Railway that runs from Minehead to Bishops Lydeard near Taunton. A return trip on this railway would cost £19.

I stopped outside of a house just by the railway tracks so that I could take a picture. A lady walking away from the house and up the road turned and very snottily asked me to move my car from in front of her house. I said that I was only stopping for a moment to take a photo, but she still persisted that this was her property. I feel that I am generally a polite, friendly and helpful person, but in the face of such a rude, green wellied, bossy English women I could do nothing but just ignore her. I left the car, which was actually on the public roadway not her property, took my photo and was gone in less than one minute. Quite spoiled my morning she did, but I do hope that I spoiled hers as well!

After Watchet you get to Blue Anchor where chalets are in your face on the front. There is also a view across to Minehead with the white spires of the Butlins Holiday camp, prominent and close to the town.

Dunster Castle, Somerset

Just before Minehead you get a terrific view of Dunster Castle an ancient fortified house. A castle on this site dates back to the 11th century. The castle was another one to suffer the fate of Pembroke and other castles in being destroyed by

Oliver Cromwell for having been on the wrong side in the English Civil War. The castle was in the hands of the Luttrell family from the 1600s through to 1976 when it was given over to the care of the National Trust. The old village of Dunster, I know from previous visits, is well worth seeing if you have the time. Indeed the West Somerset Railway stops in the town and can be part of a trip from Minehead.

On entering Minehead I was thrilled to see a sign, under the town name, saying "Free Parking". What a forward-looking town I thought that really welcomes visitors. I drove onto the Esplanade and pulled over and parked. I then noticed a parking machine. I mentioned to a lady purchasing a ticket at the machine that there was a sign entering the town saying Minehead has free parking. "No chance" she said. "If Minehead has free parking I have yet to find it."

Despite some of the horrors that I have seen on this trip, the Butlins camp at Minehad, though not unobtrusive, is certainly not overpowering the town. It is at the other end of the esplanade from the town itself. It has a very large white domed tented style construction and obvious amusement areas. It has been on this site for perhaps fifty years and still has a lot of very old chalets. However, they also have added some smart looking accommodation in a new apartment block. It is part of the complex but they are clearly aiming for a wider market of people who want more luxury and sophisticated accommodation alongside the amusements that are provided. Based on my observation of a group of people walking along the esplanade toward the town from the camp, I got the impression that they also provide venues for conferences.

On driving into the main part of Minehead, I realised that I had not before been into the town and I was pleasantly surprised by what I saw. Immediately off the esplanade is a tree-lined boulevard with restaurants and cafes. If the sun had been shining this could almost have been in France.

There is no sandy beach to speak of at Minehead, but I guess that people come for the air and its location, right on the edge of Exmoor and Lorna Doone country.

I continued on and came to Porlock Weir, an unusual little place. The beach here is black pebbles and it and the water look very uninviting. However the two pubs did look inviting and were clearly very busy as it was Father's Day.

Pub at Porlock Weir, Somerset

The natural pebble sea barrier that protects the small harbor had been breached in recent years by storms. A wooden barrier appears to have been erected to fill the breach and hope that the pebble barrier rebuilds itself. The sailboats in the harbor were all resting firmly on the mud. If you had a boat in Porlock and wanted to go sailing you could only do so on a day and time when the tide was in. I know from experience that a boat spends a lot of its time unused in the harbour. If the sun shone and you did decide that you wanted to use it, then you could be thwarted here, and indeed along most of the estuaries I have seen, by the tide.

There was notice on the edge of the beach put up by the Porlock Manor Estate saying that DEFRA (Department for the Environment, Food and Agricultural Affairs) had designated the beach as a swimming beach, which had clearly surprised and alarmed the Estate. They had put up this notice advising people of the strong tides and dangers of swimming here. They made fairly cynical comments about DEFRA and clearly were annoyed as being designated a bathing beach, which meant that they were required to take regular water samples for analysis under EU regulations. I guess they will be voting "Leave" then!

According to the Anglo Saxon Chronicles Harold Godwinson (later King Harold) raided Porlock Weir in 1052, having sailed from Ireland where he had been in exile. In 1051 Earl Godwin, Harold's father, despite his daughter being married to Edward the Confessor, fell out with the King over his refusal to act on the King's demand that he punish the people of Dover for having upset the visiting Count of Boulogne. Godwin's refusal caused him to be exiled by Edward and he went to Flanders, while two of his sons, one being Harold, fled to Dublin. Harold's raid on Porlock in 1052 was his reentering England. He marched toward London with his retinue gaining so much popular support on the way that Edward was forced to recognise the popularity of the Godwin family and restore the Earldom to Godwin. When Earl Godwin died in Flanders in 1053, Harold became the Earl and then later, as we saw at Hastings, on the death of his brother in law, Edward the Confessor, he took on the mantle of King of England (but only briefly!).

Leaving Porlock for Lynmouth I drove on a very narrow road that led to a private toll road. Unfortunately when I got there, there was a gate firmly closed across the road. Obviously father was having his lunch on this his special day and was not to be disturbed. I did a twelve-point turn and headed back to Porlock Weir now taking the higher road out. This was very difficult with switchbacks and tight bends, but I eventually arrived at the pretty little village of Lynmouth.

In August 1952 Lynmouth was the site of a major disaster. Nine inches of rain fell in the space of 24 hours. The area is very rocky and so the water gathered quickly and surged down into the village, which is at the bottom of a steep river gulley. The wall of water took away thirty nine houses and a total of thirty four people lost their lives in Lynmouth and nearby.

Lynmouth today is a pretty village. It has a funicular railway running up its steep cliffs to the village of Lynton, which sits above. I have traveled on this in the past but today I felt that I did not have time. I stopped on a yellow no-parking line to take a photograph and a lady driver in a motor caravan came across and tapped on my window. I thought that she was going to be like the other crabby woman I had met that morning and complain about where I had stopped, but no, she said that they were just about to leave and would I like her parking spot. What a nice lady. At this part of the village there were not many places to park, but the few that were here were free for up to 2 hours. Though I had not intended to stop I decided to take up her offer, so I thanked her and then parked in the spot she vacated. Next to the funicular was a smart café so I went in and had an excellent ham and brie quiche and a pot of tea, all for £5.

Funicular Railway at Lynmouth, North Devon

Feeling refreshed I then set off for Ilfracombe. The road from Porlock is a notorious one, not just for its tight bends but also because of its gradient that is 1 in 3. You are warned about this and have to drive in a low gear, but there are still considerable hazards from the numerous free roaming sheep, that are as dumb as their Scottish cousins and think nothing of suddenly leaping out into the road. Having driven the road out of Applecross just a few days ago though, this descent held no fears. It is really a piece of cake. It even has a white line down the centre and two cars can pass easily.

Ilfracombe was very, very wet, when I arrived, yet the town was buzzing with people. Brits expect rain when they go on holiday, so no one had stayed inside and the streets were bright with many different coloured cagoules. I had been to Ilfracombe a number of times for "house parties" when I was younger, but I found nothing familiar or that I recognised. I also could find nowhere to park and there was a traffic warden (on a wet Father's Day Sunday!) clearly enjoying his day and writing parking tickets. A great Father's day gift for some no doubt. On the sea front I saw two round towers, which looked like a cross between oast houses and brick kilns. It turned out that these were purpose built as a theatre and had no age or history to them.

Prior to the 1820s Ilfracombe had no beaches that could be accessed, which limited its attraction as a holiday destination. So a number of Welsh miners were employed to cut four tunnels through the cliffs to provide the town with access to a beach. The tunnels led to two bathing pools, which were strictly segregated between women and men. The women were required to swim with costumes that covered their whole bodies; but men were free to dress as they liked and most swam naked.

Britain's oldest working lighthouse is here in Ilfracombe. It sits on top of an old chapel on Lantern Hill and has been working ever since the seventeenth century, though I daresay they have changed the candle a few times.

Despite the rain I stopped, briefly, at the harbour and took a quick photograph of Verity a controversial statue made by the equally controversial artist Damien Hirst, who lives in nearby Combe Martin. The statue stands on the quay and is a good marker for ships entering the harbour. At 20 metres tall it is the highest statue in Britain. It depicts a naked women standing on law books with the sword of truth held aloft. What is more controversial than her being naked is that she is also pregnant and one side is cut away to show her anatomy and the fetus within the womb.

"Verity" at Ilfracombe Harbour, North Devon

Driving on in the torrential rain the next place is Woola-
combe, which has one of the most popular and longest (at
3 miles) surfing beaches in the country. Indeed, last year it
was voted as the best beach in Britain. It's near neighbour,
Croyde, also has a well populated surfing beach and there is
a third long beach, at Saunton Sands in Croyde Bay. We have
some close friends that have a second home in Croyde, with
their main home being on the border of Gloucestershire and
Worcestershire. I 'phoned to see if they were home, but they
were holding an open day in the garden of their main house
(where it was not raining) and would not be coming down to
Croyde until the next day, so unfortunately I missed them. The

walks along the cliffs at Croyde are spectacular and there is a lovely view towards Baggy Point and the island of Lundy in the distance in the middle of the channel.

In continuing rain I followed the coast to the fairly large town of Barnstaple. This is not really a coastal town as it is at the head of the River Taw estuary, however it is a good place to visit and explore. It has nice architecture facing the river and in the town it has numerous old buildings including a Pannier Market building that is the place for an excellent indoor produce and craft market. One of the prettiest train rides in the country is to travel from Exmouth on the east coast of Devon (where I started my journey) to Barnstaple on the west coast. The rail line is known as the Tarka Line after a famous book about an otter called Tarka. You follow the rivers Yeo and Taw along your journey and travel through cosy little English villages, with wonderful names like Eggesford, Kings Nympton and Umberleigh. The journey takes about an hour and a quarter and allows you to easily, during a day out, experience both the Atlantic and Channel coasts of Devon and the wonderful scenery in between.

After Barnstaple I moved on to Appledore and Westward Ho! There is a quay at Appledore that has a long maritime history. From the quay you look across to Braunton. These two villages form the junction and the estuary mouth for both the River Taw and the River Torridge. Appledore also has a good-sized shipyard that has built a number of Royal Navy ships and also ships for the Irish navy.

Westward Ho! (and a small town in Quebec) are the only towns in the world with an exclamation mark after their name. Westward Ho! is actually named after Charles Kingsley's book of the same name which is a story based on the nearby town of Bideford. Westward Ho! is really a manufactured place and was built specifically to attract tourists who might want to try and find a connection with the writings of Kingsley.

I had one last place that I really wanted to visit, the village of Clovelly, which is built down a steep cliff to the ocean with a small harbour at the bottom. Its main street is extremely steep, cobbled and drops 400 feet. It was still teeming with rain when I got to Clovelly. You cannot take a vehicle into the town and goods are dragged down the street from the car park above using wooden sledges. Tourists can walk down or travel astride a donkey. I arrived at the car park intending to walk down into the village, but was surprised to find that there is now an "entrance fee" of £7. The women at the desk said she would reduce this to £4 as the village was going to close in less than 30 minutes. I have in the past visited the village and there is not much there when you get to the bottom. The attraction is the cute pathway down and the donkeys.

Your £7 allows you access to the little shops that will sell you all those tourist items that you feel you must have at the time, but then never use or see after approximately one nano second of getting them home. I decided to drive on.

I tried to get out to Hartland Point but the low cloud, heavy rain and increasingly strong winds made it a fruitless journey. I therefore pushed on to Bude where just as I arrived at my B&B so did my friend Pete. We ate dinner in a horrible pub about two miles away. It was highly recommended on Google, but I think the "good comments" were likely to have been placed by the Landlord's wife and friends; we certainly did not feel it appropriate to make any good comments.

Tomorrow, with Pete as my guide, we move deeper into Cornwall.

Bude to St. Just

Miles 138

Cornish Surf, Nr. Padstow, North Cornwall

Today I have a companion once again in my good friend Pete. Pete will be my guide and scribe over the next two days. Pete and I met and became friends in Wargrave, but about four years ago he and his wife moved their main home to Cornwall, though retaining a small property in Wargrave. Having taken early retirement from a job in the City of London, Pete was for a number of years Chairman of Yeldall Manor in Wargrave a Christian residential rehabilitation Centre for men with alcohol and drug addictions. They carry out a tremendous work and have helped hundreds of men to restore their lives and return to family, jobs and society.

Our day started as it ended yesterday, damp and dull, but we planned to enjoy it anyway.

One of the glories of Britain is definitely the coast of Cornwall. Surely one of the most dramatic and picturesque anywhere, with ancient fishing villages, that have remained largely unchanged over the centuries and roads that similarly have remained largely unchanged!

Of surprise to me was to find that Bude actually has a canal. It runs south from Bude, following approximately alongside the River Neet, until it then joins up with the River itself about two miles inland. The sea lock at the end gives access from the canal to the sea at certain tides. The canal was built to carry small barges loaded with sand from the beach to put on the land and improve the soil further inland. Despite its export though, Bude has sufficient sand remaining for there to be an excellent beach. It just wasn't a good day to spend on it!

As we left Bude the drizzle turned into torrential rain. We drove along the cliff tops and came over the other side to Widemouth Bay another premier surfing beach. Despite the heavy rain there were surfers in the water. I suppose they are going to be wet anyway so why should rain bother them.

Crackington Haven was our next destination. The warm air was saturated and we ran into fog. In the clag we found a farmhouse B&B that Pete and his family stayed at back in 1977. At that time Pete's son was one year old and the farmer's son also the same age. Today that son is running the farm and the B&B. As it was his parents that Pete met, he did not think that it was worth knocking on the door to talk to the son who would almost certainly not remember him.

A few miles below Crackington Haven is Boscastle. In August 2004 both Crackington Haven and Boscastle were the sites of a massive flash flood, caused by heavy rainfall. One hundred homes were destroyed and eighty vehicles and several boats were washed into the sea. Fortunately no lives were lost, partly because the flood occurred during the daytime and not at night when people were in bed. It made for dramatic TV footage though. Once again, as with Lynmouth, the villages are located at the base of a valley with rock cliffs above them and a narrow river channel running through the village.

In continuing heavy rain we drove on to Tintagel. Legend suggests that Tintagel, with its ruined castle, might be the place where King Arthur was born. There is even a cave purporting to have been used by Merlin. Of course no one can prove any of this, or even if King Arthur actually existed, but it provides a magnate for tourists.

Tintagel Castle could never have been associated with the legendary King Arthur who is reported to have lived in the 6th century. The ruins today are of a castle actually built in the 13th century by Richard, Earl of Cornwall, who was the brother of Henry III. Richard wanted to stake his claim in Cornwall and ensure he could claim his taxes. He chose this spot due to its historic claims to King Arthur and thereby sought to take some of this magic upon himself. He even claimed (somewhat improbably without any proof) that Arthur had been conceived on this very ground. His castle though was purely symbolic and poorly built with thin walls that now are leaning as if about to fall into the sea.

What was discovered here in the mid 1980s however, suggests that Tintagel was at one time a wealthy place, probably with a harbour that traded, perhaps tin, for goods from the Mediterranean countries. A fire on the headland took away a lot of the vegetation and revealed the remains of around fifty buildings. Significant erosion of the cliffs and land has occurred so there may well have been many more buildings here. Excavations since the 1980s have uncovered pottery that can be dated as having originated in Byzantium from the middle of the 6th century. The finds are now in Truro Museum. This would confirm that there was a potentially large settlement here with strong trading links to the Mediterranean and the Middle East. The time would be right for this to tie into the legend of Arthur. It is quite possible that the ruler of this area may indeed be the genesis of the legends.

You can walk down the cliff to visit the ruins or take a taxi ride in a Land Rover. The rain kept us from walking down the rocky path.

One interesting sight in the village was a baker's shop where the bread and scones are made, in full view of everyone, in the shop window. I'm sure that this gives confidence to customers who buy here.

Eight miles further on and down very narrow lanes, we came to Port Isaac. This is the mythical Port Wen of the television series Doc Martin and the small village makes the most of the hundreds of tourists that come along to see where he and the other characters inhabit the village. We actually, inadvisably, drove down into the village and it has extremely narrow streets with no ability to park. Having squeezed past the tourists and almost lost the wing mirrors against the walls, we drove the circuit, as there was no space to turn around and came back and used the car park above the town. It did mean though that we had driven the road closest to the ocean! The footpath from the car park into the village provides an excellent view of the small harbour and in particular Doc Martin's house across the valley. You can actually book this house (named Fern Cottage) for a self-catering weekend or longer. It has two bedrooms but will set you back (currently) £206 per night.

The village is tiny and you can see everything within fifteen minutes. The only obvious Doc Martin artifact is a neck brace, worn by Mrs. Tishell the fictional Pharmacist that is now around the neck of the figurehead of Lord Nelson on the wall above the shop used in the series.

We stopped for a coffee in a café that used to be a Methodist chapel and still contains the upper balcony, now used as a gallery for handicrafts. We were persuaded by the waitress to try the saffron cake with our coffee. Excellent and I would love to try this again.

Doc Martin's house & surgery (the small one), Port Isaac,
North Cornwall

Just after Port Isaac is Port Quinn. This is apparently where Martin Clunes, who plays Doc Martin, likes to walk his dog. He is a great dog lover in real life, but fans of the show may be aware that this is not the case in the program with Doc Martin objecting to having been adopted by a stray dog, who stays with him no matter how hard he tries to lose it.

Around the Point is Polzeath, another very popular surfing beach. Again lots of surfers were in the water. The sun was now beginning to break through the clouds.

Polzeath is just outside the River Camel estuary. Further along the estuary is the village of Rock. The Halifax Building Society published a survey in 2010 that placed Rock as the fourth least affordable place in Britain, while Padstow, which faces it across the estuary, was named as the second least affordable place. Rock has been nicknamed "Chelsea on Sea" by the Daily Telegraph. (This is the second place on this trip that has been given this same nickname). What drives the house unaffordability is the out-of-towners who buy homes here and use them only for holidays. Forty percent of houses in Rock are holiday homes.

There is excellent sand here, lots of it, forming both a beach and a number of sand bars and boating is extremely popular. In May 2013 an awful boating tragedy occurred here when a family in a RIB were all thrown into the water when the father apparently fell onto the throttle and the steering wheel, causing the boat to accelerate and turn sharply.

The family of six were all thrown into the water. The father, mother and an eight year old daughter were struck by the boat as it went round and round in circles at high speed. The father and daughter were killed and the mother lost a leg. The three other children were uninjured. The mother now devotes her life campaigning for boating safety and encouraging boat operators to use the engine "kill cord" which will stop the engine if the operator falls overboard.

Padstow, North Cornwall

We had to travel up the estuary to Wadebridge to cross the river Camel and then drive back down to reach Padstow. Parking was difficult to find but after a five minute patient wait for a lady to water and feed her puppy, she drove off and we moved into her space. Padstow is nicknamed "Padstein" after the famous chef Rick Stein who owns at least three restaurants here and a cooking school. We went into a hall that had a local craft food and drink market and also a show of art from local artists. Here Pete recognised one of the artists who used to live in Wargrave. I purchased a bottle of locally made cider.

There were a lot of dogs and puppies in town with their owners. It was really nice to have so many wagging tails and wet noses all wanting to greet me. One of the great things about Britain is that dogs are welcome in most places, especially in pubs. This is not the case in Vancouver and I feel that the city is the poorer because of it.

One other distinct difference between Britain and Canada was exemplified by a visit to Boots the chemist in

Padstow. My back was painful and I asked for a product containing paracetamol (acetaminophen) along with a muscle relaxant. No such product exists and the muscle relaxant available in North America is considered a prohibited substance in Britain. However, I can purchase over the counter in Britain, cough syrups, such as Pholcodeine, containing large quantities of codeine. This product is banned in North America because of fears of misuse. Indeed you can be arrested if you enter the country with this product in your luggage. Conversely paracetamol can only be sold in limited quantities in Britain as, although an excellent drug, it is highly toxic if used beyond the recommended daily dose. In North America the dangers of acetaminophen (paracetamol), usually called Tylenol, are not addressed and you can easily purchase bottles of tablets that contain at least fifteen times the fatal dose!

This coast contains numerous bays that are magnets for surfers. Harlyn Bay, just around the headland from Padstow, is one such bay with spectacular rocky outcrops pushing out into the ocean and dividing the bays. This is seen again at Porthcothan Bay and Mawgan Porth. The area has Watergate Bay, a very large bay that Jamie Oliver has recently "blessed" by opening a new restaurant here! Cornwall seems to be coming the food mecca of Britain.

Newquay is the largest town on this coast and has two superb bays, Newquay Bay and Fistral Bay, either side of the headland. Newquay is known as the surfing capital of Britain with the main surfing beach being at Fistral Bay. This was bathed in spectacular sunshine and had huge waves when we stopped there. It was very noticeable that Fistral had excellent weather, but looking behind us, back over the land, dark clouds were present.

Fistral Beach, Newquay, Cornwall

The last time I was in Newquay was for my honeymoon! The town has grown in size since that time. It is still a magnet for holidaymakers, but has unfortunately also become a popular place for stag and hen parties and for youngsters seeking an alcohol fueled weekend.

We continued on to Perranporth, where Pete said that he had spent many of his childhood holidays. We found a parking spot close to the three-mile long beach and brewed a cup of tea.

Perranporth is named after St. Piran the patron saint of Cornwall. St. Piran died in 480 and is believed to have come, like so many, from Ireland. Not much is known about him. An oratory built by him, which became covered by the sand, was excavated in 1910, but then left alone and is once again under the sands. His symbol is a white cross on a black background and has become the county flag and symbol of Cornwall. St. Pirin is also the patron Saint of tin miners, of whom I suspect that there are now none left – certainly in Cornwall! It is said that he brought with him the secrets of extracting tin from ore, which had become lost in Cornwall, so that the industry was revived – but has since died again.

In Perranporth I came across my first Unisex loo. It is about the size of any other public toilet but with mainly stalls inside, plus urinals for men at the far end. There were both men and women using it. It felt strange at first but after a few moments I thought no more about it and everyone there seemed relaxed about it also. It was also free and relatively clean.

After Perranporth and with time marching on we continued along the coast by whatever road is closest to the ocean. Sometimes it is very close, at other times it took us quite a bit inland. We drove through St. Agnes, Porthtowan and Portreath. All very small, but all with nice beaches and lots of people and surfers.

Pete got me to stop at one place, close to Gwithian that I would not have seen just driving by. We stopped the car and walked to the cliff edge, unfenced and crumbly. Below us was a dramatic sea cliff and rocky bay known as "Hell's Mouth". Such places feel almost eerie as your mind keeps saying to you how awful it would be if you slipped and fell. Having had experience in the last 12 months of slipping and falling (and breaking things) I did not get as close to the edge as I might otherwise have done! The views from here were across to Godrevey Point and the lighthouse.

Gwithian itself has a pub called the Red River Inn, which goes back to the colour of the river in the days when mining effluence leached into it.

We continued on and drove around Hayle to arrive at our next destination of Carbis Bay with St. Ives behind it. St. Ives is a major holiday destination and rightly so because of its gorgeous position.

St. Ives, North Cornwall

However this has been another place where the demand for second homes has pushed house prices up to a level that local young people cannot afford to buy. In May of 2016, people who did not have permanent residence there owned one in four of all of the homes in St. Ives. A recent vote by residents has been to restrict the building of new second homes. Presumably this means that only locals can buy new builds, which will thus limit the market for new properties and keep their price down. How they will then prevent a local person buying cheaply one of these properties and then making a killing by selling it on, I don't know, unless there are legal covenants in place in respect of resale being only to a local. Apparently a local building company has made a legal challenge to this decision and it is to be seen if this can be implemented. What will happen is that existing homes

426

will be in greater demand and in a restricted market prices will presumably rise even further.

It is difficult to know how to deal with this sort of situation. I mentioned earlier that in one area in Scotland people had formed a development corporation to access grants and other funding to purchase land and build lower cost housing for locals. In Vancouver a review of utility bills highlighted where condos in the city were not lived in all year round (at least 25%) which suggested that these properties were not occupied full time. It is now being mooted that a higher property tax be applied to such houses/condos as a means of making it less attractive to have them unoccupied and hopefully resulting in more properties being available to rent in the city, or, to tax non residents at a higher rate on the property purchase price. There is no easy answer, it is all a supply and demand market, but I do have some sympathy with a young person or family that has grown up in an area and want to continue living there, but can't afford to buy a house. It has in the past led to drastic reactions, such as in Wales where a number of years ago, holiday homes were targeted and fire bombed.

Travelling further south from St. Ives you come across a number of old mines with their distinctive chimneys. These were copper rather than tin mines. All of the old mines appear to have romantic names, usually always starting with the word "wheal" as in Wheal Grace and Wheal Leisure, which are in the Poldark TV series. The word wheal though, is old Cornish meaning "a place of work." It quite takes away the romance when you know that!

We stopped and looked at the ruin of the Carn Galver mine, which is now managed by the National Trust.

Carn Galver tin mine

Cornish tin miners were highly sought after around the world for their skills and experience. Many mines closed down for parts of the year, especially when water entered the mines and could not be pumped out quickly enough. So, many miners left the county for work overseas where they could earn more money.

In 1812, the Cornish engineer Richard Trevithick developed the high pressure condensing steam engine, known as the "Cornish Engine" which was highly efficient and revolutionised the pumping of water from the mines. The invention

428

was eventually sold (and copied) all over the world and though helping the Cornish tin miners and mine owners greatly, also served to hasten their demise as competition from other parts of the world eventually rendered Cornish tin uneconomic to mine.

Moving on we now headed along the coast road, with beautiful views almost all the way, to find our B&B for the night in St. Just. This was the most expensive B&B I have so far stayed in (by about £10) but it was also one of the best. Very professionally done. Nice light coloured carpets (why do many B&Bs seem to have horrible carpets, usually in heavy dark red colours?) with every facility in the room you could require. They even had a bar and the daily newspapers to read. It does not take much to lift a B&B from being ordinary to exceptional. The lady running this knew how to do that and thus could charge more.

In booking B&Bs I find Trip Advisor, or other similar web sites, to be quite helpful in choosing where to stay, though I sometimes feel that my standards must be higher than others as my experience does not necessarily match those of the comments. If you read the visitors book in most B&Bs you can see that people generally, especially when they know the host will see it, only write positive things. In a couple of B&Bs that I stayed in the comments said "wonderful stay, lovely host" when probably what they wanted to write was "this place is shabby and dirty and the host was grumpy and did not shave and I will never come again". I wanted to write the latter at one of my B&Bs but decided to say nothing!

The B&B was close to the airport that flew to the Isles of Scilly. Due to fog and rain planes had not been able to fly the night before and we had at least one couple in the B&B who had been forced to spend an overnight in St. Just rather than in the (expensive) B&B they had booked on Scilly. I have in the past tried to book a vacation on the Isles of Scilly but to do this you need to book months in advance and be prepared to pay a high price.

Recently, being unable to find a suitable place on the Scillys my wife and I flew to Majorca (beautiful island) from Exeter instead and had a wonderful time. This example highlights the fact that with so many local airports around the UK, providing low cost flights to warm and sunny climes, the British B&B has to keep its standards up if it wants to keep its trade.

We went for dinner in St. Just and had a good meal in a local pub. The restaurant was very nice, but the staff clearly were not well trained and the cheery manager really could have shaved before he came into work. Dirty face, dirty hands, dirty food goes through one's mind! After our meal we moved into the bar and watched a very lack luster performance from England in a nil nil draw against Slovakia in the Euro16 tournament.

Tomorrow Pete assures me will be a short day mileage wise, but a long day in terms of driving, not only because of the narrow roads, but also because there is so much to see.

St. Just to Feock

Miles 107

St. Michael's Mount, Marazion, Cornwall

Today was a long day, but a good one. Mileage was limited but there were so many beautiful places to stop at, usually at the end of very narrow roads. I also reached the final cardinal compass point of my journey.

We left our nice B&B after a great breakfast where we both had smoked haddock and poached egg, the healthiest breakfast so far on the trip!

431

Our first destination was Sennen Cove. This is an old fishing village and was at one time the most important seine net fishing place in Cornwall. It is now, of course, a very popular surfing place lying at the southern end of Whitesand Beach. It is heavily dependent on tourism and only a few fishing boats now remain focusing on Mullet rather than the old more traditional herring and pilchards that no longer arrive in the numbers as once they did. In the olden times a watcher, known as a Huer, would be posted, often in a small tower, to watch for the shoals of herring coming into the bay. These were known as Silver Darlings, which reminded me that in the Orkneys, they use the same term. The fishing boats would then go out and spread their seine nets around the shoal and they would be hauled in to the shore. In 1977 apparently 17,000 pounds of herring were caught on one occasion. Mainly due to overfishing, there is now no seining for herring as there are few herring left.

The village has, by the beach, an old round building called of course the "Round House" that used to house the capstan wheel that would draw the boats up the beach. It was also where the herring would be pressed and the oil obtained. It is now an art gallery. Across the road is a house called "The Old Saltings" which no doubt was the place that the fish were salted down for preservation.

As expected, there is an RNLI lifeboat station here, this one holding a Tamar Class lifeboat and a smaller inshore vessel. I have actually been on board a Tamar Class vessel when this was the one on station at Exmouth. A friend of mine, who was the mechanic on board, took me into the spacious engine room that he apparently travelled in during operations. I know I would have been sick if I had to make a journey sitting down there! It is a big boat and able to take very heavy seas. RNLI lifeboats are required to be able to reach any vessel in distress up to 50 miles out to sea within two hours of the call out, so mariners can have a lot of confidence that if they get into difficulties someone will soon be with them to help them.

Sennen was also famous at one time for having a sea rescue dog, a Newfoundland called Bilbo, who was part of the local beach lifeguards group and he began his work in 2005. This group were taken over by the RNLI in 2008 and then, unfortunately Bilbo was stripped of his job. This was because of two things; firstly, dogs were prohibited from being on the beach during the summer months and secondly the RNLI rule was that only one person (or dog) could travel on the quad bike that went down to the water! There was a petition to have him reinstated, but unfortunately Bilbo died in 2015 before he could get his job back. Newfoundlands are bred as water dogs. They have webbed feet and a natural instinct for assisting people in difficulties in the water.

After Sennen Cove we experienced the only ugly part of the day, a visit to Land's End. This is just a tourist trap with a visitor center (read, place to sell tourist tat) and for which you are expected to pay £5 to park and go into their shop. Avoid it! It is not anyway the most southerly point of Britain (as John O' Groats is also not the most northerly). It is actually the most westerly point on mainland England. (Ardnamurchan Point being the most westerly point on mainland Britain). Also, the headland is fairly non-descript. There was no place to turn around so we had to drive in. The turn around point and exit are clearly marked as no doubt most people think the same as us and don't want to stay!

We motored on around the point and came to Porth-curno. Porthcurno beach looks as lovely as most of the Cornish beaches, but otherwise quite non-descript. However, there is history and mystery beneath its golden sands. Porthcurno and its beach are famous in the world of communications. Under the sands here are cables, put in in 1870 that were the first in the world to carry communications under the ocean as far away as the United States and India. On the cliff top is a museum that was at one time the nerve centre of this great operation. Between the two world wars this site was built up to fourteen cables and was the largest such station in the world. During the war a number of tunnels were excavated (by tin miners) to house the communications equipment and this operated through until 1970. The tunnels today form part of the museum. In the days of morse code, operators initiated contact with each other by sending out the morse for the letters PK, standing for Porthcurnow. (Cornwall is known locally as Kernow, hence the use of the letter K). This then became accepted as the standard contact between morse operators anywhere in the world.

Right next to Porthcurnow and on the cliff above the beach is the famous open air Minack Theatre. This has literally been carved out of the rock and has the most stupendous setting along the lines of a Roman style amphitheater. The theater was the brainchild of Rowena Cade who owned a house on the cliff and in 1973 allowed her garden to be used as the setting for a production of the Tempest. The theater grew over the years from this one production and now as many as 80,000 people a year come to see plays performed here. The actors are usually touring companies who make this a "must stop at" place to perform. Apparently productions go ahead whatever the weather and if you go you should take a cushion to sit on and a blanket in case it gets chilly.

We drove on and down into Lamorna Cove with the lovely named pub called Lamorna Wink just before it. From there we moved on to Mousehole (pronounced Mowzal). It was here that the Welsh poet Dylan Thomas spent his honeymoon in 1938. Mousehole holds a food festival in December and the famous fish dish "Star Gazey Pie" originated here, being a fish pie with fish heads added, pointing up through the crust.

Mousehole

One of the most poignant things associated with Mousehole is the Penlee lifeboat disaster of December 19th 1981. Although technically in Mousehole, the lifeboat station was named after Penlee Point, just beside the village, where the boat was based. The lifeboat was called out to attempt to rescue the crew of the Union Star a new freighter on its maiden voyage, taking fertilizer from Holland to Dublin. It had a crew of five on board, plus the wife and two stepdaughters of the captain. When off Wolf Rock, 18 miles out to sea, the ships engines failed, due to ingress of seawater. A nearby tugboat offered to tow them, but would have claimed salvage. By the time the Captain had contacted the ship's owners and received permission to accept the tow, the ship had been blown by the storm across Mounts Bay and close to the rocks at Lamorna.

An RAF Sea King helicopter attempted to lift off the crew, but with winds gusting at up to 90mph this proved impossible. The Sea King helicopter was flown that night by a US Air force pilot on secondment. The same helicopter itself was later flown in the Falklands War by Prince Andrew and is now on display at the RNAS Museum at Yeovilton.

The Penlee lifeboat, the Solomon Brown was called out to make the rescue and take off the crew. The Solomon Brown was an open forty-seven foot boat built twenty years earlier and with engine power sufficient only to make 9 knots. Waves at this time were reported to be up to sixty feet high. The helicopter pilot reported seeing the Solomon Brown come alongside the ship and despite being thrown by the sea up onto the ships deck and then washed off again, it managed to get the Captain's wife, two daughters and one other crew member on board. The Coxswain radioed, "We've got four" but that was the last message ever heard. All eight crew on the lifeboat and all eight people on board the Union Star were lost.

Within 24 hours of the disaster twenty-three volunteers came forward to man a replacement vessel. A memorial and flower garden are now in place where the lifeboat station used to be. The replacement lifeboat was moved to a new station at Newlyn. Two days before the disaster Charlie Greenhaugh, a crewmember who was lost, had turned on the village's Christmas lights. After the disaster the lights were turned off, but his widow asked for them to be turned back on again. Since this time the Christmas lights at Mousehole are turned off for one hour at 8.00pm on 19th December as a mark of respect for the lost men.

Newlyn, which now is conjoined with Penzance, has the largest remaining fishing fleet in Cornwall. Penzance is the terminus of the Great Western Railway and has regular train service every day to and from London. Penzance was the birthplace of Maria Bramwell, who became the mother of Charlotte, Emily and Anne Bronte.

In Mount's Bay is the famous St. Michael's Mount, which has similarities to Mont St. Michel on the western coast of France. The UK version has a castellated house, rather than an Abbey, which is what is atop the French version. At low tide St. Michael's Mount can be reached, on foot, by a causeway from Marazion village.

Marazion from St. Michael's Mount

It was low tide when we arrived so with the assistance of a very helpful parking attendant who, because of his injured leg (caused by a motorcycle accident) and use of a crutch, took pity on my bad back and allowed us to park close to the causeway, so we were able to walk across to the island. We followed other people taking a diagonal short cut across the soft sands, which was better for my back than the cobbled causeway. However, what none of us knew until we got there was that the sandy beach had two streams of water running across it, so we had to either get our feet wet or jump them. I chose the latter course, but regretted it when my feet landed and jarred my back further. The National Trust manages St Michael's Mount, so I got further value from my reciprocal membership of the Scottish National Trust that I had taken out at Culloden.

The house was very interesting and the site dates back to at least the 12th century. The island probably had a monastery from the 8th to 11th century and King Edward the Confessor actually gave it to the Abbey of Mont St. Michel in France, in 1060. It stayed under their control until the 14th century when it was passed to Syon Abbey near London. The Mount was fought over and besieged a number of times in various internal English conflicts. In 1659 the Mount was sold to Colonel John St.Aubyn and has been in his family ever since. When control was passed to the National Trust in 1954, along with a large endowment, the family retained a 999-year lease to continue to live in the property.

Once on the island you find that all of the pathways up to the house are rough cobbles. There is apparently a small funicular railway within a tunnel that can be used to take luggage up to the house. It is still operating, but used only rarely. It was not visible when we were there.

From Marazion we drove on with the intention of finding ice creams! We found these in Porthleven, close to Helston. Porthleven along with Mullion Cove are the only two harbours on the western side of the Lizzard Peninsula. In the winter storms of 2014, the harbor wall at Porthleven was breached. Porthleven was once the home of Wing Commander Guy Gibson who led and was killed during the famous Dam Buster raid during World War II.

Near to Porthleven is RNAS Culdrose, which until 2015 was the main Air Sea Rescue base. Air Sea rescue has now been privatised and the contract awarded to Bristow Aviation. This has caused a number of naval helicopter pilots to leave the service, some joining Bristow.

Mullion Cove was also hit and damaged by the storm of 2014 and the sea wall has not yet been repaired. Originally the harbour was built as a haven for pilchard fishing boats.

Kynance Cove, Cornwall

Pete next took me to Kynance Cove, which I have to say is spectacular. The BBC has described it as one of the most beautiful stretches of coastline in the South West. They are certainly not exaggerating. I viewed it only from above not having the time, or the ability because of my back, to walk down to the beach. Within the car park (National Trust) and seemingly oblivious to cars and people, were a herd of Devon Red Poll cattle, all lying down and enjoying the sunshine!

We then came to Lizard Point. This is the most southerly point on the UK mainland and is the last of my cardinal points that I wanted to reach. It is also spectacular. Indeed I would use the word breathtaking, especially in the bright and warm sunshine that greeted us. Again this is another National Trust protected part of the coastline.

Pete's wife, Sue, was recently here for a period of time as the *artist in residence*. She is a wonderful amateur artist working in most materials. She was based right at the Point, in a small hut alongside the café. The aim of the National Trust was to demonstrate how art draws attention to nature. This proved to be so successful that this is to become an on-going feature at the Lizard with various artists showcasing their talents. Also at the Point were some National Trust volunteers with telescopes ready to show visitors interesting creatures of the rocks and small islets. There were seals, gannets, Kittiwakes and I managed to get a reasonable photograph of an oyster catcher way down on the rocks below.

As Pete had been here a number of times before he was able to show me how I could park at the bottom of the track rather than in the main car park higher up. But be warned if you do decide to drive down to the bottom, coming back up, with other cars and pedestrians coming down, is nigh on impossible as the track is so narrow! After afternoon tea (you can tell we had a very sophisticated and pleasant day!) we were lucky in navigating our way back up the track and so drove on to Coverack with a diversion to the charming little village with the lovely name of Cadgwith. This is positioned in a small cove and is a popular stop over on the South West Coastal Path. The main beach here is shingle although there is a second smaller beach a short walk away with some sand. Given that most villages in England have a church that is a few hundred years old, it was interesting to note that here the Anglican Church is a much more recent and modest affair, being a blue painted wooden building erected no doubt in an attempt to take the Church to the people. There is apparently a noted singing group, the Cadgwith Singers, who perform locally and often can be found in the village pub.

Pete and Sue are both in a local choir and will be performing on Saturday in Coverack our next destination. This is another small fishing village, which makes most of its revenues from walkers and holidaymakers. The old lifeboat station, with its slipway down into the water, is a prominent building. There is no longer a lifeboat here, the building now being a seafood restaurant.

The next part of the journey was extreme in respect of the narrow lanes. Samantha had us drive one lane, which for two miles had no passing places and the grass was brushing the doors on both sides. As luck would have it we saw no other vehicle until we literally got to the end where we pulled in to let three vehicles pass in the opposite direction.

Helford is on the north east tip of the Lizard Peninsula and is a small and pretty little place overlooking Helford Passage (Helford River). There is a passenger only ferry (shame

441

for us) across the river. There were many small boats and dinghies moored up to the floating jetty, presumably for people to access their sailboats placed on swinging moorings in the center of the river.

Needing to be in Feock in time for Pete to get to choir practice we rushed through the premier sailing and boating town of Falmouth (which I will return to). The Falmouth estuary is a Ria (flooded river valley) and forms the third deepest natural harbor in the world.

I will now be taking a few days R&R with Pete and Sue in Feock, a charming little village further up the estuary, before Marilyn joins me on Thursday and we then together complete the journey back to Exmouth on Saturday and Sunday.

Lizard Point, Cornwall

Feock to Falmouth (again)

Miles 45

Flying a "Leave" Flag

Today will potentially be a very significant day for Britain in that this is the day in which Britain votes in the "Brexit" referendum on whether to remain in or leave the EU.

More significant for me though at a personal level is that today is the day that my wife Marilyn comes to join me, after thirty days being apart. I am due to meet her from the train, at lunchtime, at Truro station.

443

I woke up to a lovely Cornish summer morning in Feock. Feock is adjacent to the beautiful National Trust gardens at Trelissik that are a definite must visit if you are in the area. It is also the location of the King Harry Ferry, which is to be our passage across to St. Mawes tomorrow and our journey further up the coast. Cornwall is a place where lots of Saints were revered and the names of many villages and towns clearly show this. Indeed the village of Feock was once called St. Feock. The greater majority of these Cornish Saints all came from Ireland and established a Celtic form of Christianity, the same as on Iona with St. Columba and on Holy Island with St. Aidan. Here in Cornwall there are repeated legends of the Saints having arrived in coracles sitting on a rock. A coracle is a small boat, often round, made of willow and covered by animal hide. The rock perhaps was used as ballast to keep the craft stable. They would have had to choose a period of very calm weather to safely row across the Irish Sea to Britain. No doubt the remains of many erstwhile Saints lie under the waters of the Irish Sea and the Atlantic if this truly was how they travelled.

St Columba is known to have slept using a rock as his pillow, so it is possible that the rock was more symbolic than just ballast and was a way of keeping their spiritual lives as comfortless as possible. Certainly the Celtic form of Christianity favoured hardship as a way of confirming selflessness.

After one day's R&R with Pete & Sue in Feock, a very pleasant lie in and a lovely healthy breakfast, I made my way to Truro station, getting there a good thirty minutes early. Having drunk possibly two whole pots of tea I decided to use the toilets on the station platform. This turned out to be a highly praiseworthy event and a demonstration that the British loo can be done right. The toilets were actually the other side of the ticket barrier, but the young women at the gate said I could use them as long as I made sure I was back before the train arrived. Strictly speaking I needed to have a ticket to be on the platform. She could easily have said no, but she trusted my word and I think showed a great customer attitude. These turned out to be the most immaculately clean and free public toilets I have found on the whole of my journey. At least that is for the gentleman's toilets, though I am sure the same would hold true for the ladies. As I walked in, the place smelt very fresh, the sinks, urinals and every piece of porcelain in the building was sparkling and shiny. There was "blue" flush cleaner in evidence everywhere. The floors were dry and immaculate and I saw no graffiti.

As you will have already noted, this journey has for me thrown up an unexpected topic of the state of the British Loo and its availability and cost across Britain. There was a time in Britain when you had to spend a penny, literally, to use a public toilet, at least the cubicle. I remember my grandmother vociferously complaining about the unfairness of it next to men. So charging to use a loo is not a new phenomenon, however, for probably the last thirty years or so, the recognition that it is a public service and necessary to encourage hygiene, in almost every case toilets became free to use. This trend seems to be reversing. Where a public toilet already existed, many have now reverted to charging again. Also it seems, many have been removed, or new ones not built and the provision of them passed over to the expectation that people can use supermarkets or cafes. In my experience, the only one you can count on in this respect is Tesco. To remove or charge for public conveniences goes against the British spirit of being hospitable and is the polar opposite of portraying yourself as welcoming visitors.

There are those communities, such as Applecross, that have wonderfully clean establishments and politely ask for a donation. There is Perranporth, which is very forward looking and provides free unisex loos. There was the toilet in the Old Chapel Café in Port Isaac that had "twinned" with and supported the provision of a public toilet in India. This latter one I think is a great example and draws the users attention to the fact that there are many places in the world where public conveniences don't even exist. I'm happy for my penny to go towards supporting this cause. There is now of course the British Toilet Association, which strives to raise the standards of the British public Loo by giving recognition to those people who do the excellent job of maintaining and cleaning them. Most people are proud of the job they do, no matter what it is and the standard at which they perform. This is also true for the "porcelain workers" but who maybe don't get the recognition for doing such a necessary job. The BTA are seeking to raise the standards by shining a light and recognising the workers.

Anyway, back to Truro station. As I passed back through the ticket gate I felt it important to say to the young women to please pass on my congratulations to the person who cleaned the toilets. A few minutes later I heard her say to a man walking though the barrier "You have had someone praise you on the state of the toilets." Clearly this was the man responsible, so I went up to him and personally thanked him. I think he was a bit taken aback as I am sure that he does one of those jobs that people take for granted; but it was good to pass on personally my appreciation. I think if everyone gave praise where it's due, especially for those jobs that not everyone wants to do, then they will be encouraged and keep on providing the service that we all want to have. Praise where it is due probably has more impact on job performance than tipping.

The train arrived punctually and I was overjoyed to be reunited with my wife once again. As I had been writing a daily blog of my journey she was very much up to date with my news so I listened to all of her and the family's news as we returned to Feock and our hosts. After a nice lunch Marilyn and I took the afternoon on our own and went into Falmouth, which I had hurried through too quickly on Tuesday.

Leaving Feock to drive to Falmouth, you pass a sign for the delightfully named village of "Come To Good". It is very small, just a hamlet and nobody quite knows how it got its name. Some think it is a derivation of "the Coombe by the dwelling in the Wood", whereas others suggest it is called this because of the Quakers who's Friends Meeting House is in the village. Wherever it comes from I think it is a wonderful name for a community and must generate a lot of conversations when an inhabitant has to give their address.

Before you get to Falmouth you pass through the small town of Penryn, which is almost fully joined up to Falmouth. You can park and take a water taxi from here (or a bus if you don't like water) directly into Falmouth Quay. I saw nothing special enough in Penryn that would cause me to want to make a particular point of visiting it, but I am sure the car park and ferry generates local income from tourists.

Falmouth itself is noted for sailing and there are a lot of yachts in the harbour. There is also a luxury ship building yard, owned by entrepreneur Peter de Savery, who at one time had plans for expanding the whole of the waterfront in Falmouth and smartening it up. I don't know whether he changed his mind, or ran out of money, or the town council blocked the plans, but it clearly did not happen. The town around the harbour, though not unpleasant, is not particularly attractive and the shops are not ones that you would go out of your way to visit, mainly aimed at loosening the wallets of tourists.

Fal Estuary and Carrick Roads, Falmouth, Cornwall

Falmouth has always been noted as a place for Art education. Recently the famous Dartington Hall arts establishment, in Devon closed its doors and the Art College has now been relocated here to Falmouth.

Drive out of the town with the ocean on your left and you come to Castle Drive. At its end, at the point, you will come to Pendennis Castle, which affords wonderful views across Carrick Roads and towards St. Mawes on the opposite coast. This is not the traditional magnificent turreted castle with ramparts and drawbridge, but was built mainly as a gun battery to fire onto any enemy ships that might dare to try and enter Falmouth harbour and Carrick Roads. Pendennis Castle was built by Henry VIII in 1542 and is twinned with St. Mawes Castle, a similar structure on the opposite bank. Together the guns of both castles could cover the width of the ocean entrance.

Pendennis Castle, Falmouth, Cornwall

The Royalists held Pendennis Castle during the English Civil War. The future Charles II briefly stayed here before fleeing to the Scilly Isles and then to France. The Castle surrendered to Parliamentary forces in 1646 after all supplies had been cut off and the garrison was starving. It has the distinction of being the last but one castle in England to hold out against Cromwell's troops; the last being Wallingford Castle in Oxfordshire, which held out until July 1646 and the last of all in Britain was Harlech, in Wales that held out until March 1647. After its surrender the castle was not slighted due to its strategic defensive importance. The castle has a long history of usage, right up to the Second World War, but has now been "decommissioned" and is in the care of English Heritage and open to the public.

449

St. Mawes Lighthouse from Pendennis

Further out of town on the cliff road, which follows on from the route around Castle Drive, are some very smart homes and hotels. Indeed one of them, the St. Michael's Hotel used to be owned by friends of ours. Following a family tragedy and then a later fire, the hotel was sold. In the hotel grounds are now being built luxury apartments with a pool and spa. This will be a superb place to live, if you can afford it, once completed.

The beach in front is called Gyllyngvase beach and legend has it that is was named after William Aethlin, who was the grandson of William the Conqueror and son of Henry I and heir to the throne. He was drowned when the ship he was on hit rocks off Honfleur on a journey back from France in November 1120. According to local legend, William is buried on this beach, though no evidence exists. In Cornish Gilen Vas means shallow bay, but it is also suggested that the name comes from a corruption of Guillaume, French for William and Vase meaning grave. William's death put the crown of England in jeopardy as Henry had no other legitimate male heirs so he nominated his daughter, Matilda to become Queen on his death. The Barons agreed to his request, but on Henry's death they reneged on their oath and Henry's nephew Stephen, who was also a grandson of William the Conqueror, was crowned as King. The long drawn out conflict that followed was known as the Anarchy and only settled when Matilda agreed to give up her claim provided that her son, Henry would become King Henry II on the death of Stephen

We left Falmouth continuing along the beach road around to Maenporth. Here there is a good surfing beach and also an apartment complex, which has in its base an excellent restaurant having wonderful views from its patio across to the beach.

This completed the coastal places that I had too quickly passed through on Tuesday, so we set off back to our hosts. We had not gone far when, on a steep and very narrow lane, we met two tractors coming towards us, both with wide equipment attached to the front. We assumed it was cabbage harvesting equipment, as they looked like multiple large colanders turned upside down, no doubt to collect and cut the head of the cabbage. You would need to be very exact in planting and spacing the young cabbage plants if you want to later pick them mechanically with this equipment. Needless to say we and the other four vehicles behind me all had to back up, quite some distance, to let them pass. I'm sure some farmers get great pleasure in having to inconvenience the "grockles" who invade their roads.

On this evening Pete & Sue had to go out for a prior commitment, so Marilyn and I took a bottle of wine and some cheese down to Feock beach after supper. While we were there a young women drove up in her car and got out and was looking around apparently expecting to meet someone. Then to her surprise, her boyfriend drove right up to the beach in a small powerboat with a bottle of champagne and whisked her out into the Bay. Sitting there with our own bottle of wine we shared in our own equally romantic moment.

Boats at anchor, Loe Beach, Feock

Tomorrow, Friday, Pete & Sue plan to take us on a tour of the Roseland Peninsula, and St. Mawes, just a ferry ride from their house across the water and our next coastal destination. I am particularly looking forward to this, which will "knock off" 50 miles of driving that I otherwise would have to do.

Pete decided to stay up through the night to listen to the results of the referendum on whether or not Britain should leave the EU!

Feock to St. Austell

Miles 50

Veryan, Roseland Peninsula, Cornwall

Today we woke up to the news that the referendum vote had come down in favour of leaving the EU. The vote was 52% voting to leave, 48% voting to remain. Though this is a 4% difference, the number of people who turned the majority was actually only 2.7% of those who voted. To me this is too narrow a margin to give rise to such a significant outcome.

In a General Election it is similarly a "first past the post" winner. However, in a General Election you only have to live with the consequences for a maximum of 5 years, in this case the outcome is final and there is, apparently, no going back.

Having seen hundreds of "Leave" posters around the UK and only six (yes six) posters saying "Remain" I had a suspicion that the Leave camp would win this, especially as the polls were giving it as a very slight win to the Remain camp. Recent experience both here and in Canada would suggest that people polled will either not be honest with their answers, or, deliberately hope to send a protest message to "frighten" one side or the other. Either way (and it could be that the pollsters actually don't get their samples right), my straw poll, based on posters seen and asking my B&B hosts which way they intended to vote, continued to indicate to me that 'Leave' might win.

Having lived outside of the UK for longer than 15 years (although still spending a lot of weeks every year in the UK) I was unable to vote in the referendum. I remain though strongly British and this is partly the reason why I have been doing my coastal trip. If I had voted I would have voted to remain in the EU. There are lots of reasons for this, some were thought through and I believe very rational, some just emotional. No matter my view, there will now be the very real issue of uncertainty and this is something that markets don't like. In uncertain times, markets will go down, which means the economy will weaken, which impacts everyone. A weak economy leads to opportunities for other countries to take advantage of the situation and compromises are then made that will have long-term consequences. I imagine that there will be a lot of anger amongst the other EU member states and negotiations to leave will be bitter and protracted and Britain will not have an easy ride.

The campaign, by both sides, contained lots of "fear mongering" and down right inaccuracies. At the end of the day I think people voted purely on gut feel and emotion and very few people really understood the implications of what they were being asked to vote for. Probably this is true in most elections, but the swing either way is not usually driven by facts but by emotion, often based on very tenuous facts, or "remembered hurts". Indeed part of the folklore in Britain is that if anything is not right then it must be the fault of the bureaucrats in Brussels. I think a lot of the people who voted to leave, really wanted to make a protest against "the system" and politicians in general, but they did not actually expect that this would be the outcome.

So Britain is now moving into unknown waters, with probably huge economic repercussions, when the reality is that this is probably not truly what the majority of people wanted. Yes a lot did vote to leave, but many I suspect wanted just to protest but did not expect their vote to have such an impact.

David Cameron has to take a lot of the blame for the outcome of the vote. He boldly claimed that he was going to get a better deal for Britain from Europe and I think he thought that he would be like Margaret Thatcher in this respect. He rashly threatened the EU that if Britain did not get what it wanted it would hold a referendum that might result in Britain leaving – he got what he wished for. The EU was somewhat between a rock and a hard place. If it gave in to Britain's demands then it would face pressure from the other member states to also have concessions. If it stood firm and Britain did have a referendum, resulting in a vote to leave, then other member states, such as France and Holland might also have to bow to internal political pressures and similarly hold votes on leaving. This could then see the end of the EU. The EU gambled on Britain voting to stay in; Cameron also gambled on the same outcome. Both parties lost. The result is now political instability and a lack of direction as no one can fully predict where this all might lead. What is certain is that Europe wont be coming back to say, "OK, we'll give in after all, please stay." There will be a lot of EU "payback" in the short term that can only hurt Britain further.

The leave campaign in Britain was hijacked by the political ambitions of Boris Johnson, a controversial character. He was until recently the Lord Mayor of London. He was at Eton at the same time as Cameron and there has always been intense rivalry between them. Boris is seen by many as a clown and his private life has been notorious. However, he is one of those people that if he fell down a sewer he would come up holding a gold coin. Without Boris, the Leave campaign would have had no real public leader, as the only other notable person was Nigel Farage, a non-elected right-winger whose main focus was on scaring the population on the subject of immigration. This was the key emotional issue in all of the debates (and fanned by the tabloid press) but at the end of the day I personally think that it was more the general public's uneducated views on the EU and the attitude of "let's protest about them" that made the difference.

Within my family there have been strong opposing views as to whether or not the right outcome was achieved and some are elated about the outcome. However two members of my family have since said, "I voted to leave, but I never thought that it would happen." This also seems to be the view of many others that have spoken on television and there is now a new phrase, instead of "Brexit" (Britain's exit from the EU) the phrase "Regrexit" (wished we had not voted to leave) is being termed. This describes those people who voted Leave as a protest against the EU, but did not really want it to happen in reality and now that it has happened, they are fearful of the outcome.

The people I feel most sorry for are the younger generation. The voting split, as to what age group voted for which camp, clearly shows that it was young people who voted to remain in Europe and the older generation who voted to leave. As one woman on television said "I feel awful that I voted to leave and have spoiled the opportunity that my children and grand children clearly wanted. It is their inheritance I have ruined." One young man wrote to the Spectator and said that he felt "I have been screwed by my parents".

75% of young people (under age 35) who voted, voted to remain, though more older people voted than younger people. I think this shows that it is the older age group who have built up this dislike of the EU and want to have things "as they used to be". It seems to be a sign of growing old when people hearken back to what they see as the "good old days" while young people see the opportunities for being in Europe and see it as their future. There were lots of things in the "old days" that I enjoyed and still miss, but would I change my lot today for what I had thirty years ago? No way.

The immediate fall-out has been the resignation (though not until a new leader has been chosen) by David Cameron and the push to also oust Jeremy Corbyn the Labour Party leader. David Cameron clearly could not stay on, but in choosing to go only when the Conservative Party have chosen a new leader is probably a tactic to try and ensure that the party have time to mobilise to keep Boris from being elected as leader. The majority of Tories certainly do not like Boris, but if they think he can win another election victory for the Conservative Party then he will get supported.

The Labour Party meanwhile fears the prospect of a General Election in the next few months. This could be called to get the country to confirm the new Prime Minister from whoever is chosen leader of the Conservative party. Most Labour politicians feel that Jeremy Corbyn is unelectable and so are seeking to oust him now to find a new more credible leader who would have a better chance to stand in opposition to whoever becomes Tory Leader.

My money is on Theresa May for the Tories and Hilary Benn as Labour leader.

There is one other party who could benefit from all of this, the Liberal Democrats. The Liberal Party grew out of the Whigs whose origins were as aristocrats back in the time of Charles II. They went through a number of breakaways and restructurings to form the present day party. They were strong at the beginning of the 20th century and were in government during the First World War. However, they lost out on the rise of the Labour Party in the 1920s and they became the alternative third party of British politics. They gained a measure of influence in government again in 2010 when they made an alliance with David Cameron's Conservatives to allow him to form a government. However their supporters did not forgive them for this and abandoned them in the 2015 election. The few MPs that are left are the only party to consistently say that Britain should remain in Europe despite the referendum. As Cameron lost the vote and the government are forced by the referendum to seek to "Leave" and as Jeremy Corbyn urged voters to respect the referendum also, the Liberals are the only party that can campaign on a platform that they will ignore the vote and seek to remain in Europe. Perhaps this is their chance to once again get back into power.

The other big issue in all of this is Scotland. The Scottish Parliament is now dominated by the Scottish National Party, who captured virtually all of the Labour vote in the last election. Their leader, Nicola Sturgeon, says they are going to begin the process to potentially have a new independence referendum. People in Scotland voted overwhelmingly to remain in Europe and she feels that by gaining independence they can continue to do so. The Leave vote will have been a godsend for them if it results in independence for Scotland. The fear is that this will also drive calls for Northern Ireland to break away from the United Kingdom and join with Ireland. Northern Ireland of course has a geographical problem, in that it is the only part of the UK that shares a border with another EU country, the Republic of Ireland.

The Queen must be deeply worried at the potential break up of her realm, united since James I in 1603. During my trip I have come across so much of the history of how the fragmented parts of these British Isles eventually came together under one rule with monarchs who had not only English, but also Scottish, Welsh and indeed European ancestry. It has long been a united nation of people of all backgrounds and origins. The potential for a breakup of a union that has existed for almost 500 years, is a real one.

Clearly only a few hours have elapsed and there are many pieces still moving and the implications are not clear. However, what is certain is that this was a historic vote and Britain is now on a different course and it will be a few years before anyone can really tell whether or not the right choice was made. All one can say is that today is a day of real shock in Britain.

The King Harry Ferry, Feock, Cornwall

But – moving on! The King Harry Ferry is only a five minute drive from Feock and is a short and inexpensive way to cross the River Fal and arrive on the Roseland Peninsula. The ferry saves at least a forty-minute drive around.

Our first stop off from the ferry was at St. Just in Roseland a very pretty little church, set in a semi-tropical garden. The church dates back to a 6th century Celtic church though the present building is 13th century and is built close to the water's edge. The interior of the church although pretty is quite plain and lacking the large stained glass windows of many other churches. However, it all feels very peaceful.

In 1872 the church underwent restoration and the then Bishop of Exeter arrived on board HMS Ganges to rededicate it. This is also another link back to British Columbia in that HMS Ganges was a ship that was involved in the San Juan boundary dispute between the United States and Britain and was based at Esquimalt in Victoria on what was then known as the Colony of Vancouver Island. The dispute almost resulted in a war, started by an American soldier shooting a pig belonging to the Governor of San Juan Island. The resultant stand-off between each side was eventually arbitrated by the German Kaiser Wilhelm I of Germany who "gave away" the San Juan Islands to America, much to the disappointment today of British Columbians. An interesting aside about the "pig war" is the American troops stationed on San Juan Island were commanded by a Colonel George Pickett, who was the very same one who led the disastrous Pickett's charge at the battle of Gettysburg, that turned the American Civil War in favour of the Unionists.

The sub-tropical gardens surrounding the church came about in the 19th century when a parishioner, supported by the then Rector, planted a large collection of tropical plants in the grounds. These thrived in the warm climate and the proximity of the water. Over time the graveyard was extended throughout the "forest" and now graves are set amongst the trees, pathways, streams and pond. It is a tranquil scene. There is also a tree to which people affix messages of memories of loved ones in the branches. One very moving tribute was to a young baby with the words "In memory of (babies name); born sleeping".

This would be a lovely church within which to get married, as was to be the case the day after our visit and the flower

461

designers were busy at work. It is one of those churches where the bride could arrive by boat, though you would have to check on the state of the tide on the day of the wedding as you could otherwise have a very muddy wedding dress!

St.Just-In-Roseland Cemetery, Cornwall

From St. Just we drove just a short distance down into St. Mawes. The town was holding sailing races while we were there, though most of the sailors seemed to be having a Cornish pasty and coffee on land when we arrived. The sailboats were all of the same class (unknown to me) and had bright logos on their top sail. We joined them in a pastry and coffee, served in a very haphazard and confused manner from an old hut by some of the locals. The oldest family bakery in Cornwall is here in St. Mawes, possibly this was it.

Facing the ocean we saw a renowned boutique hotel, owned by Alex Polizzi, a hotelier known for her television program "The Hotel Inspector". This would I'm sure be a lovely place to stay and I may do so at some future time.

We also noted that there had been a bargain sale going on in the town but we had arrived too late for it. The petrol pumps on the harbour front showed that they had been selling petrol at 2 shillings and sixpence a gallon, which equates to approximately 12 pence per litre in new money. Unfortunately they had sold out before we got there, indeed probably 50 years before we got there!

St. Mawes Castle, Cornwall

St. Mawes is named after the Celtic Saint Maudez, who though probably having come from Ireland, is also venerated in Brittany in France.

The buildings in St. Mawes are a mix of old and 1950s style architecture. In the main car park, a parade of shops, with flats above, looked particularly depressing and by the amount of weeds growing in the gutters, I imagine that they get a lot of damp problems. This is an eyesore in an otherwise very pretty place.

Keep on the harbour road and you will reach St. Mawes Castle. This is the other half of the "pair", along with Pendennis Castle, of fortified gun emplacements, built by Henry VIII to protect Falmouth harbour.

Portscatho, Cornwall

Our next stop was Portscatho, a lovely little village with two beaches. Above the main beach there is a small cliff side garden, which is a lovely place to sit and admire the view. At this point the South West Coastal Path enters the village. It is just beside a United Church and Methodist Chapel that provides a coffee urn and honesty box for visitors, a lovely, very Christian thing to do. The village seems very much self-contained having a butcher, a baker, a gallery, pub and restaurant. I did not see a grocer, so perhaps Tesco Direct supplies the rest.

A little further up the coast is Veryan, which has an unusual pair of round cottages either side of the road as you enter the village. There is a similar pair also as you exit the village. They were apparently built round so that the devil has no corners in which to hide. The village has a mill dating back to the 16th century, now a visitor attraction and place to eat. In the 19th century the local Vicar was very influential. He not only persuaded the villagers to attend church regularly but also built a school for boys and later one for girls where they could learn "female tasks".

Outside the village is Carne Beacon reputed to be the burial place of the Cornish King Gerranius. Fable has it that he is buried inside a golden boat with silver oars, but no one has yet found this. Perhaps it is like the site at Sutton Hoo in Sussex where similarly there was an ancient mound that one day was excavated. What was found were the remains of an ancient King, buried with his treasure, inside his longship.

We stopped and had afternoon tea; saffron cake and scones with Cornish clotted cream of course, at The Nare restaurant/hotel overlooking the lovely Gerran's bay.

We later briefly stopped at Portloe. Looking down onto the beach here there were two adjacent pubs, both seemingly doing a good trade. One of the local houses, no doubt claiming a nautical connection, had the figurehead from the prow of a ship affixed to its wall.

Port Holland was next and is a bay within the private estate of Caerhayes Castle. This is more of a castellated manor house than a castle and dates back to the 13th century. John

Nash, the architect of Buckingham Palace, designed the current building in 1810. Though not open when we were there it has apparently the largest collection of magnolia species in the country. It was here that on taking a picture of the pastoral scene I got the lucky photographic shot of a crow that decided to land and sit on the head of one of the Red Devon cattle.

Our next village was Goran Haven and this proved to be a real pleasant surprise. The harbour wall encloses a lovely sandy beach. The water is shallow and we deemed it to be a perfect place to take young children. Adjacent to the harbour is a fish and chip shop serving excellent fish and with an honesty policy about letting you have trays etc to take to the beach, trusting you to return them. We bought four portions of cod and chips and sat on the sea wall in the sunshine and ate these for our supper. At the suggestion of the fish and chip shop owner we went to the pub a few doors away and obtained four glasses of lager to wash down the food! Something that would be prohibited in Vancouver. Our meal drew the attention of the local seagulls and we tried to ignore them. They caused consternation though when they attempted to eat a picnic laid out on a blanket nearby and guarded only by a small child. The gulls obviously saw the small human as no threat and swarmed the picnic. The parents had to race back to save the poor child and shoo them away, but they didn't leave hungry!

One very nice thing in Goran Haven was the old red telephone box that has been turned into a small lending library for second hand books; a nice community thing to do we thought.

We realised only as we were leaving the village that Goran Haven used to be the home of an Aunt and Uncle of my wife; they ran the local dairy. Her Uncle was at one time also the Mayor of St. Austel and achieved some national notoriety when he resigned his membership of the Conservative party in protest against Margaret Thatcher's leadership style.

From Goran Haven we followed the coast road as best we could. At Pentewen were the obligatory static caravans, but they were set out away from the beauty of the coastline.

We first saw Mevagissey from above, from Port Mellon. Mevagissey has two harbours, the inner and the outer and though some fishing vessels are still based here, there is little of the fishing industry surviving. Although at first sight, the name of the town would suggest it is not named after or associated with any saints, the name Mevagissey actually comes from two Irish saints, St. Meva and St. Issay. Their names are joined by the Cornish word "hag" which means "and", hence Mev-hag-issay.

Although the RNLI name is very evident in the town, surprisingly there is now no RNLI station here. I say surprisingly because it has seemed that almost every place on my coastal journey, be it small village or town, has an RNLI lifeboat. The station was originally at Port Mellon and then moved into Mevagissey. However, in 1930, Fowey, across the bay, was equipped with a motorized lifeboat and so the Mevagissey station was closed and the building is now used as an aquarium. We were a few days too early for "Feast Week" which is held in Mevagissey at the end of June. This is a celebration of food, fun and the famous Cornish Floral Dance.

Mevagissey, Cornwall

We finally followed the road up to St. Austell joining the A390 to turn and take the quick road back to Feock. Tomorrow I will return along this road to arrive at this same point in St. Austell for the penultimate part of my journey.

St. Austell to Thurlestone

Miles 135

Fine House in Fowey, Cornwall

We said our goodbyes to our very generous hosts, Pete & Sue and returned to St. Austell to start our day, beginning at Porthpean and Charlestown, where we had ended the drive yesterday.

Charlestown is a small harbour to the south of St. Austell. It was originally in private hands and from the early 1800s through to 2000 was a dock for the export of china clay. However, through various changes in use and bankruptcies it passed into the hands of a company called Square Sail Ventures that now use it as a base for their "tall ships". The harbour is also hired out for films and TV programs, such as Poldark, where it passes for the old City of Truro. The main ship here is the "Phoenix". The town also has a museum – the Shipwreck, Rescue and Heritage Centre.

We attempted to go down to Carlyon Bay, but there was a swimming event going on and parking was very restricted, so we turned around in the car park and moved on. The swim apparently was for various age groups and involved a mass start from the beach for a 2km sea swim. There are three beaches in Carlyon Bay and the area outside of the bay has nice homes. The heyday of Carlyon Bay with its large concert venue has now passed and there are plans in place to build a large number of luxury homes here. Planning restrictions and appeals from both developers and locals has meant that everything has been stalled since 2011.

Charlestown and Carlyon Bay are really the costal areas of St Austell so we did not go further into the town but instead headed for Fowey (pronounced Foy). To get to Fowey you pass through the dockland area of Par. Originally this was the shipment point for copper but from the mid nineteenth century until 2007, china clay was the main product shipped from here. There are plans to redevelop this area into a marina with luxury residential properties. Near to Par (but not coastal) is the Eden Project, which opened in 2000 to mark the Millenium. This is built within an old china clay pit and looks like a large wasp's nest with its hexagonal geodetic biodomes, the insides of which contain plants from all around the world.

Fowey, Cornwall

Fowey is built around the mouth of the River Fowey and again has a history as a port for metal ores and china clay, though in competition with nearby Par. It was only with the coming of the railway to Fowey that their fortunes increased. In 1943 Fowey was the main loading point for ammunition for the US troops that landed on Omaha Beach on D Day. The town has very narrow streets with virtually no parking and visitors are encouraged to use the large car park above the town and walk down. There are some fine old buildings here and the Parish Church is dedicated to St. Fimbarrus, who may be synonymous with St. Barry and was another one of the many early Irish priests who brought Celtic Christianity to Cornwall.

471

We drove through the narrow streets and headed for the car ferry, which crosses the River Fowey and delivers vehicles to Boddinick a tiny village on the opposite bank. The boatman hardly has time to take the fee of £1.50 before you arrive at the other side.

Polruan, slightly south of Boddinick, is immediately across the river from Fowey. It has a blocktower, paired with one in Fowey and was used to guard the harbour from attack by sea. A chain was attached to the two towers and could be raised to block enemy vessels. Daphne Du Maurier, the writer, once lived in the town. The entrance down into the village is a very steep road. A passenger only ferry runs between the village and Fowey.

Crumpelhorn Inn, Polperro, Cornwall

Journeying along the coast road you then come to Crumplehorn, with its large pub and a water wheel still turning on its wall. This Inn was, in the late 17th and early 18th centuries, the haunt of the richest smuggler in Cornwall, one

Zephaniah Job, who was never caught for his activities. He made so much money from the trade that he even printed his own bank notes. Zephania was more the mastermind and funder of the operations and preferred to do business at the Inn rather than on the beach. He became very fat from the trade, both physically as well as in his pocket. He made money not only from supporting smuggling, but also from the pilchard trade and the funding of Privateer ships that were able to capture French ships during the Napoleonic War.

Zephaniah came to Polperro in 1770 as a fugitive from St Agnes. Here he had worked as a Captain in the mines but following a fight, where another person was badly beaten, Zephania fled and came to the tiny village of Polperro. The people here were uneducated and to make a living he tried to start a school, but there was little interest in this and he turned to bookkeeping for a lot of the local fishermen. Because he could write he became the agent acting between the smugglers and the merchants on the Island of Guernsey, who supplied most of the tax free goods that were brought into the country.

Smuggling grew into major business due in part to poverty and the introduction of high duties on certain goods. In Cornwall, miners would get laid off at certain times of the year, such as in the summer when there was insufficient water for the mine wheels. They were then without money for their families, so they turned to other means, smuggling being an obvious option. The presence of fishing boats and the geography of their coastal location allowing for undetected importation of goods.

As a means of raising government revenue, particularly to refill the Exchequer after the long war of American Independence, duties were placed on certain imported goods, making their resale price very high. Tax on tea was 125%, brandy 250% and salt 400%. For the Cornish fishermen, the placing of duty on French salt was a particular stimulus to their smuggling activities. Salt was much needed for the preservation of the pilchards and without it the fish would rot and be worthless. French salt was considered to be the best for the purpose and was cheap to buy and available in quantity, so a tax on salt increased their costs significantly and threatened their very livelihood. To obtain these goods without paying the duty represented somewhat of a necessity for them. In 1783 when William Pitt the Younger became Prime Minister he reduced duties significantly and for a while smuggling abated, but the war with France ten years later saw a reversal of this and salt duty increased again. As the product came from France, the government had a double reason to tax and restrict it.

Guernsey one of the Channel Islands, off the coast of France, but owned by Britain, was, by long tradition, a tax-free area and could sell goods duty free. The Cornish fisherman would travel there directly, or meet ships half way and take on board large quantities of salt. Initially it was just salt, but over time other highly taxed items such as brandy, tea and tobacco, with their wider market across the country, offered further opportunity for making an income and so became part of the staple of smuggled goods. Zephaniah assisted certain fishermen, who became the leading smugglers, by financing larger boats so they could carry more goods. The Privateer vessels that he later helped finance, only further supported the smuggling trade as they were fast and could outrun most revenue vessels.

Smuggling of high value goods was considered a necessity for life in Cornwall. If and when arrested, Cornish juries would frequently find smugglers not guilty when they came to court.

Though not without its violence at times, smuggling of untaxed goods in such a way was not as deadly or dark a story as that of wrecking. Many coastal landowners had the right of salvage of any ships and their cargoes that came up onto their shores. As the locals did the salvaging, the value of the goods was shared with them to a degree. This therefore encouraged people, especially on the west coast of Cornwall, to lure ships onto the coast, often with false lights, so that they could be wrecked and provide rich pickings. This resulted in much loss of life as the survivors were either unattended or, in some cases, killed to ensure that the wreckers could not be identified. They were also killed to prevent the coastal land-owner finding out the real value of the goods collected and so be denied his share.

In 1805 the Channel Islands gave up supplying the smugglers, who then turned to the port of Roscoff in France as the main source of products. Ironically today a ferry still runs between Cornwall and Roscoff. If and when Britain leaves the EU, no doubt smuggling and the avoidance of duty and taxes will once again become commonplace on this route.

As Britain's manufacturing and exports rose in the early to mid 1800s so duties on imports were significantly reduced. This along with the rise and influence of the Methodist Church, which denounced smuggling as immoral, played a major part in the abatement of smuggling.

Zephaniah Job died in 1822, rich, but unmarried and with no family. On his death the villagers of Polperro came together and held a bonfire on the beach of his papers, which having been meticulously kept by Zephaniah, could provide evidence of all of their involvement. His story only really became known about one hundred and fifty years after his death when a quantity of his papers that missed the fire, were discovered hidden away in the Crumplehorn Inn.

Crumplehorn is the entrance to Polperro, a popular tourist destination. We managed to drive a little way into the town before finding it restricted and so had to turn back and go up out of the town to a large car park. To park here costs £4 and then you can either walk a half-mile into the town or take a shuttle bus at £2 return fare. The last time we came here we had an elderly person on board, but there was no allowance to take elderly or disabled people closer into the town, it is the car park and walk, or shuttle bus, or nothing.

We decided to first have some lunch (2 large pasta salads, purchased earlier at Tesco in St Austell for £2) and then take the shuttle bus into Polperro. After eating our lunch we had both changed our mind and did not feel that it was worth the £8 for two people to visit, take a couple of photos (showcase their town!) and then leave. From other people's photos it is certainly a quaint old fishing village, but honestly it did not look unique enough to want to spend £8 to visit it. This reminded me of Clovelly on the north Devon coast that charge £7 per person for you to enter their village. There are too many other lovely and quaint places that you don't have to pay to visit so why pay to go to Polperro? Maybe I will visit it from the ocean someday and see if I have really missed something special, but I don't think so. I can quite understand that the roads are too narrow for cars, but paying money to visit so that I can then spend more money in their town, forget it. No doubt this money is seen today as the replacement for the money that used to come into the town from smuggling!

Heading to Looe we came across Porthallow and Talland. Again narrow lanes but there was a cute little café just up from the beach at Talland Bay where we had afternoon tea. This is right on the South West Coastal Path and no doubt is a popular place for walkers.

By the time we got to Looe the tide was out and the boats were high and dry. This is despite the name Looe being derived from a Cornish word meaning deep-water inlet! It seems to have been a feature of my trip that the tide is often out, especially noticeable where the harbour is built around an estuary.

Looe, Cornwall

Looe is divided by the river into East and West Looe, the town being mainly on the west side of the river. I have been to Looe a number of times and feel that I know it fairly well.

Last time we were here we had an excellent lunch cooked by a young and up and coming chef. Looe is now mainly a small fishing and tourist town, but over the years its fortunes have risen and fallen in accordance with the demand for minerals such as tin and arsenic. In the 1960s and 70s Looe was one of the many Cornish seaside towns to which artists flocked "because of the light."

Following eastwards along the coast the next seaside place is Seaton. This seems so very different from any of the other Cornish seaside towns. Like its namesake in East Devon, it is quite open to the sea and feels a little bit bleak. It is certainly not a "cosy" place. The beach here also seems "sad" being grey coloured shale. This was the start of the "open windswept geography" that now went all the way towards Rame Head where the Sound leading into Plymouth begins.

We passed through Crafthole and Portwrinkle, with its golf course on the ocean edge. Portwrinkle, was another of the Cornish pilchard villages that was significantly impacted by the high duties placed on salt, leading to their taking up smuggling.

Just beyond Portwrinkle is Whitsand Bay.

At Freathy we saw a large holiday home/lodge camp on the cliffs, which made me realise that this was almost the only one I had seen for a number of days. It is no doubt popular with the citizens of Plymouth. The area seemed moor like and windswept.

We then saw an imposing and rather ominous military "fortress". This is Tregantle Fort, which commands a military firing range. Most of the open country here was marked with red and white poles to warn that this was a military area and that live firing might take place.

Tregantle Fort is an hexagonal shaped construction built in 1865 as part of the sea defences for Plymouth. It was designed to have 22 guns and 1000 men barracked there, but only 7 guns were ever fitted and its use has mainly been only as a rifle firing range.

We followed the cliff road all around Rame Head and Mount Edgecumbe and eventually arrived on the other side of the Tregantle fortress and the entry into Millbrook. Millbrook, which overlooks Plymouth, appears to be a naval town.

After Millbrook we followed the road into Torpoint and the ferry across to Plymouth.

Plymouth, Devon

This ferry was the cheapest we had taken all day at £1.40. The ticket seller said that this was because the company also owned the Tamar Bridge, which provides an alternative to the ferry. If the ferry were to charge more, it would mean less traffic on the ferry and the potential loss of their jobs.

Plymouth is very much a naval town and its presence still dominates its economy. The naval dockyards are at

Devonport, which at one time was a town separate from Plymouth. In 1914 Plymouth (once called Sutton) was merged with Devonport and Stonehouse into one town, all called Plymouth. Because of the naval presence it was heavily bombed during the second world war and the town still had evidence of this as recently as the 1980s.

Plymouth is known as the place where in 1588 Sir Francis Drake was playing bowls on the Hoe when he was advised of the approach of the Spanish Armada. He is famously reported to have said that he had time to finish his game as the wind was not favourable for the Spanish fleet.

The story of the defeat of the Spanish Armada remains legendary in Britain. King Philip of Spain had been married to Mary, Elizabeth I's sister. After Mary's death he had asked Elizabeth to marry him, but she had refused seeing it as only a ploy for Spain to take over England and return it once again to the control of the Pope. Philip's fleet was 130 ships whereas Drake and Lord Howard, who was the main naval commander, could only command 70. However, the English fleet was faster and more maneuverable and in fierce fighting sank 77 of the Spanish galleons. The Spanish fleet then scattered, some of it, finding it hard to turn around in the English Channel, sailed all the way up the east coast of Britain and around Scotland and then back down the west coast. The weather took its toll of many of them. It is less well known that Philip of Spain twice more sent armadas to attack Britain, but both also failed due to bad weather rather than English cannons.

Plymouth is also the place where in 1620 the Pilgrim Fathers (eventually) set out for the New World. The Pilgrim Fathers actually had their origins in 1586 in a small village,

Scrooby, in Nottinghamshire and were a group of Puritans. Unlike others of this name they believed that they should be completely separate from the Church of England and thus became known as Separatists. In 1606 a group moved to Leiden in Holland to continue to worship as they wanted to without harassment.

In 1620 a number of factors came together that determined that some of the group would move to America. Increasing old age and poor finances meant that many of the group had returned to England. The elders also began to fear that Holland was too liberal in its way of living and was a bad influence on their children. They thus began to explore countries to move to and found support to go to America from British trading interests who would assist colonists to take on land at the expense of the Dutch traders.

Eventually a number of them set sail in the *Speedwell* a vessel that was part of the fleet that sailed against the Armada. They landed at Southampton where they met up with the *Mayflower*. This was a larger ship and had on board other colonists that were being supported by investors. Both ships set sail but the *Speedwell* began leaking and they had to put in to Dartmouth for repairs. After setting out again the *Speedwell* continued to leak so they landed this time at Plymouth, where it was decided to abandon the *Speedwell* and continue on with a reduced number aboard the *Mayflower*. Of the original separatists who set out from Leiden, only 28 of their number, plus their children were able to travel on the *Mayflower*, the remainder returning to Leiden. Thus the majority of people on board the *Mayflower* were not in fact Puritan separatists, but "ordinary" settlers seeking a new life.

We attempted to drive up to the Hoe, but unfortunately it

is not accessible to cars so we stopped below it in a pub car park.

The Pub was packed with people enjoying the views across to Drakes Island. Drakes Island was where Sir Francis Drake sailed from in 1577 on his round the world voyage, returning here in 1580. In 1583 Drake was made Governor of the island and it then was named after him. The island had originally been made a fortress in 1549 to protect the harbour. From 1642 to 1648 Plymouth was a Parliamentarian stronghold, besieged by the Royalists. When the Monarchy was restored in 1660, Charles II had Drakes Island used as a prison for ex Parliamentarian supporters from Plymouth and its surrounds. The island was owned by the military until 1995 when it was sold to a businessman. He wanted to build a hotel on it, but has never yet received planning permission so it today is somewhat derelict.

Drake's Island, Plymouth, Devon

On the Hoe prominently stands Smeaton's Tower. This is the upper portion of the old Eddystone Lighthouse, built by John Smeaton in 1759, and replaced in 1877. It was transported back from the Eddystone, brick by brick and reassembled here on the Hoe.

Moving on from Plymouth, the next part of our journey we knew would take us along country lanes and up and down little peninsulas.

Our first destination was Wembury, and although there is a small village of this name the area around is also called Wembury. We once had relatives living here and so were able to find our way along the lanes to the village and the beach. One thing I particularly remember about Wembury, when I attended a family wedding here, is the bird song. It is loud and beautiful. This is quite unlike Vancouver, where bird song is actually a rarity. This is mainly because the city has pine trees rather than deciduous ones that song birds need to provide cover. Also, it is possibly due to the over abundance of crows and other raptors.

From Wembury we were able to look out to sea and view close in, the Mewstone, a particular feature of the area and often used by the navy for invasion practice. We could also just about make out the Eddystone Lighthouse out to sea, 9 nautical miles south of Rame head.

We had to drive up out of Wembury and then come down the other side of the estuary to reach Newton Ferrers a very pretty (and expensive) little town.

Opposite this and reachable on foot at low tide is the village of Noss Mayo. To get to it by car is about a four-mile narrow lane drive. There is an excellent pub here serving great food and if the time is right you can park on the beach.

Provided you keep an eye on the tide table and don't drink too much this is a safe way to park your car and eat at the pub.

From here we drove through Mothercombe and then, about thirteen miles in total, back up to the main road so that we could cross the River Erme and come down its other side to Bigbury-on-Sea. Apparently a lot of South West Coastal Path walkers get caught out here as they assume that there is a ferry across the Erme. There isn't one. It is either, arrive at low tide and wade across or, walk thirteen miles to get around it!

Burgh Island, South Devon

Bigbury-on-Sea has nothing going for it other than it is the landward side of Burgh Island. Burgh Island is a true island, when the tide comes in. It is separated from the mainland by a sandy causeway, which is easy to walk across at low tide. However, when the tide comes in, which it does from both sides of the sandy beach, there is a tall tractor like machine that takes people to and from the island. On the island is the famous art deco style Burgh Island Hotel. This has featured in many an Agatha Christie "Poirot" movie and was the setting for her story *"And then there were none"*. It was built as a house by an industrialist in 1930 and only later became a hotel. The Beatles have stayed here and so have Edward and Mrs. Simpson and Noel Coward.

The final part of our journey required us to retrace our steps, back up this time the estuary of the River Avon (not the famous one) and then down again to reach Thurlestone, where our B&B for the night was located. This proved to be a bit of let down for us as we were imagining much more luxury than it was. It's name promised sea views, but did not deliver. It was also the only B&B on my trip that did not have an en-suite bathroom. It was also the most expensive B&B as well (by almost £20). We had had difficulty in getting a booking for this night as being a weekend everyone wanted to let only to people who would book two nights. I had not actually experienced this anywhere else on my UK trip.

We ate at the Pub in the village, which is owned by and attached to the hotel. This was OK but not particularly special. I had expected a menu with more variety. They let themselves down at the end when having ordered strawberries and ice cream for dessert, after twenty minutes waiting they had still not arrived. So, we cancelled them, paid for what we did eat and left.

I spent most of the night sleeping on the floor as my back problem, which started due to my fall in Whithorn more than 10 days ago, was still with me and the bed was too soft.

Altogether a very busy driving day, made especially enjoyable by the presence of my wife. It was also a day of stark contrast in geography between Cornwall and this part of Devon.

Thurlestone to Exmouth

Miles 116

Hope Cove, South Devon

Today was the last day of my round Britain coastal trip. When I arrived back at Exmouth I had driven the whole coast of mainland Britain (plus some islands) and covered a distance of around 5060 miles.

We allowed ourselves the luxury of a good English breakfast and a late start and set off from Thurlestone at 9.00am. We firstly went down into the village to look at the ocean that we had been assured by the name of our B&B we should have been able to see from our room! In the center of the Bay is a distinctive large rock arch, though to me it looked more like one stack of rocks had fallen over onto another one. It is called the "thirled stone" which is what gives the village its name.

We drove through the lanes to Galmpton and then into Hope Cove, which has both an inner and an outer beach. I remember this area from when I came here with my parents aged seven years old for a holiday. We stayed in a caravan just a few miles away at Salcombe. During the flight of the Spanish Armada one of the ships was wrecked here on the beach. The residents at that time saw the opportunity of a prize from the wreck. They were quite violent men and the 140 survivors were lucky not to have been killed on the beach, although perhaps more likely, it was the fact that there were such a large number of Spaniards, most of them soldiers that stayed the hand of the Hope Cove residents. The survivors were taken prisoner and later sentenced to death; but this was stayed and eventually they were returned to Spain on payment of a large ransom.

We then drove up onto Bolberry Down where there are large communications aerials and lots and lots of rabbits. The views from up here were spectacular right along the coast and out to sea. Here you can walk in one direction to Bolt Head and in the other direction to Bolt Tail.

We then drove down into Soar Cove. We firstly looked at the Soar Cove Hotel who were that afternoon going to be holding a "Gin and Jazz" festival in the grounds. We very much wished that we could have had the time to stay for this as we both like gin and jazz! The Cove itself is a small sandy beach, which can only be reached by foot.

Salcombe, our next destination is a famous yachting town and is now said to be the most expensive town in England in which to buy property as "out of towners" snap up almost anything that comes onto the market. Salcombe estuary is like Falmouth in that it is a Ria, or drowned river valley, so it does not dry out and thus is a sailing mecca.

Water Tractor Taxi Salcombe, Devon

We drove into the town via Coombe, South Sands and North Sands. It was at North Sands that I came as a child and the beach still looks very much the same. It was here that I discovered that my Mickey Mouse wristwatch (my first ever one) was not waterproof! At that time you had to walk a mile into Salcombe town, but today, if you want to, you can take a "water tractor taxi".

Salcombe still has a small fishing industry based on shellfish harvesting, but no traditional fishing boats are now based here. Almost every vessel is a pleasure craft. Just before the mouth of the estuary is a sand bar and it is said that this is what inspired Alfred Lord Tennyson to write his famous poem "Crossing the Bar". It starts: *Sunset and evening Star and one clear call for me! And may there be no moaning of the bar, when I put out to sea.*

We drove into the town, again very restricted as to where you can drive and park. We found a small side street by the water and stopped to buy a coffee. There was a small jetty and I noticed something moving on it, which turned out to be a fledgling seagull that had fallen out of its nest. I spied the nest up on a nearby roof and his/her brother/sister still up there. There were a number of gulls flying around and we assumed that one was the mother of the chick. Marilyn went into the coffee shop (on whose roof was the nest) to let them know and see if they could help. The lady came out and said that this chick had actually fallen out almost a week ago and at that time could not even walk. She had put it on a sack by the house, expecting it to die, but the parents obviously had been continuing to feed it and it was still alive and now walking. Clearly the best thing to do was to leave it to nature.

Notable residents of Salcombe are the singer Kate Bush and Mary Berry the star of the great British Bake Off, who has a holiday home here.

Across from Salcombe is the small hamlet of East Portlemouth, linked to Salcombe by a foot ferry. We decided to visit it as when I was fourteen years old, I came to a boy's camp here and I remember being buried, voluntarily, in the sand on East Portlemouth Beach. The journey to East Portlemouth was again complicated in that we had to drive all the way up to Kingsbridge at the top of the estuary, before driving down the other side, a distance of about fifteen miles. Kingsbridge is not strictly a coastal town, but I have to mention how charming it is. It is clean and smart and the river here is full of lots of moored small craft. It reminded me somewhat of Henley-On-Thames, near where I used to live, in the way in which the water and the boats beautified the town.

Once on the other side of the estuary the roads were again single track and as we entered East Portlemouth they were not much wider than the wing mirrors on the car. We drove all the way down to the car park, which was as far as the road went. Indeed once committed to driving down the road you would have to go all the way to the bottom as it would be virtually impossible to turn around. At the top of the road it had said parking charge was £7.50, which probably puts off a lot of people. What it did not say was that it was a National Trust car park and now being members (courtesy of the Scottish National Trust) we would not have to pay. When we got there a very friendly lady acting as the volunteer parking attendant met us. She allowed us to stop and take a photo and not park and gave us good advice as the route to take to reach our next destination.

We turned around and set off back up the lane. This time we met a vehicle coming the other way and as luck would have it, right by the entrance to a house so I could edge mostly off the road into its gateway. The vehicle was a Tesco delivery van! As the van squeezed past, I had my window open and his was open also. I commented to the driver that I bet that most of his deliveries were to houses that lived in very small lanes. He laughed and said that it was not most houses, it was all of them!

I thought that this might just about be it for narrow lanes. I was wrong. We had to go to Start Point and the lighthouse, as this was a distinctive coastal feature. We traveled for one and a half miles and got almost to the car park before meeting another vehicle. This driver opted to reverse back, a good 200 yards to find somewhere for me to pass. When we got to the car park I was surprised at just how many cars were there. All had braved the road.

Having taken the obligatory photograph we turned around and started back. This was when we met not one, not two, but four cars all coming towards us and wanting to get into the car park. For a moment it was stalemate as to who should move as I had two cars also behind me. One of the four cars ahead of me reversed a little so that I could squeeze into the soft hedge, but the cars behind me all had to reverse back into the car park. With my mirrors folded I sat still while the four vehicles crept past me with no more than an inch between us. Once past I set off again, knowing that it was one and a quarter miles to the next slightly wider road and praying that I would not meet anyone else coming in. Fortunately I didn't. Whatever happened with the other cars coming out that had been behind me I don't know.

At the next cross roads and based on what the car park lady at East Portlemouth had advised, we turned right. A good decision! Straight over at the crossroads, on the road we might have taken, we could see a stationary car towing a caravan facing another stationary car towing a caravan that was traveling in the other direction. There was no way either could reverse. I expect that they are both still there now. Just as well they are able to sleep in the caravans!

Through the lanes we eventually came to Beesands on the coast. The pub in Beesands, the Cricket Inn, is noted for being the place that Mick Jagger and Keith Richards of the Rolling Stones made their first public appearance!

Torcross, just further on, is a very interesting place. It is at the end of a two-mile long beach. The road runs right beside the beach while on the other side of the road, the inland side and separated only by the road, is a large expanse of fresh water, known as Slapton Ley. This area is protected and unique for its bird life. There is concern today that eventually a large storm will breach the land between them and the sea then inundate the freshwater, destroying its habitat.

Torcross is noted for a double tragedy that occurred during World War II. In late 1943 the whole area around Torcross was evacuated, people being told to leave their homes by the army, without any explanation being given. Indeed they were unable to return for almost two years.

Torcross became a training ground for the D-Day Landings as the topography of its beach was thought to be similar to Utah beach in Normandy. On April 27th 1944 as part of a continuing series of exercises, known as Operation Tiger, taking place over a nine-day period, troops were to be landed on the beach under fire. The instructions were not to advance beyond a certain point until a specified time. However, due to incorrect communication channels having been given to the landing craft and the warships that were to shell the beaches, the troops had already moved into the target area when shelling began. At least 300 servicemen on the beach were killed by friendly fire. On the following day, in the evening of April

28th the second tragedy occurred. A night exercise was planned and a convoy of vessels, three miles long, set out to sail from Portland to Torcross. Nine German fast attack E boats, alerted by the heavy radio traffic, came into the convoy and sunk two tank landing ships with the loss of 946 American servicemen.

At the time both of these incidents were hushed up for fear that it might give away to the enemy that a beach landing invasion was being planned. After the war though it continued to be kept secret and it was only much later that the facts came out and an investigation took place.

Operation Tiger Memorial at Slapton Sands, Devon

Today at Slapton Sands, due to the persistence of one man, a tank was salvaged from one of the sunken tank landing ships and is now on display as a memorial to all of the men lost during the tragedy of Operation Tiger. Even today the number of men who died in these two events is still not accurately known. The tank monument states that 749 men died on the ships, whereas another account says the number is 946. Together the number of men killed in these two events was greater than the number of men who were killed in the landings on Utah Beach, which saw the heaviest of all of the invasion casualties. The names of those killed in Operation Tiger were added to the list of those killed on Utah Beach.

From Slapton Sands we drove along the coast road driving up the hill to Strete and then past Blackpool Sands. Last Christmas we went as a family on Boxing Day onto the beach here and had mince pies and champagne!

Stoke Fleming is the village above Blackpool Sands where I came as a teenager to a Boy's Camp and still remember today how much fun it was. I also remember, that it was on a walk from Stoke Fleming to Slapton Sands that another boy, with a then magical transistor radio, announced to us all that Marilyn Monroe had died.

Dartmouth, Devon

We entered Dartmouth from the southern end via Warfleet and signs pointing to the Castle. Now there is not much left of the castle at Dartmouth and it sits on a strategic point where cannon could be turned onto any enemy ships trying to get into the port. It was never a large castle and was paired up with a castle on the opposite bank at Kingswear. As with other fortifications, such as at Fowey, a heavy chain joined the castles and was stretched up across the entrance to block the harbour at night.

During World War II, after the rescue of the British and French troops at Dunkirk, my father, who was in the Royal Artillery, was posted to coastal defence in Dartmouth and was actually based at the castle for some time. I remember him taking me there as a young boy when to his surprise he saw large ancient cannons still lying on the ground outside the castle just where he and others had had to move them to make room for anti-aircraft weapons. They are no longer there today.

Dartmouth is a flourishing, smart and lively, boating town with a strong naval tradition. It is still the home of the Royal Naval College where junior officers are trained and inducted into the service. Edward III established the College in the 11th century. The town has a long history as a port and was a major embarkation point back in the time of the Crusades in the 12th century.

My parents actually met in Dartmouth, during World War II. My Father was stationed here after Dunkirk and my Mother came down on a short holiday from the factory in Cheltenham where she worked making aircraft instruments. She had moved to Cheltenham from the East End of London after the original factory was bombed in the Blitz. They got married in 1944 as my father knew that he would be going back to France and she would at least get a pension if he was killed. After the war he joined the factory where my Mother worked and thus I was born in Cheltenham.

Marilyn and I both like Dartmouth and it is a favourite place for us to visit when we can. You can take an excellent boat trip from Totnes, down the River Dart to Dartmouth. On the way you can stop at Greenway the holiday home of Agatha Christie. (Greenway was once owned by Sir Walter Raleigh and his half brother Sir Humphrey Gilbert.) Once in Dartmouth you link to a ferry across to Kingswear, followed by a steam train to Paignton. In Paignton you then take a bus back to Totnes making a circular tour. A great day out.

We took the higher of the two chain ferries from Dartmouth across to Kingswear. For the distance travelled this was, at £5.60, the most expensive ferry ride on the whole of my coastal trip around Britain!

From Kingswear we headed across to the coast at Berry Head just above the fishing port of Brixham, famous particularly for its crab. It still has an active fishing fleet and fish from here every day goes out to the top restaurants in the area. It was here that Prince William of Orange and his wife Mary, the daughter of James II, landed on November 5th, 1688, to begin their march to London and jointly take over the crown of England.

From this point our journey on narrow country lanes was done (hurray!). It is possible for us now to drive alongside the ocean, on good roads, through the seaside towns of Paignton and Torquay and almost all the way into Exmouth.

I recalled also another wartime story from my father about when he was stationed in Paignton. He had been on night duty manning an anti-aircraft gun on the sea front. In the morning they were stood down and another crew took up the duty. Each new crew on taking over had to fire a test round with the gun. The new crew did this, but the shell must have been faulty and it exploded in the gun and all the crew were killed. It could have been him if they had used just one more shell.

A not too dissimilar thing happened to a Fogden cousin of mine, who was killed before I got to know him. He was flying a Sea Fury off the deck of HMS Glory, an aircraft carrier, in the Yellow Sea, during the Korean War, a few days before Christmas 1952. When they started patrol they had to fire a burst from the in-wing mounted 20mm machine guns. He did so and his wing was seen to explode and he crashed into the sea and was killed. It was suggested that it was caused by old ammunition, manufactured in 1943, jamming in the gun.

Paignton is very much a family holiday resort that, though it has very nice beaches, has seen better days. It is still lively but it no longer has the glory or the attractiveness that it once had.

Torquay Marina, Devon

On leaving Paignton the houses become more elegant as you get closer into Torquay. Torquay also, like most UK seaside resorts, experienced a big down turn when cheap overseas flights came along. It is coming back though. The older retired and fairly wealthy folk that populate a lot of Torquay did not disappear (though I imagine they did turn over!) and this kept the town alive. This is still the case today. However, the town now focuses on long weekend, more upmarket, luxury breaks and business conferences to keep it moving forward. There is also a very active theatre in Torquay.

Just above the sea front and to the south is the village of Cockington that seems frozen in time with its thatched cottages.

The coastal road through the town (and you have to search it out) goes across Daddyhole Plain, a favourite viewing spot for Marilyn's grandfather.

The road continues right along the cliffs, past large houses with lovely sea views over Thatcher Rock and on into Babbacombe. Here there is a fun funicular railway down to the beach and a wonderful model village.

From Babbacombe it is mainly a direct drive along the coast, with expansive views over the ocean, to Shaldon, with its low bridge across the Teign Estuary into Teignmouth. Shaldon is very narrow if you decide to drive through the village, but it is possible and takes you up to the Ness where there is parking and a tunnel down to the beach, claimed, as they all are, to have been used by smugglers.

This area again is a place of my family holidays as a child. Teignmouth still has a pier and sea front with light entertainments. It is popular with seniors and families, but probably not as popular as Paignton for family holidays, though I'm not sure that it really wants to be. There are no caravan parks in evidence in Teignmouth, whereas Paignton has quite a number, mainly on the Totnes side of the town. The beach here is sandy, sort of. Its not good "digging" sand such as at Goodrington Beach in Paignton, but it is a nice beach to laze on.

Fresh Shellfish at Teignmouth Pier

After Teignmouth the road continues along the coast to Dawlish. The town fronts right onto the main Great Western Railway line which runs between it and the beach. This all seems in harmony though and certainly train travelers get a magnificent view of both the small town and the ocean. In the winter storms of February 2014 the railway line was left hanging in the air when the sea washed away all of the ground beneath it. This completely cut railway links between London and Penzance and significant efforts were made to reconstruct the sea wall and defences to enable the line to reopen. This was done by early April; however, there is now consideration being given to creating a new inland railway route.

Personally I cannot see this happening any time soon. The impact of taking farmland and homes would create a real outcry and the cost of new bridges over rivers and motorways will probably fall outside of any post European membership budget. I love traveling on this section of railway and hope that it remains running here for many years to come.

Just outside of Dawlish on the north side is Dawlish Warren. For over sixty years this has been a holiday area and it is populated with hundreds of chalets and static caravans. I remember coming here on Boxing Day in the early 1970s, with other family members, and racing the go-carts. I was pleasantly surprised to see that they are still operating.

The Warren itself is an area of extensive sand dunes, covered today with lovely yellow and purple flowers and obviously a place people like to walk and run their dogs. The footpath along the sea wall is well maintained and provides excellent views across the Bay to Exmouth and my final destination of Orcombe Point. The estuary of the Exe at Exmouth is rapidly silting up, having now caused the lifeboat to be moved to a new station closer to the ocean. There is a large sand bar growing out that looks as if it is getting close to joining up Exmouth with Dawlish. Obviously the flow of the river will prevent a complete joining but it may allow a bridge to be constructed before too long.

Dawlish Warren is also the end of the wonderful Exe River Trail that stretches from Exmouth up one side of the river, crossing over at Countess Weir at Exeter and then following the river on its other bank down to Dawlish. This is now becoming well used by walkers and cyclists, though from experience I would anticipate that some separation system will have to be put in place, or cyclists forced to slow down in some way. Many of them ride too fast and walkers (especially with small children) are unable to hear them coming up behind until it is too late. If a new bridge were built, even a pedestrian one, across the sandbar, it would then be a wonderful circular route.

From Dawlish Warren the road continues along the Exe to the little village of Cockwood with its wonderful Anchor Inn pub offering excellent pub grub. The village has a small boat harbour that dries on low tide.

At this point you rejoin the main rode at Starcross, where you can catch a passenger only ferry across to Exmouth. The Pub here is called the Atmospheric Railway in remembrance of Brunel's attempts to have an air driven railway line. The technology employed by Brunel was not new but he introduced many modifications in an attempt to allow the trains to run faster and carry more loads. The principle was that a narrow pipe would be laid in the centre of the rail lines, with a slit in the top, into which would fit a valve connected to a piston on the front carriage of the train. Without the need for coal fired locomotives significant cost savings were thought possible. Leather seals along the pipe slit would allow the train connector to move along the central pipe with the leather flaps opening in front and closing behind, as it moved, to maintain the pressure. The pressure created behind the valve and the vacuum ahead of it would propel the train forward.

After significant technical issues and introduction of new designs, the first trains began operating in September

1847 and the line was fully functional from Exeter to Newton Abbot by March 1848. The highest speed recorded by a train was 64mph. The railway though continued to experience technical problems. Pipe bores were changed and during the winter the leather froze and became hard thus causing air pressure failures. Grease used to keep the leather supple and prevent it cracking in dry weather would apparently attract rats that would eat the leather, again causing air leakage. In September 1848 the railway company abandoned the atmospheric railway and returned to steam driven locomotives. It had operated for only one year.

Shortly after Starcross we turned off to follow the sign for Powderham Church. This is a back road around Powderham Castle, home to the Earl of Devon. We were at one time acquaintances of his Aunt, the Lady Elizabeth, who attended our church in Wargrave. This road eventually joins the main road again, close to Kenton and leads on to join the A379 at Countess Weir. After following this road for a mile you turn back down the other bank of the Exe and head for Topsham.

In 1286 the Countess of Devon, apparently anxious over how much trade went through the port at Topsham, decided to make the upper stretch of the River Exe navigable so that ships could come right into the City of Exeter. A weir and canal system were constructed at her expense and the city then became a major port in its own right.

Topsham was the original Roman port for Exeter from the first to the fifth century AD. It became a major cotton trading hub with Holland and a number of Dutch merchants houses are still in evidence today. These houses were constructed from Dutch bricks that were used as ballast by the vessels coming from Holland to load up with cotton. This is similar to what occurred in the old city of Quebec where a lot of the buildings are built from Bristol stone, used as ballast by ships coming from England to collect furs and other goods from Canada.

Another Canadian connection with Topsham is through the Franklin expedition, which was lost trying to find the North West Passage around Canada. One of Franklin's ships, HMS Terror, was built in Topsham. HMS Erebus, the other one of Franklin's lost ships was discovered in Canadian arctic waters in 2014 and the search for HMS Terror was continuing. Both Erebus and Terror had previously been on a four-year expedition to the Antarctic with Captain John Ross before they went to the Arctic with Franklin. It is known that they became trapped in the ice and eventually were abandoned by their crews. The crews survived for some time on the rations taken off the ships, however many of them apparently died of lead poisoning from the lead used to seal the canned foods, whilst the remainder perished in the cold wilderness.

HMS Terror was originally built as a mortar firing ship. It is the bombs that she fired at the American Fort McHenry during the War of Independence that are immortalized in the American national anthem, the Star Spangled Banner. The words *"and the rockets red glare, the bombs bursting in air, gave proof through the night that our flag was still there"* reflect the mortars fired by HMS Terror. (The Terror has since been located, on September 16, 2016, lying in seventy feet of water off the coast of King William Island in the appropriately named Terror Bay).

From Topsham the road follows the Exe Estuary and leads through Lympstone, with its Royal Marine Commandoes training barracks, then Exton and finally into Exmouth.

I had mixed emotions as I arrived back into Exmouth. I felt a great sense of achievement, mixed with relief that I had managed to drive this safely and without incident. I also felt somewhat sad that it was now all over.

I again drove the length of Exmouth's Esplanade, this time in cloudy weather and finally stopped the car at the end, by Orcombe Point.

I had left this same spot just 34 days ago and after a journey of 5068 miles, it did feel good to be back home. I have gained many treasured memories and a real insight into this beautiful and very varied land that is Britain. I have discovered places where my ancestors lived and died. I have experienced wonderful weather and met wonderful people. I continue to feel proud that this is the country of my birth and my roots and feel now so much more connected to my heritage. It has also been a discovery of so much of the history of Britain. It really has come alive, as I have visited castles and places where Kings and Queens have lived and where intrigue and plots have been carried out.

Back at Orcombe Point, Exmouth – Journey's End!

It certainly has been a momentous and historical time to undertake such a journey. The Brexit vote will now change so much, perhaps even the very union of Britain that has existed since 1603. Ironically my journey has confirmed to me that Britain's origins are in Europe and seeking independence is a denial (certainly a misunderstanding) of all of our common ancestry. But, I suppose that it must now be considered as part of Britain's future direction and new stories will I am sure be written.

All that remains is for me to now try and make sense of all of the photos and video – and perhaps plan to do it all again. If I do, then I will take more time to relax, stop and enjoy the view, wallow in the history and rejoice in my ancestry.

Appendix of Kings and Queens

Dates	Kings & Queens of England & Great Britain	Lineage
871-899	Alfred the Great	Son of Aethelwulf
King of Wessex. Considered to be first Anglo Saxon King. Capital Winchester. Reign spent mainly fighting the Danes. Buried Winchester, now lost.		
899-924	Edward the Elder	Son of Alfred
Strong King who united all Anglo Saxon Kingdoms. Buried Hyde Abbey.		
924-939	Aethelstan	Son of Edward
Considered first true King of all England. Defeated and reclaimed last Viking stronghold in York. Buried Malmesbury.		
939-946	Edmund I	Son of Edward, half brother to Aethelstan
Lost Northumbria to the Danes, but later recovered. Treaty with Malcolm I of Scotland ensured safe borders. Assassinated. Buried Glastonbury.		
946-955	Eadred	Son of Edward, half brother to Aethelstan
Continued battles in Northumbria, winning control. Burnt Ripon Abbey. Buried Winchester.		
955-959	Eadwig	Son of Edmund
Married his 3rd cousin but annulled by Archbishop (later Saint) Dunstan who fled to France. Died at age 18. Buried Winchester.		

507

959-975	Edgar the Peaceful	Son of Edmund

Earlier made King of lands north of Thames by Nobles who disliked Eadwig. His coronation (in Bath) is the model for today's service. Buried Glastonbury.

975-978	Edward the Martyr	Son of Edgar (probably illegitimate)

Right to be King disputed by Nobles and Aethelred. Monasteries stripped by Nobles. Murdered in Corfe Castle. Buried Wareham later Woking.

978-1013	Aethelred the Unready	Son of Edgar

Became King at aged 12. Had to pay allegiance to Danish King Sweyn. Massacred many Danes living in England so Sweyn invades.

1013-1014	Sweyn Forkbeard	Harald Bluetooth

Invades and Aethelred flees, but Sweyn dies after 1 year. His Son, Canut, is in Northern England but returns to Denmark to raise an army. Buried Denmark.

1014 -1016	Aethelred (the Unready)	Son of Edgar

Returned from exile when Sweyn dies. Dies before Canut invades. His widow Emma later marries Canut to save the lives of her two sons. Buried Old St Paul's Cathedral. Now lost

1016	Edmund Ironside	Son of Aethelred by first wife

Defeated by Canut. Canut allows him to rule Wessex, but he only lives for one more year. Buried Glastonbury.

1016-1035	Canut	Son of Sweyn Forkbeard

Invaded England, but took 18 months to gain full control. His second wife is Emma, widow of Aethelstan. They have a son, Harthacanut. Buried Winchester.

1035-1040	Harold Harefoot	Son of Canut by an earlier wife

Only ruled half of England as Emma insisted Harthacanut, who was in Denmark fighting invading Swedes, should also rule half. Buried St. Clement Danes, London.

APPENDIX OF KINGS AND QUEENS

| 1040-1042 | Harthacanut | Son of Canut & Emma |

Shared the throne until half brother Harold dies. Has Harold's body thrown in sewer as sign that he usurped him. Buried Winchester.

| 1042-1066 | Edward the Confessor | Son of Aethelred and Emma |

Became King on death of his younger half-brother. Married the daughter of Earl Godwin the most powerful Lord in England. Buried Westminster Abbey.

| 1066 | Harold Godwinson | Son of Earl Godwin & brother-in-law to Edward |

Present at Edward's death. Claimed that Edward named him as his heir on his deathbed. Had no bloodline to the throne. Killed by William. Possibly buried Bosham.

| 1066 | Edgar Aethling | Grandson of Edmund Ironside |

Bloodline to throne as nephew of Edward. Named King by the Lords on death of Harold, but they then bowed to the might of William. Edgar flees to Scotland where his sister Margaret was married to King Malcolm.

| 1066-1087 | William I (the Conqueror) | Cousin of Edward |

Claimed that Edward had earlier promised him the throne so he invaded. Barons had elected Edgar but conceded to William. Buried Caen, France.

| 1087-1100 | William II | Son of William I |

Died in hunting accident and his brother Henry took the throne. Buried Winchester.

| 1100-1135 | Henry I | Son of William the Conqueror |

Married Matilda, daughter of Margaret & Malcolm of Scotland, who was niece of Edgar. His son, William, drowned so his daughter, also called, Matilda is named as his heir. Buried Reading Abbey.

| 1135-1141 | Stephen of Blois | Grandson of William the Conqueror |

Chosen by Lords instead of Matilda. He was seen as a warrior and she was living in France. Matilda invades and he is captured.

509

| 1141 | Matilda (disputed) | Daughter of Henry I |

Husband is Count of Anjou. She is never crowned. Stephen her prisoner but Country remains divided and fighting continues. Buried Bec (Rouen) France.

| 1141-1154 | Stephen of Blois | Grandson of William the Conqueror |

Stephen is released in exchange for Matilda's half brother. Stephen's son dies and he agrees with Matilda that he will reign but that the heir will be her son Henry. Buried Faversham Abbey.

| 1154-1189 | Henry II | Grandson of Henry I |

First Plantagenet King. Marries Eleanor ex-wife of King of France. Thomas Becket murdered. First son, also called Henry, rebels but later dies. Buried Fontevraud Abbey, France

| 1189-1199 | Richard I (The Lionheart) | 2nd son of Henry II |

Lived mainly in France and spent little time in England. The Crusader King. Imprisoned in Europe. Dies of septic wound following a crossbow accident. Buried Fontevraud Abbey, France

| 1199-1216 | John 1 | Youngest son of Henry II |

Ruled England in Richard's absence. The King John of the legend of Robin Hood. Forced by Barons to sign Magna Carta. Buried Worcester Cathedral.

| 1216 | Louis the Lion of France (disputed) | Son of Phillip II of France |

King of France. Invited by Barons to invade and remove John. Supported by Scottish King, Alexander II. However John dies and Barons decide his son Henry should be King, so Louis returns to France.

| 1216-1272 | Henry III | Son of John I |

Became unpopular. Barons led by Simon DeMontfort rebelled and captured him. His son Edward then defeated DeMontfort at Evesham and Henry was freed. Buried Westminster Abbey.

| 1272-1307 | Edward I (Longshanks) | Son of Henry III |

Warrior King. Known as the Hammer of the Scots. Built mighty castles in Wales. Established Parliament. Expelled the Jews from England for not financing his wars. Buried Westminster Abbey.

| 1307-1327 | Edward II (of Caernarvon) | Son of Edward I |

Married Isabella, daughter of the King of France. Defeated by the Scots at Bannockburn. Eventually usurped by Isabella and her lover Lord Mortimer and son, also Edward made King. He was murdered at Berkley Castle. Buried Gloucester Cathedral.

| 1327-1377 | Edward III | Son of Edward II |

King at age 14 and initially under the influence of his Mother and Mortimer. After 2 years had Mortimer executed. Built England into powerful military nation. Heir Edward, the Black Prince, dies. Third son is John of Gaunt, Duke of Lancaster. Buried Westminster Abbey.

| 1377-1399 | Richard II | Grandson of Edward II |

King at age 10 upon death of his father, Edward, who died before becoming King. Deposed by Henry IV, son of his Uncle, John of Gaunt. Buried Kings Langley then later Westminster Abbey.

| 1399-1413 | Henry IV (Bolingbroke) | Grandson of Edward III and son of John of Gaunt |

First King whose native language was English. First King of House of Lancaster. Deposed cousin Edward after he had banished him and confiscated his lands. Buried Canterbury Cathedral.

| 1413-1422 | Henry V | Son of Henry IV |

Victor over French at Battle of Agincourt. Married the daughter of the King of France and was heir to French throne. Died and his widow married a courtier, Owen Tudor. Buried Westminster Abbey.

| 1422-1461 | Henry VI | Son of Henry V |

King of England & France at age 9 months. War of the Roses between the Houses of Lancaster & York began in 1460. Suffered bouts of mental illness. Son and heir, Richard of York killed in battle.

511

| 1461-1470 | Edward IV | Grandson of Henry VI
Son of Richard of York |

Had acted as Regent during Henry VI's bouts of illness. Took Henry prisoner and seized the throne.

| 1470-1471 | Henry VI (6 months) | Son of Henry V |

Freed by Earl of Warwick and restored to throne. Edward IV fled to Flanders but came back with an army and again seized the throne. Died, possibly murdered, while prisoner in the Tower of London. Buried Windsor Castle.

| 1471-1483 | Edward IV | Grandson of Henry VI.
Son of Richard of York |

Defeated the Lancastrians at Tewkesbury in 1471 ending the Wars of the Roses. Became the first Yorkist King. Buried Windsor Castle.

| 1483 | Edward V | Son of Edward IV |

Never crowned. One of the Princes in the Tower and allegedly murdered by his Uncle Richard of Gloucester, who seized the throne. Burial unkown.

| 1483-1485 | Richard III | Grandson of Henry VI.
Son of Richard of York |

Killed his nephew Edward V and took throne. Killed at Battle of Bosworth Field by Henry Tudor. Buried Leicester Cathedral.

| 1485-1509 | Henry VII | Son of Edmund Tudor. Half
brother to Henry VI |

First Tudor King. No bloodline to throne. Last King to win throne of England in battle. Married Elizabeth of York, daughter of Edward IV, uniting Houses of Lancaster and York. Buried Westminster Abbey.

| 1509-1547 | Henry VIII | Son of Henry VII |

Broke from the Catholic Church over wish to divorce his first wife. Had 6 wives, two daughters and one son. Buried Windsor Castle.

| 1547-1553 | Edward VI | Son of Henry VIII |

Son of Jane Seymour Henry VIII's third wife. Died at age 16. Named Jane Grey as his heir as did not want Catholic sister Mary to be his heir. Buried Westminster Abbey.

July 1553	Lady Jane Grey	Gt. Granddaughter of Henry VII

Reluctantly reigned for 9 days in July, before ceding to Mary. Kept prisoner in the Tower of London and executed in 1554 aged 16. Buried St. Peter ad Vinicula, London

1553-1558	Mary I (Bloody Mary)	Daughter of Henry VIII

First Queen of England. People supported her so Jane Grey never ruled and was beheaded. Persecuted Protestants. Married King Phillip of Spain, whose father was her maternal cousin. No heirs. Buried Westminster Abbey.

1558-1603	Elizabeth I	Daughter of Henry VIII

Protestant. Never married. Time of Drake & Raleigh. Phillip of Spain asked to marry her but she refused. His invasion Armada was defeated. Buried Westminster Abbey.

1603-1625	James I of England and VI of Scotland	Son of Mary Queen of Scots & Lord Darnley

King of Scotland in 1567 when mother Mary abdicated. King of England from 1603 uniting both crowns. Catholics tried to kill him in Gunpowder Plot. Buried Westminster Abbey.

1625-1649	Charles I	Son of James I/VI (Sister Elizabeth Stuart)

Fell out with Parliament over his powers. Married a Catholic. English Civil War 1642-1648 saw him ousted by Cromwell. Beheaded 1649. Buried Windsor Castle.

1649-1658	Oliver Cromwell (Lord Protector)

Fervent Puritan. Committed genocide of Catholics and Jews in Britain and Ireland. Invaded Scotland after they declared Charles II as their King

1658-1659	Richard Cromwell

Ineffective. Known as Tumbledown Dick. Lords seek restoration of Monarchy.

1660-1685	Charles II	Son of Charles I

Invaded England but defeated by Cromwell at Worcester. Fled to France. Invited in 1660 to return by Lords and restore the monarchy. Considered to be a reluctant Protestant. No legitimate heirs. Buried Westminster Abbey.

1685-1688	James II	Son of Charles I

Brother of Charles II. Married a Catholic and Nobles feared a Catholic heir.
Had a son, James Stuart (the Old Pretender).
Nobles invited his daughter Mary to depose him. Buried Paris.

1688-1694	Mary II (Joint with William III)	Daughter of James II & Granddaughter of Charles I

Married to Protestant cousin, William of Orange, of Netherlands. English protestants
invited her and William to invade and seize crown. Joint ruler with her husband. No
children. Buried Westminster Abbey.

1688-1702	William III	Grandson of Charles I

Ruled after Mary's death. Suppressed Irish catholic uprisings in support of James
II. Known as King Billy. Act of Settlement in 1701 banned Catholics from throne of
England. Buried Westminster Abbey.

1702-1714	Anne	Daughter of James II

Younger sister of Mary. Despite 17 pregnancies no heir survived. Buried
Westminster Abbey.

1714-1727	George I	Gt. Grandson of James I

German. 2nd Cousin to Anne but closest Protestant relative. Jacobites tried to have
James Stuart elected, but failed. Buried Hanover, Germany.

1727-1760	George II	Son of George I

Last King born outside England. Last King to fight in battle. Put down final Jacobite
rebellion, led by Bonnie Prince Charlie, at Culloden. Buried Westminster Abbey.

1760-1820	George III	Grandson of George II

Latterly suffered severe mental illness and son ruled as Regent. Buried Windsor Castle.

1820-1830	George IV	Son of George III

Led extravagant life. Only daughter died so brother succeeded him.
Buried Windsor Castle.

514

1830-1837	William IV	Son of George III

Brother of George III. King at age 64. No legitimate children. Buried Windsor Castle.

1837-1901	Victoria	Granddaughter of George III

Niece of William IV. German husband. Albert. The Industrial age. Significant expansion of British Empire. 2nd longest serving Monarch. Buried Frogmore, Windsor.

1901-1910	Edward VII	Son of Victoria

Reformed the military. Friends with France. Poor relationship with his cousin, Wilhelm II of Germany. Buried Windsor Castle.

1910-1936	George V	2nd Son of Edward VII

King during 1st World War. Renamed Royal House as Windsor. Buried Windsor Castle.

1936	Edward VIII (Abdicated)	Son of George V

Did not like protocol. Married a divorcee and gave up throne. Buried Frogmore, Windsor.

1936-1952	George VI	Son of George V

King during 2nd World War. Formation of Commonwealth. Heavy smoker. Died of lung cancer. Buried Windsor Castle.

1952-	Elizabeth II	Daughter of George VI

Longest serving British Monarch

515

Royal Houses of England & Britain	
House of Wessex	871 - 1014 (not 1013) then 1042 - 1066
House of Denmark	1013 then 1015 - 1042
House of Normandy	1066 - 1154
House of Plantagenet	1154 - 1485 (York and Lancaster)
House of Tudor	1485 - 1603
House of Stuart	1603 - 1649
Interregnum	1649 - 1659
House of Stuart	1660 -1714
House of Hanover	1714 - 1837
House of Saxe Coburg Gotha	1837 - 1910
House of Windsor	1910 - Present

Kings & Queens of Scotland up to Union with England		
843-858	Kenneth I (MacAlpin)	Drest, King of the Picts

King of the Picts & claimed founder of Kingdom of Alba. Maybe a Gaul. Norse settlements increased in his time. Born & buried on Iona.

| 858-862 | Donald I | Brother to Kenneth |

King of Picts for only 4 years. Died at Scone. Buried on Iona.

| 862-877 | Constantine I | Son of Kenneth |

Increased Viking raids during his time. Died in battle. Buried on Iona

| 877-878 | Aed | Son of Kenneth |

Ruled for one year before being overthrown by Giric. Buried on Iona.

| 878-889 | Giric or Gregory (Joint rule) | Possibly Son of Donald I |

Little known of his origins. Possibly a cousin of Eochaid. Disputed that he was son of Donald who was allegedly childless

| 878-889 | Eochaid (Joint) | Grandson of Kenneth |

Mother possibly daughter of Kenneth. Disputed that he was joint King and Giric may have ruled alone.

| 889-900 | Donald II | Son of Constantine I |

Possibly overthrew Giric to take throne. Killed at Dunnottar, possibly by Vikings. Buried on Iona.

| 900-943 | Constantine II | Son of Aed |

2nd longest reign. In his time the country was first called Scotland. At times submitted to Aethelstan in England. Abdicated in favour of his nephew. Buried on Iona.

943-954	Malcolm I	Son of Donald II

King when Constantine abdicated as son Indulf was too young to take over. Died in battle with the English. Buried on Iona.

954-962	Indulf (or Illulb)	Son of Constantine II

Died fighting against Vikings. Buried on Iona

962-966	Dub (or Duff)	Son of Malcolm I

Brother of Kenneth II. Allegedly killed by Cuilen at Forres. Kenneth II claimed by some to have become King at this time. Descendants are the MacDuffs. Burial unknown.

966-971	Cuilen (possibly joint with Amlaib)	Son of Indulf

Brother of Amlaib. Slain, possibly by King of Strathclyde in revenge for rape of his daughter by Cuilen. Buried St Andrews.

971-977	Amlaib (possibly joint with Cuilen)	Son of Indulf

Brother to Cuilen. Killed by Kenneth II

(966)/971-995	Kenneth II	Son of Malcolm I

Potentially became King after brother Dub in 966. Fought against Cuilen and Amlaib and they may never have ruled.

995-997	Constantine III	Son of Cuilen

Last heir of Aed. Murdered Kenneth II and took the throne. Killed by Kenneth III. No heirs. Buried Iona.

997-1005	Kenneth III	Son of Dub (Nephew of Kenneth II)

Killed in battle by Malcolm II. Granddaughter, Gruoch, later marries MacBeth. Buried Iona

| 1005-1034 | Malcolm II | Son of Kenneth II |

Mother, possibly Irish. 3 daughters. Eldest had heir, Duncan. 2nd daughter had son Thorfinn. 3rd daughter had son MacBeth. Buried Iona.

| 1034-1040 | Duncan I | Grandson of Malcolm II |

Killed in raid on MacBeth's lands in Moray. Possibly his wife Sybil, is sister of Earl of Northumbria and becomes wife of Macbeth, but she dies soon after. Buried Iona

| 1040-1057 | MacBeth | Grandson of Malcolm II |

His second wife was Gruoch who already had a son, Lulach. Killed in battle with Malcolm & Earl of Northumbria. Buried on Iona.

| 1057-1058 | Lulach | Grandson of Kenneth II |

Briefly reigned after his stepfather was killed, but killed by Malcolm. Buried on Iona

| 1058-1093 | Malcolm III | Son of Duncan I |

Seized throne from MacBeth and Lulach. 2nd wife was Margaret, granddaughter of Aethelred and sister to Edgar Aethling. Their grandson became Henry I of England. Malcolm and his son Edward killed while invading Northumbria. Margaret died soon after and later became St. Margaret. Buried Dunfermline.

| 1093-1094 | Donald III | Son of Duncan I |

Brother to Malcolm. Expelled Margaret's children when Malcolm died and he took the throne. They were exiled to their brother in law Henry I.
Buried Dunfermline then later Iona.

| 1094 | Duncan II (short) | Son of Malcolm III |

Overthrew Donald with English help but killed shortly after they left. Buried Dunfermline.

| 1094-1097 | Donald III | Son of Duncan I |

Resumed the throne but overthrown by his nephew Edgar. Buried Dunfermline then later iona.

| 1097-1107 | Edgar | 4th Son of Malcolm III |

His elder brother Edmond was supporter of Donald so deemed unfit to be King. Settled Norwegian claims to Hebrides. No heirs. Buried Dunfermline.

| 1107-1124 | Alexander I | 5th Son of Malcolm III |

Married illegitimate daughter of Henry I. Buried Dunfermline.

| 1124-1153 | David I | 6th son of Malcolm III |

Lived in Court of Henry I in England while in exile. His son, Henry Earl of Northumberland died so grandson David was his heir. Supported claim of Matilda, his niece and daughter of Henry I, to the English throne instead of Stephen. Buried Dunfermline.

| 1153-1165 | Malcolm IV | Grandson of David I |

Died at age 24 of Paget's Disease. Earldom of Northumbria taken off him by Henry II. Buried Dunfermline.

| 1165-1214 | William I | Grandson of David I |

Tried to regain Northumbria but captured by Henry II. Released on agreement to pay taxes to Henry. Buried Arbroath.

| 1214- 1249 | Alexander II | Son of William I |

Invaded England in plot to unseat King John and put King Louis of France on the throne. John died so Barons chose his son as King over Louis. Buried Melrose.

| 1249-1286 | Alexander III | Son of Alexander II |

Married daughter of Henry III. Fought Norwegians and reclaimed Isle of Man and the Western Isles. Died in a riding accident. Buried Dunfermline.

| 1286-1290 | Margaret of Norway | Granddaughter of Alexander III |

Alexander's son died leaving his granddaughter as heir. She was the daughter of King of Norway but died in Orkney en route to Scotland. Buried Bergen.

| 1290-1292 | Interregnum | |

Number of claimants were considered. Edward I asked to choose and he selected John Balliol over Robert de Brus.

| 1292-1296 | John Balliol (John I) | Gt. Gt. nephew of William I |

Edward influenced and ruled him. Scottish Council upset and sign treaty (Auld Alliance) with France. Edward I invades. John deposed. Buried France.

| 1296-1306 | 2nd Interregnum | |

(1297-1298)
William Wallace leads Scottish rebellion. Resigns in favour of Robert the Bruce. Betrayed in 1305 and brutally killed by Edward I.

| 1306-1329 | Robert I (the Bruce) | 4th great grandson of David I |

Killed his rival John Comyn. Fought against Edward 1. Defeated Edward II at Battle of Bannockburn. Buried Dunfermline.

| 1329-1371 | David II | Son of Robert I |

Age 5 when became King, but only ruled at 16. Married daughter of Edward II. No children. Invaded England in support of French but captured and prisoner for 11 years until ransomed. Buried Holyrood Abbey.

| 1371-1390 | Robert II | Grandson of Robert I (by mother) |

King at age 55. Gained back Scottish lands held by English. Lost his authority in a coup by his son. Buried Scone Abbey.

| 1390-1406 | (John) Robert III | Son of Robert II |

Born John but took name Robert on becoming King. Had little authority. Injured in battle so brother Robert & Son David act for him. Buried Paisley.

| 1406-1437 | James I | Son of Robert III |

Brother David dies. Heir, but forced to flee. Captured, prisoner of Henry IV for 18 years. Considered English. Later assassinated by Uncle. Buried Perth.

521

| 1437-1460 | James II | Son of James I |

Escapes murder attempt and is King at age 6. Dies when artillery piece explodes next to him at siege of Roxburgh Castle. Buried Holyrood.

| 1460-1488 | James III | Son of James II |

Unpopular King. Gains Orkneys & Shetland by unpaid dowry. Killed in battle by Parliamentary opponents. Buried Stirling.

| 1488-1513 | James IV | Son of James II |

Wife Margaret Tudor, daughter of Henry VII. Opportunistically invaded England when Henry VIII was invading France. Killed at the Battle of Flodden. The last Monarch in Britain to be killed in battle. Burial uncertain.

| 1513-1542 | James V | Son of James IV |

First controlled by Mother and stepfather, Earl of Angus. On death of Mother, tried to carry out an invasion of England, but failed. Buried Holyrood.

| 1542-1567 | Mary I Queen of Scots) | Daughter of James V |

Widow of King of France. Unpopular in Scotland. Flees to England after death of husband. Executed by Elizabeth I. Buried Peterborough then later Westminster Abbey.

| 1567-1625 | James VI of Scotland, I of England | Son of Mary Queen of Scots |

King of Scotland in 1567 when mother Mary abdicated. King of England from 1603 uniting both crowns. Father of Charles I. Buried Westminster Abbey.

Royal Houses of Scotland	
House of Alpin	843 - 1034
House of Dunkeld	1034 - 1057
House of Moray	1057 - 1058
House of Dunkeld	1058 - 1286
House of Serre (Norway)	1286 - 1290
Interregnum	1290 - 1292
House of Balliol	1292 - 1296
Interregnum	1296 - 1306
House of Bruce	1306 - 1371
House of Stuart	1371 - 1649

CPSIA information can be obtained
at www.ICGtesting.com
Printed in the USA
LVHW02s0538030118
561593LV00004B/5/P

9 781773 740065